NYSTCE
060

CST
Students with Disabilities
Teacher Certification Exam

By: Sharon Wynne, M.S
Southern Connecticut State University

"And, while there's no reason yet to panic, I think it's only prudent that we make preparations to panic."

XAMonline, INC.
Boston

XAMOnline, Inc.
21 Orient Ave.
Melrose, MA 02176
Toll Free 1-800-509-4128
Email: info@xamonline.com
Web www.xamonline.com
Fax: 1-781-662-9268

Library of Congress Cataloging-in-Publication Data

Wynne, Sharon A.
    CST Students with Disabilities 060: Teacher Certification / Sharon A. Wynne. -2nd ed.
    ISBN 978-1-58197-860-5
    1. CST Students with Disabilities 060.   2. Study Guides.   3. NYSTCE
    4. Teachers' Certification & Licensure.   5. Careers

Disclaimer:
The opinions expressed in this publication are the sole works of XAMonline and were created independently from the National Education Association, Educational Testing Service, or any State Department of Education, National Evaluation Systems or other testing affiliates.

Between the time of publication and printing, state specific standards as well as testing formats and website information may change that is not included in part or in whole within this product. Sample test questions are developed by XAMonline and reflect similar content as on real tests; however, they are not former tests. XAMonline assembles content that aligns with state standards but makes no claims nor guarantees teacher candidates a passing score. Numerical scores are determined by testing companies such as NES or ETS and then are compared with individual state standards. A passing score varies from state to state.

Printed in the United States of America   œ-1

NYSTCE: CST Students with Disabilities 060
ISBN: 978-1-58197-860-5

Table of Contents

ACKNOWLEDGEMENTS
Special Education

Recognizing the hard work in the production of our study guides we would like to thank those involved. The credentials and experience fulfilling the making of this study guide, aided by the professionalism and insight of those who expressed the subject mastery in specialized fields, is valued and appreciated by XAMonline. It results in a product that upholds the integrity and pride represented by modern educators who bear the name **TEACHER**.

Providers of foundational material

Founding authors 1996	Kathy Schinerman
	Roberta Ramsey
Pre-flight editorial review	Paul Sutliff
Pre-flight construction :	Brittany Good
	Harris Brooks Hughes
Authors 2006	Paul Sutliff
	Beatrice Jordan
	Marisha Tapera
	Kathy Gibson
	Twya Lavender
Sample Test Rational	Sidney Findley

XAMonline Editorial and Production acknowledgements

Project Manager	Sharon Wynne
Project Coordinator	Twya Lavender
Series Editor	Mary Collins
Editorial Assistant	Virginia Finnerty
Marketing Manager	John Wynne
Marketing support	Maria Ciampa
Cover design	Brian Messenger
Sales	Justin Dooley
Production Editor	David Aronson
Typist	Julian German
Manufacturing	Chris Morning/Midland Press
E-Books	Kristy Gipson/Lightningsource
Cover Administrator	Jenna Hamilton

INTRODUCTION

This one-volume study guide was designed for professionals preparing to take a teacher competency test in special education or in any field in which the principles of special education are a part of the test content. Objectives specific to the field of special education were obtained from state departments of education and federal territories and dependencies across the nation. Educators preparing to take tests in the various areas of special education should find the manual helpful, for the objectives and the scope of the discussions concerning each objective cover a wide range of the field.

The study guide offers many benefits to the person faced with the necessity of making a qualifying score on a competency test in special education. A large number of source materials must be covered in order to study the conceptual knowledge reflected by the objectives listed in each state study guide. These objectives encompass the major content of the special education field. The term "objective" may be called "competency" in some states. These terms are synonymous and refer to an item of professional knowledge for mastery.

Many prominent textbooks used by preservice teacher training programs nationwide were researched for the content of this book. Other important resources (e.g. books, journal articles, and media) were included in the discussions about the objectives. The compilation of this research alleviates the hardship imposed on a teacher who attempts to accumulate, as one individual preparing for an examination, the vast body of professional material. This one-volume study guide highlights the current knowledge and accepted concepts of the field of special education, thus reducing the massive amount of material, which would need to be assembled if one did not have it between a single set of covers.

The book is organized by major topical sections. These topics often correspond with course titles and textbooks in pre-service teacher training programs. The objectives and discussions about them comprise the main content within each section. The discussions feature important information from textbooks in the field of special education, reported in the books in a synthesized and summarized form. Specific references have been given for charts and quoted materials, which were included to enhance understanding of conceptual discussions. Complete reference citations can be located in the reference listings. A glossary of terms is located at the end of each topical section. The definitions are stated in the contextual usage of special education.

Finally, questions specific to the discussion of each objective have been written to help determine if the reader understands that material. Correctness of responses to questions can be checked for immediate accuracy in the Answer Key section. Test questions are written as teaching mechanisms and appear in the style and format to cover those used on tests by any state.

Though this manual is comprehensive, it in no way purports to contain all the research and applied techniques in every area of exceptionality. Research generates new applications, and continuing in-service education is a requirement for all special education professionals. This manual gives the reader a one-volume summary of the fundamentals known and practiced at the time of writing.

About the Test

The New York teacher Certification examinations are criterion referenced and objective based test, developed using textbooks, New York State learning standards and curriculum guides; teacher education curricula and certification standards. The purpose of the test is to identify teachers who demonstrate an appropriate level of knowledge and skill that are important to teach effectively in New York State public schools.

The exam accessed the knowledge and skills of the following areas:

Subarea I. Understanding and Evaluating Students with Disabilities (Skills 1.01-5.08)
Subarea II. Promoting Student Learning and Development in a Collaborative Learning Community (Skill 6.01-13.08)
Subarea III. Working in a Collaborative Professional Environment (14.01-17.06)
Subarea IV. Promoting Student Learning and Development in a Collaborative Learning Community: Constructed-Response Assignment (Objectives from Subarea II will be used to create the constructed-response assignment)

There are approximately 90 multiple-choice test questions and one constructed-response (written) assignment. The majority of the test is Subarea II (42% of the test). Subarea I is 27% of the test. Subarea III is 21% of the test. Subarea IV is 10% of the test.

Passing score
An examinee's multiple-choice score and scores on any constructed-response assignments are added together to obtain the total test score. A score of 220 is the minimum passing score for each test. An examinee with a total test score of 220 or above passes the test.

Location, Cost, and Registration

At the time of the creation of this study guide, the cost of taking this test is $88. Registration can occur by phone, mail, or internet. The sites and dates of testing are located on www.nystce.nesinc.com. Please also refer to this site for more specific information about registration.

Great Study and Testing Tips!

What to study in order to prepare for the subject assessments is the focus of this study guide but equally important is *how* you study.

You can increase your chances of truly mastering the information by taking some simple, but effective steps.

1. Some foods aid the learning process. Foods such as milk, nuts, seeds, rice, and oats help your study efforts by releasing natural memory enhancers called CCKs (*cholecystokinin*) composed of *tryptopha*n, *choline*, and *phenylalanine*. All of these chemicals enhance the neurotransmitters associated with memory. Before studying, try a light, protein-rich meal of eggs, turkey, and fish. All of these foods release the memory enhancing chemicals. The better the connections, the more you comprehend.

Likewise, before you take a test, stick to a light snack of energy boosting and relaxing foods. A glass of milk, a piece of fruit, or some peanuts all release various memory-boosting chemicals and help you to relax and focus on the subject at hand.

2. Learn to take great notes. A by-product of our modern culture is that we have grown accustomed to getting our information in short doses (i.e. TV news sound bites or USA Today style newspaper articles.)

Consequently, we've subconsciously trained ourselves to assimilate information better in neat little packages. If your notes are scrawled all over the paper, it fragments the flow of the information. Strive for clarity. Newspapers use a standard format to achieve clarity. Your notes can be much clearer through use of proper formatting. A very effective format is called the *"Cornell Method."*

Take a sheet of loose-leaf lined notebook paper and draw a line all the way down the paper about 1-2" from the left-hand edge.

Draw another line across the width of the paper about 1-2" up from the bottom. Repeat this process on the reverse side of the page.

Look at the highly effective result. You have ample room for notes, a left hand margin for special emphasis items or inserting supplementary data from the textbook, a large area at the bottom for a brief summary, and a little rectangular space for just about anything you want.

3. Get the concept then the details. Too often we focus on the details and don't gather an understanding of the concept. However, if you simply memorize only dates, places, or names, you may well miss the whole point of the subject.

A key way to understand things is to put them in your own words. If you are working from a textbook, automatically summarize each paragraph in your mind. If you are outlining text, don't simply copy the author's words.

Rephrase them in your own words. You remember your own thoughts and words much better than someone else's, and subconsciously tend to associate the important details to the core concepts.

4. Ask Why? Pull apart written material paragraph by paragraph and don't forget the captions under the illustrations.

Example: If the heading is "Stream Erosion", flip it around to read "Why do streams erode?" Then answer the questions.

If you train your mind to think in a series of questions and answers, not only will you learn more, but it also helps to lessen the test anxiety because you are used to answering questions.

5. Read for reinforcement and future needs. Even if you only have 10 minutes, put your notes or a book in your hand. Your mind is similar to a computer; you have to input data in order to have it processed. *By reading, you are creating the neural connections for future retrieval.* The more times you read something, the more you reinforce the learning of ideas.

Even if you don't fully understand something on the first pass, *your mind stores much of the material for later recall.*

6. Relax to learn so go into exile. Our bodies respond to an inner clock called biorhythms. Burning the midnight oil works well for some people, but not everyone.

If possible, set aside a particular place to study that is free of distractions. Shut off the television, cell phone, pager and exile your friends and family during your study period.

If you really are bothered by silence, try background music. Light classical music at a low volume has been shown to aid in concentration over other types.

Music that evokes pleasant emotions without lyrics are highly suggested. Try just about anything by Mozart. It relaxes you.

7. Use arrows not highlighters. At best, it's difficult to read a page full of yellow, pink, blue, and green streaks.

Try staring at a neon sign for a while and you'll soon see my point, the horde of colors obscure the message.

A quick note, a brief dash of color, an underline, and an arrow pointing to a particular passage is much clearer than a horde of highlighted words.

8. Budget your study time. Although you shouldn't ignore any of the material, *allocate your available study time in the same ratio that topics may appear on the test.*

Testing Tips:

1. Get smart, play dumb. **Don't read anything into the question.** Don't make an assumption that the test writer is looking for something else than what is asked. Stick to the question as written and don't read extra things into it.

2. Read the question and all the choices _twice_ before answering the question. You may miss something by not carefully reading, and then re-reading both the question and the answers.

If you really don't have a clue as to the right answer, leave it blank on the first time through. Go on to the other questions, as they may provide a clue as to how to answer the skipped questions.

If later on, you still can't answer the skipped ones . . . **_Guess._**
The only penalty for guessing is that you _might_ get it wrong. Only one thing is certain; if you don't put anything down, you will get it wrong!

3. Turn the question into a statement. Look at the way the questions are worded. The syntax of the question usually provides a clue. Does it seem more familiar as a statement rather than as a question? Does it sound strange?

By turning a question into a statement, you may be able to spot if an answer sounds right, and it may also trigger memories of material you have read.

4. Look for hidden clues. It's actually very difficult to compose multiple-foil (choice) questions without giving away part of the answer in the options presented.

In most multiple-choice questions you can often readily eliminate one or two of the potential answers. This leaves you with only two real possibilities and automatically your odds go to Fifty-Fifty for very little work.

5. Trust your instincts. For every fact that you have read, you subconsciously retain something of that knowledge. On questions that you aren't really certain about, go with your basic instincts. **Your first impression on how to answer a question is usually correct.**

6. Mark your answers directly on the test booklet. Don't bother trying to fill in the optical scan sheet on the first pass through the test.

Just be very careful not to miss-mark your answers when you eventually transcribe them to the scan sheet.
7. Watch the clock! You have a set amount of time to answer the questions. Don't get bogged down trying to answer a single question at the expense of 10 questions you can more readily answer.

THIS PAGE BLANK

Pre-test

1. Which is an educational characteristic common to students with mild intellectual learning and behavioral disabilities? *(Skill 1.01) (Easy)*

   A. Show interest in schoolwork
   B. Have intact listening skills
   C. Require modification in classroom instruction
   D. Respond better to passive than to active learning tasks

2. Zero Reject requires all children with disabilities be provided with what? *(Skill 1.01) (Average)*

   A. Total exclusion of Functional exclusion
   B. Adherence to the annual local education agency (LEA) reporting.
   C. Free, appropriate public education
   D. Both b and c.

3. Joey is in a mainstreamed preschool program. One of the means his teacher uses in determining growth in adaptive skills is that of observation. Some questions about Joey's behavior that she might ask include: *(Average) (Skill 1.01)*

   A. Is he able to hold a cup?
   B. Can he call the name of any of his toys?
   C. Can he reach for an object and grasp it?
   D. All of the above

4. Individuals with mental retardation can be characterized as: *(Skill 1.01) (Rigorous)*

   A. Often indistinguishable from normal developing children at an early age
   B. Having a higher than normal rate of motor activity
   C. Displaying significant discrepancies in ability levels
   D. Uneducable in academic skills

5. Which of the following statements about children with an emotional/ behavioral disorder is true? *(Skill 1.01) (Average)*

   A. They have very high IQs
   B. They display poor social skills
   C. They are academic achievers
   D. Mature understanding of concepts

6. Which behavior would be expected at the mild level of emotional/behavioral disorders? *(Skill 1.01) (Average)*

   A. Attention seeking
   B. Inappropriate affect
   C. Self-Injurious
   D. Poor sense of identity

7. **All of the following EXCEPT one are characteristics of a student who is Emotionally Disturbed?** *(Skill 1.01)* *(Average)*

A. Socially accepted by peers.
B. Highly disruptive to the classroom environment.
C. Academic difficulties.
D. Areas of talent overlooked by a teacher

8. **Echolalia is a characteristic of what?** *(Skill 1.01) (Average)*

A. Autism
B. Mental Retardation
C. Social Pragmatic Disorder
D. ADHD

9. **Children are engaged in a game of charades. Which type of social-interpersonal skill is the teacher most likely attempting to develop?** *(Skill 1.01) (Rigorous)*

A. Sensitivity to others
B. Making behavioral choices in social situations
C. Social maturity
D. All of the above

10. **Johnny just hit Sarah for no apparent reason. What condition listed below could allow a conclusion that this action it was related to his disability.** *(Skill 1.04)* *(Rigorous)*

A. Hearing Impairment
B. Learning disabled with Central Auditory Processing issues.
C. Social Pragmatic Disorder
D. Obsessive Compulsive Disorder

11. **Five-year-old Tom continues to substitute the "w" sound for the "r" sound when pronouncing words; therefore, he often distorts words e.g., "wabbit" for "rabbit" and "wat" for "rat." His articulation disorder is basically a problem in:** *(Skill 1.04) (Easy)*

A. Phonology
B. Morphology
C. Syntax
D. Semantics

12. **Which of the following is untrue about the ending "er?"** *(Skill 1.04) (Rigorous)*

A. It is an example of a free morpheme
B. It represents one of the smallest units of meaning within a word
C. It is called an inflectional ending
D. When added to a word, it connotes a comparative status

13. Which component of language involves language content rather than the form of language? *(Skill 1.04)* *(Average)*

A. Phonology
B. Morphology
C. Semantics
D. Syntax

14. Television, movies, radio, and newspapers contribute the public's poor understanding of disabilities by: *(Skill 1.05)* *(Average)*

A. Only portraying those who look normal.
B. Portraying the person with the disability as one with incredible abilities.
C. Showing emotionally disturbed children
D. Portraying all people in wheel chairs as independent.

15. The definition for "Other Health Impaired (OHI)" in IDEA: *(Skill 1.05) (Average)*

A. Is the definition that accepts heart conditions.
B. Includes deafness, blindness or profound mental retardation
C. includes Autism and PDD.
D. Includes cochlear implants.

16. Which of the following is true about autism? *(Skill 2.02)* *(Easy)*

A. It is caused by having cold, aloof or hostile parents
B. Approximately 4 out of 10 people have autism
C. It is a separate exceptionality category in IDEA
D. It is a form of mental illness

17. Antwon is in your 12:1:1 in a 10th grade Regent program. You begin to wonder if a functional program would be best when you not the student's? *(Skill 2.02)* *(Average)*

A. Lack of ability to comprehend inferences.
B. Stuttering
C. Delayed processing.
D. Difficulties understanding concrete examples

18. Which of the following is a possible side-effect of an Anti-depressant? *(Skill 2.04)* *(Rigorous)*

A. Anxiety
B. Aggression
C. Tremors
D. Restlessness

19. Mrs. Stokes has been teaching her third-grade students about mammals during a recent science unit. Which of the following would be true of a criterion-referenced test she might administer at the conclusion of the unit? *(Skill 3.01) (Average)*

   A. It will be based on unit objectives
   B. Derived scores will be used to rank student achievement.
   C. Standardized scores are effective of national performance samples
   D. All of the above

20. For which of the following purposes is a norm-referenced test least appropriate? *(Skill 3.01) (Average)*

   A. Screening
   B. Individual program planning
   C. Program evaluation
   D. Making placement decisions

21. The extent to which a test measures what its authors or users claim that it measures is called its: *(Skill 3.01) (Rigorous)*

   A. Validity
   B. Reliability
   C. Normality
   D. Acculturation

22. What do the 9th and 10th Amendments to the U.S. Constitution state about education? *(Skill 3.02) (Easy)*

   A. That education belongs to the people
   B. That education is an unstated power vested in the states
   C. That elected officials mandate education
   D. That education is free

23. Michael's teacher complains that he is constantly out of his seat. She also reports that he has trouble paying attention to what is going on in class for more than a couple of minutes at a time. He appears to be trying, but his writing is often illegible, containing many reversals. Although he seems to want to please, he is very impulsive and stays in trouble with his teacher. He is failing reading, and his math grades, though somewhat better, are still below average. Michael's psychometric evaluation should include assessment for: *(Skill 3.02) (Average)*

   A. Mild mental retardation
   B. Specific learning disabilities
   C. Mild behavior disorders
   D. Hearing impairment

24. **Which of the following is an example of an Alternative Assessment?**
(Skill 3.05) *(Rigorous)*

A. Testing skills in a "real world" setting in several settings.
B. Pre-test of student knowledge of fractions before beginning Wood Shop.
C. Answering an Essay question that allows for creative thought.
D. A compilation of a series of tests in a Portfolio.

25. **The No Child Left Behind Act (NCLB) affected students with Limited English Proficiency (LEP) by :** *(Skill 3.05)* *(Rigorous)*

A. Requiring these students to demonstrate English Language Proficiency before a High School Diploma is granted.
B. Providing allowances for schools not to require them to take and pass state Reading Exams (RCTs) if the students were enrolled in US schools for less than a year.
C. Providing allowances for these students to opt out of state math tests if the student was enrolled in a US school for less than one year.
D. Both B and C.

26. **When you need to evaluate a students work ethics, you should give what assessment?** *(Skill 3.05)* *(Rigorous)*

A. Naturalistic
B. Dynamic
C. Performance Based
D. Criterion referenced

27. **Autism is a disorder characterized by:** *(Skill 3.07)* *(Easy)*

A. Distorted relationships with others
B. Perceptual anomalies
C. Self-stimulation
D. All of the above

28. **IDEA 2004 states that evaluations of student eligibility should?** *(Skill 3.07)* *(Average Rigor)*

A. Be At intervals with teacher discretion
B. use a variety of assessment tools and strategies.
C. Should only address the area of determined need.
D. Conducted annually

29. **Safeguards against bias and discrimination in the assessment of children include:** *(Skill 3.07) (Easy)*

A. The testing of a child in Standard English
B. The requirement for the use of one standardized test
C. The use of evaluative materials in the child's native language or other mode of communication
D. All testing performed by a certified, licensed, psychologist

30. **Which of these factors relate to eligibility for learning disabilities?** *(Skill 4.01)* **(Easy)**

A. A discrepancy between potential and performance
B. Sub-average intellectual functioning
C. Social deficiencies or learning deficits that are not due to intellectual, sensory, or physical conditions
D. Documented results of behavior checklists and anecdotal records of aberrant behavior

31. **In general, characteristics of the learning disabled include:** *(Skill 4.01) (Easy)*

A. A low level of performance in a majority of academic skill areas
B. Limited cognitive ability
C. A discrepancy between achievement and potential
D. A uniform pattern of academic development

32. **As a separate exceptionality category in IDEA, autism:** *(Skill 4.01) (Average Rigor)*

A. Includes emotional/behavioral disorders as defined in federal regulations
B. Adversely affects educational performance
C. Is thought to be a form of mental illness
D. Is a developmental disability that affects verbal and non-verbal communication

33. **Which of the following must be provided in a written notice to parents when proposing a child's educational placement?** *(Skill 4.01 (Easy)*

A. A list of parental due process safeguards
B. A list of current test scores
C. A list of persons responsible for the child's education
D. A list of academic subjects the child has passed

34. Students who receive special services in a regular classroom with consultation, generally have academic and/or social-interpersonal performance deficits at which level of severity? (Skill 4.01) (Easy)

    A. Mild
    B. Moderate
    C. Severe
    D. Profound

35. The <u>greatest number of</u> students receiving special services are enrolled primarily in: (Skill 4.01) (Average Rigor)

    A. The regular classroom
    B. The resource room
    C. Self-contained classrooms
    D. Special schools

36. The most restrictive environment in which an individual might be placed and receive instruction is that of: (Skill4.01) (Easy)
    A. Institutional setting
    B. Homebound instruction
    C. Special schools
    D. Self-contained special classes

37. A test, which measures students' skill development in academic content areas, is classified as an _____ test. (Skill 4.02) (Average Rigor)

    A. Achievement
    B. Aptitude
    C. Adaptive
    D. Intelligence

38. The Key Math Diagnostic Arithmetic Test is an individually administered test of math skills. It is comprised of fourteen subtests which are classified into the major math areas of content, operations, and applications for which subtest scores are reported. The test manual describes the population sample upon which the test was normed, and reports data pertaining to reliability and validity. In addition, for each item in the test, a behavioral objective is presented. From the description, it can be determined that this achievement test is: (Skill 4.02) (Average Rigor)

    A. Individually administered
    B. Criterion-referenced
    C. Diagnostic
    D. All of the above

39. Which of the following is an example of tactile perception? (Skill 4.05) (Average Rigor)
    A. Making an angel in the snow with one's body
    B. Running a specified course
    C. Identifying a rough surface with eyes closed
    D. Demonstrating aerobic exercises

40. **Which of the following activities best exemplifies a kinesthetic exercise in developing body awareness?** *(Skill 4.05) (Average Rigor)*

   A. Touching materials of different textures
   B. Singing with motions "Head and Shoulder's Knees and toes."
   C. Identifying geometric shapes being drawn on one's back
   D. Making a shadow-box project

41. **Which of the following teaching activities is least likely to enhance observational learning in students with special needs?** *(Skill 4.05) (Rigorous)*

   A. A verbal description of the task to be performed, followed by having the children immediately attempt to perform the instructed behavior
   B. A demonstration of the behavior, followed by an immediate opportunity for the children to imitate the behavior
   C. A simultaneous demonstration and explanation of the behavior, followed by ample opportunity for the children to rehearse the instructed behavior
   D. Physically guiding the children through the behavior to be imitated, while verbally explaining the behavior

42. **Acculturation refers to the individual's:** *(Skill 4.07) (Rigorous)*

   A. Gender
   B. Experiential background
   C. Social class
   D. Ethnic background

43. **According to IDEA 2004, the IEP team is composed of:** *(Skill 5.01) (Average Rigor)*

   A. The student's Special Education Teacher and Psychiatrist
   B. The student's parents/guardians and their lawyer
   C. Content Specialist and the CASE
   D. The student's parent(s)/guardians and those providing the related services.

44. **What components of the IEP are required by law?** *(Skill 5.02) (Average Rigor)*

    A. Present level of academic and functional performance; statement of how the disability affects the student's involvement and progress; evaluation criteria and timeliness for instructional objective achievement; modifications of accommodations
    B. Projected dates for services initiation with anticipated frequency, location and duration; statement of when parent will be notified; statement of annual goals
    C. Extent to which child will not participate in regular education program; transitional needs for students age 14.
    D. All of the above.

45. **CSE meetings are held for different reasons. Which of the following would be a reason to hold a CSE meeting?** *(Skill 5.05) (Average Rigor)*

    A. Moving from one school to another within the school district.
    B. Temporary placement in inclusion.
    C. A teacher requests a child to be removed from his/her class.
    D. Transition to post-secondary school life.

46. **Vocational training programs are based on all of the following ideas except:** *(Skill 5.06) (Average Rigor)*

    A. Students obtain career training from elementary through high school
    B. Students acquire specific training in job skills prior to exiting school
    C. Students need specific training and supervision in applying skills learned in school to requirements in job situations
    D. Students obtain needed instruction and field-based experiences that help them to be able to work in specific occupations

47. **In career education specific training and preparation required for the world of work occurs during the phase of:** *(Skill 5.06) (Average Rigor)*

    A. Career Awareness
    B. Career Exploration
    C. Career Preparation
    D. Daily Living and Personal-Social Interaction

48. What is most descriptive of vocational training in special education? (Skill 5.06) (Easy)

A. Trains students in intellectual disabilities solely
B. Segregates students with and without disabilities in vocational training programs
C. Only includes students capable of moderate supervision
D. Instruction focuses upon self-help skills, social-interpersonal skills, motor skills, rudimentary academic skills, simple occupational skills, and lifetime leisure and occupational skills

49. Teachers must keep meticulous records. They are required to share all of them with the student's parent/guardian EXCEPT: (Skill 5.08) (Rigorous)

A. Daily Attendance Record
B. Grade reports.
C. Teacher's personal notes.
D. Discipline notice placed in cumulative record.

50. In establishing your behavior management plan with the students it is best to: (Skill 6.01) (Average Rigor)

A. Have rules written and in place on day one.
B. To hand out a copy of the rules to the students on day one.
C. Have separate rules for each class on day one.
D. Have students involved in creating the rules on Day one.

51. Students with Autistic tendencies can be more successful academically by the teacher: (Skill 6.01) (Average Rigor)

A. Ignoring inappropriate behaviors.
B. Allowing them to go out of the room during instruction.
C. Keeping a calendar on the board of expected transitions.
D. Asking the CSE for a 1:1 Aide.

52. Which tangible reinforcer would Mr. Whiting find to be most effective with teenagers? (Skill 6.01) (Easy)

A. Plastic whistle
B. Winnie-the-Pooh book
C. Free Homework Pass
D. Toy ring

53. Charise comes into your room and seems to know every button to push to get you upset with her. What would be a good intervention? *(Skill 6.01) (Rigorous)*

   A. Nonverbal Interactions
   B. Self-monitoring
   C. Proximity Control
   D. Planned Ignoring

54. Which of the following is a good example of a generalization? *(Skill 6.03) (Average Rigor)*

   A. Jim has learned to add and is now ready to subtract
   B. Sarah adds sets of units to obtain a product
   C. Bill recognizes a vocabulary word on a billboard when traveling
   D. Jane can spell the word "net" backwards to get the word "ten"

55. What can you do to make create a good working environment with a classroom assistant? *(Skill 6.05) (Rigorous)*

   A. Planning lessons with the assistant.
   B. Writing a contract that clearly defines his/her responsibilities in the classroom.
   C. Remove previously given responsibilities.
   D. All of the above

56. One of the most important goals of the Special Education Teacher is to foster and create with the student: *(Skill 6.05) (Easy)*

   A. Handwriting skills.
   B. Self-Advocacy
   C. An increased level of reading
   D. Logical reasoning

57. A paraprofessional has been assigned to assist you in the classroom. What action on the part of the teacher would lead to a poor working relationship? *(Skill 6.08) (Average Rigor)*

   A. Having the paraprofessional lead a small group.
   B. Telling the paraprofessional what you expect him/her to do.
   C. Defining classroom behavior management as your responsibility alone.
   D. Taking an active role in his/her   evaluation.

58. Mrs. Freud is a Consultant Teacher. She has two students with Mr. Ricardo. Mrs. Freud should: *(Skill 7.01) (Average Rigor)*

   A. Co-Teach
   B. Spend two days a week in the classroom helping out.
   C. Discuss lessons with the teacher and suggest modifications before class.
   D. Pull her students out for instructional modifications.

59. Which of the following would be classified as _direct_ rather than indirect _services_ that a specially trained special education teacher would provide to regular education teachers? *(Skill 7.01)* *(Rigorous)*

A. Answer questions about a particular child's academic or social-inter-personal needs
B. Teach a math unit on measurement
C. Assist with selecting special materials for a student
D. Develop math worksheets tailored to meet a student's needs

60. Which is a less than ideal example of collaboration in successful inclusion? *(Skill 7.01)* *(Rigorous)*

A. Special education teachers are part of the instructional team in a regular classroom
B. Special education teachers are informed of the lesson before hand and assist regular education teachers in the classroom
C. Teaming approaches are used for problem solving and program implementation
D. Regular teachers, special education teachers, and other specialists or support teachers co-teach

61. If a student is predominantly a visual learner, he may learn more effectively by: *(Skill 7.01)* *(Easy)*

A. Reading aloud while studying
B. Listening to a cassette tape
C. Watching a DVD
D. Using body movement

62. _____ is a method used to increase student engaged learning time by having students teach other students. *(Skill 7.02)* *(Easy)*

A. Collaborative learning
B. Engaged learning time
C. Allocated learning time
D. Teacher consultation

63. Presentation of tasks can be altered to match the student's rate of learning by: *(Skill 7.06)* *(Rigorous)*

A. Describing how much of a topic is presented in one day and how much practice is assigned, according to the student's abilities and learning style
B. Using task analysis, assign a certain number of skills to be mastered in a specific amount of time
C. Introducing a new task only when the student has demonstrated mastery of the previous task in the learning hierarchy
D. Using standardized assessments to measure skills..

64. All of the following are suggestions for altering the presentation of tasks to match the student's rate of learning except: *(Skill 7.06) (Average Rigor)*

A. Teach in several shorter segments of time rather than a single lengthy session
B. Continue to teach a task until the lesson is completed in order to provide more time on task
C. Watch for nonverbal cues that indicate students are becoming confused, bored, or restless
D. Avoid giving students an inappropriate amount of written work

65. In which of the following ways does an effective teacher utilize pacing as a means of matching a student's rate of learning? *(Skill 7.06) (Rigorous)*

A. Selected content is presented based upon prerequisite skills, then presented in modified measures of time.
B. Tasks are presented during optimum time segments
C. Special needs students always require smaller steps and learning segments regardless of the activity or content
D. Teacher utilizes tier assessment after present materials

66. John learns best through the auditory channel, so his teacher wants to reinforce his listening skills. Through which of the following types of equipment would instruction be most effectively presented? *(Skill 9.06) (Easy)*

A. Overhead projector
B. CD Player
C. PC
D. VHS or DVD player.

67. In which way is a computer like an effective teacher? *(Skill 8.06) (Rigorous)*

A. Provides immediate feedback
B. Sets the pace at the rate of the average student
C. Produces records of errors made, only
D. Record attendance.

68. During which written composition stage are students encouraged to read their stories aloud to others? *(Skill 8.06) (Average Rigor)*

A. Planning
B. Drafting
C. Revising/editing
D. Sharing/publication

69. Which assistive device can be used by those who are visually impaired to assist in their learning? *(Skill 8.06) (Rigorous)*

    A. Soniguide
    B. Personal companion
    C. Closed circuit television
    D. ABVI

70. Which electronic device enables persons with hearing impairments to make and receive phone calls? *(Skill 8.06) (Average Rigor)*

    A. Personal companion
    B. Telecommunication Device for the Deaf (TDD)
    C. Deafnet
    D. Hearing aids

71. When teaching a student, who is predominantly auditory, to read, it is best to: *(Skill 9.01) (Rigorous)*

    A. Stress sight vocabulary
    B. Stress phonetic analysis
    C. Stress the shape and configuration of the word
    D. Stress rapid reading

72. Cognitive learning strategies include: *(Skill 9.04) (Rigorous)*

    A. Reinforcing appropriate behavior
    B. Teaching students how to manage their own behavior in school
    C. Heavily structuring the learning environment
    D. Generalizing learning from one setting to another

73. Most children entering school are not developmentally ready to understand concepts such as? *(Skill 10.02) (Rigorous)*

    A. Zero symbol
    B. Equalizing.
    C. Joining
    D. Patterns

74. The effective teacher varies her instructional presentations and response requirements depending upon: *(Skill 10.02) (Easy)*

    A. Student needs
    B. The task at hand
    C. The learning situation
    D. All of the above

75. A money bingo game was designed by Ms Johnson for use with her middle grade students. Cards were constructed with different combinations of coins pasted on each of the nine spaces. Ms. Johnson called out various amounts of change (e.g. 30 cents) and students were instructed to cover the coin combinations on their cards which equaled the amount of change (e.g. two dimes and two nickels, three dimes, and so on). The student who had the first bingo was required to add the coins in each of the spaces covered and tell the amounts before being declared the winner. Five of Ms. Johnson's sixth graders played the game the ten minute free activity time following math the first day the game was constructed. Which of the following attributes are present in this game in this situation? *(Skill 10.02) (Easy)*

A. Accompanied by simple, uncomplicated rules
B. Of brief duration, permitting replay
C. Age appropriateness
D. All of the above

76. Modeling is an essential component of which self-training approach? *(Skill 10.04) (Rigorous)*

A. Self-instructional training
B. Self-monitoring
C. Self-reinforcing
D. Self-punishing

77. Strategies specifically designed to move the learner from dependence to independence include: *(Skill 10.04) (Rigorous)*

A. Assessment, planning, implementation, and reevaluation
B. Demonstration, imitation, assistance, prompting, and verbal instruction
C. Cognitive modeling and self-guidance through overt, faded overt and covert stages
D. b and c

78. Which of the following questions most directly evaluates the utility of instructional material? *(Skill 10.05) (Rigorous)*

A. Is the cost within budgetary means?
B. Can the materials withstand handling by students?
C. Are the materials organized in a useful manner?
D. Are the needs of the students met by the use of the materials?

79. Alan has failed repeatedly in his academic work. He needs continuous feedback in order to experience small, incremental achievements. What type of instructional material would best meet this need? *(Skill 11.01) (Rigorous)*

A. Programmed materials
B. Audiotapes
C. Materials with no writing required
D. Worksheets

80. After purchasing what seemed to be a very attractive new math kit for use with her students who have learning disabilities, Ms. Davis discovered her students could not use the kit unless she read the math problems and instructions to them, as the readability level was higher than the majority of the students' functional reading capabilities. Which criterion of the materials selection did Ms. Davis most likely fail to consider when selecting this math kit? *(Skill 11.01) (Average Rigor)*

A. Durability
B. Relevance
C. Component Parts
D. Price

81. _____is a skill that teachers help students develop to sustain learning throughout life *(Skill 11.01) (Rigorous)*

A. Work ethic
B. Basic Math Computation
C. Reading
D. Critical thinking

82. Which of the following is an example of cross-modal perception involving integrating visual stimuli to an auditory verbal process? *(Skill 11.02) (Rigorous)*

A. Following spoken directions
B. Describing a picture
C. Finding certain objects in pictures
D. b and c

83. Bob shows behavior problems like lack of attention, out of seat and talking out. His teacher has kept data on these behaviors and has found that Bob is showing much better self-control since he has been self-managing himself through a behavior modification program. The most appropriate placement recommendation for Bob at this time is probably: *(Skill 11.03) (Average Rigor)*

A. Any available part-time special education program
B. The regular classroom solely
C. A behavior disorders resource room for one period a day
D. A specific learning disabilities resource room for one period a day

84. In order for a student to function independently in the learning environment, which of the following must be true? (Skill 11.03) (Average Rigor)

A. The learner must understand the nature of the content
B. The student must be able to do the assigned task
C. The teacher must communicate the task to the learner
D. The student must complete the task.

85. The social skills of students in mental retardation programs are likely to be appropriate for children of their mental age, rather than chronological age. This means that the teacher will need to do all of the following except: (Skill 11.03) (Easy)

A. Model desired behavior
B. Provide clear instructions
C. Expect age appropriate behaviors
D. Adjust the physical environment when necessary

86. A functional curriculum includes: (Skill 11.04) (Average Rigor)

A. Regents curriculum
B. Life Skills
C. Remedial Academics
D. Vocational placement.

87. An individual with disabilities in need of employability training, as well a job, should be referred to what governmental agency for assistance? (Skill 11.07 (Average Rigor)

A. OMRDD
B. VESID
C. Social Services
D. ARC

88. A good method to teach ethical understanding to those in the functional curriculum is: (Skill 12.01) (Rigorous)

A. Modeling
B. The Unfinished Story.
C. Handouts
D. Questionnaire

89. Social maturity may be evidenced by the student's: (Skill 12.01) (Easy)

A. Recognition of rights and responsibilities (his own and others)
B. Display of respect for legitimate authority figures
C. Formulation of a valid moral judgment
D. Demonstration of all of the above

90. **What can a teacher plan that will allow him/her to avoid adverse situations with students?** *(Skill 12.03) (Rigorous)*

    A. Lessons
    B. Recess
    C. Environment
    D. Class schedule

91. **Which of the following is the first step you should take to prepare to teach preparation for social situations?** *(Skill 12.01) (Easy)*

    A. Allow students to plan event.
    B. Lecture
    C. Anticipate possible problems
    D. Take your students to the anticipated setting.

92. **Children with disabilities are least likely to improve their social-interpersonal skills by:** *(Skill 12.01) (Rigorous)*

    A. Developing sensitivity to other people
    B. Making behavioral choices in social situations
    C. Developing social maturity
    D. Talking with their sister or brother.

93. **A Life Space Interview is used for?** *(Skill 13.01) (Rigorous)*

    A. Transition to Exit Interview.
    B. Analysis of proficiency levels.
    C. Maintenance of acceptable behavior.
    D. To create awareness of distorted perceptions.

94. **Target behaviors must be:** *(Skill 13.01) (Easy)*

    A. Observable
    B. Measurable
    C. Definable
    D. All of the above

95. **A Behavioral Intervention Plan (BIP):** *(Skill 13.03) (Rigorous)*

    A. Should be written by a team.
    B. Should be reviewed annually.
    C. Should be written by the teacher who is primarily responsible for the student.
    D. Should consider placement.

96. **Janelle is just as "antsy" as Jaquan who has ADHD. You want to keep a good eye on them so you put them in the same corner. Later you suspect Amanda also has ADHD and you move her to the same area.. You are creating:** *(Skill 12.04) (Average Rigor)*

    A. Self-fulfilling prophecy.
    B. cooperative learning circle.
    C. disordered support group
    D. A buffer zone to observe and direct behavior centrally.

97. **Acceptance of disabilities by parents and siblings is most influenced by?** *(Skill 13.05) (Rigorous)*

    A. Social Economic Status (SES)
    B. The severity of the disability.
    C. The culture of the family.
    D. Media portrayal of the disability.

98. **The opportunity for a student with a disability to attend a class as close to the normal as possible describes:** *(Skill 13.06) (Easy)*

    A. Least Restrictive Environment
    B. Normalization
    C. Mainstreaming
    D. Deinstitutionalization

99. **Which of the following examples would be considered of highest priority when determining the need for the delivery of appropriate special education and related services?** *(Skill 13.06) (Rigorous)*

    A. A ten-year-old girl with profound mental retardation who is receiving education services in a state institution.
    B. A six-year-old girl who has been diagnosed as autistic is placed in a special education class within the local school. Her mother wants her to attend residential school next year, even though the girl is showing progress.
    C. An eight-year-old boy is repeating first grade for the second time and exhibits problems with toileting, gross motor functions, and remembering number and letter symbols. His regular classroom teacher claims the referral forms are too time-consuming and refuses to complete them. He also refuses to make accommodations because he feels every child should be treated alike.
    D. A twelve-year-old boy with mild disabilities who was placed in a behavior disorders program, but displays obvious perceptual deficits (e.g. reversal of letters and symbols, and inability to discriminate sounds). He originally thought to have a learning disability, but did not meet state criteria for this exceptionality category, based on results of standard scores. He has always had problems with attending to a task, and is now beginning to get into trouble during seatwork time. His teacher feels that he will eventually become a real behavior problem. He receives social skills training in the resource room one period a day.

100. The most important steps in writing a Functional Behavioral Assessment (FBA) is: *(Skill 13.07) (Rigorous)*

   A. Establish a replacement behavior
   B. Establish levels of interventions.
   C. Establish antecedents related or causative to the behavior.
   D. Establish assessment periods of FBA effectiveness.

101. The best resource a teacher can have to reach a student is? *(Skill 14.01) (Rigorous)*

   A. Contact with the parents/guardians.
   B. A successful behavior modification Exam.
   C. A listening ear.
   D. Gathered scaffold approach to teaching.

102. You should do to prepare for a parent-teacher conference by: *(Skill 14.02) (Average Rigor)*

   A. Memorizing student progress/grades.
   B. Anticipating questions.
   C. Scheduling the meetings during your lunch time.
   D. Planning a tour of the school.

103. Lotzie is not labeled as needing special education services and appears unable to function on grade level in both academics and socially. He is in 9th grade reading picture books, and consistently displays immature behavior that can be misinterpreted. You have already observed these behaviors. What should be done first? *(Skill 14.02) (Rigorous)*

   A. Establish a rapport with the parents.
   B. Write a CSE referral.
   C. Plan and discuss possible interventions with the teacher.
   D. Address the class about acceptance.

104. You note that a child in your class is expressing discomfort when placing his back against a chair. You ask him if he is OK, and he says its nothing. You notice what appears to be a belt mark on his shoulder. What is the first thing you should do? *(Skill 14.04) (Rigorous)*

   A. Send the child to the nurse.
   B. Contact an Administrator.
   C. Call Child Protective's
   D. Follow the school policy.

105. You are monitoring the cafeteria and you noticed Joshua stuffing his pockets with food. Not just snack food, but lunch items as well. You suspect:. *(Skill 14.04) (Average Rigor)*

   A. Joshua has Obsessive Compulsive Disorder (OCD).
   B. Joshua may not be getting fed at home.
   C. Joshua is just an average growing boy.
   D. Joshua is trying to be funny.

106. What determines whether a person is entitled to protection under Section 504? *(Skill 15.01) (Average Rigor)*

   A. The individual must meet the definition of a person with a disability
   B. The person must be able to meet the requirements of a particular program in spite of his or her disability
   C. The school, business or other facility must be the recipient of federal funding assistance
   D. All of the above

107. Which is **NOT** a step teachers use to establish cooperative learning groups in the classroom? The teacher: *(Skill 15.01) (Rigorous)*

   A. Selects Members of Each Learning Group
   B. Directly Teaches Cooperative Group Skills
   C. Assigns Cooperative Group Skills
   D. Has Students Self-Evaluate Group Efforts

108. The _____ modality is most frequently used in the learning process. *(Skill 15.02) (Rigorous)*

   A. Auditory
   B. Visual
   C. Tactile
   D. All of the Above

109. Some environmental elements which influence learning styles include all except: *(Skill 15.02) (Rigorous)*

   A. Light
   B. Temperature
   C. Design
   D. Motivation

110. Janiay requires Occupational Therapy and Speech Therapy services. She is your student. What must you do to insure her services are met? (Skill 15.04) (Rigorous)

   A. Watch the services being rendered.
   B. Schedule collaboratively.
   C. Ask for services to be given in a push-in model.
   D. Ask them to train you to give the service.

111. Included in data brought to the attention of Congress regarding the evaluation procedures for education of students with disabilities was the fact that? (Skill 15.07) (Easy)

   A. There were a large number of children and youths with disabilities in the United States
   B. Many children with disabilities were not receiving an appropriate education
   C. Many parents of children with disabilities were forced to seek services outside of the public realm
   D. All of the above

112. What TWO student behaviors are indicative of a possible crisis? (Skill 15.07) (Average Rigor)

   A. Bullying and socially active.
   B. Uncontrolled and intermittent periods of laughter and rage.
   C. High academic performance and gang activity
   D. Victim of violence and uncontrolled anger

113. The Individuals with Disabilities Education Act (IDEA) was signed into law in and later reauthorized to its current in what years? (Skill 16.01) (Easy)

   A. 1975 and 2004
   B. 1980 and 1990
   C. 1990 and 2004
   D. 1995 and 2001

114. How was the training of Special Education teachers changed by the No Child Left Behind Act of 2002? (Skill 16.01) (Average Rigor)

   A. Required all Special Education teachers to be certified in reading and math
   B. Required all Special Education teachers to take the same coursework as general education teachers
   C. If a Special Education teacher is teaching a core subject, he or she must meet the standard of a highly qualified teacher in that subject.
   D. All of the above

115. Which of the following is a specific change of language in IDEA? (Skill 16.01) (Average Rigor)

   A. The term "Disorder" changed to "Disability"
   B. The term "Children" changed to "Children and Youth"
   C. The term "Handicapped" changed to "Impairments"
   D. The term "Handicapped" changed to "With Disabilities"

116. Which component changed with the reauthorization of the Education for all Handicapped Children Act of 1975 (EHA) 1990 EHA Amendment? (Skill 16.01) (Average Rigor)

   A. Specific terminology
   B. Due Process Protections
   C. Non-Discriminatory Reevaluation Procedures
   D. Individual Education Plans

117. Which is untrue about the Americans with Disabilities Act (ADA)? (Skill 16.01) (Easy)

   A. It was signed into law the same year as IDEA by President Bush
   B. It reauthorized the discretionary programs of EHA
   C. It gives protection to all people on the basis of race, sex, national origin, and religion
   D. It guarantees equal opportunities to persons with disabilities in employment, public accommodations, transportation, government services, and telecommunications.

118. Requirements for evaluations were changed in IDEA 2004 to reflect that no 'single' assessment or measurement tool can be used to determine special education qualification, furthering that a disproportionate representation of what types of students? (Skill 16.01) (Average Rigor)

   A. Disabled
   B. Foreign
   C. Gifted
   D. Minority and Bilingual

119. IEPs continue to have multiple sections; one section, present levels now addresses what? *(Skill 16.01) (Easy)*

    A. Academic achievement and functional performance
    B. English as a second language
    C. Functional performance
    D. Academic achievement

120. What is true about IDEA? In order to be eligible, a student must:
    (Skill 16.01) (Easy)

    A. Have a medical disability
    B. Have a disability that fits into one of the categories listed in the law
    C. Attend a private school
    D. Be a slow learner

121. Free Appropriate Public Education (FAPE) describes Special Education and related services as? *(Skill 16.01) (Easy)*

    A. Public expenditure and standard to the state educational agency
    B. Provided in conformity with each student's individualized education program, if the program is developed to meet requirements of the law.
    C. Include preschool, elementary and/or secondary education in the state involved
    D. All of the above.

122. Jane is a third grader. Mrs. Smith, her teacher, noted that Jane was having difficulty with math and reading assignments. The results from recent diagnostic tests showed a strong sight vocabulary, strength in computational skills, but a weakness in comprehending what she read. This weakness was apparent in mathematical word problems as well. The multi-disciplinary team recommended placement in a special education resource room for learning disabilities two periods each school day. For the remainder of the school day, her placement will be: *(Skill 16.01) (Easy)*

    A. In the Regular Classroom
    B. At a Special School
    C. In a Self-Contained Classroom
    D. In a Resource Room for Mental Retardation

123. **Legislation in Public Law 94 – 142 attempts to:** *(Skill 16.01)* *(Rigorous)*

    A. Match the child's educational needs with appropriate educational services
    B. Include parents in the decisions made about their child's education
    C. Establish a means by which parents can provide input
    D. All of the above

124. **Manifest Determination CSEs should first:** *(Skill 16.01)* *(Average Rigor)*

    A. Make a decision on whether to return the student to placement
    B. Determine if the disability was a cause of the behavior.
    C. Evaluate the placement for possible needed change.
    D. Examine past behaviors.

125. **A Mother is upset that her child is not being helped and asks you about the difference between the t 504 Plan and an IEP. What is the difference?** *(Skill 16.01)* *(Rigorous)*

    A. 504 Plan requires classification, IEP requires labeling.
    B. 504 Plan requires provides no services just adaptations.
    C. 504 Plan is better for children who have ADHD.
    D. 504 plan provides little interventions/services, while an IEP is more intensive providing more services such as a special class.

126. **Which legislation has forced public and private facilities to accommodate those who are physically disabled?** *(Skill 16.01)* *(Easy)*

    A. ADA
    B. IDEA
    C. 504 Plan
    D. PL 105-17

127. **You have been asked to work with a teacher who states Special Education students do not belong in her room and she refuses to work with them. What should you remind her of?** *(Skill16.01)* *(Easy)*

    A. Confidentiality responsibility
    B. FAPE
    C. Part 200
    D. All of the above

128. The clock time from request for intervention to a determination of eligibility is: *(Skill 16.01) (Rigorous)*

    A. 30 school days
    B. 60 school days
    C. 30 calendar days
    D. 60 calendar days.

129. Which of the following must be completed first before testing occurs:
    (Skill 16.01) (Average Rigor)

    A. Teacher consult on student needs
    B. Pre-CSE Conference.
    C. Parental Permission for each test.
    D. All of the above

130. Effective transition was included in: *(Skill 16.01) (Rigorous)*

    A. American's with Disabilities Act (ADA)
    B. IDEA
    C. FERPA
    D. Public Law 130-999

131. IDEA defines children with a disability as children evaluated in accordance with what? *(Skill 16.01) (Average Rigor)*

    A. Those who because of their impairments, need education and related services.
    B. Those who because of their disabilities will not succeed in the regular education environment.
    C. Those who because of their impairments are in need of supports to accommodate them in the classroom.
    D. Those who are impaired and need physical or educational environmental assistance.

132. School Administrators understand special education and the reasons for the classes but may ask for you to? *(Skill 17.01) (Rigorous)*

    A. Keep them up to date on changing laws relevant to special education.
    B. Share your Paraprofessional with other teachers.
    C. Provide staff workshops
    D. Become a Parent Liaison

133. Miss Carol asks you for help. She has noted that her regular education student, Amanda, does not seem able to follow 3-step directions. What can you do? *(Skill 17.01) (Average Rigor)*

    A. Ask if the student was supposed placed in a blended classroom.
    B. Tell Miss Carol the student is a special education student.
    C. Observe Amanda and help the teacher make a referral to CSE.
    D. Offer to trade your student who is ready for inclusion for Amanda who needs

134. IDEA defines children with a disability as children evaluated in accordance with what? *(Skill 16.01) (Average Rigor)*

    A. Those who because of their impairments, need education and related services.
    B. Those who because of their disabilities will not succeed in the regular education environment.
    C. Those who because of their impairments are in need of supports to accommodate them in the classroom.
    D. Those who are impaired and need physical or educational environmental assistance.

135. A Pre-CSE coordinates and participates in due diligence through what process? *(Skill 16.01) (Rigorous)*

    A. Child study team meets first time without parents
    B. Teachers take child learning concerns to the school counselor
    C. School counselor contact parents for permission to perform screening assessments
    D. All of the above

136. The definition of Assistive Technology devices was amended in the IDEA reauthorization of 2004 to exclude what? *(Skill 16.01) (Average Rigor)*

    A. iPods other hand-held devices
    B. Computer enhanced technology
    C. Surgically implanted devices
    D. Braille and/or special learning aids

Pre-test Answer Key

1.	C	35.	A	69.	C	103.	A
2.	D	36.	A	70.	B	104.	D
3.	D	37.	A	71.	B	105.	A
4.	A	38.	D	72.	B	106.	D
5.	B	39.	C	73.	A	107.	D
6.	A	40.	B	74.	D	108.	D
7.	A	41.	A	75.	D	109.	D
8.	A	42.	B	76.	A	110.	B
9.	A	43.	D	77.	D	111.	D
10.	C	44.	D	78.	C	112.	D
11.	B	45.	D	79.	A	113.	C
12.	A	46.	A	80.	B	114.	C
13.	C	47.	C	81.	D	115.	D
14.	B	48.	D	82.	B	116.	A
15.	A	49.	C	83.	B	117.	B
16.	C	50.	D	84.	B	118.	D
17.	D	51.	C	85.	C	119.	A
18.	C	52.	C	86.	B	120.	B
19.	A	53.	D	87.	B	121.	D
20.	B	54.	C	88.	B	122.	A
21.	A	55.	A	89.	D	123.	D
22.	A	56.	B	90.	C	124.	B
23.	B	57.	C	91.	C	125.	D
24.	A	58.	C	92.	D	126.	A
25.	A	59.	B	93.	D	127.	D
26.	A	60.	B	94.	D	128.	C
27.	D	61.	C	95.	A	129.	C
28.	B	62.	A	96.	A	130.	B
29.	D	63.	C	97.	C	131.	C
30.	A	64.	B	98.	B	132.	A
31.	C	65.	A	99.	C	133.	C
32.	D	66.	B	100.	C	134.	C
33.	A	67.	A	101.	A	135.	D
34.	A	68.	C	102.	B	136.	C

Pre-test Rigor Table

Number	Level of Question	Skill Reference		Number	Level of Question	Skill Reference
1	Easy Rigor	1.01		36	Average Rigor	4.01
2	Average Rigor	1.01		37	Easy Rigor	4.01
3	Easy Rigor	1.01		38	Average Rigor	4.02
4	Rigorous	1.01		39	Average Rigor	4.02
5	Average Rigor	1.01		40	Average Rigor	4.05
6	Average Rigor	1.01		41	Average Rigor	4.05
7	Average Rigor	1.01		42	Rigorous	4.05
8	Average Rigor	1.01		43	Rigorous	4.07
9	Rigorous	1.01		44	Average Rigor	5.01
10	Rigorous	1.04		45	Average Rigor	5.02
11	Rigorous	1.04		46	Average Rigor	5.05
12	Easy Rigor	1.04		47	Average Rigor	5.06
13	Rigorous	1.04		48	Average Rigor	5.06
14	Average Rigor	1.04		49	Easy Rigor	5.06
15	Average Rigor	1.05		50	Rigorous	5.08
16	Easy Rigor	2.02		51	Average Rigor	6.01
17	Average Rigor	2.02		52	Average Rigor	6.01
18	Average Rigor	2.02		53	Easy Rigor	6.01
19	Rigorous	2.04		54	Rigorous	6.01
20	Average Rigor	3.01		55	Average Rigor	6.03
21	Average Rigor	3.01		56	Rigorous	6.05
22	Rigorous	3.01		57	Easy Rigor	6.05
23	Easy Rigor	3.02		58	Average Rigor	6.08
24	Average Rigor	3.03		59	Average Rigor	7.01
25	Rigorous	3.05		60	Rigorous	7.01
26	Rigorous	3.05		61	Rigorous	7.01
27	Rigorous	3.05		62	Easy Rigor	7.01
28	Easy Rigor	3.07		63	Easy Rigor	7.02
29	Average Rigor	3.07		64	Rigorous	7.06
30	Easy Rigor	3.07		65	Average Rigor	7.06
31	Easy Rigor	4.01		66	Rigorous	7.06
32	Easy Rigor	4.01		67	Easy Rigor	8.06
33	Average Rigor	4.01		68	Rigorous	8.06
34	Easy Rigor	4.01		69	Average Rigor	8.06
35	Easy Rigor	4.01		70	Rigorous	8.06
				71	Average Rigor	8.06
				72	Rigorous	9.01

73	Rigorous	9.04		105	Rigorous	14.04
74	Rigorous	10.01		106	Average Rigor	14.04
75	Easy Rigor	10.02		107	Average Rigor	15.01
76	Easy Rigor	10.02		108	Rigorous	15.01
77	Rigorous	10.04		109	Rigorous	15.02
78	Rigorous	10.04		110	Rigorous	15.02
79	Rigorous	10.05		111	Rigorous	15.04
80	Rigorous	11.01		112	Easy Rigor	15.07
81	Average Rigor	11.01		113	Average Rigor	15.07
82	Rigorous	11.01		114	Easy Rigor	16.01
83	Rigorous	11.02		115	Average Rigor	16.01
84	Average Rigor	11.03		116	Average Rigor	16.01
85	average Rigor	11.03		117	Average Rigor	16.01
86	Easy Rigor	11.03		118	Easy Rigor	16.01
87	Average Rigor	11.04		119	Average Rigor	16.01
88	Average Rigor	11.07		120	Easy Rigor	16.01
89	Rigorous	12.01		121	Easy Rigor	16.01
90	Easy Rigor	12.01		122	Easy Rigor	16.01
91	Rigorous	12.03		123	Easy Rigor	16.01
92	Easy Rigor	12.1		124	Average Rigor	16.01
93	Rigorous	12.1		125	Rigorous	16.01
94	Rigorous	13.01		126	Rigorous	16.01
95	Easy Rigor	13.01		127	Average Rigor	16.01
96	Rigorous	13.03		128	Rigorous	16.01
97	Average Rigor	13.04		129	Easy Rigor	16.01
98	Rigorous	13.05		130	Easy Rigor	16.01
99	Easy Rigor	13.06		131	Rigorous	16.01
100	Rigorous	13.06		132	Average Rigor	16.01
101	Rigorous	13.07		133	Rigorous	16.01
102	Rigorous	14.01		134	Rigorous	17.01
103	Average Rigor	14.02		135	Rigorous	3.01, 7.02
104	Rigorous	14.02		136	Rigorous	

Rationales with Sample Questions

DIRECTIONS: Read each item and select the best response

1. **Which is an educational characteristic common to students with mild intellectual learning and behavioral disabilities?** *(Skill 1.01) (Easy)*

    A. Show interest in schoolwork
    B. Have intact listening skills
    C. Require modification in classroom instruction
    D. Respond better to passive than to active learning tasks

Answer: C. Require modification in classroom instruction

Here are some of the characteristics of students with mild learning and behavioral disabilities are as follows: Lack of interest in schoolwork; prefer concrete rather than abstract lessons; weak listening skills; low achievement; limited verbal and/or writing skills; respond better to active rather than passive learning tasks; Have areas of talent or ability often overlooked by teachers; prefer to receive special help in regular classroom; higher dropout rate than regular education students; achieve in accordance with teacher expectations; require modification in classroom instruction; and are easily distracted.

2. **Zero Reject requires all children with disabilities be provided with what?** *(Skill 1.01) (Average)*

    A. Total exclusion of Functional exclusion
    B. Adherence to the annual local education agency (LEA) reporting.
    C. Free, appropriate public education
    D. Both b and c.

Answer: D. Both B and C.

The principle of zero reject requires that all children with disabilities be provided with a free, appropriate public education and the LEA reporting procedure locates, identifies and evaluates children with disabilities within a given jurisdiction to ensure their attendance in public school.

3.   Joey is in a mainstreamed preschool program. One of the means his teacher uses in determining growth in adaptive skills is that of observation. Some questions about Joey's behavior that she might ask include: *(Average) (Skill 1.01)*

   A. Is he able to hold a cup?
   B. Can he call the name of any of his toys?
   C. Can he reach for an object and grasp it?
   D. All of the above

Answer: D. All of the above

Here are some characteristics of individual with mental retardation or intellectual Disabilities:
   - IQ of 70 or below
   - Limited cognitive ability; delayed academic achievement, particularly in language-related subjects
   - Deficits in memory which often relate to poor initial perception, or inability to apply stored information to relevant situations
   - Impaired formulation of learning strategies
   - Difficulty in attending to relevant aspects of stimuli: slowness in reaction time or in employing alternate strategies.

4.   **Individuals with mental retardation can be characterized as:** *(Skill 1.01) (Rigorous)*

   A. Often indistinguishable from normal developing children at an early age
   B. Having a higher than normal rate of motor activity
   C. Displaying significant discrepancies in ability levels
   D. Uneducable in academic skills

Answer: A. Often indistinguishable from normal developing children at an early age.

Here are some characteristics of individual with mental retardation or intellectual Disabilities:
   - IQ of 70 or below
   - Limited cognitive ability; delayed academic achievement, particularly in language-related subjects
   - Deficits in memory which often relate to poor initial perception, or inability to apply stored information to relevant situations
   - Impaired formulation of learning strategies
   - Difficulty in attending to relevant aspects of stimuli: slowness in reaction time or in employing alternate strategies

5.   **Which of the following statements about children with an emotional/ behavioral disorder is true?** *(Skill 1.01) (Average)*

    A. They have very high IQs
    B. They display poor social skills
    C. They are academic achievers
    D. Mature understanding of concepts

Answer: B. They display poor social skills

Children who exhibit mild behavioral disorders are characterized by:
- Average or above average scores on intelligence tests
- Poor academic achievement; learned helplessness
- Unsatisfactory interpersonal relationships
- Immaturity; attention seeking

Aggressive, acting-out behavior: (hitting, fighting, teasing, yelling, refusing to comply with requests, excessive attention seeking, poor anger control, temper tantrums, hostile reactions, defiant use of language) OR
Anxious, withdrawn behavior: (infantile behavior, social isolation, few friends, withdrawal into fantasy, fears, hypochondria, unhappiness, crying).

6.   **Which behavior would be expected at the mild level of emotional/behavioral disorders?** *(Skill 1.01) (Average)*

    A. Attention seeking
    B. Inappropriate affect
    C. Self-Injurious
    D. Poor sense of identity

Answer: A. Attention seeking

See rationale to question 19.

7. **All of the following EXCEPT one are characteristics of a student who is Emotionally Disturbed?** *(Skill 1.01) (Average)*

A. Socially accepted by peers.
B. Highly disruptive to the classroom environment.
C. Academic difficulties.
D. Areas of talent overlooked by a teacher

Answer: A. Socially accepted by peers.

While a child may be socially accepted by peers, children who are emotionally disturbed tend to alienate those around them, and are often ostracized.

8. **Echolalia is a characteristic of what?** *(Skill 1.01) (Average)*

A. Autism
B. Mental Retardation
C. Social Pragmatic Disorder
D. ADHD

Answer: A. Autism

Echolalia is echoing/repeating the speech of others, which is a characteristic of autism.

9. **Children are engaged in a game of charades. Which type of social-interpersonal skill is the teacher most likely attempting to develop?** *(Skill 1.01) (Rigorous)*

A. Sensitivity to others
B. Making behavioral choices in social situations
C. Social maturity
D. All of the above

Answer: A Sensitivity to others

Children with disabilities often perceive facial expressions and gestures differently to their nondisabled peers, due to their impairment. The game of charades, a guessing game, would help them develop sensitivity to others.

10. Johnny just hit Sarah for no apparent reason. What condition listed below could allow a conclusion that this action it was related to his disability. *(Skill 1.04) (Rigorous)*

    A. Hearing Impairment
    B. Learning disabled with Central Auditory Processing issues.
    C. Social Pragmatic Disorder
    D. Obsessive Compulsive Disorder

Answer: C. Social Pragmatic Disorder

A Social pragmatic disorder interferes with the students ability to correctly process social cues. It is possible that Johnny misinterpreted an action as an insult or a threat to his person.

11. Five-year-old Tom continues to substitute the "w" sound for the "r" sound when pronouncing words; therefore, he often distorts words e.g., "wabbit" for "rabbit" and "wat" for "rat." His articulation disorder is basically a problem in: *(Skill 1.04) (Easy)*

    A. Phonology   s
    B. Morphology
    C. Syntax
    D. Semantics

Answer: B. ~~Morphology~~ *Phonology*
Consenent replacement is classic

Morphemes are the smallest units of language with meaning. They are root words or stand alone words.

12. Which of the following is untrue about the ending "er?" *(Skill 1.04) (Rigorous)*

    A. It is an example of a free morpheme
    B. It represents one of the smallest units of meaning within a word
    C. It is called an inflectional ending
    D. When added to a word, it connotes a comparative status

Answer: A. It is an example of a free morpheme

Morpheme: the smallest unit of meaningful language. "Er" on its own, has no meaning.

13.　Which component of language involves language content rather than the form of language? *(Skill 1.04) (Average)*

   A. Phonology
   B. Morphology
   C. Semantics
   D. Syntax

Answer: C. Semantics

Semantics involves specifics regarding word usage.

14.　Television, movies, radio, and newspapers contribute the public's poor understanding of disabilities by: *(Skill 1.05) (Average)*

   A. Only portraying those who look normal.
   B. Portraying the person with the disability as one with incredible abilities.
   C. Showing emotionally disturbed children
   D. Portraying all people in wheel chairs as independent.

Answer: B. Portraying the person with the disability as one with incredible abilities.

Many movies, TV shows, etc. only show a person with a disability who has "overcome" his/her disability with a talent. The hype over "J-Mac," a student with Autism at Greece Athena making several baskets is an example. The media only showed his incredible talent, and ignored any struggles he may have had.

15.　The definition for "Other Health Impaired (OHI)" in IDEA: *(Skill 1.05) (Average)*

   A. Is the definition that accepts heart conditions.
   B. Includes deafness, blindness or profound mental retardation
   C. includes Autism and PDD.
   D. Includes cochlear implants.

Answer: A. Is the definition that accepts heart conditions.

OHI includes a variety of reasons and diagnoses including heart conditions.

16.   **Which of the following is true about autism?** *(Skill 2.02) (Easy)*

   A. It is caused by having cold, aloof or hostile parents
   B. Approximately 4 out of 10 people have autism
   C. It is a separate exceptionality category in IDEA
   D. It is a form of mental illness

Answer: C. It is a separate exceptionality category in IDEA

In IDEA, the 1990 Amendment to the Education for All Handicapped Children Act, autism was classified as a separate exceptionality category. It is thought to be caused by a neurological or biochemical dysfunction. It generally becomes evident before age 3. The condition occurs in about 4 of every 10,000 persons. Smith and Luckasson, 1992, describe it as a severe language disorder which affects thinking, communication, and behavior. They list the following characteristics:

- **Absent or distorted relationships with people**—inability to relate with people except as objects, inability to express affection, or ability to build and maintain only distant, suspicious or bizarre relationships.
- **Extreme or peculiar problems in communication**—absence of verbal language or language that is not functional such as echolalia (parroting what one hears), misuse of pronouns (e.g. he for you or I for her), neologisms (made-up meaningless words or sentences), talk that bears little or no resemblance to reality.
- **Self-stimulation**—repetitive stereo-typed behavior that seems to have no purposes other than providing sensory stimulation. this may take a wide variety of forms, such as swishing saliva, twirling objects, patting one's cheeks, flapping one's arms, staring,…etc.
- **Self-injury**—repeated physical self-abuse, such as biting, scratching, or poking oneself, head banging, …etc
- **Perceptual anomalies**—unusual responses or absence of response to stimuli that seem to indicate sensory impairment or unusual sensitivity.

17.   **Antwon is in your 12:1:1 in a 10th grade Regent program. You begin to wonder if a functional program would be best when you not the student's?** *(Skill 2.02) (Average)*

   A. Lack of ability to comprehend inferences.
   B. Stuttering
   C. Delayed processing.
   D. Difficulties understanding concrete examples

Answer: D. Difficulties understanding concrete examples

Typical concrete operations are developed from age 6 to age 12.

18.   Which of the following is a possible side-effect of an Anti-depressant? *(Skill 2.04)* *(Rigorous)*

   A. Anxiety
   B. Aggression
   C. Tremors
   D. Restlessness

Answer: C. Tremors

Tremors is one indicator of a possible side-effect of an Anti-depressant,

19.   **Mrs. Stokes has been teaching her third-grade students about mammals during a recent science unit. Which of the following would be true of a criterion-referenced test she might administer at the conclusion of the unit?** *(Skill 3.01)* *(Average)*

   A. It will be based on unit objectives
   B. Derived scores will be used to rank student achievement.
   C. Standardized scores are effective of national performance samples
   D. All of the above

 Answer: A. It will be based on unit objectives

Criterion-referenced tests measure the progress made by individuals in mastering specific skills. The content is based on a specific set of objectives rather than on the general curriculum. Criterion-referenced tests provide measurements pertaining to the information a given student needs to know and the skills that student needs to master. Norm-referenced tests have a large advantage over criterion-referenced tests when used for screening or program evaluation. Norm-referenced tests provide a means of comparing a student's performance to the performance typically expected of others of his age.

20. **For which of the following purposes is a norm-referenced test least appropriate?** *(Skill 3.01) (Average)*

    A. Screening
    B. Individual program planning
    C. Program evaluation
    D. Making placement decisions

Answer: B. Individual program planning

An example of this is assessing a new student to figure out which reading group he/she would be a good fit.

21. **The extent to which a test measures what its authors or users claim that it measures is called its:** *(Skill 3.01) (Rigorous)*

    A. Validity
    B. Reliability
    C. Normality
    D. Acculturation

Answer: A. Validity

Validity is the degree or extent to which a test measures what it was designed or intended to measure. Reliability is the extent to which a test is consistent in its measurements.

22. **What do the 9th and 10th Amendments to the U.S. Constitution state about education?** *(Skill 3.02) (Easy)*

    A. That education belongs to the people
    B. That education is an unstated power vested in the states
    C. That elected officials mandate education
    D. That education is free

Answer: A. That education belongs to the people

The concept of unstated power regarding education was instituted. It was felt that some education should be state specific. The refusal of states to provide services for those needing special education services, and a need for financial support encouraged the federal government to take a more involved stance.

23. **Michael's teacher complains that he is constantly out of his seat. She also reports that he has trouble paying attention to what is going on in class for more than a couple of minutes at a time. He appears to be trying, but his writing is often illegible, containing many reversals. Although he seems to want to please, he is very impulsive and stays in trouble with his teacher. He is failing reading, and his math grades, though somewhat better, are still below average. Michael's psychometric evaluation should include assessment for:** *(Skill 3.02)* *(Average)*

A. Mild mental retardation
B. Specific learning disabilities
C. Mild behavior disorders
D. Hearing impairment

Answer: B. Specific learning disabilities

Here are some of the characteristics of persons with learning disabilities:
- Hyperactivity: a rate o motor activity higher than normal
- Perceptual difficulties: visual, auditory, and hap tic perceptual problems
- Perceptual-motor impairments: poor integration of visual and motor systems, often affecting fine motor coordination.
- Disorders of memory and thinking: memory deficits, trouble with problem-solving, concept formation and association, poor awareness of own metacognitive skills (learning strategies)
- Impulsiveness: acts before considering consequences, poor impulse control, often followed by remorselessness.
- Academic problems in reading, math, writing or spelling; significant discrepancies in ability levels.

24. **Which of the following is an example of an Alternative Assessment?** *(Skill 3.05) (Rigorous)*

A. Testing skills in a "real world" setting in several settings.
B. Pre-test of student knowledge of fractions before beginning Wood Shop.
C. Answering an Essay question that allows for creative thought.
D. A compilation of a series of tests in a Portfolio.

Answer: A. Testing skills in a "real world" setting in several settings.

Naturalistic Assessment is a form of alternative assessment that requires testing in actual application settings of life skills. The skill of using money correctly could be correctly assessed in this method by taking the student shopping in different settings.

25. **The No Child Left Behind Act (NCLB) affected students with Limited English Proficiency (LEP) by :** *(Skill 3.05) (Rigorous)*

   A. Requiring these students to demonstrate English Language Proficiency before a High School Diploma is granted.
   B. Providing allowances for schools not to require them to take and pass state Reading Exams (RCTs) if the students were enrolled in US schools for less than a year.
   C. Providing allowances for these students to opt out of state math tests if the student was enrolled in a US school for less than one year.
   D. Both B and C,

Answer: A. Requiring these students to demonstrate English Language Proficiency before a High School Diploma is granted.

NCLB requires Special Education content area teachers to be just as equally qualified as their counterparts. They must have a "Highly Qualified" status.

26.   When you need to evaluate a students work ethics, you should give what assessment? *(Skill 3.05) (Rigorous)*

   A. Naturalistic
   B. Dynamic
   C. Performance Based
   D. Criterion referenced

Answer: A. Naturalistic

Work ethics are social skills. Social skills, are best evaluated over time in their natural surroundings.

27.   Autism is a disorder characterized by: *(Skill 3.07) (Easy)*

   A. Distorted relationships with others
   B. Perceptual anomalies
   C. Self-stimulation
   D. All or the above

Answer: D. All or the above

In IDEA, the 1990 Amendment to the Education for All Handicapped Children Act, autism was classified as a separate exceptionality category. It is thought to be caused by a neurological or biochemical dysfunction. It generally becomes evident before age 3. The condition occurs in about 4 of every 10,000 persons. Smith and Luckasson, 1992, describe it as a severe language disorder which affects thinking, communication, and behavior. They list the following characteristics:

- **Absent or distorted relationships with people**—inability to relate with people except as objects, inability to express affection, or ability to build and maintain only distant, suspicious or bizarre relationships.
- **Extreme or peculiar problems in communication**—absence of verbal language or language that is not functional such as echolalia (parroting what one hears),misuse of pronouns (e.g. he for you or I for her), neologisms (made-up meaningless words or sentences), talk that bears little or no resemblance to reality.
- **Self-stimulation**—repetitive stereo-typed behavior that seems to have no purposes other than providing sensory stimulation. this may take a wide variety of forms, such as swishing saliva, twirling objects, patting one's cheeks, flapping one's arms, staring,…etc.
- **Self-injury**—repeated physical self-abuse, such as biting, scratching, or poking oneself, head banging, …etc
- **Perceptual anomalies**—unusual responses or absence of response to stimuli that seem to indicate sensory impairment or unusual sensitivity.

28.	IDEA 2004 states that evaluations of student eligibility should? *(Skill 3.07) (Average Rigor)*

A.	Be At intervals with teacher discretion
B.	use a variety of assessment tools and strategies.
C.	Should only address the area of determined need.
D.	Conducted annually

Answer: B. use a variety of assessment tools and strategies.

Evaluation to determine eligibility should not be made using one tool or addressing a previously thought need alone. Other issues and needs may be found by using a variety of assessment tools.

29.	Safeguards against bias and discrimination in the assessment of children include: (Skill 3.07) (Easy)

A.	The testing of a child in Standard English
B.	The requirement for the use of one standardized test
C.	The use of evaluative materials in the child's native language or other mode of communication
D.	All testing performed by a certified, licensed, psychologist

Answer: C. The use of evaluative materials in the child's native language or other mode of communication

The law requires that the child be evaluated in his native language, or mode of communication. The idea that a licensed psychologist evaluates the child does not meet the criteria if it is not done in the child's normal mode of communication.

30. **Which of these factors relate to eligibility for learning disabilities?** *(Skill 4.01) (Easy)*

    A. A discrepancy between potential and performance
    B. Sub-average intellectual functioning
    C. Social deficiencies or learning deficits that are not due to intellectual, sensory, or physical conditions
    D. Documented results of behavior checklists and anecdotal records of aberrant behavior

Answer: A. A discrepancy between potential and performance

Tests need to show a discrepancy between potential and performance. Classroom observations and samples of student work (such as impaired reading ability) also provide indicators of possible learning disabilities. Eligibility for services in behavior disorders requires documented evidence of social deficiencies or learning deficits that are not due to intellectual, sensory, or physical conditions. Any student undergoing multidisciplinary evaluation is usually given an intelligence test, diagnostic achievement tests, and social and/or adaptive inventories. Answers b, c and d are symptoms displayed before testing for eligibility. Some students who display these symptoms do fail the tests and are not categorized as eligible to receive services.

31. **In general, characteristics of the learning disabled include:** *(Skill 4.01) (Easy)*

    A. A low level of performance in a majority of academic skill areas
    B. Limited cognitive ability
    C. A discrepancy between achievement and potential
    D. A uniform pattern of academic development

Answer: C. A discrepancy between achievement and potential

The individual with a specific learning disability exhibits a discrepancy between achievement and potential.

32. **As a separate exceptionality category in IDEA, autism:** *(Skill 4.01)* *(Average Rigor)*

   A. Includes emotional/behavioral disorders as defined in federal regulations
   B. Adversely affects educational performance
   C. Is thought to be a form of mental illness
   D. Is a developmental disability that affects verbal and non-verbal communication

Answer: D. Is a developmental disability that affects verbal and non-verbal communication

Autism effects interacting with others, because communication is moderately to profoundly impaired.

33. **Which of the following must be provided in a written notice to parents when proposing a child's educational placement?** *(Skill 4.01* *(Easy)*

   A. A list of parental due process safeguards
   B. A list of current test scores
   C. A list of persons responsible for the child's education
   D. A list of academic subjects the child has passed

Answer: A. A list of parental due process safeguards

Written notice must be provided to parents prior to a proposal or refusal or refusal to initiate or make a change in the child's identification, evaluation or educational placement. Notices must contain:
   • A listing of parental due process safeguards.
   • A description and a rationale for the chosen action.
   • A detailed listing of components (e.g. tests, records, reports) which were
   • the basis for the decision.
   • Assurance that the language and content of the notices were understood by the parents.

34. **Students who receive special services in a regular classroom with consultation, generally have academic and/or social-interpersonal performance deficits at which level of severity?** *(Skill 4.01) (Easy)*

  A. Mild
  B. Moderate
  C. Severe
  D. Profound

Answer: A. Mild

The majority of students receiving special services are enrolled primarily in regular classes. Those with mild learning and behavior problems exhibit academic and/or social interpersonal deficits that are often evident only in a school-related setting. These students appear no different to their peers, physically.

35. **The greatest number of students receiving special services are enrolled primarily in:** *(Skill 4.01) (Average Rigor)*
  A. The regular classroom
  B. The resource room
  C. Self-contained classrooms
  D. Special schools

Answer: A. The regular classroom

See previous question.

36. **The most restrictive environment in which an individual might be placed and receive instruction is that of:** *(Skill4.01) (Easy)*

  A. Institutional setting
  B. Homebound instruction
  C. Special schools
  D. Self-contained special classes

Answer: A. Institutional setting

Individuals, who require significantly modified environments for care treatment and accommodation, are usually educated in an institutional setting. They usually have profound/multiple disorders.

37. A test, which measures students' skill development in academic content areas, is classified as an _____ test. *(Skill 4.02) (Average Rigor)*

A. Achievement
B. Aptitude
C. Adaptive
D. Intelligence

Answer: A. Achievement

Achievement tests directly assess students' skill development in academic content areas. It measures the degree to which a student has benefited education and/or life experiences compared to others of the same age or grade level. They may be used as diagnostic tests to find strengths and weaknesses of students. They may be used for screening, placement progress evaluation, and curricular effectiveness.

38. **The Key Math Diagnostic Arithmetic Test is an individually administered test of math skills. It is comprised of fourteen subtests which are classified into the major math areas of content, operations, and applications for which subtest scores are reported. The test manual describes the population sample upon which the test was normed, and reports data pertaining to reliability and validity. In addition, for each item in the test, a behavioral objective is presented. From the description, it can be determined that this achievement test is:** *(Skill 4.02) (Average Rigor)*

A. Individually administered
B. Criterion-referenced
C. Diagnostic
D. All of the above

Answer: D. All of the above

The test has a limited content designed to measure to what extent the student has mastered specific areas in math. The expressions "individually administered" and "diagnostic" appear in the description of the test.

39.	Which of the following is an example of tactile perception? *(Skill 4.05) (Average Rigor)*

A. Making an angel in the snow with one's body
B. Running a specified course
C. Identifying a rough surface with eyes closed
D. Demonstrating aerobic exercises

Answer: C. Identifying a rough surface with eyes closed

Tactile: having to do with touch.

40.	Which of the following activities best exemplifies a kinesthetic exercise in developing body awareness? *(Skill 4.05) (Average Rigor)*

A. Touching materials of different textures
B. Singing with motions "Head and Shoulder's Knees and toes."
C. Identifying geometric shapes being drawn on one's back
D. Making a shadow-box project

Answer: B.
Kinesthetic: having to do with body movement.

41.	Which of the following teaching activities is least likely to enhance observational learning in students with special needs? *(Skill 4.05) (Rigorous)*

A. A verbal description of the task to be performed, followed by having the children immediately attempt to perform the instructed behavior
B. A demonstration of the behavior, followed by an immediate opportunity for the children to imitate the behavior
C. A simultaneous demonstration and explanation of the behavior, followed by ample opportunity for the children to rehearse the instructed behavior
D. Physically guiding the children through the behavior to be imitated, while verbally explaining the behavior

Answer: A. A verbal description of the task to be performed, followed by having the children immediately attempt to perform the instructed behavior

Students are given verbal instructions only. The children are not given a chance to observe, or see, the behavior so that they can imitate it. Some of the students may have hearing deficiencies.

42.   Acculturation refers to the individual's: *(Skill 4.07) (Rigorous)*

   A. Gender
   B. Experiential background
   C. Social class
   D. Ethnic background

Answer: B. Experiential background

A person's culture has little to do with gender, or social class, or ethnicity. A person is the product of his experiences. Acculturation: differences in experiential background.

43.   According to IDEA 2004, the IEP team is composed of: *(Skill 5.01) (Average Rigor)*

   A. The student's Special Education Teacher and Psychiatrist
   B. The student's parents/guardians and their lawyer
   C. Content Specialist and the CASE
   D. The student's parent(s)/guardians and those providing the related services.

Answer: D. The student's parent(s)/guardians and those providing the related services.

It is a parent's right to be at the meeting. Parents should be present, but often are not. Should the parent not be present an attempt should be made to contact the parent/guardian to see if they want to postpone the meeting. Those who deliver the services the student receives also must be present.

44. **What components of the IEP are required by law?** *(Skill 5.02)* *(Average Rigor)*

A. Present level of academic and functional performance; statement of how the disability affects the student's involvement and progress; evaluation criteria and timeliness for instructional objective achievement; modifications of accommodations
B. Projected dates for services initiation with anticipated frequency, location and duration; statement of when parent will be notified; statement of annual goals
C. Extent to which child will not participate in regular education program; transitional needs for students age 14.
D. All of the above.

Answer: D. All of the above.

IEPs state 14 elements that are required, review them in Skill 1.3 under IEP. Educators must keep themselves apprised of the changes and amendments to laws such as IDEA 2004 with addendums released in October of 2006.

45. **CSE meetings are held for different reasons. Which of the following would be a reason to hold a CSE meeting?** *(Skill 5.05)* *(Average Rigor)*

A. Moving from one school to another within the school district.
B. Temporary placement in inclusion.
C. A teacher requests a child to be removed from his/her class.
D. Transition to post-secondary school life.

Answer: D. Transition to post-secondary school life.

Temporary placement does not require a CSE, it does however require a parental/guardian signature. The temp placement of services should be reviewed at a CSE for its success to discuss permanent placement. Post-school transition is one of the most important CSE's held. It discusses services the student may/will need to be successful in the post-school environment.

46. **Vocational training programs are based on all of the following ideas except:** *(Skill 5.06) (Average Rigor)*

   A. Students obtain career training from elementary through high school
   B. Students acquire specific training in job skills prior to exiting school
   C. Students need specific training and supervision in applying skills learned in school to requirements in job situations
   D. Students obtain needed instruction and field-based experiences that help them to be able to work in specific occupations

Answer: A. Students obtain career training from elementary through high school

Vocational education programs or transition programs prepare students for entry into the labor force. They are usually incorporated into the work-study at the high school or post-secondary levels. They are usually focused on job skills, job opportunities, and skill requirements for specific jobs, personal qualifications in relation to job requirements, work habits, money management, and academic skills needed for specific jobs.

47. **In career education specific training and preparation required for the world of work occurs during the phase of:** *(Skill 5.06) (Average Rigor)*

   A. Career Awareness
   B. Career Exploration
   C. Career Preparation
   D. Daily Living and Personal-Social Interaction

Answer: C. Career Preparation

Curricular aspects of career education include:
- career awareness: diversity of available jobs
- career exploration: skills needed for occupational groups
- career preparation: specific training and preparation required for the world of work

48. **What is most descriptive of vocational training in special education?** *(Skill 5.06) (Easy)*

A. Trains students in intellectual disabilities solely
B. Segregates students with and without disabilities in vocational training programs
C. Only includes students capable of moderate supervision
D. Instruction focuses upon self-help skills, social-interpersonal skills, motor skills, rudimentary academic skills, simple occupational skills, and lifetime leisure and occupational skills

Answer: D. Instruction focuses upon self-help skills, social-interpersonal skills, motor skills, rudimentary academic skills, simple occupational skills, and lifetime leisure and occupational skills

Persons with disabilities are mainstreamed with nondisabled students where possible. Special sites provide training for those persons with more severe disabilities who are unable to be successfully taught in an integrated setting. Specially trained vocational counselors monitor and supervise student work sites.

49. **Teachers must keep meticulous records. They are required to share all of them with the student's parent/guardian EXCEPT:** *(Skill 5.08) (Rigorous)*

A. Daily Attendance Record
B. Grade reports.
C. Teacher's personal notes.
D. Discipline notice placed in cumulative record.

Answer: C. Teacher's personal notes.

Information on students that a teacher writes down for his/her own reference do not have to be shared with parents. However the teacher may choose to share these notes with the parent/guardian..

50.   **In establishing your behavior management plan with the students it is best to:** *(Skill 6.01) (Average Rigor)*

    A. Have rules written and in place on day one.
    B. To hand out a copy of the rules to the students on day one.
    C. Have separate rules for each class on day one.
    D. Have students involved in creating the rules on Day one.

Answer: D. Have students involved in creating the rules on Day one.

Rules are easier to follow when you not only know the reason they are in place, you took part in creating them. It may be good to already to have a few rules pre-written and then to discuss if they cover all the rules the students have created. If not,, it is possible you may want to modify your set of pre-written rules.

51.   **Students with Autistic tendencies can be more successful academically by the teacher:** *(Skill 6.01) (Average Rigor)*

    A. Ignoring inappropriate behaviors.
    B. Allowing them to go out of the room during instruction.
    C. Keeping a calendar on the board of expected transitions.
    D. Asking the CSE for a 1:1 Aide.

Answer: C. Keeping a calendar on the board of expected transitions.

Students with Autism tend to express an inability to transition unless that transition is already expected. Placing calendars and schedule where they can be seen are important.

52.   **Which tangible reinforcer would Mr. Whiting find to be most effective with teenagers?** *(Skill 6.01) (Easy)*

    A. Plastic whistle
    B. Winnie-the-Pooh book
    C. Free Homework Pass
    D. Toy ring

Answer: C. Free Homework Pass

Students in thie teens often want something that will assist their grades. Freebies such as this are incredible tangible rewards.

53. **Charise comes into your room and seems to know every button to push to get you upset with her. What would be a good intervention?** *(Skill 6.01) (Rigorous)*

   A. Nonverbal Interactions
   B. Self-monitoring
   C. Proximity Control
   D. Planned Ignoring

Answer: D. Planned Ignoring

Planned Ignoring takes control from the student and tends to reduce the irritating behaviors as they do not draw the attention they were employed to receive.

54. **Which of the following is a good example of a generalization?** *(Skill 6.03) (Average Rigor)*

   A. Jim has learned to add and is now ready to subtract
   B. Sarah adds sets of units to obtain a product
   C. Bill recognizes a vocabulary word on a billboard when traveling
   D. Jane can spell the word "net" backwards to get the word "ten"

Answer: C. Bill recognizes a vocabulary word on a billboard when traveling

Generalization is the occurrence of a learned behavior in the presence of a stimulus other than the one that produced the initial response. It is the expansion of a student's performance beyond the initial setting. Students must be able to expand or transfer what is learned to other settings (e.g., reading to math word problems, resource room to regular classroom). Generalization may be enhanced by the following:

- Use many examples in teaching to deepen application of learned skills
- Use consistency in initial teaching situations, and later introduce variety in format, procedure and use of examples
- Have the same information presented by different teachers, in different settings, and under varying conditions
- Include a continuous reinforcement schedule at first, later changing to delayed and intermittent schedules as instruction progresses
- Teach students to record instances of generalization and to reward themselves at that time
- Associate naturally occurring stimuli when possible

55. **What can you do to make create a good working environment with a classroom assistant?** *(Skill 6.05) (Rigorous)*

   A. Planning lessons with the assistant.
   B. Writing a contract that clearly defines his/her responsibilities in the classroom.
   C. Remove previously given responsibilities.
   D. All of the above

Answer: A. Planning lessons with the assistant..

Planning with your classroom assistant shows that you respect his//her input , and allows you to see where he/she feels confident.

56. **One of the most important goals of the Special Education Teacher is to foster and create with the student:** *(Skill 6.05) (Easy)*

   A. Handwriting skills.
   B. Self-Advocacy
   C. An increased level of reading
   D. Logical reasoning

Answer: B. Self-Advocacy

When a student achieves the ability to recognize his/her deficits and knows how to correctly advocate for his/her needs, the child has learned one of the most important skills of his/her life.

57. **A paraprofessional has been assigned to assist you in the classroom. What action on the part of the teacher would lead to a poor working relationship?** *(Skill 6.08) (Average Rigor)*

   A. Having the paraprofessional lead a small group.
   B. Telling the paraprofessional what you expect him/her to do.
   C. Defining classroom behavior management as your responsibility alone.
   D. Taking an active role in his/her evaluation.

Answer: C. Defining classroom behavior management as your responsibility alone.

When you do not allow another adult in the room to enforce the class rules, yoyu create an environment where the other adult is seen as someone not to be respected. No one wants to be in a work environment where they do not feel respected..

58.   Mrs. Freud is a Consultant Teacher. She has two students with Mr. Ricardo. Mrs. Freud should: *(Skill 7.01) (Average Rigor)*

    A. Co-Teach
    B. Spend two days a week in the classroom helping out.
    C. Discuss lessons with the teacher and suggest modifications before class.
    D. Pull her students out for instructional modifications.

Answer: C. Discuss lessons with the teacher and suggest modifications before class.

Consultant teaching provides the least interventions possible for the success of the academic child. Pushing in or pulling out are not essential components. However, an occasional observation as a classroom observer who does not single out any students may also be helpful to providing modifications for the student.

59.   **Which of the following would be classified as direct rather than indirect services that a specially trained special education teacher would provide to regular education teachers?** *(Skill 7.01) (Rigorous)*

    A. Answer questions about a particular child's academic or social-inter-personal needs
    B. Teach a math unit on measurement
    C. Assist with selecting special materials for a student
    D. Develop math worksheets tailored to meet a student's needs

Answer: B. Teach a math unit on measurement

Indirect services are those given when special education personnel consult with regular classroom teachers to assist them in teaching students with mild disabilities who are enrolled fulltime in their regular classrooms. Direct services are those in which personnel work with the students in the classroom to remediate difficulties.

60. **Which is a less than ideal example of collaboration in successful inclusion?** *(Skill 7.01) (Rigorous)*

   A. Special education teachers are part of the instructional team in a regular classroom
   B. Special education teachers are informed of the lesson before hand and assist regular education teachers in the classroom
   C. Teaming approaches are used for problem solving and program implementation
   D. Regular teachers, special education teachers, and other specialists or support teachers co-teach

Answer: B. Special education teachers are informed of the lesson before hand and assist regular education teachers in the classroom

In an Inclusive classroom, all students need to see both teachers as equals. This situation places the Special Education teacher in the role of a Paraprofessional/Teacher Aide.

61. **If a student is predominantly a visual learner, he may learn more effectively by:** *(Skill 7.01) (Easy)*

   A. Reading aloud while studying
   B. Listening to a cassette tape
   C. Watching a DVD
   D. Using body movement

Answer: C. Watching a DVD

Visual learners use their sense of sight, which is the sense being used to watch a DVD.

62. **_____is a method used to increase student engaged learning time by having students teach other students.** *(Skill 7.02) (Easy)*

   A. Collaborative learning
   B. Engaged learning time
   C. Allocated learning time
   D. Teacher consultation

Answer: A. Collaborative learning

Collaborative Learning is a method for increasing student learning time by having students teach other students.

63. **Presentation of tasks can be altered to match the student's rate of learning by:** *(Skill 7.06) (Rigorous)*
    A. Describing how much of a topic is presented in one day and how much practice is assigned, according to the student's abilities and learning style
    B. Using task analysis, assign a certain number of skills to be mastered in a specific amount of time
    C. Introducing a new task only when the student has demonstrated mastery of the previous task in the learning hierarchy
    D. Using standardized assessments to measure skills..

Answer: C. Introducing a new task only when the student has demonstrated mastery of the previous task in the learning hierarchy

Pacing is the term used for altering of tasks to match the student's rate of learning. This can be done in two ways; altering the subject content and the rate at which tasks are presented.

64. **All of the following are suggestions for altering the presentation of tasks to match the student's rate of learning except:** *(Skill 7.06) (Average Rigor)*

    A. Teach in several shorter segments of time rather than a single lengthy session
    B. Continue to teach a task until the lesson is completed in order to provide more time on task
    C. Watch for nonverbal cues that indicate students are becoming confused, bored, or restless
    D. Avoid giving students an inappropriate amount of written work

Answer: B. Continue to teach a task until the lesson is completed in order to provide more time on task

This action taken does not alter the subject content; neither does it alter the rate at which tasks are presented.

65. **In which of the following ways does an effective teacher utilize pacing as a means of matching a student's rate of learning?** *(Skill 7.06) (Rigorous)*

    A. Selected content is presented based upon prerequisite skills, then presented in modified measures of time.
    B. Tasks are presented during optimum time segments
    C. Special needs students always require smaller steps and learning segments regardless of the activity or content
    D. Teacher utilizes tier assessment after present materials

Answer: A. Selected content is presented based upon prerequisite skills, then presented in modified measures of time.

Pacing utilizes a scaffold approach to teaching with modified time periods of presentation of new material..

66. **John learns best through the auditory channel, so his teacher wants to reinforce his listening skills. Through which of the following types of equipment would instruction be most effectively presented?** *(Skill 9.06) (Easy)*

    A. Overhead projector
    B. CD Player
    C. PC
    D. VHS or DVD player.

Answer: B. CD Player

A CD player would help sharpen and further develop his listening skills as he is an auditory learner.

67. **In which way is a computer like an effective teacher?** *(Skill 8.06)* *(Rigorous)*

   A. Provides immediate feedback
   B. Sets the pace at the rate of the average student
   C. Produces records of errors made, only
   D. Record attendance.

Answer: A. Provides immediate feedback

While modern technology programs declare they can mark attendance by a persons presence at a PC station, it ignores the fact a student can be present and not on the computer.,

68. **During which written composition stage are students encouraged to read their stories aloud to others?** *(Skill 8.06)* *(Average Rigor)*

   A. Planning
   B. Drafting
   C. Revising/editing
   D. Sharing/publication

Answer: C. Revising/editing

It is encouraged at this stage as both the child and the audience will distinguish errors and make corrections. The child also learns to accept constructive criticism.

69. **Which assistive device can be used by those who are visually impaired to assist in their learning?** *(Skill 8.06)* *(Rigorous)*

   A. Soniguide
   B. Personal companion
   C. Closed circuit television
   D. ABVI

Answer: C. Closed circuit television

CCTV is used to enlarge material such as worksheets and books so that it can appear in a "readable size..

70.   **Which electronic device enables persons with hearing impairments to make and receive phone calls?** *(Skill 8.06) (Average Rigor)*

   A. Personal companion
   B. Telecommunication Device for the Deaf (TDD)
   C. Deafnet
   D. Hearing aids

Answer: B. Telecommunication Device for the Deaf (TDD)

TDDs are available throughout the world today. Many public telephones now carry this feature in a small box under the phone.

71.   **When teaching a student, who is predominantly auditory, to read, it is best to:** *(Skill 9.01) (Rigorous)*

   A. Stress sight vocabulary
   B. Stress phonetic analysis
   C. Stress the shape and configuration of the word
   D. Stress rapid reading

Answer: B. Stress phonetic analysis

Sensory modalities are one of the physical elements that affect learning style. Some students learn best through their visual sense (sight), others through their auditory sense (hearing) and still others by doing, touching and moving (tactile-kinesthetic). Auditory learners generally listen to people, follow verbal directions, and enjoy hearing records, cassette tapes, and stories. Phonics has to do with sound, an auditory stimulus.

72.   **Cognitive learning strategies include:** *(Skill 9.04) (Rigorous)*

   A. Reinforcing appropriate behavior
   B. Teaching students how to manage their own behavior in school
   C. Heavily structuring the learning environment
   D. Generalizing learning from one setting to another

Answer: B. Teaching students how to manage their own behavior in school

Engaging students as participants in learning is an example of creating metacognitive learning.

73. **Most children entering school are not developmentally ready to understand concepts such as?** *(Skill 10.02) (Rigorous)*

   A. Zero symbol
   B. Equalizing.
   C. Joining
   D. Patterns

Answer: A.

Understanding the concept of zero requires an understanding of place value.

74. **The effective teacher varies her instructional presentations and response requirements depending upon:** *(Skill 10.02) (Easy)*

   A. Student needs
   B. The task at hand
   C. The learning situation
   D. All of the above

Answer: D. All of the above

Differentiated instruction, and meeting the needs of the group as a whole must cater to the students mode of learning to be successful.

75. **A money bingo game was designed by Ms Johnson for use with her middle grade students. Cards were constructed with different combinations of coins pasted on each of the nine spaces. Ms. Johnson called out various amounts of change (e.g. 30 cents) and students were instructed to cover the coin combinations on their cards which equaled the amount of change (e.g. two dimes and two nickels, three dimes, and so on). The student who had the first bingo was required to add the coins in each of the spaces covered and tell the amounts before being declared the winner. Five of Ms. Johnson's sixth graders played the game the ten minute free activity time following math the first day the game was constructed. Which of the following attributes are present in this game in this situation?** *(Skill 10.02) (Easy)*

   A. Accompanied by simple, uncomplicated rules
   B. Of brief duration, permitting replay
   C. Age appropriateness
   D. All of the above

Answer: D. All of the above

Games and puzzles should also be colorful and appealing, of relevance to individual students, and appropriate for learners at different skill levels, in order to sustain interest and motivational value.

76. **Modeling is an essential component of which self-training approach?** *(Skill 10.04) (Rigorous)*

   A. Self-instructional training
   B. Self-monitoring
   C. Self-reinforcing
   D. Self-punishing

Answer: A. Self-instructional training

Cognitive modeling: The adult model performs a task while verbally instructing himself
Self-instruction: The child performs the task while instructing himself, silently or overtly
Self-monitoring: Refers to procedures by which the learner records whether or not he is engaging in certain behaviors, particularly those that would lead to increased academic achievement and/or social behavior

77. **Strategies specifically designed to move the learner from dependence to independence include:** *(Skill 10.04) (Rigorous)*

 A. Assessment, planning, implementation, and reevaluation
 B. Demonstration, imitation, assistance, prompting, and verbal instruction
 C. Cognitive modeling and self-guidance through overt, faded overt and covert stages
 D. B and C

Answer: D. B and C

Both are correct, as demonstration is a form of modeling.

78. **Which of the following questions most directly evaluates the utility of instructional material?** *(Skill 10.05) (Rigorous)*

 A. Is the cost within budgetary means?
 B. Can the materials withstand handling by students?
 C. Are the materials organized in a useful manner?
 D. Are the needs of the students met by the use of the materials?

Answer: C. Are the materials organized in a useful manner?

It is a question of utility or usefulness.

79. **Alan has failed repeatedly in his academic work. He needs continuous feedback in order to experience small, incremental achievements. What type of instructional material would best meet this need?** *(Skill 11.01) (Rigorous)*

 A. Programmed materials
 B. Audiotapes
 C. Materials with no writing required
 D. Worksheets

Answer: A. Programmed materials

Programmed materials are best suited as Alan would be able to chart his progress as he achieves each goal. He can monitor himself and take responsibility for his successes.

80. **After purchasing what seemed to be a very attractive new math kit for use with her students who have learning disabilities, Ms. Davis discovered her students could not use the kit unless she read the math problems and instructions to them, as the readability level was higher than the majority of the students' functional reading capabilities. Which criterion of the materials selection did Ms. Davis most likely fail to consider when selecting this math kit? (Skill 11.01) (Average Rigor)**

   A. Durability
   B. Relevance
   C. Component Parts
   D. Price

Answer: B. Relevance

Relevance is the only cognitive factor, listed. Since her students were learning disabled, she almost certainly would have considered the kit's durability and component parts. She did not have to consider price. That would be taken care of by the district.

81. **_____is a skill that teachers help students develop to sustain learning throughout life (Skill 11.01) (Rigorous)**

   A. Work ethic
   B. Basic Math Computation
   C. Reading
   D. Critical thinking

Answer: D. Critical thinking

Critical thinking sustains the ability of a person to learn from life, books, and experience.

82. **Which of the following is an example of cross-modal perception involving integrating visual stimuli to an auditory verbal process?** *(Skill 11.02) (Rigorous)*

   A. Following spoken directions
   B. Describing a picture
   C. Finding certain objects in pictures
   D. b and c

Answer: B. Describing a picture

We see (visual modality) the picture and use words (auditory modality) to describe it.

83. **Bob shows behavior problems like lack of attention, out of seat and talking out. His teacher has kept data on these behaviors and has found that Bob is showing much better self-control since he has been self-managing himself through a behavior modification program. The most appropriate placement recommendation for Bob at this time is probably:** *(Skill 11.03) (Average Rigor)*

   A. Any available part-time special education program
   B. The regular classroom solely
   C. A behavior disorders resource room for one period a day
   D. A specific learning disabilities resource room for one period a day

Answer: B. The regular classroom solely

Bob is able to self-manage himself and is very likely to behave like the other children in the regular classroom. The classroom is the least restrictive environment.

84. **In order for a student to function independently in the learning environment, which of the following must be true?** *(Skill 11.03) (Average Rigor)*

   A. The learner must understand the nature of the content
   B. The student must be able to do the assigned task
   C. The teacher must communicate the task to the learner
   D. The student must complete the task.

Answer: B. The student must be able to do the assigned task

Together with the above, the child must be able to ask for and obtain assistance if necessary.

85. **The social skills of students in mental retardation programs are likely to be appropriate for children of their mental age, rather than chronological age. This means that the teacher will need to do all of the following except:** *(Skill 11.03) (Easy)*

   A. Model desired behavior
   B. Provide clear instructions
   C. Expect age appropriate behaviors
   D. Adjust the physical environment when necessary

Answer: C. Expect age appropriate behaviors

Age appropriate means mental age appropriate, not chronological age appropriate.

86. **A functional curriculum includes:** *(Skill 11.04) (Average Rigor)*

   A. Regents curriculum
   B. Life Skills
   C. Remedial Academics
   D. Vocational placement.

Answer: B. Life Skills

While a, c and, d may be utilized in the functional curriculum, the curriculum may not be considered functional without addressing life skills.

87. **An individual with disabilities in need of employability training, as well a job, should be referred to what governmental agency for assistance?**
    (Skill 11.07 (Average Rigor)

    A. OMRDD
    B. VESID
    C. Social Services
    D. ARC

Answer: B. VESID

VESID stands for Vocational and Educational Services for Individuals with Disabilities.

88. **A good method to teach ethical understanding to those in the functional curriculum is:** *(Skill 12.01) (Rigorous)*

    A. Modeling
    B. The Unfinished Story.
    C. Handouts
    D. Questionnaire

Answer: B. The Unfinished Story.

The Unfinished story ends where an ethical judgement should take place and allows for the students to discuss what the right choice should be.

89. **Social maturity may be evidenced by the student's:** *(Skill 12.01) (Easy)*

    A. Recognition of rights and responsibilities (his own and others)
    B. Display of respect for legitimate authority figures
    C. Formulation of a valid moral judgment
    D. Demonstration of all of the above

Answer: D. Demonstration of all of the above

Some additional evidence of social maturity:
- The ability to cooperate
- Following procedures formulated by an outside party
- Achieving appropriate levels of independence

90.   **What can a teacher plan that will allow him/her to avoid adverse situations with students?** *(Skill 12.03) (Rigorous)*

A. Lessons
B. Recess
C. Environment
D. Class schedule

Answer: C. Environment

The only preventative control over adverse situations is that which a teacher has over his/her room. From simple things such as moving desk assignments to moving distractions and creating time-out areas are environmental issues teachers can control.

91.   **Which of the following is the first step you should take to prepare to teach preparation for social situations?** *(Skill 12.01) (Easy)*

A. Allow students to plan event.
B. Lecture
C. Anticipate possible problems
D. Take your students to the anticipated setting.

Answer: C. Anticipate possible problems

Look at all the things that could go wrong first. Chances are that if you are not prepared an embarrassing situation could occur.

92.   **Children with disabilities are least likely to improve their social-interpersonal skills by:** *(Skill 12.01) (Rigorous)*

A. Developing sensitivity to other people
B. Making behavioral choices in social situations
C. Developing social maturity
D. Talking with their sister or brother.

Answer: D. Talking with their sister or brother.

The social skills of the child are known in the family, and seen as "normal" for him/her. Regular conversation with a family member would be the least conducive to improving social skills. Remember, the purpose in building social-interpersonal skills, is to improve a person's ability to maintain interdependent relationships between persons.

93. **A Life Space Interview is used for?** *(Skill 13.01) (Rigorous)*

   A. Transition to Exit Interview.
   B. Analysis of proficiency levels.
   C. Maintenance of acceptable behavior.
   D. To create awareness of distorted perceptions.

Answer: D. To create awareness of distorted perceptions.

Life Space Interviews are given in a here-and-now fashion. Often they employ role plays to increase awareness of misunderstandings, and can be used to prepare a student for mediation.

94. **Target behaviors must be:** *(Skill 13.01) (Easy)*

   A. Observable
   B. Measurable
   C. Definable
   D. All of the above

Answer: D. All of the above

Behaviors must be observable, measurable and definable in order to be assessed and changed.

95. **A Behavioral Intervention Plan (BIP):** *(Skill 13.03) (Rigorous)*

   A. Should be written by a team.
   B. Should be reviewed annually.
   C. Should be written by the teacher who is primarily responsible for the student.
   D. Should consider placement.

Answer: A. Should be written by a team.

IDEA 2004, establishes that the BIP is a team intervention. Part 200 also establishes this. Writing BIPs without a team approach does not allow the behavior to truly be addressed as a team.

96.   Janelle is just as "antsy" as Jaquan who has ADHD. You want to keep a good eye on them so you put them in the same corner. Later you suspect Amanda also has ADHD and you move her to the same area.. You are creating: *(Skill 12.04) (Average Rigor)*

A. Self-fulfilling prophecy.
B. cooperative learning circle.
C. disordered support group
D. A buffer zone to observe and direct behavior centrally.

Answer: A. Self-fulfilling prophecy.

When you treat students like they have a disability you may be creating a disability. Amanda and Janelle may not have ADHD, but you are placing them in a group where ADHD behavior is rewarded by attention. You are then creating a Self-fulfilling prophecy.

97.   Acceptance of disabilities by parents and siblings is most influenced by? *(Skill 13.05) (Rigorous)*

A. Social Economic Status (SES)
B. The severity of the disability.
C. The culture of the family.
D. Media portrayal of the disability.

Answer: C. Media portrayal of the disability.

The cultural influence on the family has the largest impact on their understanding of the disability.

98. **The opportunity for a student with a disability to attend a class as close to the normal as possible describes:** *(Skill 13.06) (Easy)*

    A. Least Restrictive Environment
    B. Normalization
    C. Mainstreaming
    D. Deinstitutionalization

Answer: B. Normalization

Normalization is a term coined in the early 1980s to describe a goal of creating conditions of care and environment as close to normal. This description tore down the concept of "institutionalization" in favor of community residence placement. A sample of the move away from Institutionalization is the closing of most of NYS Monroe Developmental Center in Rochester, NY. Least Restrictive Environment refers directly to student placement.

99.   **Which of the following examples would be considered of highest priority when determining the need for the delivery of appropriate special education and related services?** *(Skill 13.06) (Rigorous)*

A. A ten-year-old girl with profound mental retardation who is receiving education services in a state institution.
B. A six-year-old girl who has been diagnosed as autistic is placed in a special education class within the local school. Her mother wants her to attend residential school next year, even though the girl is showing progress.
C. An eight-year-old boy is repeating first grade for the second time and exhibits problems with toileting, gross motor functions, and remembering number and letter symbols. His regular classroom teacher claims the referral forms are too time-consuming and refuses to complete them. He also refuses to make accommodations because he feels every child should be treated alike.
D. A twelve-year-old boy with mild disabilities who was placed in a behavior disorders program, but displays obvious perceptual deficits (e.g. reversal of letters and symbols, and inability to discriminate sounds). He originally thought to have a learning disability, but did not meet state criteria for this exceptionality category, based on results of standard scores. He has always had problems with attending to a task, and is now beginning to get into trouble during seatwork time. His teacher feels that he will eventually become a real behavior problem. He receives social skills training in the resource room one period a day.

Answer: C. An eight-year-old boy is repeating first grade for the second time and exhibits problems with toileting, gross motor functions, and remembering number and letter symbols. His regular classroom teacher claims the referral forms are too time-consuming and refuses to complete them. He also refuses to make accommodations because he feels every child should be treated alike.

No modifications are being made, so the child is not receiving any services whatsoever.

100. **The most important steps in writing a Functional Behavioral Assessment (FBA) is:** *(Skill 13.07) (Rigorous)*

    A. Establish a replacement behavior
    B. Establish levels of interventions.
    C. Establish antecedents related or causative to the behavior.
    D. Establish assessment periods of FBA effectiveness.

Answer: C. Establish antecedents related or causative to the behavior.

An FBA will only be successful if antecedents are recognized. Avoidance of situations, and training/cultivating of replacement behaviors then become possible..

101. **The best resource a teacher can have to reach a student is?** *(Skill 14.01) (Rigorous)*

    A. Contact with the parents/guardians.
    B. A successful behavior modification Exam.
    C. A listening ear.
    D. Gathered scaffold approach to teaching.

Answer: A. Contact with the parents/guardians.

Parents are often the best source of information on their children. They generally know if a behavior management technique will be successful. They also can inform you of influences outside of school that may affect school performance and behavior.

102. **You should do to prepare for a parent-teacher conference by:** *(Skill 14.02) (Average Rigor)*

    A. Memorizing student progress/grades.
    B. Anticipating questions.
    C. Scheduling the meetings during your lunch time.
    D. Planning a tour of the school.

Answer: B. Anticipating questions.

It pays to anticipate parent questions. It makes you more likely to be able to answer them. It is also possible that your anticipating them may be a way for you to plan what to speak to the parent about.

103. Lotzie is not labeled as needing special education services and appears unable to function on grade level in both academics and socially. He is in 9th grade reading picture books, and consistently displays immature behavior that can be misinterpreted. You have already observed these behaviors. What should be done first? *(Skill 14.02) (Rigorous)*

    A. Establish a rapport with the parents.
    B. Write a CSE referral.
    C. Plan and discuss possible interventions with the teacher.
    D. Address the class about acceptance.

Answer: A. Establish a rapport with the parents.

When a student enters 9th grade in a poor placement such as this, it is not unusual for the parents to have been opposed to special education. The best way to help the student is to establish a rapport with the parents. You need to help them see why their child would benefit from special education services.

104. You note that a child in your class is expressing discomfort when placing his back against a chair. You ask him if he is OK, and he says its nothing. You notice what appears to be a belt mark on his shoulder. What is the first thing you should do? *(Skill 14.04) (Rigorous)*

    A. Send the child to the nurse.
    B. Contact an Administrator.
    C. Call Child Protective's
    D. Follow the school policy.

Answer: D. Follow the school policy.

You are required to report all suspected abuse and neglect to CPS. Most schools have policies in place regarding this issue. Most school policies request giving prior notice to an Administrator before calling CPS. This action allows for easier communication between you, CPS and the school. Depending on the abuse the child may need to see the nurse immediately. You may also have to judge the child's reaction before requesting him/her to go to the nurse.

105. You are monitoring the cafeteria and you noticed Joshua stuffing his pockets with food. Not just snack food, but lunch items as well. You suspect:. *(Skill 14.04) (Average Rigor)*

A. Joshua has Obsessive Compulsive Disorder (OCD).
B. Joshua may not be getting fed at home.
C. Joshua is just an average growing boy.
D. Joshua is trying to be funny.

Answer: A. Joshua has Obsessive Compulsive Disorder (OCD).

Hording food is a symptom of neglect. The child wants to save the food because he will
not have anything to eat after school, or before school.. Inform your administrator of your suspicion and collaborate with other teachers to get a better picture of what is going on..

106. What determines whether a person is entitled to protection under Section 504? *(Skill 15.01) (Average Rigor)*

A. The individual must meet the definition of a person with a disability
B. The person must be able to meet the requirements of a particular program in spite of his or her disability
C. The school, business or other facility must be the recipient of federal funding assistance
D. All of the above

Answer: D. All of the above

To be entitled to protection under Section 504, an individual must meet the definition of a person with a disability, which is: any person who (i) has a physical or mental impairment which substantially limits one or more of that person's major life activities, (ii) has a record of such impairment, or (iii) is regarded as having such an impairment. Major life activities are: caring for oneself, performing manual tasks, walking, seeing, hearing, speaking, breathing, learning, and working. The person must also be "otherwise qualified," which means that the person must be able to meet the requirements of a particular program in spite of the disability. The person must also be afforded "reasonable accommodations" by recipients of federal financial assistance.

107. **Which is NOT a step teachers use to establish cooperative learning groups in the classroom? The teacher:** *(Skill 15.01) (Rigorous)*

    A. Selects Members of Each Learning Group
    B. Directly Teaches Cooperative Group Skills
    C. Assigns Cooperative Group Skills
    D. Has Students Self-Evaluate Group Efforts

Answer: D. Has Students Self-Evaluate Group Efforts

According to Henley et al, there are four steps to establishing cooperative learning groups:
1. The teacher selects members of each learning group
2. The teacher directly teaches cooperative group skills
3. The teacher assigns cooperative group activities
4. The teacher evaluates group efforts

108. **The _____ modality is most frequently used in the learning process.** *(Skill 15.02) (Rigorous)*

    A. Auditory
    B. Visual
    C. Tactile
    D. All of the Above

Answer: D. All of the Above

The auditory, visual, and tactile modalities are the ones frequently used in the learning process. We learn through an integration of these modalities (multi-sensory approach).

109. Some environmental elements which influence learning styles include all except: *(Skill 15.02) (Rigorous)*

    A. Light
    B. Temperature
    C. Design
    D. Motivation

Answer: D. Motivation

Individual learning styles are influenced by environmental, emotional, sociological, and physical elements. Environmental include sound, light, temperature and design. Emotional elements include such as motivation, persistence, responsibility and structure. Motivation is not an environmental element.

110. Janiay requires Occupational Therapy and Speech Therapy services. She is your student. What must you do to insure her services are met?
    (Skill 15.04) (Rigorous)

    A. Watch the services being rendered.
    B. Schedule collaboratively.
    C. Ask for services to be given in a push-in model.
    D. Ask them to train you to give the service.

Answer: B. Schedule collaboratively.

Collaborative scheduling of students to receive services is both your responsibility and that of the service provider. Scheduling together allows for both your convenience and that of the service provider. It also will provide you with an opportunity to make sure the student does not miss important information.

111. **Included in data brought to the attention of Congress regarding the evaluation procedures for education of students with disabilities was the fact that?** *(Skill 15.07) (Easy)*
    A. There were a large number of children and youths with disabilities in the United States
    B. Many children with disabilities were not receiving an appropriate education
    C. Many parents of children with disabilities were forced to seek services outside of the public realm
    D. All of the above

Answer: D. All of the above

All three factors, and many more, have driven Congress to act.

112. **What TWO student behaviors are indicative of a possible crisis?** *(Skill 15.07) (Average Rigor)*

    A. Bullying and socially active.
    B. Uncontrolled and intermittent periods of laughter and rage.
    C. High academic performance and gang activity
    D. Victim of violence and uncontrolled anger

Answer: D. Victim of violence and uncontrolled anger
While a student may display one behavior indicating he/she maybe be entering a crisis state for the school to be concerned about, often two or more signs are displayed. Victims of violence that display uncontrolled rage may be seen as a crisis waiting to happen.

113. **The Individuals with Disabilities Education Act (IDEA) was signed into law in and later reauthorized to its current in what years?** *(Skill 16.01) (Easy)*

    A. 1975 and 2004
    B. 1980 and 1990
    C. 1990 and 2004
    D. 1995 and 2001

Answer: C. 1990 and 2004

IDEA, Public Law 101-476 is a consolidation and reauthorization of all prior Special Education mandates, with amendments. It was signed into law by President Bush on October 30, 1990. Revision of IDEA occurred in 2004, IDEA was re-authorized as the Individuals with Disabilities Education Improvement Act of 2004 (IDEIA 2004) is commonly referred to as IDEA 2004. IDEA 2004 (effective July 1, 2005).

114. **How was the training of Special Education teachers changed by the No Child Left Behind Act of 2002?** *(Skill 16.01) (Average Rigor)*

   A. Required all Special Education teachers to be certified in reading and math
   B. Required all Special Education teachers to take the same coursework as general education teachers
   C. If a Special Education teacher is teaching a core subject, he or she must meet the standard of a highly qualified teacher in that subject.
   D. All of the above

Answer: C. If a Special Education teacher is teaching a core subject, he or she must meet the standard of a highly qualified teacher in that subject.

In order for special education teachers to be a students sole teacher of a core subject they must meet the professional criteria of NCLB. They must be *highly qualified*, that is certified or licensed in their area of special education and show proof of a specific level of professional development in the core subjects that they teach. As special education teachers received specific education in the core subject they teach, they will be better prepared to teach to the same level of learning standards as the general education teacher.

115. **Which of the following is a specific change of language in IDEA?** *(Skill 16.01) (Average Rigor)*

   A. The term "Disorder" changed to "Disability"
   B. The term "Children" changed to "Children and Youth"
   C. The term "Handicapped" changed to "Impairments"
   D. The term "Handicapped" changed to "With Disabilities"

Answer: D. The term "Handicapped" changed to "With Disabilities"

"Children" became "individuals", highlighting the fact that some students with special needs were adolescents not just "children". The word "handicapped" was changed to "with disabilities", denoting the difference between limitations imposed by society, (handicap) and an inability to do certain things (disability). "With disabilities" also demonstrates that the person is thought of first, and the disabling condition is but one of the characteristics of the individual.

116. **Which component changed with the reauthorization of the Education for all Handicapped Children Act of 1975 (EHA) 1990 EHA Amendment?**
(Skill 16.01) (Average Rigor)

A. Specific terminology
B. Due Process Protections
C. Non-Discriminatory Reevaluation Procedures
D. Individual Education Plans

Answer: A. Specific terminology

See answer above.

117. **Which is <u>untrue</u> about the Americans with Disabilities Act (ADA)?**
(Skill 16.01) (Easy)

A. It was signed into law the same year as IDEA by President Bush
B. It reauthorized the discretionary programs of EHA
C. It gives protection to all people on the basis of race, sex, national origin, and religion
D. It guarantees equal opportunities to persons with disabilities in employment, public accommodations, transportation, government services, and telecommunications.

Answer: B. It reauthorized the discretionary programs of EHA

EHA is the precursor of IDEA, the Individuals with Disabilities Education Act. ADA, however, is Public Law 101 – 336, the Americans with Disabilities Act, which gives civil rights protection to all individuals with disabilities in private sector employment, all public services, public accommodations, transportation and telecommunications. It was patterned after the Rehabilitation Act of 1973.

118. Requirements for evaluations were changed in IDEA 2004 to reflect that no 'single' assessment or measurement tool can be used to determine special education qualification, furthering that a disproportionate representation of what types of students? *(Skill 16.01) (Average Rigor)*

    A. Disabled
    B. Foreign
    C. Gifted
    D. Minority and Bilingual

Answer: D. Minority and Bilingual

IDEA 2004 recognized that there exists a disproportionate representation of minorities and bilingual students and that pre-service interventions that are *scientifically based on early reading programs, positive behavioral interventions and support,* and early intervening services may prevent some of those children from needing special education services.

119. IEPs continue to have multiple sections; one section, present levels, now addresses what? *(Skill 16.01) (Easy)*

    A. Academic achievement and functional performance
    B. English as a second language
    C. Functional performance
    D. Academic achievement

Answer: A. Academic achievement and functional performance

Individualized Education Plans (IEPS) continue to have multiple sections. One section, present levels, now addresses academic achievement and functional performance. Annual IEP goals must now address the same areas.

120. **What is true about IDEA? In order to be eligible, a student must:** *(Skill 16.01) (Easy)*

    A. Have a medical disability
    B. Have a disability that fits into one of the categories listed in the law
    C. Attend a private school
    D. Be a slow learner

Answer: B. Have a disability that fits into one of the categories listed in the law

IDEA is a legal instrument, thus it is defined by law. Every aspect in the operation of IDEA is laid out in law.

121. **Free Appropriate Public Education (FAPE) describes Special Education and related services as?** *(Skill 16.01) (Easy)*

    A. Public expenditure and standard to the state educational agency
    B. Provided in conformity with each student's individualized education program, if the program is developed to meet requirements of the law.
    C. Include preschool, elementary and/or secondary education in the state involved
    D. All of the above.

Answer: D. All of the above.

FAPE states that Special Education and related services are provided at public expense; meet the standards of the state educational agency; include preschool, elementary and/or secondary education in the state involved; and are provided in conformity with each student's IEP is the program is developed to meet requirements of the law.

122. **Jane is a third grader. Mrs. Smith, her teacher, noted that Jane was having difficulty with math and reading assignments. The results from recent diagnostic tests showed a strong sight vocabulary, strength in computational skills, but a weakness in comprehending what she read. This weakness was apparent in mathematical word problems as well. The multi-disciplinary team recommended placement in a special education resource room for learning disabilities two periods each school day. For the remainder of the school day, her placement will be:** *(Skill 16.01) (Easy)*

   A. In the Regular Classroom
   B. At a Special School
   C. In a Self-Contained Classroom
   D. In a Resource Room for Mental Retardation

Answer: A. In the Regular Classroom

The resource room is a special room inside the school environment where the child goes to be taught by a teacher who is certified in the area of disability. We hope the accommodations and services provided in the resource room will help her to catch up and perform with her peers in the regular classroom.

123. **Legislation in Public Law 94 – 142 attempts to:** *(Skill 16.01) (Rigorous)*

   A. Match the child's educational needs with appropriate educational services
   B. Include parents in the decisions made about their child's education
   C. Establish a means by which parents can provide input
   D. All of the above

Answer: D. All of the above

Much of what was stated in separate curt rulings and mandated legislation was brought together into what is now considered to be the "backbone" of special education. Public Law 94 – 142, (education for All Handicapped Children Act) was signed into law by President Ford in 1975. It was the culmination of a great deal of litigation and legislation from the late 1960's to the mid 1970's , that included decisions supporting the need to assure an appropriate education to all persons regardless of race, creed, or disability. In 1990, this law was reauthorized and renamed the Individuals with Disabilities education Act, IDEA.

124. **Manifest Determination CSEs should first:** *(Skill 16.01) (Average Rigor)*

   A. Make a decision on whether to return the student to placement
   B. Determine if the disability was a cause of the behavior.
   C. Evaluate the placement for possible needed change.
   D. Examine past behaviors.

Answer: B. Determine if the disability was a cause of the behavior.

The purpose of the Manifest Determination CSE is to evaluate the behavior in light of the students disability. IDEA 2004 states that if the disability was not related to the behavior the student should be given the same punishment/result as a "regular education" student.

125. **A Mother is upset that her child is not being helped and asks you about the difference between the t 504 Plan and an IEP. What is the difference?**
   (Skill 16.01) (Rigorous)

   A. 504 Plan requires classification, IEP requires labeling.
   B. 504 Plan requires provides no services just adaptations.
   C. 504 Plan is better for children who have ADHD.
   D. 504 plan provides little interventions/services, while an IEP is more intensive providing more services such as a special class.

Answer: D. 504 plan provides little interventions/services, while an IEP is more intensive providing more services such as a special class.

504 Plans provides only a few services such as a test modification or the allowance of a child to have a fidget toy. IEPs are needed for to receive modified instruction and more services to assist the students academic success.

126. **Which legislation has forced public and private facilities to accommodate those who are physically disabled?** *(Skill 16.01) (Easy)*

    A. ADA
    B. IDEA
    C. 504 Plan
    D. PL 105-17

Answer: A. ADA

To date many accommodations to public facilities such as sidewalks, public transit, and public bathrooms have been made because of the expressed needs which were legislated in the American's With Disabilities Act.

127. **You have been asked to work with a teacher who states Special Education students do not belong in her room and she refuses to work with them. What should you remind her of?** *(Skill16.01) (Easy)*

    A. Confidentiality responsibility
    B. FAPE
    C. Part 200
    D. All of the above

Answer: D. All of the above

All of the above listed items of law specifically refer to that a child's confidentiality and FAPE must be granted.

128. **The clock time from request for intervention to a determination of eligibility is:** *(Skill 16.01) (Rigorous)*

    A. 30 school days
    B. 60 school days
    C. 30 calendar days
    D. 60 calendar days.

Answer: C. 30 calendar days.

IDEA 2004 changed the clock from 30 school days to 30 calendar days.

129. **Which of the following must be completed first before testing occurs:**
(Skill 16.01) (Average Rigor)

A. Teacher consult on student needs
B. Pre-CSE Conference.
C. Parental Permission for each test.
D. All of the above

Answer: C. Parental Permission for each test.

The only required piece by both Part 200 and IDEA 2004 is parental permission for each test.

130. **Effective transition was included in:** *(Skill 16.01) (Rigorous)*

A. American's with Disabilities Act (ADA)
B. IDEA
C. FERPA
D. Public Law 130-999

Answer: B. IDEA

With the enactment of IDEA transition services became a right.

131. **IDEA defines children with a disability as children evaluated in accordance with what?** *(Skill 16.01) (Average Rigor)*

A. Those who because of their impairments, need education and related services.
B. Those who because of their disabilities will not succeed in the regular education environment.
C. Those who because of their impairments are in need of supports to accommodate them in the classroom.
D. Those who are impaired and need physical or educational environmental assistance.

Answer: C.
IDEA defines disability as children who are mentally retarded, hard of hearing deaf, speech impaired, visually impaired, seriously emotionally disturbed, orthopedic ally impaired, other health impaired, deaf-blind, multi-handicapped, or as having specific learning disabilities, who, because of those impairments, need special education and related services .

132. School Administrators understand special education and the reasons for the classes but may ask for you to? *(Skill 17.01) (Rigorous)*

    A. Keep them up to date on changing laws relevant to special education.
    B. Share your Paraprofessional with other teachers.
    C. Provide staff workshops
    D. Become a Parent Liaison

Answer: A. Keep them up to date on changing laws relevant to special education

Many Principals and other school administrators do not keep up on the changing laws regarding children with special needs. They may need you to keep them up to date. Keeping up to date with changing special education law is your professional responsibility.

133. Miss Carol asks you for help. She has noted that her regular education student, Amanda, does not seem able to follow 3-step directions. What can you do? *(Skill 17.01) (Average Rigor)*

    A. Ask if the student was supposed placed in a blended classroom.
    B. Tell Miss Carol the student is a special education student.
    C. Observe Amanda and help the teacher make a referral to CSE.
    D. Offer to trade your student who is ready for inclusion for Amanda who needs

Answer: C. Observe Amanda and help the teacher make a referral to CSE.

Remember you are a colleague of the teacher not an Administrator. If the student is labeled an IEP should already be with the teacher, and she would have told you the child is labeled as having special needs. Trading students would violate LRE for Amanda, as well as anger parents who have not signed for an evaluation or for placement.

134. **IDEA defines children with a disability as children evaluated in accordance with what?** *(Skill 16.01) (Average Rigor)*

   A. Those who because of their impairments, need education and related services.
   B. Those who because of their disabilities will not succeed in the regular education environment.
   C. Those who because of their impairments are in need of supports to accommodate them in the classroom.
   D. Those who are impaired and need physical or educational environmental assistance.

Answer: C.

IDEA defines disability as children who are mentally retarded, hard of hearing deaf, speech impaired, visually impaired, seriously emotionally disturbed, orthopedic ally impaired, other health impaired, deaf-blind, multi-handicapped, or as having specific learning disabilities, who, because of those impairments, need special education and related services .

135. **A Pre-CSE coordinates and participates in due diligence through what process?** *(Skill 16.01) (Rigorous)*

   A. Child study team meets first time without parents
   B. Teachers take child learning concerns to the school counselor
   C. School counselor contact parents for permission to perform screening assessments
   D. All of the above

Answer: D. All of the above

The **Pre-CSE** coordinates and participates in due diligence through a process that includes teachers or parents concerns about academic or functional development goes to the counselor who then obtain a permission for screening assessments of child's skills And, the results determine need, if needed child study team meets without parents first.

136. The definition of Assistive Technology devices was amended in the IDEA reauthorization of 2004 to exclude what? *(Skill 16.01) (Average Rigor)*

    A. iPods other hand-held devices
    B. Computer enhanced technology
    C. Surgically implanted devices
    D. Braille and/or special learning aids

Answer: C. Surgically implanted devices

The definition of Assistive technology devices was amended to exclude devices that are surgically implanted (i.e. cochlear implants), and clarified that students with assistive technology devices shall not be prevented from having special education services. Assistive technology devices may need to be monitored by school personnel, but schools are not responsible for the implantation or replacement of such devices surgically.

SUBAREA I.   UNDERSTANDING AND EVALUATING STUDENTS WITH
                DISABILITIES

COMPETENCY 0001   UNDERSTAND CHARACTERISTICS OF INDIVIDUALS
                  WITH DISABILITIES.

Skill 1.01   Identify types, etiologies, and characteristics of various
                disabilities.

The Causation and Prevention of a Disability

No one knows exactly what causes learning disabilities. There is a wide range of possibilities that makes it almost impossible to pinpoint the exact cause. Listed below are some factors that can be attributed to the development of a disability.

Problems in Fetal Brain Development: During pregnancy, things can go wrong in the development of the brain that can alter how the neurons form or interconnect. Throughout pregnancy, brain development is vulnerable to disruptions. If the disruption occurs early, the fetus may die, or the infant may be born with widespread disabilities and possibly mental retardation. If the disruption occurs later, when the cells are becoming specialized and moving into place, it may leave errors in the cell makeup, location, or connections. Some scientists believe that these errors may later show up as learning disorders.

Genetic Factors: Learning disabilities can run in families, which shows that there may be a genetic link. For example, children who do not have certain reading skills, such as hearing the separate sounds of words, are likely to have a parent with a similar problem. A parent's learning disability can take a slightly different form in the child. Due to this, it is unlikely that specific learning disorders are directly inherited.

Environment: Additional reasons for why learning disabilities appear to run in families stem from the family environment. Parents with expressive language disorders may talk less to their children, or their language may be muffled. In this case, the lack of a proper role model for acquiring good language skills causes the disability.

Tobacco, Alcohol, and Other Drug Use: Many drugs taken by the mother pass directly to the fetus during pregnancy. Research shows that a mother's usage of cigarettes, alcohol, or other drugs during pregnancy may have damaging effects on the unborn child. Mothers who smoke during pregnancy are more likely to have smaller birth weight babies. Newborns who weigh less than 5 pounds are more at risk for learning disorders. Heavy alcohol use during pregnancy has been linked to fetal alcohol syndrome, a condition resulting in low birth weight, intellectual impairment, hyperactivity, and certain physical defects.

<u>Problems During Pregnancy or Delivery</u>: Complications during pregnancy can also cause learning disabilities. The mother's immune system can react to the fetus and attack it as if it were an infection. This type of problem appears to cause newly-formed brain cells to settle in the wrong part of the brain. In addition, during delivery, the umbilical cord can become twisted and temporarily cut off oxygen to the fetus, resulting in impaired brain functions.

<u>Toxins in the Environment</u>: New brain cells and neural networks are produced for a year after the child is born. These cells are vulnerable to certain disruptions. There are certain environmental toxins that may lead to learning disabilities. Cadmium and lead are becoming a leading focus of neurological research. Cadmium is used in making some steel products. It can get into the soil and then into the foods we eat. Lead was once common in paint and gasoline and is still present in some water pipes.

Children with cancer who have been treated with chemotherapy or radiation at an early age can also develop learning disabilities. This is very prevalent in children with brain tumors who received radiation to the skull.

In order to prevent disabilities from occurring, information on the causes of disabilities should be widely available so that parents can take the necessary steps to safeguard their children from conception up until the early years of life. While some of the causes of disabilities are unavoidable or incidental, there are many causes that can be prevented.

Identify the Characteristics of Emotionally Disturbed Children

Children with emotional disturbances or behavioral disorders are not always easy to identify. It is, of course, easy to identify the acting-out child who is constantly fighting, who cannot stay on task for more than a few minutes, or who shouts obscenities when angry. It is not always easy to identify the child who internalizes his or her problems, on the other hand, or may appear to be the "model" student, but suffers from depression, shyness, or fears. Unless the problem becomes severe enough to impact school performance, the internalizing child may go for long periods without being identified or served.

Studies of children with behavioral and emotional disorders indicate that children with these disorders share some general characteristics:

Lower academic performance: While it is true that some emotionally disturbed children have above average IQ scores, the majority are behind their peers in measures of intelligence and school achievement. Most score in the "slow learner" or "mildly mentally retarded" range on IQ tests, averaging about 90. Many have learning problems that exacerbate their acting out or "giving-up" behavior. As the child enters secondary school, the gap between him or her and non-disabled peers widens until the child may be as many as 2 to 4 years behind in reading and/or math skills by high school. Children with severe degrees of impairment may be difficult to evaluate.

Social skills deficits: Students with deficits may be uncooperative, selfish in dealing with others, unaware of what to do in social situations, or ignorant of the consequences of their actions. This may be a combination of lack of prior training, lack of opportunities to interact, and dysfunctional value systems and beliefs learned from their family.

Classroom behaviors: Often, emotionally disturbed children display classroom behavior that is highly disruptive to the classroom setting. Emotionally disturbed children are often out of their seat or running around the room, hitting, fighting, or disturbing their classmates, stealing or destroying property, defiant and noncompliant, and/or verbally disruptive. They do not follow directions and often do not complete assignments.

Aggressive behaviors: Aggressive children often fight or instigate their peers to strike back at them. Aggressiveness may also take the form of vandalism or destruction of property. Aggressive children also engage in verbal abuse.

Delinquency: As emotionally disturbed, acting-out children enter adolescence, they may become involved in socialized aggression (i.e., gang membership) and delinquency. Delinquency is a legal term, rather than medical, and describes truancy and actions that would be criminal if they were committed by adults. Not every delinquent is classified as emotionally disturbed, but children with behavioral and emotional disorders are especially at risk for becoming delinquent because of their problems at school (the primary place for socializing with peers), deficits in social skills that may make them unpopular at school, and/or dysfunctional homes.

Withdrawn behaviors: Children who manifest withdrawn behaviors may consistently act in an immature fashion or prefer to play with younger children. They may daydream or complain of being sick in order to "escape". They may also cry often, cling to the teacher, ignore those who attempt to interact, or suffer from fears or depression.

Schizophrenia and psychotic behaviors: Children may have bizarre delusions, hallucinations, incoherent thoughts, and disconnected thinking. Schizophrenia typically manifests itself between the ages of 15 and 45, and the younger the onset, the more severe the disorder. These behaviors usually require intensive treatment beyond the scope of the regular classroom setting.

Gender: Many more boys than girls are identified as having emotional and behavioral problems, especially hyperactivity and attention deficit disorder, autism, childhood psychosis, and problems with undercontrol (aggression, socialized aggression). Girls, on the other hand, have more problems with overcontrol (i.e., withdrawal and phobias). Boys are much more prevalent than girls in problems with mental retardation and language and learning disabilities.

Age Characteristics: When they enter adolescence, girls tend to experience affective or emotional disorders such as anorexia, depression, bulimia, and anxiety at twice the rate of boys, which mirrors the adult prevalence pattern.

Family Characteristics: Having a child with an emotional or behavioral disorder does not automatically mean that the family is dysfunctional. However, there are family factors that create or contribute to the development of behavior disorders and emotional disturbance.

- Abuse and neglect
- Lack of appropriate supervision
- Lax, punitive, and/or lack of discipline
- High rates of negative types of interaction among family members
- Lack of parental concern and interest
- Negative adult role models
- Lack of proper health care and/or nutrition
- Disruption in the family

Children with Mild Learning, Intellectual, and Behavioral Disabilities

Some characteristics of students with mild learning and behavioral disabilities are as follows:

- Lack of interest in schoolwork
- Prefer concrete rather than abstract lessons
- Possess weak listening skills
- Low achievement; limited verbal and/or writing skills
- Respond better to active rather than passive learning tasks
- Have areas of talent or ability often overlooked by teachers
- Prefer to receive special help in regular classroom
- Higher dropout rate than regular education students
- Achieve in accordance with teacher expectations
- Require modification in classroom instruction and are easily distracted

Identify characteristic of students who have a Learning Disability:

- Hyperactivity: a rate of motor activity higher than normal
- Perceptual difficulties: visual, auditory, and perceptual problems
- Perceptual-motor impairments: poor integration of visual and motor systems, often affecting fine motor coordination
- Disorders of memory and thinking: memory deficits, trouble with problem-solving, concept formation and association, poor awareness of own metacognitive skills (learning strategies)
- Impulsiveness: act before considering consequences, poor impulse control, often followed by remorselessness
- Academic problems in reading, math, writing or spelling; significant discrepancies in ability levels

Identify characteristics of individuals with Mental Retardation or Intellectual Disabilities:

- IQ of 70 or below
- Limited cognitive ability; delayed academic achievement, particularly in language-related subjects
- Deficits in memory which often relate to poor initial perception or inability to apply stored information to relevant situations
- Impaired formulation of learning strategies
- Difficulty in attending to relevant aspects of stimuli; slowness in reaction time or in employing alternate strategies

Identify characteristics of individuals with Autism:

This exceptionality appears very early in childhood. Six common features of autism are:

- **Apparent sensory deficit** –The child may appear not to see or hear or react to a stimulus, then react in an extreme fashion to a seemingly insignificant stimulus.
- **Severe affect isolation**—The child does not respond to the usual signs of affection such as smiles and hugs.
- **Self-stimulation** – Stereotyped behavior takes the form of repeated or ritualistic actions that make no sense to others, such as hand flapping, rocking, staring at objects, or humming the same sounds for hours at a time.
- **Tantrums and self-injurious behavior (SIB)** – Autistic children may bite themselves, pull their hair, bang their heads, or hit themselves. They can throw severe tantrums and direct aggression and destructive behavior toward others.

- **Echolalia** (also known as "parrot talk")—The autistic child may repeat what is played on television, for example, or respond to others by repeating what was said to him. Alternatively, he may simply not speak at all.
- **Severe deficits in behavior and self-care skills**—Autistic children may behave like children much younger than themselves.

Skill 1.02 **Demonstrating familiarity with similarities and differences among individuals with disabilities, including levels of severity and multiple disabilities**

IDEA 2004 defines *a child with a disability as having mental retardation, a hearing impairment (including deafness), a speech or language impairment, a visual impairment (including blindness), a serious emotional disturbance (referred to in this part as emotional disturbance), an orthopedic impairment, autism, traumatic brain injury, an other health impairment, a specific learning disability, deaf-blindness, or multiple disabilities, and who, by reason thereof, needs special education and related services.*

Eligibility for special education services is based on a student having one of the above disabilities (or a combination thereof) and demonstration of educational need through professional evaluation.

Seldom does a student with a disability fall into only one of the characteristics listed in IDEA 2004. For example, a student with a hearing impairment may also have a specific learning disability, or a student on the autism spectrum may also demonstrate a language impairment. In fact, language impairment is inherent in autism. Sometimes the eligibility is defined as multiple disabilities (with one listed as a primary eligibility on the IEP and the others listed as secondary). Sometimes there are overlapping needs that are not necessarily listed as a secondary disability.

Teachers of special education students should be aware of the similarities between areas of disabilities, as well as the differences.

Students with disabilities (in all areas) may demonstrate difficulty in social skills. For a student with a hearing impairment, social skills may be difficult because of not hearing social language. However, the emotionally disturbed student may have difficulty because of a special type of psychological disturbance. An autistic student, as a third example, would be unaware of the social cues given with voice, facial expression, and body language. Each of these students would need social skill instruction but in a different way.

Students with disabilities (in all areas) may demonstrate difficulty in academic skills. A student with mental retardation will need special instruction across all areas of academics while a student with a learning disability may need assistance in only one or two subject areas.

Students with disabilities may demonstrate difficulty with independence or self-help skills. A student with a visual impairment may need specific mobility training while a student with a specific learning disability may need a checklist to help in managing materials and assignments.

Special Education Teachers should be aware that although students across disabilities may demonstrate difficulty in similar ways, the causes may be very different. For example, some disabilities are due to specific sensory impairments (hearing or vision), some due to cognitive ability (mental retardation), and some due to neurological impairment (autism or some learning disabilities). The reason for the difficulty should be a consideration when planning the program of special education intervention.

Additionally, Special Education Teachers should be aware that each area of disability has a range of involvement. Some students may have minimal disability and require no services. Others may need only a few accommodations and have a 504 plan. Some may need an IEP that outlines a specific special education program which might be implemented in an inclusion/resource program, self-contained program, or in a residential setting.

A student with ADD may be able to participate in the regular education program with a 504 plan that outlines a checklist system to keep the student organized and additional communication between school and home. Other students with ADD may need instruction in a smaller group with fewer distractions and would be better served in a resource room.

Special educators should be knowledgeable of the cause and severity of the disability and its manifestations in the specific student when planning an appropriate special education program. Because of the unique needs of the child, such programs are documented in the child's IEP – Individualized Education Program.

Skill 1.03 Analyzing similarities and differences (e.g., cognitive, physical, language, social, emotional) among individuals with and without disabilities

Normality in child behavior is influenced by society's attitudes and cultural beliefs about what is normal for children (e.g., the motto for the Victorian era was "Children should be seen and not heard"). However, criteria for what is "normal" involves consideration of these questions:

- **Is the behavior age appropriate?** An occasional tantrum may be expected for a toddler, but is not typical for a high school student.
- **Is the behavior pathological in itself?** Drug or alcohol use would be harmful to children, regardless of how many engage in it.
- **How persistent is the problem?** A kindergarten student initially may be afraid to go to school. However, if the fear persisted into first or second grade, then the problem would be considered persistent.
- **How severe is the behavior?** Self-injurious, cruel, and extremely destructive behaviors would be examples of behaviors that require intervention.
- **How often does the behavior occur?** An occasional tantrum in a young child or a brief mood of depression in an adolescent would not be considered problematic. However, if the behaviors occur frequently, that behavior would not be characteristic of normal child development.
- **Do several problem behaviors occur as a group?** Clusters of behaviors, especially severe behaviors that occur together, may be indicative of a serious problem, such as schizophrenia.
- **Is the behavior sex-appropriate?** Cultural and societal attitudes towards gender change over time. While attitudes towards younger boys playing with dolls or girls preferring sports to dolls have relaxed, children eventually are expected as adults to conform to the expected behaviors for males and females.

Certain stages of child development have their own sets of problems, and it should be kept in mind that short-term undesirable behaviors can and will occur over these stages. Child development is also a continuum, and children may manifest these problem behaviors somewhat earlier or later than their peers.

About 15-20% of the school-aged population between 6 and 17 years old receive special education services.. The categories of learning disabilities and emotional disturbance are the most prevalent. Exceptional students are very much like their peers without disabilities. The main difference is that they have an intellectual, emotional, behavioral, or physical deficit that significantly interferes with their ability to benefit from education.

(You may also refer back to skill 1.01 for more information about the characteristics found in students with disabilities.)

Skill 1.04   Demonstrating knowledge of typical, delayed, and disordered communication patterns among individuals with disabilities

Language is the means whereby people communicate their thoughts, make requests, and respond to others. Communication Competence is an interaction of cognitive competence, social knowledge, and language competence. Communication problems may result from, in any or all of these areas, which directly impact the student's ability to interact with others. Language consists of several components, each of which follows a sequence of development. Brown and colleagues were the first to describe language as a function of developmental stages rather than age (Reid, 1988, p. 44). He developed a formula to group the mean length of utterances (sentences) into stages. Counting the number of morphemes per 100 utterances, one can calculate a mean length of utterance, MLU. Total number of morphemes / 100 = MLU e.g. 180/100 = 1.8

Summary of Brown's findings about MLU and language development:

Stage	MLU	Developmental Features
L	1.5-2.0	14 basic morphemes (e.g., in, on, articles, possessives)
LI	2.0-2.5	Beginning of pronoun use, auxiliary verbs
LII	2.5-3.0	Language form approximate adult forms. Beginning of questions and negative statements
Lv	3.0-3.5	Use of complex (embedded)sentences
V	3.5-4.0	Use of compound sentences.

Components of Language

Language learning is composed of five components. Children progress through developmental stages through each component.

Phonology

Phonology is the system of rules about sounds and sound combinations for a language. A phoneme is the smallest unit of sound that combines with other sounds to make words. A phoneme, by itself, does not have a meaning; it must be combined with other phonemes. Problems in phonology may be manifested as developmental delays in acquiring consonants, or reception problems, such as misinterpreting words because a different consonant was substituted.

Morphology

Morphemes are the smallest units of language that convey meaning. Morphemes are root words or free morphemes that can stand alone (e.g., walk), and affixes (e.g., ed, s, ing). Content words carry the meaning in a sentence, and functional words join phrases and sentences. Generally, students with problems in this area may not use inflectional endings in their words, may not be consistent in their use of certain morphemes, or may be delayed in learning morphemes such as irregular past tenses.

Syntax

Syntax rules, commonly known as grammar, govern how morphemes and words are correctly combined. Wood (1976) describes six stages of syntax acquisition (Mercer, p. 347).

- **Stages 1 and 2**—Birth to about 2 years: Child is learning the semantic system.
- **Stage 3**—Ages 2 to 3 years: Simple sentences contain subject and predicate.
- **Stage 4**—Ages 2 ½ to 4 years: Elements such as question words are added to basic sentences (e.g., where) and word order is changed to ask questions. The child begins to use "and" to combine simple sentences, and the child begins to embed words within the basic sentence.
- **Stage 5**—About 3 ½ to 7 years: The child uses complete sentences that include word classes of adult language. The child is becoming aware of appropriate semantic functions of words and differences within the same grammatical class.
- **Stage 6**—About 5 to 20 years: The child begins to learn complex sentences and sentences that imply commands, requests, and promises.

Syntactic deficits are manifested by the child using sentences that lack length or complexity for a child that age. The child may have problems understanding or creating complex sentences and embedded sentences.

Semantics

Semantics is language content: objects, actions, and relations between objects. As with syntax, Wood (1976) outlines stages of semantic development:

Stage 1—Birth to about 2 years: The child is learning meaning while learning his first words. Sentences are one word, but the meaning varies according to the context. Therefore, "doggie" may mean, "This is my dog." or "There is a dog." or "The dog is barking."

Stage 2—About 2 to 8 years: The child progresses to two-word sentences about concrete actions. As more words are learned, the child forms longer sentences. Until about age 7, things are defined in terms of visible actions. The child begins to respond to prompts (e.g., pretty/flower), and at about age 8, the child can respond to a prompt with an opposite (e.g., pretty/ugly).

Stage 3—Begins at about age 8: The child's word meanings relate directly to experiences, operations, and processes. Vocabulary is defined by the child's experiences, not the adult's. At about age 12, the child begins to give "dictionary" definitions, and the semantic level approaches that of adults.

Semantic problems take the form of:

- Limited vocabulary
- Inability to understand figurative language or idioms; interprets literally
- Failure to perceive multiple meanings of words, changes in word meaning from changes in context, resulting in incomplete understanding of what is read
- Difficulty understanding linguistic concepts (e.g., before/after), verbal analogies, and logical relationships such as possessives, spatial, and temporal
- Misuse of transitional words such as "although" or "regardless"

Pragmatics

Commonly known as the speaker's intent, pragmatics is used to influence or control actions or attitudes of others. **Communicative competence** depends on how well one understands the rules of language, as well as the social rules of communication, such as taking turns and using the correct tone of voice.

Pragmatic deficits are manifested by failures to respond properly to indirect requests after age 8 (e.g., "Can't you turn down the TV?" elicits a response of "No" instead of "Yes" and the child turning down the volume). Children with these deficits have trouble reading cues that indicate the listener does not understand them. Whereas a person would usually notice this and adjust one's speech to the listener's needs, the child with pragmatic problems does not do this. Pragmatic deficits are also characterized by inappropriate social behaviors such as interruptions or monopolizing conversations. Children may use immature speech and have trouble sticking to a topic. These problems can persist into adulthood, affecting academic, vocational, and social interactions. Problems in language development often require long-term interventions and can persist into adulthood.

Certain problems are associated with different grade levels:

Preschool and Kindergarten: The child's speech may sound immature and the child may not be able to follow simple directions and often cannot name things such as the days of the week and colors. The child may not be able to discriminate between sounds and the letters associated with the sounds. The child might substitute sounds and have trouble responding accurately to certain types of questions. The child may play less with his peers or participate in non-play or parallel play.

Elementary School: Problems with sound discrimination persist, and the child may have problems with temporal and spatial concepts (e.g,. before/after). As the child progresses through school, he may have problems making the transition from narrative to expository writing. Word retrieval problems may not be very evident because the child begins to devise strategies such as talking around the word he cannot remember or using fillers and descriptors. The child might speak more slowly, have problems sounding out words, and get confused with multiple-meaning words. Pragmatic problems show up in social situations such as failure to correctly interpret social cues and adjust to appropriate language, inability to predict consequences, and inability to formulate requests to obtain new information.

Secondary School: At this level, difficulties become more subtle. The child lacks the ability to use and understand higher-level syntax, semantics, and pragmatics. If the child has problems with auditory language, he may also have problems with short-term memory. Receptive and/or expressive language delays impair the child's ability to learn effectively. The child often lacks the ability to organize/categorize the information received in school. Problems associated with pragmatic deficiencies persist, but because the child is aware of them, he becomes inattentive, withdrawn, or frustrated.

Skill 1.05   Recognizing how social and cultural factors (e.g., beliefs, traditions, values) may affect attitudes about disabilities and the relationship among student, family, and school

As cultures place varying value on education or on the role of genders, different views may be taken of individuals with disabilities, appropriate education, career goals, and the individual's role in society. The special educator must first become familiar with the cultural representations of her students and the community in which she teaches. As she demonstrates respect for the individual student's culture, she will build the rapport necessary to work with the student, family, and community to prepare him for future productive work, independence, and possible post-secondary education or training (IDEA 2004).

While society has "progressed," and many things are more acceptable today than they were yesterday, having a disability still carries a stigma. Historically, people with disabilities have been ostracized from their communities. Up until the 1970s, a large number of people with special needs were institutionalized at birth because their relatives either did not know what to do, they felt embarrassed to admit they had a child with a disability, or they gave in to the cultural peer pressure to put their "problem" away. Sometimes this meant hiding a child's disability, which may even have meant locking a child in a room in the house. Perhaps the worst viewpoint society had expressed up to the 1970s, and which still prevails today, is that the person with "special needs" is unable to contribute to society.

Today, American society has left the "must institutionalize" method for a "normalize" concept. Houses in local communities have been purchased for the purpose of providing supervision and/or nursing care that allows for people with disabilities to have "normal" social living arrangements. Congress passed laws that have allowed those with disabilities to access public facilities. American society has widened doorways, added special bathrooms, etc. The regular education classroom teacher is now learning to accept and teach students with special needs. America's media today has provided education and frequent exposure of people with special needs. The concept of acceptance appears to be occurring for those with physically noticeable handicaps.

> Learn more about **Disability in Cross-Cultural Perspective:**
> http://www.disabilityworld.org

But the appearance of those with special needs in media such as television and movies generally are those who rise above their "label" as disabled because of an extraordinary skill. Most people in the community are portrayed as accepting the "disabled" person when that special skill is noted. In addition, those who continue to express revulsion or prejudice towards the person with a disability often express remorse when the special skill is noted or if peer pressure becomes too intense. This portrayal often ignores those with learning and emotional disabilities who appear normal by appearance and who often feel and suffer from the prejudices.

The most significant group any individual faces is their peers. Pressure to appear normal and not "needy" in any area is still intense from early childhood to adulthood. During teen years, when young people are beginning to "express their individuality," the very appearance of walking into a Special Education classroom often brings feelings of inadequacy and labeling by peers that the student is "special". Being considered normal is the desire of all individuals with disabilities, regardless of the age or disability. People with disabilities today, as many years ago, still measure their successes by how their achievements mask/hide their disabilities.

The most difficult cultural/community outlook on those who are disabled comes in the adult work world where disabilities of persons can become highly evident, often causing those with special needs to have difficulty in finding work and keeping their jobs. This is a particularly difficult place for those who have not learned to self advocate or accommodate for their area(s) of special needs.

COMPETENCY 0002   UNDERSTAND THE EFFECTS OF DISABILITIES ON HUMAN DEVELOPMENT AND LEARNING.

Skill 2.01   Demonstrating knowledge of typical patterns of human development (e.g., physical, sensory, motor, cognitive, language, social, emotional)

Social Emotional

Children whose behavior deviates from society's standards for normal behavior for certain ages and stages of development fall into the social emotional category of disability. Behavioral expectations vary from setting to setting; for example, it is acceptable to yell on the football field, but not as the teacher is explaining a lesson to the class. Different cultures have their standards of behavior, further complicating the question of what constitutes a behavioral problem. People also have their personal opinions and standards for what is tolerable and what is not. Some behavioral problems are openly expressed; others are inwardly directed and not very obvious. As a result of these factors, the terms behavioral disorders and emotional disturbance have become almost interchangeable.

While almost all children at times exhibit behaviors that are aggressive, withdrawn, or otherwise inappropriate, the IDEA definition of serious emotional disturbance focuses on behaviors that persist over time, are intense, and which impair a child's ability to function in society. The behaviors must not be caused by temporary stressful situations or other causes (i.e., depression over the death of a grandparent or anger over the parents' impending divorce). In order for a child to be considered seriously emotionally disturbed, he or she must exhibit one or more of the following characteristics over a **long period of time** and to a **marked degree** that **adversely affects** a child's educational performance.

- Inability to learn that cannot be explained by intellectual, sensory, or health factors
- Inability to maintain satisfactory interpersonal relationships
- Inappropriate types of behaviors
- General pervasive mood of unhappiness or depression
- Physical symptoms or fears associated with personal or school problems
- Schizophrenic children are covered under this definition, and social maladjustment by itself does not satisfy this definition unless it is accompanied by one of the other conditions of SED.

The diagnostic categories and definitions used to classify mental disorders come from the American Psychiatric Association's publication, *Diagnostic and Statistical Manual of Mental Disorders* (DSM-IV), the handbook that is used by psychiatrists and Psychologists. The DSM-IV is a multi-axial classification system consisting of dimensions (axes) coded along with the psychiatric diagnosis. The axes are:

Axis I   Principal psychiatric diagnosis (e.g., overanxious disorder)

Axis II   Developmental problems (e.g., developmental reading disorder)

Axis III   Physical disorders (e.g., allergies)

Axis IV   Psychosocial stressors (e.g., divorce)

Axis V   Rating of the highest level of adaptive functioning (includes intellectual and social). Rating is called Global Assessment Functioning (GAF) score.

While the DSM-III diagnosis is one way of diagnosing serious emotional disturbance, there are other ways of classifying the various forms that behavior disorders manifest themselves. The following tables summarize some of these classifications.

Externalizing Behaviors	Internalizing Behaviors
Aggressive behaviors expressed outwardly toward others	Withdrawing behaviors that are directed inward to oneself
Manifested as hyperactivity, persistent aggression, irritating behaviors that are impulsive and distractible	Social withdrawal
Examples: hitting, cursing, stealing, arson, cruelty to animals, hyperactivity	Depression, fears, phobias, elective mutism, withdrawal, anorexia and bulimia

Well-known instruments used to assess children's behavior have their own categories (scales) to classify behaviors. The following table illustrates the scales used in some of the most widely-used instruments.

Walker Problem Identification Checklist	Burks' Behavior Rating Scales (BBRS)	Devereux Behavior Rating Scale (adolescent)	Revised Behavior Problem Checklist (Quay & Peterson)
Acting out	Excessive self-blame	Unethical behavior	Major scales
Withdrawal	Excessive anxiety	Defiant-resistive	Conduct Disorder
Distractibility	Excessive withdrawal	Domineering-sadistic	Socialized aggression
Disturbed peer relations	Excessive dependency	Heterosexual interest	Attention problems; immaturity
Immaturity	Poor ego strength	Hyperactive expansive	Anxiety—withdrawal
	Poor physical strength	Poor emotional control	
	Poor coordination	Need approval, dependency	Minor scales
	Poor intellectuality	Emotional disturbance	Psychotic behavior
	Poor academics	Physical inferiority--timidity	Motor excess
	Poor attention	Schizoid withdrawal	
	Poor impulse control	Bizarre speech and cognition	
	Poor reality contact	Bizarre actions	
	Poor sense of identity		
	Excessive suffering		
	Poor anger control		
	Excessive sense of persecution		

	Excessive aggressiveness		
	Excessive resistance		
	Poor social conformity		

Disturbance may also be categorized in degrees: mild, moderate, or severe. The degree of disturbance will affect the type and degree of interventions and services required by emotionally handicapped students. Degree of disturbance also must be considered when determining the least restrictive environment and the services named for free, appropriate education for these students. An example of a set of criteria for determining the degree of disturbance is the one developed by P.L. Newcomer:

	DEGREE	OF	DISTURBANCE
CRITERIA	Mild	Moderate	Severe
Precipitating events	Highly stressful	Moderately stressful	Not stressful
Destructiveness	Not destructive	Occasionally destructive	Usually destructive
Maturational appropriateness	Behavior typical for age	Some behavior untypical for age	Behavior too young or too old
Personal functioning	Cares for own needs	Usually cares for own needs	Unable to care for own needs
Social functioning	Usually able to relate to others	Usually unable to relate to others	Unable to relate to others
Reality index	Usually sees events as they are	Occasionally sees events as they are	Little contact with reality
Insight index	Aware of behavior	Usually aware of behavior	Usually not aware of behavior
Conscious control	Usually can control behavior	Occasionally can control behavior	Little control over behavior
Social responsiveness	Usually acts appropriately	Occasionally acts appropriately	Rarely acts appropriately

Source: *Understanding and Teaching Emotionally Disturbed Children and Adolescents*, (2nd ed., p. 139), by P.L. Newcomer, 1993, Austin, TX: Pro-De. Copyright 1993. Reprinted with permission.

Language Development and Behavior

(Refer to skill 1.04 for language development.)

Cognitive Development

Children go through patterns of learning, beginning with pre-operational thought processes, and then move to concrete operational thoughts. Eventually, they begin to acquire the mental ability to think about and solve problems in their heads because they can manipulate objects symbolically. Children of most ages can use symbols, such as words and numbers to represent objects and relations, but they need concrete reference points. It is essential that children be encouraged to use and develop the thinking skills that they possess in solving problems that interest them. The content of the curriculum must be relevant, engaging, and meaningful to the students.

The teacher of special needs students must have a general knowledge of cognitive development. Although children with special needs' cognitive development rate may be different than other children, a teacher needs to be aware of some of the activities of each stage as part of the basis to determine what should be taught and when it should be taught.

The following information about cognitive development was taken from the Cincinnati Children's Hospital Medical Center at www.cincinattichildrens.org.

Some common features indicating a progression from more simple to more complex cognitive development include the following:

Children (ages 6-12)

Begin to develop the ability to think in concrete ways
Concrete operations are operations performed in the presence of the object and events that are to be used. Examples: how to combine (addition), separate (subtract or divide), order (alphabetize and sort/categorize), and transform (change things such as 25 pennies=1 quarter) objects and actions

Adolescence (ages 12-18)

Adolescence marks the beginning development of more complex thinking skills, including abstract thinking, the ability to reason from known principles (form own new ideas or questions), the ability to consider many points of view according to varying criteria (compare or debate ideas or opinions), and the ability to think about the process of thinking.

What cognitive developmental changes occur during adolescence?

During adolescence (between 12 and 18 years of age), the developing teenager acquires the ability to think systematically about all logical relationships within a problem. The transition from concrete thinking to formal logical operations occurs over time. Every adolescent progresses at varying rates in developing his ability to think in more complex ways. Each adolescent develops his own view of the world. Some adolescents may be able to apply logical operations to school work long before they are able to apply them to personal dilemmas. When emotional issues arise, they often interfere with an adolescent's ability to think in more complex ways. The ability to consider possibilities, as well as facts, may influence decision making in either positive or negative ways.

Some common features indicating a progression from more simple to more complex cognitive development include the following:

Early Adolescence

During early adolescence, the use of more complex thinking is focused on personal decision making in school and home environments, including the following:

Begins to demonstrate use of formal logical operations in schoolwork.
Begins to question authority and society standards.
Begins to form and verbalize his own thoughts and views on a variety of topics, usually more related to his own life, such as:

- Which sports are better to play

- Which groups are better to be included in

- What personal appearances are desirable or attractive

- What parental rules should be changed

Middle Adolescence

With some experience in using more complex thinking processes, the focus of middle adolescence often expands to include more philosophical and futuristic concerns, including the following:

- Often questions more extensively.
- Often analyzes more extensively.
- Thinks about and begins to form his own code of ethics.
- Thinks about different possibilities and begins to develop own identity. Thinks about and begins to systematically consider possible future goals.
- Thinks about and begins to make his own plans.
- Begins to think long term.
- Use of systematic thinking begins to influence relationships with others.

Late Adolescence

During late adolescence, complex thinking processes are **used to focus on** less self-centered concepts, as well as personal decision making, including the following:

- Increases thoughts about more global concepts such as justice, history,
- Politics, and patriotism.
- Develops idealistic views on specific topics or concerns.
- Debates and develops intolerance of opposing views.
- Begins to focus thinking on making career decisions.
- Begins to focus thinking on emerging role in adult society.

What encourages healthy cognitive development during adolescence?

The following suggestions will help to encourage positive and healthy cognitive development in the adolescent:

- Include adolescents in discussions about a variety of topics, issues, and current events.
- Encourage adolescents to share ideas and thoughts with adults.
- Encourage adolescents to think independently and develop their own ideas.
- Assist adolescents in setting their own goals.
- Compliment and praise adolescents for well-thought-out decisions.
- Assist adolescents in re-evaluating poorly made decisions for themselves.
- Stimulate adolescents to think about possibilities of the future.

Physical Development, Including Motor and Sensory

It is important for the teacher to be aware of the physical stage of development and how the child's physical growth and development affect the child's learning. Factors determined by the physical stage of development include: ability to sit and attend, the need for activity, the relationship between physical skills and self-esteem, and the degree to which physical involvement in an activity (as opposed to being able to understand an abstract concept) affects learning.

Children with physical impairments possess a variety of disabling conditions. Although there are significant differences among these conditions, similarities also exist. Each condition usually affects one particular system of the body: the cardiopulmonary system (i.e., blood vessels, heart, and lungs) or the musculoskeletal system (i.e., spinal cord, brain nerves). Some conditions develop during pregnancy, birth, or infancy because of the known or unknown factors, which may affect the fetus or newborn infant. Other conditions occur later due to injury (trauma), disease, or factors not fully understood.

In addition to motor disorders, individuals with physical disabilities may have multi-disabling conditions such as concomitant hearing impairments, visual impairments, perceptual disorders, speech defects, behavior disorders, or mental handicaps, performance, and emotional responsiveness. Some characteristics which may occur with individuals with physical disabilities and other health impairments are:

1. Lack of physical stamina; fatigue
2. Chronic illness; poor endurance
3. Deficient motor skills; normal movement may be prevented
4. May cause physical limitations or impede motor development; a prosthesis or an orthosis may be required
5. Mobility and exploration of one's environment may be limited
6. Limited self-care abilities
7. Progressive weakening and degeneration of muscles
8. Frequent speech and language defects; communication may be prevented; echolatia orthosis may be present
9. May experience pain and discomfort throughout the body
10. May display emotional (psychological) problems which require treatment
11. Social adjustments may be needed; may display maladaptive social behavior
12. May necessitate long-term medical treatment
13. May have embarrassing side effects from certain diseases or treatment
14. May exhibit erratic or poor attendance patterns

In 1981, the condition of autism was moved from the exceptionality category to the seriously emotionally disturbed to that of other health impaired by virtue of a change in language in the original definitions under Public Law 94-142 (*Education of Handicapped Children*, *Federal Register*, 1977). With IDEA in 1990, autism was made into a separate exceptionality category.

Skill 2.02   Recognizing the implications of various disabilities for physical, sensory, motor, cognitive, language, social, and/or emotional development and functioning

Student with a disability means a student with a disability who has not attained the age of 21 prior to September 1st and who is entitled to attend public schools and who, because of mental, physical or emotional reasons, has been identified as having a disability and who requires special services and programs approved by the department. The terms used in this definition are defined as follows:

(1) *Autism* means a developmental disability significantly affecting verbal and nonverbal communication and social interaction, generally evident before age 3, that adversely affects a student's educational performance. Other characteristics often associated with autism are engagement in repetitive activities and stereotyped movements, resistance to environmental change or change in daily routines, and unusual responses to sensory experiences. The term does not apply if a student's educational performance is adversely affected primarily because the student has an emotional disturbance. A student who manifests the characteristics of autism after age 3 could be diagnosed as having autism if the criteria in this paragraph are otherwise satisfied.

(2) *Deafness* means a hearing impairment that is so severe that the student is impaired in processing linguistic information through hearing, with or without amplification, that adversely affects a student's educational performance.

(3) *Deaf-Blindness* means concomitant hearing and visual impairments, the combination of which causes such severe communication and other developmental and educational needs that they cannot be accommodated in special education programs solely for students with deafness or students with blindness.

(4) *Emotional Disturbance* means a condition exhibiting one or more of the following characteristics over a long period of time and to a marked degree that adversely affects a student's educational performance:

(i) an inability to learn that cannot be explained by intellectual, sensory, or health factors;

(ii) an inability to build or maintain satisfactory interpersonal relationships with peers and teachers;

(iii) inappropriate types of behavior or feelings under normal circumstances;

(iv) a generally pervasive mood of unhappiness or depression; or

(v) a tendency to develop physical symptoms or fears associated with personal or school problems.

The term includes schizophrenia. The term does not apply to students who are socially maladjusted unless it is determined that they have an emotional disturbance.

(5) *Hearing Impairment* means an impairment in hearing, whether permanent or fluctuating, that adversely affects the child's educational performance but that is not included under the definition of *deafness* in this section.

(6) *Learning Disability* means a disorder in one or more of the basic psychological processes involved in understanding or in using language, spoken or written, which manifests itself in an imperfect ability to listen, think, speak, read, write, spell, or do mathematical calculations. The term includes such conditions as perceptual disabilities, brain injury, minimal brain dysfunction, dyslexia, and developmental aphasia. The term does not include learning problems that are primarily the result of visual, hearing, or motor disabilities, of mental retardation, of emotional disturbance, or of environmental, cultural, or economic disadvantage.

(7) *Mental Retardation* means significantly sub-average general intellectual functioning, existing concurrently with deficits in adaptive behavior and manifested during the developmental period, that adversely affects a student's educational performance.

(8) *Multiple Disabilities* means concomitant impairments (such as mental retardation-blindness, mental retardation-orthopedic impairment, etc.), the combination of which cause such severe educational needs that they cannot be accommodated in a special education program solely for one of the impairments. The term does not include deaf-blindness.

(9) *Orthopedic Impairment* means a severe orthopedic impairment that adversely affects a student's educational performance. The term includes impairments caused by a congenital anomaly (*e.g.*, clubfoot, absence of some member, etc.), impairments caused by disease (*e.g.*, poliomyelitis, bone tuberculosis, etc.), and impairments from other causes (*e.g.*, cerebral palsy, amputation, and fractures or burns which cause contractures).

(10) *Other Health Impairment* means having limited strength, vitality, or alertness, including a heightened alertness to environmental stimuli, that results in limited alertness with respect to the educational environment, that is due to chronic or acute health problems, including but not limited to a heart condition, tuberculosis, rheumatic fever, nephritis, asthma, sickle cell anemia, hemophilia, epilepsy, lead poisoning, leukemia, diabetes, attention deficit disorder, or attention deficit hyperactivity disorder, or Tourette's syndrome, which adversely affects a student's educational performance.

(11) *Speech or Language Impairment* means a communication disorder, such as stuttering, impaired articulation, a language impairment, or a voice impairment, that adversely affects a student's educational performance.

(12) *Traumatic Brain Injury* means an acquired injury to the brain caused by an external physical force or by certain medical conditions such as stroke, encephalitis, aneurysm, anoxia, or brain tumors with resulting impairments that adversely affect educational performance. The term includes open or closed head injuries or brain injuries from certain medical conditions resulting in mild, moderate, or severe impairments in one or more areas, including cognition, language, memory, attention, reasoning, abstract thinking, judgment, problem solving, sensory, perceptual, and motor abilities, psychosocial behavior, physical functions, information processing, and speech. The term does not include injuries that are congenital or caused by birth trauma.

(13 *Visual Impairment including blindness* means an impairment in vision that, even with correction, adversely affects a student's educational performance. The term includes both partial sight and blindness.

Skill 2.03   Demonstrating familiarity with development issues that may affect individuals with disabilities

To effectively assess and plan for the developmental needs of individuals with disabilities, Special Education Teachers should first be familiar with the development of the typically developing child. Developmental areas of speech and language, fine and gross motor skills, cognitive abilities, emotional development, and social skills should be considered.

If a six-year-old child who is missing her front teeth is referred for speech therapy for mispronunciation of words with the /th/ sound, the cause is the lack of teeth. Without a place to place the tongue, the /th/ cannot be pronounced correctly. Thus, speech therapy would not be warranted. Rather, a typical development stage must be passed.

A second grade student may have difficulty buttoning clothing. Because that is a skill that is typically mastered around age four, a developmental delay in fine motor skills may be present. It is appropriate for the special educator to request consultation and possibly formal evaluation of the child's needs.

In addition to being aware of the ages of typical developmental milestones, the Special Education Teacher should consider the sequence in which the skills are acquired. While not all children go through every step of development (some children never seem to crawl), most follow the typical sequence. In an example of language development, children name objects with single words long before they form phrases or sentences. In other words, a child cannot understand how to form the sentence *I see a cat on the fence* before he can accurately voice *cat* when he sees a cat or a picture of one.

Sometimes the disability itself will hinder or prevent a child from accomplishing a developmental task. A child with a visual-spatial difficulty may not be able to see the components of a certain letter in print. Given a handwriting program that shows the parts of a letter made with wooden pieces may provide the link to the child mastering that letter formation.

The key to understanding the role of development and the needs of the special education student is being knowledgeable of typical development and seeing such skills in a number of typically developing students. This is another benefit of the inclusion classroom. Given a foundation of developmental understanding and knowledge of the specific child's disability [refer to skill 1.01], the Special Education Teacher can better assess and implement an appropriate education program to meet the unique needs of the child.

Skill 2.04   Recognizing the possible effects of medications on student learning, developing, and functioning (e.g., cognitive, physical, social, emotional)

Students with disabilities who take medications often experience medication side effects that can impact their behavior and educational development. Teachers may perceive the child as unmotivated or drowsy, not fully understanding the cognitive effects that medications can have on a child.

Some medications may impair concentration, which can lead to poor processing ability, lower alertness, and cause drowsiness and hyperactivity. Students who take several medications may have an increased risk of behavioral and cognitive side effects.

The students' parents should let the school know when the students are beginning or changing their medication so they can look out for possible side effects.

There are three different classes of antidepressants that students can take. One type is called the selective serotonin-reuptake inhibitors (SSRIs). The SSRIs block certain receptors from absorbing serotonin. Over time, SSRIs may cause changes in brain chemistry. The side effects of SSRIs include dry mouth, insomnia or restless sleep, increased sweating, and nausea. It can also cause mood swings in people with bipolar disorders.

A second type of antidepressant that may be used is the tricyclic antidepressants. They are considered good for treating depression and obsessive-compulsive behavior. They cause similar side effects to the SSRIs, such as sedation, tremor, seizures, dry mouth, light sensitivity, and mood swings in people with bipolar disorders.

A third type of antidepressant is the monoamine oxidase inhibitors (MAOIs). They are not as widely used as the other two types because many have unpleasant and life-threatening interactions with many other drugs, including common over-the-counter medications. People taking MAOIs must also follow a special diet because these medications interact with many foods. The list of foods to avoid includes chocolate, aged cheeses, and more.

Stimulants are often prescribed to help with attention deficit disorder and attention deficit hyperactivity disorder. The drugs can have many side effects, including agitation, restlessness, aggressive behavior, dizziness, insomnia, headache, or tremor.

In severe cases of anxiety, an anti-anxiety medication (tranquilizer) may be prescribed. Most tranquilizers have a potential for addiction and abuse. They tend to be sedating and can cause a variety of unpleasant side effects, including blurred vision, confusion, sleepiness, and tremors.

If educators are aware of the types of medication that their students are taking, along with the myriad of side effects, they will be able to respond more positively when some of the side effects of the medication change their students' behavior, response rate, and attention span.

COMPETENCY 0003   UNDERSTAND TYPES AND CHARACTERISTICS OF ASSESSMENT INSTRUMENTS AND METHODS.

Skill 3.01   Recognizing basic concepts and terminology used in assessment

The following terms are frequently used in behavioral and academic testing and assessment. They represent basic terminology and not more advanced statistical concepts.

Baseline—This is also known as establishing a baseline. This procedure means collecting data about a target behavior or performance of a skill before certain interventions or teaching procedures are implemented. Establishing a baseline will enable a person to determine if the interventions are effective.

Criterion-Referenced Test—A test in which the individual's performance is measured against mastery of curriculum criteria rather than comparison to the performance of other students. Criterion-referenced tests may be commercially or teacher made. Since these tests measure what a student can or cannot do, results are especially useful for identifying goals and objectives for IEPs and lesson plans.

Curriculum-Based Assessment—Assessment of an individual's performance of objectives of a curriculum, such as a reading or math program. The individual's performance is measured in terms of what objectives were mastered.

Duration recording—Measuring the length of time a behavior lasts, i.e., tantrums, time out of class, or crying.

Error Analysis—The mistakes on an individual's test are noted and categorized by type. For example, an error analysis in a reading test could categorize mistakes by miscues, substituting words, omitted words or phrases, and miscues that are self corrected.

Event recording—The number of times a target behavior occurs during an observation period.

Formal Assessment—Standardized tests that have specific procedures for administration, norming, scoring, and interpretation. These include intelligence and achievement tests.

Frequency—The number of times a behavior occurs in a time interval, such as out-of-seat behavior, hitting, and temper tantrums.

Frequency Distribution—Plotting the scores received on a test and tallying how many individuals received those scores. A frequency distribution is used to visually determine how the group of individuals performed on a test, to illustrate extreme scores, and to compare the distribution to the mean or other criterion.

Informal Assessment—Non-standardized tests such as criterion-referenced tests and teacher-prepared tests. There are no rigid rules or procedures for administration or scoring.

Intensity—The degree of a behavior as measured by its frequency and duration.

Interval recording—This technique involves breaking the observation into an equal number of time intervals, such as 10-second intervals during a 5-minute period. At the end of each interval, the observer notes the presence or absence of the target behavior. The observer can then calculate a percentage by dividing the number of intervals in which the target behavior occurred by the total number of intervals in the observation period. This type of recording works well for behaviors which occur with high frequency or for long periods of time, such as on- or off-task behavior, pencil tapping, or stereotyped behaviors. The observer does not have to constantly monitor the student yet can gather enough data to get an accurate idea of the extent of the behavior.

Latency—The length of time that elapses between the presentation of a stimulus (e.g., a question) and the response (e.g., the student's answer).

Mean—The arithmetic average of a set of scores, calculated by adding the set of scores and dividing the sum by the number of scores. For example, if the sum of a set of 35 scores is 2935, dividing that sum by 35 (the number of scores), yields a mean of 83.9.

Median—The middle score: 50% of the scores are above this number, and 50% of the scores are below this number. In the example above, if the middle score were 72, 17 students would have scored less than 72, and 17 students would have scored more than 72.

Mode—The score most frequently tallied in a frequency distribution. In the example above, the most frequently tallied score might be 78. It is possible for a set of scores to have more than one mode.

Momentary time sampling—This is a technique used for measuring behaviors of a group of individuals or several behaviors from the same individual. Time samples are usually brief and may be conducted at fixed or variable intervals. The advantage of using variable intervals is increased reliability, as the students will not be able to predict when the time sample will be taken.

Multiple Baseline Design—This may be used to test the effectiveness of an intervention in a skill performance or to determine if the intervention accounted for the observed changes in a target behavior. First, the initial baseline data is collected, followed by the data during the intervention period. To get the second baseline, the intervention is removed for a period of time, and data is collected again. The intervention is then reapplied, and data is collected on the target behavior. An example of a multiple baseline design might be ignoring a child who calls out in class without raising his hand. Initially, the baseline could involve counting the number of times the child calls out before applying interventions. During the time the teacher ignores the child's call-outs, data is collected. For the second baseline, the teacher would resume the response to the child's call-outs in the way she did before ignoring. The child's call-outs would probably increase again, if ignoring actually accounted for the decrease. If the teacher reapplies the ignoring strategy, the child's call-outs would probably decrease again.

Multiple baseline designs may also be used with single-subject experiments where:

- The same behavior is measured for several students at the same time. An example would be observing off-task or out-of-seat behavior among three students in a classroom.
- Several behaviors may be measured for one student. The teacher may be observing call-outs, off-task, and out-of-seat behavior for a particular child during an observation period.
- Several settings are observed to see if the same behaviors are occurring across settings. A student's aggressive behavior toward his classmates may be observed at recess, in class, going to or from class, or in the cafeteria.

Norm-Referenced Test—An individual's performance is compared to the group that was used to calculate the performance standards in this standardized test. Some examples are the CTBS, WISC-R, and Stanford-Binet.

Operational Definition—The description of a behavior and its measurable components. In behavioral observations, the description must be specific and measurable so that the observer will know exactly what constitutes instances and non-instances of the target behavior. Otherwise, reliability may be inaccurate.

Pinpoint—Specifying and describing the target behavior for change in measurable and precise terms. "On time for class" may be interpreted as arriving physically in the classroom when the tardy bell has finished ringing, or it may mean being at the pencil sharpener, or it may mean being in one's in seat and ready to begin work when the bell has finished ringing. Pinpointing the behavior makes it possible to accurately measure the behavior.

Profile—Plotting an individual's behavioral data on a graph.

Rate—The frequency of a behavior over a specified time period, such as 5 talk-outs during a 30-minute period or typing 85 words per minute.

Raw Score—The number of correct responses on a test before they have been converted to standard scores. Raw scores are not meaningful because they have no basis of comparison to the performance of other individuals.

Reliability—The consistency (stability) of a test over time to measure what it is supposed to measure. Reliability is commonly measured in four ways:

- Test-retest method—The test is administered to the same group or individuals after a short period of time, and the results are compared.
- Alternate form (equivalent form)—This measures reliability by using alternative forms to measure the same skills. If both forms are administered to the same group within a relatively short period of time, there should be a high correlation between the two sets of scores if the test has a high degree of reliability.
- Interrater—This refers to the degree of agreement between two or more individuals observing the same behaviors or observing the same tests.
- Internal reliability—This is determined by statistical procedures or by correlating one half of the test with the other half of the test.

Standard Deviation—The standard deviation is a statistical measure of the variability of the scores. The more closely the scores are clustered around the mean, the smaller the standard deviation will be.

Standard Error of Measurement—This statistic measures the amount of possible error in a score. If the standard error of measurement for a test is + or - 3, and the individual's score is 35, then the actual score may be 32 to 35.

Standard Score—A derived score with a set mean (usually 100) and a standard deviation. Examples are T-scores (mean of 50 and a standard deviation of 10), Z-scores (mean of 0 and standard deviation of 1), and scaled scores. Scaled scores may be given for age groups or grade levels. IQ scores, for instance, use a mean of 100 and a standard deviation of 15.

Task Analysis—Breaking an academic or behavioral task down into its sequence of steps. Task analysis is necessary when preparing criterion-referenced tests and performing error analysis. A task analysis for a student learning to do laundry might include:

1. Sort the clothes by type (white, permanent press, delicate).
2. Choose a type, and select the correct water temperature and setting.
3. If doing a partial load, adjust the water level.
4. Measure the detergent.
5. Turn on the machine.

6. Load the clothes.
7. Add bleach and fabric softener at the correct time.
8. Wait for the machine to stop spinning completely before opening it.
9. Remove the clothes from the machine and place in a dryer.
(A task analysis could be done for drying and folding as well.)

Validity—The degree to which a test measures what it claims to measure, such as reading readiness, self-concept, or math achievement. A test may be highly reliable, but it will be useless if it is not valid. There are several types of validity to examine when selecting or constructing an assessment instrument.

- Content Validity examines the question of whether the types of tasks in the test measure the skill or construct the test claims to measure. That is, a test which claims to measure mastery in algebra would probably not be valid if the majority of the items involved basic operations with fractions and decimals.

- Criterion–Referenced Validity involves comparing the test results with a valid criterion. For example, a doctoral student preparing a test to measure reading and spelling skills may check the test against an established test, such as the WRAT-T or another valid criterion, such as school grades.

- Predictive Validity refers to how well a test will relate to a future criterion level, such as the ability of a reading test administered to a first-grader to predict that student's performance at third or fifth grade.

- Concurrent Validity refers to how well the test relates to a criterion measure given at the same time. For example, a new test, which probably measures reading achievement, may be given to a group that also takes the WRAR-R, which has established validity. The test results are compared using statistical measures. The recommended coefficient is 80 or better.

- Construct Validity refers to the ability of the test to measure a theoretical construct, such as intelligence, self-concept, and other non-observable behaviors. Factor analysis and correlation studies with other instruments that measure the same construct are ways to determine construct validity.

Skill 3.02   Identify types, characteristics, and methods of formal and informal assessment.

Formal assessments include standardized criterion, norm-referenced instruments, and commercially-prepared inventories, which are developmentally appropriate for students across the spectrum of disabilities. Criterion-referenced tests compare a student's performance to a previously established criterion rather than to other students from a normative sample. Norm-referenced tests use normative data for scoring, which include performance norms by age, gender, or ethnic group.

Informal assessment strategies include non-standardized instruments, such as checklists, developmental rating scales, observations, error analysis, interviews, teacher reports, and performance-based assessments that are developmentally appropriate students across disabilities. Informal evaluation strategies rely upon the knowledge and judgment of the professional and are an integral part of the evaluation. An advantage of using informal assessments is the ease of design and administration and the usefulness of information the teacher can gain about the student's strength and weaknesses.

Some instruments can be both formal and informal tools. For example, observation may incorporate structured observation instruments as well as other informal observation procedures, including professional judgment. When evaluating a child's developmental level, a professional may use a formal adaptive rating scale while simultaneously using professional judgment to assess the child's motivation and behavior during the evaluation process.

IDEA 2004 requires that a variety of assessment tools and strategies are to be utilized when conducting assessments. Before utilizing a formal or informal tool, the practitioner should make sure that the tool is the most appropriate one that can be used for that particular population group. Many assessment tools can be used across disabilities. Dependent upon the disability in question, such as blindness, autism, or hearing impairment, some assessment tools will give more information than others.

Some of the informal and formal assessments that can be used across disabilities are curriculum-based assessments, multiple baseline design, norm-referenced tests (see definitions of each in skill 3.01), and momentary time sampling.

Momentary time sampling—This is a technique used for measuring behaviors of a group of individuals or several behaviors from the same individual. Time samples are usually brief and may be conducted at fixed or variable intervals. The advantage of using variable intervals is increased reliability, as the students will not be able to predict when the time sample will betaken.

Skill 3.03 **Demonstrating familiarity with principles of and procedures for creating, selecting, evaluating, and using educational and adaptive behavior assessment instruments and methods**

Adaptive behavior refers to the knowledge, behavior, and daily living skills that are required to function effectively and independently in a number of different settings.

An adaptive behavior measure is a specific comprehensive assessment of independent living skills. The measurement of adaptive behavior assesses the skills of an individual relative to the skills of his same-age peers. It is a significant tool in eligibility consideration for students with mental handicaps and in the development of effective educational interventions.

Adaptive behaviors commonly include communication and social skills, daily living skills, personal care skills, and other skills that are needed to function at home, at school, and in the community.

> **Learn more about Behavioral Assessments:**
> http://www.specialednews.com/behavior/behavnews/CECbehavassess021900.html

Adaptive behavior measurement is important for pinpointing specific skills that need to be taught. Most students acquire adaptive behavior skills through practical experiences. Students with disabilities may need direct instruction in order to acquire the necessary adaptive behavior skills.

Measurement of adaptive behavior should take into account the student's behavior and skills in a number of settings, including the classroom, school, home, and neighborhood. In order to get an accurate assessment, the adaptive behavior should be measured by a variety of different people in different settings.

The primary method of measuring adaptive behavior is via structured interviews with teachers and parents. A person trained to administer an adaptive behavior rating scale, such as a school counselor, interviews the student's parents and teachers. The responses are recorded on a rating scale that assesses the student's skills and abilities in various settings. The information obtained from the interview is more valid when the people being interviewed are familiar with the student's knowledge and skills. It is important that parents and teachers provide the most accurate and objective assessment as possible.

Additional methods of measuring adaptive behavior include analyzing the student's records from schools, watching the student in specific circumstances, and testing the student's skills by giving him specific tasks to complete.

The rating scales are created to address the following areas:

- **Communication**—skills in communicating with others, talking, writing

- **Self-Care**—skills in toileting, eating, dressing, hygiene, and grooming

- **Home-Living**—clothing care, housekeeping, property maintenance, food preparation and cooking, planning and budgeting for shopping

- **Social**—getting along with others in social situations, interacting with others, forming relationships

- **Community Use**—travel within community, shopping, obtaining services in community (doctor, dentist, setting up utilities), public transportation

- **Self-Direction**—making choices in allocation of time and effort, following a schedule, seeking assistance, deciding what to do in new situations

- **Health and Safety**—making choices about what to eat, illness identification and treatment, avoiding danger, relationships

- **Functional Academics**—skills taught in school that are used every day, including reading, writing, computation skills, telling time, using numbers

- **Leisure**—using available time when not working or in school, choosing age-appropriate activities

- **Work**—employment skills, including work-related attitudes and social behaviors, completion of tasks, persistent effort

Some of the most common adaptive behavior instruments include the following:

Measure	Format	Useful Derived Information
American Association of Mental Retardation (AAMR) 1993	Rating scale or interview	Factor scores of Personal, Social, and Community plus 2 Maladaptive Domains
Adaptive Behavior Assessment System – second edition 2003– school, parent, and adult forms	Multiple formats including rating scale, interview, and self report for adults; multiple formats encouraged	Composite, plus scores in 10 adaptive skills areas.
Comprehensive Test of Adaptive Behavior (Revised 2000)	Rating scale with behavioral composite plus "tests" that are used if the behavior has not been observed	7 domains, self-help, home, independence, social, sensory, motor, and language/academic
Scales of Independent Behavior – Revised (1996)	Highly-structured interview conducted by professional or paraprofessional	Composite plus motor, social interaction and communication, personal living, and community living; maladaptive behaviors included
Vineland Adaptive Behavior Scales (1984)	Semi-structured interview requiring well-trained professional; school form uses a rating scale format.	Composite plus Communication, Daily Living, Motor (0-6 yrs), and Socialization. No maladaptive behavior content

Skill 3.04   Recognizing appropriate purposes, uses, and limitations of various types of assessment instruments

Types of Assessment

It is useful to consider the types of assessment procedures that are available to the classroom teacher. The types of assessment discussed below represent many of the more common types, but the list is not comprehensive.

Anecdotal Records

These are notes recorded by the teacher concerning an area of interest or concern with a particular student. These records should focus on observable behaviors and should be descriptive in nature. They should not include assumptions or speculations regarding affective areas, such as motivation or interest. These records are usually compiled over a period of several days to several weeks.

Rating Scales & Checklists

These assessments are generally self-appraisal instruments completed by the students or observation-based instruments completed by the teacher. The focus of these is frequently on behavior or affective areas, such as interest and motivation.

Questioning

One of the most frequently occurring forms of assessment in the classroom is oral questioning by the teacher. As the teacher questions the students, she collects a great deal of information about the degree of student learning and potential sources of confusion for the students. While questioning is often viewed as a component of instructional methodology, it is also a powerful assessment tool.

Formal/Informal testing

(Please refer to skill 3.02 for definitions and descriptions.)

Additional Types of tests

Tests and similar direct assessment methods represent the most easily identified types of assessment. Thorndike (1997) identifies three types of assessment instruments:

1. Standardized achievement tests
2. Assessment material packaged with curricular materials
3. Teacher-made assessment instruments
   - Pencil and paper test
   - Oral tests
   - Product evaluations
   - Performance tests
   - Effective measures (p.199)

Kellough and Roberts (1991) take a slightly different perspective. They describe "three avenues for assessing student achievement:

- a) What the learner says
- b) What the learner does, and
- c) What the learner writes..." (p.343)

Purposes for Assessment

There are a number of different classification systems used to identify the various purposes for assessment. A compilation of several lists identifies some common purposes, such as the following:

1. Diagnostic assessments are used to determine individual weaknesses and strengths in specific areas.
2. Readiness assessments measure prerequisite knowledge and skills.
3. Interest and attitude assessments attempt to identify topics of high interest or areas in which students may need extra motivational activities.
4. Evaluation assessments are generally programmed or teacher focused.
5. Placement assessments are used for the purposes of grouping students or determining appropriate beginning levels in leveled materials.
6. Formative assessments provide on-going feedback about student progress and the success of instructional methods and materials.
7. Summative assessments define student accomplishment with the intent to determine the degree of student mastery or learning that has taken place.

For most teachers, assessment purposes vary according to the situation. It may be helpful to consult several sources to help formulate an overall assessment plan. Kellough and Roberts (1991) identify six purposes for assessment. These are:

1. To evaluate and improve student learning
2. To identify student strengths and weaknesses
3. To assess the effectiveness of a particular instructional strategy
4. To evaluate and improve program effectiveness
5. To evaluate and improve teacher effectiveness
6. To communicate to parents their children's progress (p.341)

Limitations of Various Types of Assessment

The existence of various types of assessment stems from the unique needs of children with disabilities and the environments in which the disabilities are most troublesome. A student who demonstrates difficulty interacting with peers and acts impulsively may not be effectively evaluated with a portfolio. Anecdotal records, questioning, and certain checklists may give a better picture of the extent to which such peer interactions are detrimental to the student's (and others') well being and success. Conversely, a student who displays academic difficulty is better assessed with samples of work (portfolio) and carefully chosen formal tests. In short, assessments are as valuable as the appropriate choice and use thereof.

Skill 3.05   Demonstrating knowledge of alternative assessments (e.g., authentic assessment, portfolio assessment)

Special Education teachers must be associated with the various methods of Alternative Assessments in order to properly evaluate the goals and objectives of their students that are not able to be assessed by the usage of standardized tests that utilize "paper and pencil methods."

Naturalistic Assessments (informal/authentic) address the functional skills that enhance a person's independence and social interactions in a variety of settings

> **Learn More About Raising Achievement Through Alternative Assessments:**
> http://www.ed.gov/
> policy/elsec/guid/
> raising/alt-assess.html

(i.e. school, home, community, etc.). Functional skills best addressed by this method are vocational skills such as following directions, socially acceptable behavior, and measurable work ethics. Naturalistic assessment requires planning for instruction to occur in various settings. The advantages of this method include a "real world setting" while allowing for the cultural appropriate materials. The disadvantages of this method are the requirements for long-range planning and reduced efficiency in both. teaching and assessing the skill that is to measured.

Performance-Based Assessments use a form of evaluation that examines a skill that is necessary to complete a project. An example of this method would be evaluating the Math skill of "Order of Operations" by evaluating how an algebraic expression was solved. Another example would be observing how the skill of buttoning a shirt is progressing when having a student complete the task of putting a shirt on.

Portfolio Assessments are a mode of evaluation that provides a good way to document the beginning, middle, and end of a student's yearly progress. This method utilizes compiling samples of work throughout a given period of time. Portfolio Assessment is a tool often used to track academic growth/progress in writing within regular education classrooms. The portfolio assessment also provides the teacher with a way to explain a student's present levels to parents.

> **Learn More How to Ensure Equity when Giving Alternative Assessments:** http://www.ncrel.org/sdrs/areas/issues/methods/assment/as800.htm

Dynamic Assessment is a tailor made evaluation tool that looks at how a student learns and possible impediments to a student's successful completion of a goal. Dynamic Assessments look first at what must be taught and how it is taught the student. Next, possible impediments to the student's success in this goal are examined to provide possible insight as to their success/failure to meet a goal. When the impediments have been examined it is now possible to look at the goal and distinguish between performance and ability. For this reason it is an ideal method to use when evaluating student progress that may have been inhibited by a cultural norm. Identifying impediments allows for the evaluator to assess if a different teaching strategy may be more effective for students to attain objectives and goals on their IEPs.

Recommended Reading: Alternative Approaches to Assessing Young Children By Angela Losardo, Ph.D., & Angela Notari-Syverson, Ph.D. © 2001 Paul H. Brookes Publishing Co.

Skill 3.06	Demonstrating familiarity with strategies for collaborating with families and with other professionals in the assessment process

The assessment process is an essential part of developing an individualized program for students. The needs of the whole child must be considered in order to address all of the needs of each child. Therefore information should be gathered by using various sources of information.

Besides the general education teacher, a vital person or persons in the assessment process should be the parent. The parent can provide needed background information on the child, such as a brief medical, physical, and developmental history. Paraprofessionals, doctors, and other professionals are also very helpful in providing necessary information about the child.

Methods of Gathering Information

Interviews: Interviews can be in person or on paper. The related parties can be invited to a meeting to conduct the interview; if the parent does not respond after several attempts, the paper interview may be sent or mailed home.

Questionnaires: Questionnaires are also a good way of gathering information. Some questionnaires may consist of open-ended questions, and some may contain several questions that are to be answered using a rating scale. The answerer is to circle ratings ranging from 1 to 5 or 1 to 7 (Strongly Disagree to Strongly Agree).

Conferences/Meetings: With parents' permission, it may be useful to conduct a meeting one on one or in a group setting to gather information about the child. Everyone involved with the child that may be able to offer any information about the child, the child's academic progress, physical development, social skills, behavior, or medical history, and/or needs should be invited to attend.

Skill 3.07   Demonstrating an understanding of legal provisions, regulations, guidelines, and ethical concerns related to assessment, including preserving confidentiality

If instructional modifications in the regular classroom have not proven successful, a student may be referred for multidisciplinary evaluation. The evaluation is comprehensive and includes norm- and criterion-referenced tests (e.g., IQ and diagnostic tests), curriculum-based assessment, systematic teacher observation (e.g., behavior frequency checklist), samples of student work, and parent interviews. The results of the evaluation are twofold: to determine eligibility for special education services and to identify a student's strengths and weaknesses in order to plan an individual education program.

The wording in federal law is very explicit about the manner in which evaluations must be conducted and about the existence of due process procedures that protect against bias and discrimination. Provisions in the law include the following as listed.

1. The testing of children in their native or primary language unless it is clearly not feasible to do so.
2. The use of evaluation procedures selected and administered to prevent cultural or ethnic discrimination.
3. The use of assessment tools validated for the purpose for which they are being used (e.g., achievement levels, IQ scores, adaptive skills).
4. Assessment by a multidisciplinary team utilizing several pieces of information to formulate a placement decision.

Furthermore, parental involvement must occur in the development of the child's educational program. According to the law, parents must:

1. Be notified before initial evaluation or any change in placement by a written notice in their primary language describing the proposed school action, the reasons for it, and the available educational opportunities.
2. Consent, in writing, before the child is initially evaluated.

Parents may:

1. Request an independent educational evaluation if they feel the school's evaluation is inappropriate.
2. Request an evaluation at public expense if a due process hearing decision is that the public agency's evaluation was inappropriate.
3. Participate on the committee that considers the evaluation, placement, and programming of the student.

All students referred for evaluation for special education should have the results of a relatively current vision and hearing screening on file. This will determine the adequacy of sensory acuity and ensure that learning problems are not due to a vision and/or hearing problem.
All portions of the special education process, from assessment to placement, are strictly confidential to parties outside of the people who will directly be servicing the student. Under no circumstances should information be shared outside of the realm of parent/guardian and those providing related services without the consent of the parent/guardian.

Skill 3.08   Understanding the implications of limited English proficiency in the assessment of students with disabilities

The No Child Left Behind legislation includes students with limited English proficiency and students with disabilities in the accountability system and judges them by the same standard used for all other students. In the past, students with limited English proficiency (LEP) were often excluded from high-stakes, large-scale assessments because educators believed it was not in the best interest of students to take the tests. Students who have LEP and a disability have an even greater chance of their educational needs not being met. In many cases, educators will have to assess whether their problem in the classroom can be attributed to their language difficulties or to their disability, or a combination of both.

The NCLB legislation was designed to make sure that students in subgroups with low percentages of students meeting standards would receive attention in schools. Educators are concerned that excluding students from testing may be detrimental to students because it allows their needs to remain unknown. Students who are not tested may not get the services they need to improve their academic achievement. Many educational researchers now believe that LEP students and students with disabilities should be included in the assessments, when practical, to ensure that the needs of these students are not ignored.

> **Learn more about LEP Theory and Practice in Special Education:**
> http://www.specialed news.com/behavior/ behavnews/CECbeh avassess021900.html

The policies for LEP students and students with disabilities under the No Child Left Behind legislation was changed in February 2004. One change was that schools were no longer required to give students with limited English proficiency their state's reading test if the students were enrolled in a U.S. school for less than a year. Schools are still required to give those students the state's math test, but they may substitute an English-proficiency test for the reading test during the first year of enrollment.

As was the case before this change, states have a one-year grace period before they must include scores of students with limited English proficiency in the calculations for adequate yearly progress. The second rule change permits states to count students who have become proficient in English within the past two years in their calculations of adequate yearly progress.

COMPETENCY 0004   UNDERSTAND PURPOSES, METHODS, AND PROCEDURES FOR IDENTIFYING STUDENTS WITH DISABILITIES AND EVALUATING THEIR PROGRESS.

Skill 4.01   Identifying procedures used for screening, pre-referral, referral, classification, and declassification

Referral

Referral is the process through which a teacher, a parent, or some other person formally requests an evaluation of a student to determine eligibility for special education services. The decision to refer a student may be influenced by: (1) student characteristics, such as the abilities, behaviors, or skills that students exhibit (or lack of them); (2) individual differences among teachers in their beliefs, expectations, or skill in dealing with specific kinds of problems; (3) expectations for assistance with a student who is exhibiting academic or behavioral learning problems; (4) availability of specific kinds of strategies and materials; (5) parents' demand for referral or opposition to referral; and (6) institutional factors which may facilitate or constrain teachers in making referral decisions. Fewer students are referred when school districts have complex procedures for referral, psychological assessments are backlogged for months, special education classes are filled to capacity, or principals and other administrators do not fully recognize the importance of special services.

It is important that referral procedures be clearly understood and coordinated among all school personnel. All educators need to be able to identify characteristics typically exhibited by special needs students.

In New York, the student suspected of having a disability is referred to a multidisciplinary team called the Committee on Special Education (CSE) or the Committee on Preschool Special Education (CPSE). With the parents' written consent, the CSE arranges for an evaluation of the student. Based on the results of the comprehensive assessments, the committee determines the status of the student's eligibility.

Special Education Procedures

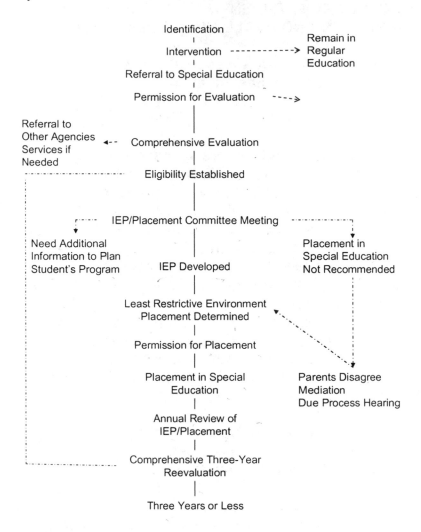

Evaluation

While some of the material here was previously stated in Skill 3.07 it is also important to be included in this section)

The evaluation is comprehensive and includes norm and criterion-referenced tests (e.g., IQ and diagnostic tests), curriculum-based assessment, systematic teacher observation (e.g., behavior frequency checklist), samples of student work, and parent interviews. The results of the evaluation are twofold: to determine eligibility for special education services and to identify a student's strengths and weaknesses in order to plan an individual education program.

The wording in federal law is very explicit about the manner in which evaluations must be conducted and about the existence of due process procedures that protect against bias and discrimination. Provisions in the law include the following as listed.

1. The testing of children in their native or primary language unless it is clearly not feasible to do so.
2. The use of evaluation procedures selected and administered to prevent cultural or ethnic discrimination.
3. The use of assessment tools validated for the purpose for which they are being used (e.g., achievement levels, IQ scores, adaptive skills).
4. Assessment by a multidisciplinary team utilizing several pieces of information to formulate a placement decision.

According to the New York Education website (www.nysed.gov), an initial evaluation to determine the student's weaknesses must include:

- A physical examination
- A psychological evaluation (if determined appropriate for school-age students, but mandatory for pre-school children)
- A social history
- Observation of the child in his or her current education setting
- Other tests or assessments that are appropriate for the child (such as a speech and language assessment or a functional behavioral assessment)
- Vocational assessments (required at age 12)

Furthermore, parental involvement must occur in the development of the child's educational program. According to the law, parents must:

1. Be notified before initial evaluation or any change in placement by a written notice in their primary language describing the proposed school action, the reasons for it, and the available educational opportunities.
2. Consent, in writing, before the child is initially evaluated.

All students referred for evaluation for special education should have on file the results of a relatively current vision and hearing screening. This will determine the adequacy of sensory acuity and ensure that learning problems are not due to a vision and/or hearing problem.

Eligibility

Eligibility is based on criteria defined in federal law or state regulations, which vary from state to state. Evaluation methods correspond with eligibility criteria for the special education classifications. For example, a multidisciplinary evaluation for a student being evaluated for intellectual disabilities would include the individual's intellectual functioning, adaptive behavior, and achievement levels. Other tests are based on developmental characteristics exhibited (e.g., social, language, and motor).

A student evaluated for learning disabilities is given reading, math, and/or spelling achievement tests, an intelligence test to confirm average or above average cognitive capabilities, and tests of written and oral language ability. Tests need to show a discrepancy between potential and performance. Classroom observations and samples of student work (such as impaired reading ability or impaired writing ability) also provide indicators of possible learning disabilities.

If considered eligible for special education services, the child's disability should be documented in a written report stating specific reasons for the decision. A meeting must be held with the CSE committee, in which the parent and other professionals are a part, to discuss the results. The status of the child's eligibility will be revealed during this meeting. If the child does qualify, the parents' permission must be received before official placement occurs. If the child does not qualify, the parent will be given information revealing why the child does not qualify. The parent will also be informed of any other programs in which the child may qualify.

Also, if the child qualifies, three-year re-evaluations of a student's progress are required by law and serve the purpose of determining the growth and changing needs of the student. During the re-evaluation, continued eligibility for services in special education must be assessed using a range of evaluation tools similar to those used during the initial evaluation. All relevant information about the student is considered when making a decision about continued eligibility or whether the student no longer needs the service and is ready to begin preparing to exit the program. If the latter is transition that is more appropriate, planning must occur.

IEP Development

The CSE committee convenes to discuss the child's current functional level, along with assessment results and information gathered from the committee. From that information, the committee agrees on the goals the child should be working toward. The committee then discusses the supports and services and modifications that the child needs to reach those goals. Finally, the committee determines where those special education services will be provided (location and placement). The location where services will be provided and the student's placement must be in the student's least restrictive environment.

Special education services occur at a variety of levels, some more restrictive than others. The largest number of students (i.e., mild disabilities) are served in settings closest to normal educational placements. Service delivery in more restrictive settings is limited to students with severe or profound disabilities, who comprise a smaller population within special education. The exception is correctional facilities, which serve a limited and restricted populace.

Options for placement of special education students are given on what we call a "cascade of services," the term coined by Deno (1970). The multidisciplinary team must be able to match the needs of the student with an appropriate placement in the cascade system of services .

Cascade System of Special Education Services

Level 1	Regular classroom, including students with disabilities able to learn with regular class accommodations, with or without medical and counseling services.
Level 2	Regular classroom with supportive services (i.e., consultation, inclusion).
Level 3	Regular class with part-time special class (i.e., itinerant services, resource room).
Level 4	Full-time special class (i.e., self-contained).
Level 5	Special stations (i.e., special schools).
Level 6	Homebound
Level 7	Residential (i.e., hospital, institution)

Adapted from 1. Deno, "Special Education as Developmental Capital." Exceptional Children 1970, 37, 239, 237 Copyright 1970 by The Council for Exceptional Children Reprinted with permission from The Council for Exceptional Children.

According to Polloway, et al. (1994), two assumptions are made when we place students using the cascade of services as a guide. First, a child should be placed in an educational setting as close to the regular classroom as possible and placed only as far away from this least restrictive environment as necessary to provide an appropriate education. Second, program exit should be a goal. A student's placement may change when the team obtains data suggesting the advisability of an alternative educational setting. As adaptive, social, cognitive, motor, and language skills are developed, the student may be placed in a lesser restrictive environment. The multidisciplinary team is responsible for monitoring and recommending placement changes when appropriate.

Declassification

The student must be evaluated to determine if he or she no longer has a disability. Declassification recommendations should be documented on the student's final IEP.

Skill 4.02 Identifying appropriate assessment instruments and methods, including alternative assessment, for monitoring the progress of individuals with disabilities

The assessment of academic achievement is an essential component of a Psychoeducational evaluation. Achievement tests are instruments that directly assess students' skill development in academic content areas. This type of test measures the extent to which a student has profited from educational and/or life experiences compared to others of the same age or grade level. Emphasis needs to be placed upon the kinds of behaviors each tests samples, the adequacy of its norms, the test reliability, and its validity.

An achievement test may be classified as a diagnostic test because the strengths and weaknesses in skill development can be defined. Typically, when used as a diagnostic tool, an achievement test measures one basic skill and its related components. For example, a reading test may measure reading recognition, reading comprehension, reading fluency, decoding skills, and sound discrimination. Each skill measured is reported in sub-classifications.

In order to render pertinent information, achievement tests must reflect the content of the curriculum. Some achievement tests assess skill development in many subject areas, while others focus upon single content areas. Within similar content areas, the particular skills assessed and how they are measured differ from test to test. The more prominent areas assessed by achievement tests include math, reading, and spelling.

Achievement test usages include screening, placement, progress evaluation, and curricula effectiveness. As screening tests, these instruments provide a wide index of academic skill development and may be used to pinpoint students for whom educational interventions may be necessary for purposes of remediation or enrichment. They offer a general idea of where to begin additional diagnostic assessment.

Achievement tests are routinely given in school districts across the nation as a means of evaluating progress. Scores of students can be compared locally, statewide, and with national norms. Accountability and quality controls can be kept in check through the reporting of scores.

Achievement tests may be norm-referenced or criterion-referenced and administered individually or within groups. Results of norm-referenced achievements tests, e.g., Peabody Individualized Achievement Test (PIAT), Wide Range Achievement Test (WRAT), thought important in making comparisons, may not provide information needed for individual program planning, types of behaviors tests, sub-skill data, or types of scores reported. Criterion-referenced achievement tests (e.g., KeyMath Diagnostic Arithmetic Test, Brigance Diagnostic Inventories) contain items that correspond with stated objectives, thus enabling identification of cognitive deficiencies. Knowledge of specific skill deficits is needed for developing individualized education plans.

Last, teachers can be provided with measures showing the effectiveness of their instruction. Progress reflected by student scores should be used to review, and often revise, instructional techniques and content. Alternative methods of delivery (i.e., presentations, worksheets, tests) can be devised to enhance instruction provided students.

(Refer to skill 3.04 and 3.05 about alternate assessment and teacher-made tests, etc.)

Skill 4.03 Recognizing the importance of assessment in placement and accommodation decisions

Each child receiving special education services is to be placed in his or her least restrictive environment. The placement of the student depends on his or her current functioning level. The student's current functioning level is determined by formal and informal assessments (see skill 3.02). Assessment information will help determine the child's least restrictive environment and give key information to assist with accommodation decisions. (See skill 5.03 for possible accommodations.)

Placement of the student could be in a wide range of settings, but the best location for the child is as close to full time in the general education class as possible, while still providing for the student's weaknesses. (See the cascade of services, also called continuum of services on skill 4.01.)

The law defines special education and identifies related services that may be required if special education is to be effective. By law, placement in a special education delivery service must be the student's least restrictive environment. Many factors determine least restrictive environment. Assessment has a large weighing on the child's least restrictive environment. If the child functions on a 1st grade level in reading, it would be hard for that student to be successful in a 5th grade reading level without accommodations and interventions. Along with the assessment information, work samples, and input from parents and support service personnel, the child's least restrictive environment will be decided.

Skill 4.04 **Interpreting and applying formal and informal assessment data (e.g., standard scores, percentile ranks, stanines, grade equivalent scores, age equivalent scores, environmental inventories, rubrics) to develop an individualized instructional program**

Having the knowledge of interpreting and applying formal and informal assessment data is very important to the development of IEPs. An individualized educational instructional program is designed around the child's strengths and weaknesses. An educator must have knowledge of interpreting formal and informal assessment data to assist him in determining some of those strengths and weaknesses.

Results of formal assessments are given in derived scores, which compare the student's raw score to the performance of a specified group of subjects. Criteria for the selection of the group may be based on characteristics such as age, sex, or geographic area. The test results of formal assessments must always be interpreted in light of what type of tasks the individual was required to perform. The most commonly used derived scores follow.

Age and Grade Equivalents are considered developmental scores because they attempt to convert the student's raw score into an average performance of a particular age or grade group.

Age equivalents are expressed in years and months, i.e., 7-3. In the standardization procedure, a mean is calculated for all individuals of the particular age who took the test. If the mean or median number of correct responses for children 7 years and 3 months was 80, then an individual whose raw score was 80 would be assigned an age-equivalent of 7 years and 3 months.

Grade Equivalents are written as years and tenths of years, e.g., 6.2 would read sixth grade, second month. Grade equivalents are calculated on the average performance of the group and have been criticized for their use to measure gains in academic achievement and to identify exceptional students.

Quartiles, Deciles, and Percentiles indicate the percentage of scores that fall below the individual's raw score. Quartiles divide the score into four equal parts; the first quartile is the point at which 25% of the scores fall below the full score. Deciles divide the distribution into ten equal parts; the seventh decile would mark the point below which 70% of the scores fall. Percentiles are the most frequently used, however. A percentile rank of 45 would indicate that the person's raw score was at the point below which 45% of the other scores fell.

Standard Scores are raw scores with the same mean (average) and standard deviation (variability of asset of scores). In the standardization of a test, about 68% of the scores will fall above or below 1 standard deviation of the mean of 100. About 96% of the scores will fall within the range of 2 standard deviations above or below the mean. A standard deviation of 20, for example, will mean that 68% of the scores will fall between 80 and 120, with 100 as the mean. The most common are T scores, z scores, stanines, and scaled scores. Standard scores are useful because they allow for direct comparison of raw scores from different individuals. In interpreting scores, it is important to note what type of standard score is being used.

Criterion-Referenced Tests and Curriculum-based Assessments are interpreted on the basis of the individual's performance on the objectives being measured. Such assessments may be commercially prepared or teacher made and can be designed for a particular curriculum or a scope and sequence. These assessments are made by selecting objectives, task analyzing those objectives, and selecting measures to test the skills necessary to meet those tasks. Results are calculated for each objective, such as Cindy was able to divide 2-digit numbers by 1-digit numbers 85% of the time and was able to divide 2-digit numbers by 2-digit numbers 45% of the time. These tests are useful for gaining insight into the types of error patterns the student makes. Because the student's performance is not compared to others in a group, results are useful for writing IEPs as well as deciding what to teach.

Skill 4.05   Identifying strategies for using assessment data and information from general education teachers, other professionals, individuals with disabilities, and parents to make instructional decisions and modify learning environments

(Please refer to skill 6.01 about modifying learning environments.)

The assessment information gathered from various sources is key to identify the strengths and the weaknesses of the student. Each test and each person will have something to offer about the child, therefore increasing the possibility of creating a well-developed plan to assist in the success of the student. The special education and general education teacher along with other professionals will use the assessment data to make appropriate instructional decisions and to modify the learning environment that it is conducive to learning.

The information gathered can be used to make some of the following instructional decisions:

I   **Classroom Organization:** The teacher can vary grouping arrangements (e.g., large group, small group, peer tutoring, or learning centers) and methods of instruction (teacher directed, student directed).

II   **Classroom Management:** The teacher can vary grading systems, vary reinforcement systems, and vary the rules (differentiate for some students).

III   **Methods of Presentation: Variation of methods include—**
   A. Content: Amount to be learned, time to learn, and concept level
   B. General Structure: advance organizers, immediate feedback, memory devices, and active involvement of students.
   C. Type of presentation: verbal or written, transparencies, audiovisual

   IV   Methods of Practice:
   A. General Structure: amount to be practiced, time to finish, group, individual, or teacher-directed, and varied level of difficulty
   B. Level of response: copying, recognition, or recall, with and without cues
   C. Types of materials: worksheets, audiovisual, texts

   V   **Methods of Testing:**
   A   Type: verbal, written, or demonstration
   B. General Structure: time to complete, amount to complete, group or individual testing
   C. Level of response: multiple choice, essay, recall of facts

Instructional Decisions

Presentation of Subject Matter:

Subject matter should be presented in a fashion that helps students <u>organize</u>, <u>understand</u>, and <u>remember</u> important information. Advance organizers and other instructional devices can help students to:

- Connect information to what is already known
- Make abstract ideas more concrete
- Capture students' interest in the material
- Help students to organize the information and visualize the relationships.

Organizers can be visual aids, such as diagrams, tables, charts, guides, or verbal cues that alert students to the nature and content of the lesson. Organizers may be used:

- **Before the lesson** to alert the student to the main point of the lesson, establish a rationale for learning, and activate background information.
- **During the lesson** to help students organize information, keep focused on important points, and aid comprehension.
- **At the close of the lesson** to summarize and remember important points.

Examples of organizers include:

- Question- and graphic-oriented study guide.
- Concept diagramming: Students brainstorm a concept and organize information into three lists (always present, sometimes present, and never present).
- Semantic feature analysis: Students construct a table with examples of the concept in one column and important features or characteristics in the opposite column.
- Semantic webbing: The concept is placed in the middle of the chart or chalkboard, and relevant information is placed around it. Lines show the relationships.
- Memory (mnemonic) devices. Diagrams, charts, and tables.

Instructional Decisions May Also Include:

Instructional modifications are tried in an attempt to accommodate the student in the regular classroom. Effective instruction is geared toward individual needs and recognizes differences in how students learn. Modifications are tailored to individual student needs. Some strategies for modifying regular classroom instruction shown on Table 1-1 are effective with at-risk students with disabilities, as well as students without learning or behavior problems.

Table 1-1 Strategies for Modifying Classroom Instruction

Strategy 1 Provide active learning experiences to teach concepts. Student motivation is increased when students can manipulate, weigh, measure, read, or write using materials and skills that relate to their daily lives.

Strategy 2 Provide ample opportunities for guided practice of new skills. Frequent feedback on performance is essential to overcome student feelings of inadequacy. Peer tutoring and cooperative projects provide non-threatening practice opportunities. Individual student conferences, curriculum-based tests, and small group discussions are three useful methods for checking progress.

Strategy 3 Provide multi-sensory learning experiences. Students with learning problems sometimes have sensory processing difficulties; for instance, an auditory discrimination problem may cause misunderstanding about teacher expectations. Lessons and directions that include visual, auditory, tactile, and kinesthetic modes are preferable to a single sensory approach.

Strategy 4 Present information in a manner that is relevant to the student. Particular attention to this strategy is needed when there is a cultural or economic gap between the lives of teachers and students. Relate instruction to a youngster's daily experience and interests.

Strategy 5 Provide students with concrete illustrations of their progress. Students with learning problems need frequent reinforcement for their efforts. Charts, graphs, and check sheets provide tangible markers of student achievement.

Skill 4.06 **Recognizing the importance to the decision-making process of background information regarding academic, medical, and family history and cultural background**

Relevant background information regarding the student's academic, medical, and family history should be used to identify students with disabilities and evaluate their progress.

An evaluation report should include the summary of a comprehensive diagnostic interview by a qualified evaluator. A combination of candidate self-report interviews, with families and others, and historical documentation, such as transcripts and standardized test scores, is recommended.

The evaluator should use professional judgment as to which areas are relevant to determining a student's eligibility for accommodations due to disabilities. In order to properly identify students with disabilities and evaluate their progress, the evaluator should include background information regarding academic, medical, cultural, and family history when making an evaluation. The evaluation should include a developmental history; relevant medical history, including the absence of a medical basis for the present symptoms; academic history including results of prior standardized testing; reports of classroom performance; relevant family history, including the primary language of the home and the candidate's current level of fluency of English; relevant psychosocial history; a discussion of dual diagnosis, alternative or co-existing mood, behavioral, neurological, and/or personality disorders, along with any history of relevant medication use that may affect the individual's learning; and exploration of possible alternatives that may mimic a learning disability.

By utilizing all possible background information in the assessment, the evaluator can rule out alternative explanations for academic problems, such as poor education, poor motivation and study skills, emotional problems, and cultural and language differences. If the student's entire background and history is not taken into account, it is not always possible to institute the most appropriate educational program for the student with disabilities.

Skill 4.07   Demonstrating knowledge of the implications of diversity with regard to assessment, eligibility, programming, and placement

Fair Assessment Practices

The issue of fair assessment for individuals from minority groups has a long history in the law, philosophy, and education. Slavia and Ysseldyke, 1995, point out three aspects of this issue that are particularly relevant to the assessment of students.

1. **Representation**
   Individuals from diverse backgrounds need to be represented in assessment materials. It is essential that persons from different cultures be represented fairly. Of equal importance is the presentation of individuals from differing genders in non-stereotypical roles and situations.

2. Acculturation

It is important that individuals from different backgrounds receive opportunities to acquire the tested skills, information, and values. When students are tested with standardization instruments, they are compared to a set of norms in order to gain an index of their relative standing and to make comparisons. We assume that the students tested are similar to those on whom the test was standardized. That is, it is assumed that their acculturation is comparable. Acculturation is a matter of educational, socioeconomic, and experiential background rather than of gender, skin color, race, or ethnic background. When it is said that a child's acculturation differs from that of the group used as a norm, what is really meant is that the experiential background differed, not simply that the child is of a different ethnic origin (Slavia & Ysseldyke, 1991). Differences in experiential background should therefore be accounted for when administering tests.

3. Language

The language and concepts that comprise test items should be unbiased. Students should be familiar with terminology and references to which the language is being made when they are administered tests, especially when the results of the tests are going to be used for decision-making purposes. Many tests given in regular grades relate to decisions about promotion and grouping of students for instructional purposes. Tests and other assessment instruments that relate to special education are generally concerned with two types of decisions: (1) eligibility and (2) program planning for individualized education.

Skill 4.08   Use ongoing assessment to evaluate and modify instruction.

Assessment skills should be an integral part of teacher training, where teachers are able to monitor student learning using pre- and post-assessments of content areas; analyze assessment data in terms of individualized support for students and instructional practice for teachers; and design lesson plans that have measurable outcomes and definitive learning standards. Assessment information should be used to provide performance-based criteria and academic expectations for all students in evaluating whether students have learned the expected skills and content of the subject area.

For example, in an Algebra I class, teachers can use assessments to see whether students have learned the prior knowledge to engage in the subject area. If the teacher provides students with a pre-assessment on algebraic expression and ascertains whether the lesson plan should be modified to include a pre-algebraic expression lesson unit to refresh student understanding of the content area, then the teacher can create, if needed, quantifiable data to support the need of additional resources to support student learning. Once the teacher has taught the unit on algebraic expression, a post-assessment test can be used to test student learning, and a mastery exam can be used to test how well students understand and can apply the knowledge to the next unit of math content learning.

Teachers can use assessment data to inform and impact instructional practices by making inferences on teaching methods and gathering clues for student performance. By analyzing the various types of assessments, teachers can gather more definitive information on projected student academic performance. Instructional strategies for teachers would provide learning targets for student behavior, cognitive thinking skills, and processing skills that can be employed to diversify student learning opportunities.

COMPETENCY 0005 UNDERSTAND PROCEDURES FOR DEVELOPING, IMPLEMENTING, AND AMENDING INDIVIDUALIZED EDUCATION PROGRAMS (IEPS) FOR STUDENTS WITH DISABILITIES.

Skill 5.01 Recognizing the rights, roles, and functions of IEP team members (e.g., Special Education Teacher, student, parents/guardians, general education teacher, speech language therapist, Occupational Therapist, school administrator)

According to IDEA 2004, the IEP team includes: the parents of a child with a disability; not less than one regular education teacher of such child (if the child is, or may be, participating in the regular education environment); not less than one Special Education Teacher, or where appropriate, not less than one special education provider of such child; a representative of the local educational agency; an individual who can interpret the instructional implications of evaluation results; at the discretion of the parent of the agency, other individuals who have knowledge or special expertise regarding the child, including related services personnel as appropriate; and whenever appropriate, the child with a disability.

The role of the representative of the local education agency is to provide or supervise the provision of specifically-designed instruction to meet the unique needs of the child. This is usually the school principal if this is the first time the child has been evaluated. If the representative is not an expert on evaluations, then one of the people who participated in the actual testing of the child must be present.

The role of the teacher is to identify the short and long term goals for the student and to give the student's current progress, including strengths and weaknesses. The school must allow any other individual whom the parent wants to invite to attend the meeting. This may be a caseworker involved with the student's family, people involved with the day-to-day care of the student, or any person whom the parent feels can contribute vital information to the meeting.

The parents or guardians can also bring someone to help them understand the IEP or the IEP process, such as a lawyer experienced with educational advocacy or a parent advocate.

There are lists of related services that may be considered during a CSE meeting. The related services are developmental, corrective, and other supportive services that are required to help a child with special needs benefit from special education. These related services can include speech pathology and audiology, psychological services, physical and occupational therapy, recreation and extracurricular activities, counseling services, and medical services for diagnostic or evaluation purposes.

The IEP should specify the services to be provided, the extent to which they are necessary, and who will provide the services. If a specialist, such as a speech teacher or Occupational Therapist will provide specific services, they should be included in the CSE team so they can give input on the types of services required, available, and what may be beneficial to the student in question. Information on how they are doing in particular specialist areas will also be included with an evaluation of student process with speech therapy and occupational therapy.

Skill 5.02   Identifying information that must be specified in an IEP (Individualized Education Programs)

It is important to understand how much the law affects the required components of the IEP. Educators must keep themselves apprised of the changes and amendments to laws, such as IDEA, and the required manner that they must be completed.   At present, the following elements are required of an IEP:

1. The student's present level of academic performance and functional performance.
2. A statement of how the disability affects the student's involvement and progress in the general education curriculum. Preschool children must have a statement explaining how the disability effects the child's participation in appropriate activities.
3. A statement of annual goals or anticipated attainments.
4. Short-term objectives are no longer required on every IEP. Students with severe disabilities or those taking an alternate assessment may need short-term objectives, which lead to the obtainment of annual goals.
5. A statement of when the parents will be notified of their child's progress, which must be at least as often as the regular education student.
6. Modifications or accommodations for participation in statewide or citywide assessments; or if it is determined that the child cannot participate, why the assessment is inappropriate for the child and how the child will be assessed.
7. Specific educational services, assistive technology, and related services, to be provided, and those who will provide them.

8.   Evaluate criteria and timeliness for determining whether instructional objectives have been achieved.
9.   Projected dates for initiating services with their anticipated frequency, location, and duration.
10. The extent to which the child will not participate in the regular education program.
11. Transition information. (See below.)

Beginning when a student is 14, and annually thereafter, the student's IEP must contain a statement of his or her transition service needs under the various components of that IEP that focus upon the student's courses of study (e.g., vocational education or advanced placement),and when appropriate, include interagency responsibilities and links for possible future assistance.

Beginning at least one year before the student reaches the age of majority under State law, the IEP must contain a statement that the student has been informed of the rights under the law that will transfer to him or her upon reaching the age of majority.

Skill 5.03   Demonstrating knowledge of supports and accommodations needed for integrating students with disabilities into various program placements

The special educator is trained to work in a team approach. This occurs from the initial identification of students who appear to deviate from what is considered to be normal performance or behavior for particular age- and grade-level students. The Special Education Teacher serves as a consultant (or as a team member, depending on the school district) to the student support team. If the student is referred, the Special Education Teacher may be asked to collect assessment data for the forthcoming comprehensive evaluation. This professional then generally serves on the multidisciplinary eligibility, individualized educational planning, and placement committees. If the student is placed in a special education setting, the special educator continues to coordinate and collaborate with regular classroom teachers and support personnel at the school-based level.

Support professionals are available at both the district- and school-based levels, and they contribute valuable services and expertise in their respective areas. A team approach between district ancillary services and local school-based staff is essential.

> **Learn more about specific support roles for those working with children who have special needs:**
> http://www.cec.sped.org/Content/NavigationMenu/ProfessionalDevelopment/CareerCenter/Job Profiles/

1. **School Psychologist.** The school Psychologist participates in the referral, identification, and program planning processes. She contributes to the multidisciplinary team by adding important observations, data, and inferences about the student's performance. As she conducts an evaluation, she observes the student in the classroom environment, takes a case history, and administers a battery of formal and informal individual tests. The Psychologist is involved as a member of a professional team throughout the stages of referral, assessment, placement, and program planning.

2. **Physical Therapist.** This person works with disorders of bones, joints, muscles, and nerves following medical assessment. Under the prescription of a physician, the therapist applies treatment to the students in the form of heat, light, massage, and exercise to prevent further disability or deformity. Physical therapy includes the use of adaptive equipment and prosthetic and orthotic devices to facilitate independent movement. This type of therapy helps individuals with disabilities to develop or recover their physical strength and endurance.

3. **Occupational Therapist.** This specialist is trained in helping students develop self-help skills (e.g., self-care, motor, perceptual, and vocational skills). The students are actively involved in the treatment process to quicken recovery and rehabilitation.

4. **Speech and Language Pathologist.** This specialist assists in the identification and diagnosis of children with speech or language disorders. In addition, she makes referrals for medical or habilitation needs, counsels family members and teachers, and works with the prevention of communicative disorders. The speech and language therapist concentrates on rehabilitative service delivery and continuing diagnosis.

5. **Administrators.** Building principals and special education directors (or coordinators) provide logistical as well as emotional support. Principals implement building policy procedures and control designation of facilities, equipment, and materials. Their support is crucial to the success of the program within the parameters of the base school. Special education directors provide information about federal, state, and local policy, which is vital to the operation of a special education unit. In some districts, the special education director may actually control certain services and materials. Role clarification, preferably in writing, should be accomplished to ensure effectiveness of program services.

6. **Guidance Counselors, Psychometrists, and Diagnosticians.** These persons often lead individual and group counseling sessions and are trained in assessment, diagnostic, and observation skills, as well as personality development and functioning abilities. They can apply knowledge and skills to multidisciplinary teams and assist in the assessment, diagnosis, placement, and program planning process.

7. **Social Worker.** The Social Worker is trained in interviewing and counseling skills. This person possesses knowledge of available community and school services and makes these known to parents. She often visits homes of students, conducts intake and assessment interviews, counsels individuals and small groups, and assists in district enforcement policies.

8. **School Nurse.** This person offers valuable information about diagnostic and treatment services. She is knowledgeable about diets, medications, therapeutic services, health-related services, and care needed for specific medical conditions. Reports of communicable diseases are filed with the health department, to which a health professional has access. A medical professional can sometimes obtain cooperation with the families of children with disabilities in ways that are difficult for the Special Education Teacher to achieve.

9. **Regular teachers and subject matter specialists.** These professionals are trained in general and specific instructional areas, teaching techniques, and overall child growth and development. They serve as a vital component to the referral process, as well as in the subsequent treatment program, if the student is determined eligible. They work with the students with special needs for the majority of the school day and function as a link to the children's special education and medical programs.

10. **Paraprofessional.** This staff member assists the special educator and often works in the classroom with the special needs students. She helps prepare specialized materials, tutor individual students, lead small groups, and provide feedback to students about their work.

Modifying materials is a great accommodation to use in order to include students in the general education classroom. Materials, usually textbooks, are usually modified because of reading level. The goal of modification is to present the material in a manner that the student can better understand while preserving the basic ideas and content. Modifications of course material may take the form of:

Simplifying Texts

a) Using a highlighter to mark key terms, main ideas, and concepts. In some cases, a marker may be used to delete nonessential content.
b) Cut and paste. The main ideas and specific content are cut and pasted on separate sheets of paper. Additional headings or other graphic aids can be inserted to help the student understand and organize material.
c) Supplement with graphic aids or tables
d) Supplement with study guides, questions, and directed preview.
e) Use self-correcting materials.
f) Allow additional time or break content material into smaller, more manageable units.

Taped Textbooks

Textbooks can be taped by the teacher or aide for students to follow along. In some cases, the students may qualify for recordings of textbooks from agencies such as Recordings for the Blind.

Parallel Curriculum

Projects, such as Parallel Alternative Curriculum (PAC) or Parallel Alternative Strategies for Students (PASS), present the content at a lower grade reading level and come with tests, study guides, vocabulary activities, and tests.

Supplementary Texts

Book publishers, such as Steck-Vaughn, publish a series of content-area texts that have been modified for reading level, amount of content presented on pages, highlighted key items, and visual aids.

ACCOMMODATIONS IN TEST-TAKING SITUATIONS

Test taking is not a pleasant experience for many students with behavioral and/or learning problems. They may lack study skills, may experience anxiety before or during a test, or may have problems understanding and differentiating the task requirements for different tests. The skills necessary to be successful vary with the type of test. Certain students have difficulty with writing answers but may be able to express their knowledge of subject matter verbally. Therefore, modifications of content area material may be extended to methods and modifications for evaluation and assessment of student progress.

Some of the ways that teachers can modify assessment for individual needs include:

- Help students to get used to timed tests with timed practice tests.
- Provide study guides before tests.
- Make tests easier to read by leaving ample space between the questions.
- Modify multiple choice tests by reducing the number of choices, reforming questions to yes-no, or using matching items.
- Modify short-answer tests with cloze (fill-in) statements, or provide a list of facts or choices that the student can choose from.
- Essay tests can be modified by using partial outlines for the student to complete, allowing additional time, or including test items that do not require extensive writing.

Skill 5.04   Analyzing issues related to the preparation and amendment of an IEP

A considerable amount of preparation and information gathering must be done prior to writing an IEP. Largely, this responsibility lies with the special educator although the school Psychologist or psychometrist may be more involved if the IEP is an initial IEP or if it is one written after an evaluation. Other school professionals who may be contributors are the Nurse, Social Worker, speech and language therapist, Occupational Therapist, physical therapist, audiologist, and technology consultant. In addition, information from outside sources of the above professions, as well as from physicians, may be included.

Initial IEPs are written only after the student completes an evaluation by a school Psychologist or psychometrist and the findings of such are that the student has a disability that adversely affects his school performance. Once eligibility for special services has been determined, the following information should be supplied for the IEP.

Identifying Information includes student's name, address, phone number, Social Security Number (if available), Medicaid number (if applicable), birth date, parents' names, parents' addresses, and parents' phone numbers. With whom the student resides (parent, guardian, foster parent) is also included.

Student Eligibility to receive special education services is indicated, as well as any secondary eligibilities.

Present Level of Functioning (including strengths and weaknesses) for social skills, communication, academic functioning, fine and gross motor skills, independent functioning, and vocational skills is recorded.

Current Vision and Hearing Screening Results are included to rule out possible impairment and the need for further assessment in these areas.

State Standards-Based Goals with Measurable Objectives should be included in areas where the student is expected to need the greatest concentration of special education.

Program Services Times will outline the amount of time that the student may receive services from various therapists (speech and language, occupational therapy, physical therapy, social work, technology, Nurse, vision and hearing), the amount of time that the student will receive special education services in the regular and special education classroom, and the amount of time the student will participate in the regular education curriculum (including time in "specials," classes such as music, PE, library, computers, art). Times are often listed in minutes per week or minutes per month.

Accommodations and Modifications (if any) that will be made to the student's educational program (special equipment needed, reduction in amount of work, assistance needed, extended time).

Student Participation in State and Local Assessments will also be included. The IEP will indicate if the student will participate in these assessments (strongly encouraged due to NCLB, No Child Left Behind) and if accommodations will be made. Accommodations may include things such as testing in a separate setting, untimed testing sessions, use of a calculator, having tests (other than a reading test) read or instructions rephrased. Use of specific assistive technology, such as an auditory trainer, must be documented. Note: If it is determined that the student cannot participate in "regular" state and local testing, then *Alternative Testing* must be marked on the IEP.

Extended School Year is considered for each student and determination is made based on whether or not the student will have difficulty regaining skills that may be lost during the summer months if extended school year is not attended.

Transportation is considered for the student, including the need for special transportation and any special equipment or personnel that may be needed.

Overall Percentage of Time in Special/Regular Education is determined, as well as the rationale of why other percentages of time (greater or lesser) were not chosen.

Parental Consent and Notification of a CSE Meeting is required. Parents should be notified in writing ten days prior to a CSE meeting. A total of three contacts should be made with the parent prior to the meeting. Parents should also be provided with a document outlining parents' rights in the special education process. Although parental consent is required for initial testing, subsequent consent is not needed unless a change in placement is being considered.

Reconvening of an IEP (Amendment) may be requested by school personnel or parents at any time that the program is considered to not be meeting the needs of the student. However, according to the IDEA 2004, changes may be made in the IEP as deemed necessary by the CPSE (Committee on Pre-school Special Education) / CSE (Committee on Special Education) committee, and as with regular IEP meetings, a parent member is not mandatory.

Multi-year CSE Meetings are now being used in some school districts when the existing program seems appropriate for the student. This is an effort to minimize paperwork and meeting times.

Three-year Re-evaluation Meetings determine the appropriateness of the student's program and the possible need for additional testing.

Skill 5.05   Demonstrating knowledge of characteristics and purposes of various CSE meetings (e.g., annual review, triennial review)

While New York State conforms to IDEA and its revisions, it is essential that all Special Education Teachers become aware of the New York State law on special education, which is Part 200 and Part 201. Part 200 defines the characteristics and purposes of the CSE meetings and is revised almost every 5 years. Part 201 covers the disciplinary procedures and protocols for students receiving special education services. For the purposes of preparing you for the NYSTCE Content Specialty Exam on Special Education, this section will take much of its information directly from both Part 200 and Part 201.

Purposes for CSE Meetings

There are 5 defined reasons for a CSE to take place.

1) *Initial*
    The initial CSE is the first CSE held on a child due to a referral on the part of school personnel or parents/guardians. Pre-school children, like those who are school age, may be evaluated for the purposes of arriving at the decision of whether or not a child's disability can be deemed to adversely affect his/her ability to learn.

2) *Annual Review*
    Once a year, reviews of IEPs are given at a CSE. The purpose of these meetings is to determine if progress is being made, and if the student's program remains appropriate. *Program* here means the students placement (i.e., Inclusion, 12:1:1, 8:1:1), test modifications, and the necessary academic and instructional interventions to aide a student's learning ability.

3) *Triennials*

This type of CSE is often deemed to be similar to an initial CSE meeting. Like the annual reviews, the triennials are also reviews but are more extensive and may require additional testing to provide verification that the student's current placement continues to be appropriate or needs to be changed. The intention of making the third-year review (triennial reviews) significant is to provide a type of "marker" at which "the whole child" must be looked at rather than a basic review of present levels of performance.

3) *Amendments--Change of Program/Placement*

It is not unusual for teachers, parents, and administrators to note possible ways to best assist a student to achieve his/her learning potential. Amendment CSEs are convened by the request of a parent or teacher. Amendment CSEs look at specific needs for change in the "immediate future". For this reason, expedited requests for CSEs are recorded as Amendment CSEs. A sample purpose for such a CSE meeting would be a mother's request to add the test modification of a scribe for her son to be put in place before his Regents Exam in three months.

4) *Manifestation Determination*

Manifestation Determination is a CSE which is held when a student has been removed from his/her academic environment for a period of more than 10 consecutive days or if the student has received a series of suspensions that add up to more than 10 school days a year. School districts often make this policy stricter by requiring a Manifestation Determination CSE when a student reaches a series of suspensions that add up to 8 academic days within a school year in order to insure compliance with Part 201.

The purpose of the CSE is to determine if the behavior that resulted in a suspension was a result of the student's disability. One example would be if a student with special needs swears at a teacher and is suspended as a result, and the CSE determines that the student's behavior is a manifestation of the student's disability, which is Tourette's Syndrome.

5) *Post School Transition*

Unfortunately, too often this type of CSE is pushed aside, and its importance is highly ignored. The last CSE before a student leaves the school district "umbrella" of special education services can be the one that provides lasting opportunities for the student. Since the student was 15 years old, transitional evaluations and statements have been important. This is the transitional CSE. It is here that students and their parents should be given what can be considered "lasting resources and supports" that will grow as the young adult with special needs steps out into society. One of the most basic of resources that teachers need to think of is the test modifications of their students. Test modifications can follow students through life, providing several occupational opportunities.

Skill 5.06 **Demonstrating understanding of the purposes and components of transition planning, including the coordination of members of various disciplines and agencies to ensure the systematic transition at all levels (birth to adulthood) of students with disabilities**

Transition planning is mandated in the Individuals with Disabilities Education Act (IDEA). The transition planning requirements ensure that planning is begun at age 14 and continued through high school. Transition planning and services focus on a coordinated set of student-centered activities designed to facilitate the student's progression from school to post-school activities. Transition planning should be flexible and focus on the developmental and educational requirements of the student at different grades and times.

Transition planning is a student-centered event that necessitates a collaborative endeavor. In reference to secondary students, the responsibilities are shared by the student, parents, secondary personnel, and postsecondary personnel, who are all members of the transition team.

In most cases when transition is mentioned, it is referring to a child 14 or over, but in some cases, children younger than 14 may need transition planning and assistance. Depending on the child's disability and its severity, a child may need assistance with transitioning to school from home or to school from a hospital or institution or any other setting. In those cases, the members of the transition team may also include doctors or Nurses, Social Workers, speech therapists, and physical therapists.

It is important that the student play a key role in transition planning. This will entail asking the student to identify preferences and interests and to attend meetings on transition planning. The degree of success experienced by the student in postsecondary educational settings depends on the student's degree of motivation, independence, self-direction, self-advocacy, and academic abilities developed in high school. Student participation in transition activities should be implemented as early as possible and no later than age 16.

In order to contribute to the transition planning process, the student should: understand his learning disability and the impact it has on learning and work; implement achievable goals; present a positive self-image by emphasizing strengths while understanding the impact of the learning disability; know how and when to discuss and ask for needed accommodations; be able to seek instructors and learning environments that are supportive; and establish an ongoing personal file that consists of school and medical records, an individualized education program (IEP), a resume, and samples of academic work.

The primary function of parents during transition planning is to encourage and assist students in planning and achieving their educational goals. Parents also should encourage students to cultivate independent decision-making and self-advocacy skills.

Transition planning involves input from four groups: the student, parents, secondary education professionals, and postsecondary education professionals. The result of effective transition from a secondary to a postsecondary education program is a student with a learning disability who is confident, independent, self-motivated, and striving to achieve career goals. This effective transition can be achieved if the team, consisting of the student, parents, and professional personnel, work as a group to create and implement effective transition plans. The transition team of a student entering the workforce may also include community members, organizations, company representatives, vocational education instructors, and job coaches.

Transition Services

Transition services will be different for each student. Transition services must take into account the student's interests and preferences. Evaluation of career interests, aptitudes, skills, and training may be considered.

The transition activities that have to be addressed, unless the CSE team finds it uncalled for, are: (a) instruction, (b) community experiences, and (c) the development of objectives related to employment and other post-school areas.

a) **Instruction** – The instruction part of the transition plan deals with school instruction. Students should have a portfolio completed upon graduation. They should research and plan for further education and/or training after high school. Education can be in a college setting, technical school, or vocational center. Goals and objectives created for this transition domain depend upon the nature and severity of the student's disability, the student's interests in further education, plans made for accommodations needed in future education and training, and identification of post-secondary institutions that offer the requested training or education.

b) **Community Experiences** – This part of the transition plan investigates how the student utilizes community resources. Resources entail places for recreation, transportation services, agencies, and advocacy services. It is essential for students to deal with the following areas:

- Recreation and leisure - examples: movies, YMCA, religious activities.
- Personal and social skills - examples: calling friends, religious groups, going out to eat.

- Mobility and transportation - examples: passing a driver's license test or utilizing Dial-A-Ride.
- Agency access - examples: utilizing a phone book and making calls.
- System advocacy - example: have a list of advocacy groups to contact.
- Citizenship and legal issues - example: registering to vote.

c) **Development of Employment** - This segment of the transition plan investigates becoming employed. Students should complete a career interest inventory. They should have chances to investigate different careers. Many work skill activities can take place within the classroom, home, and community. Classroom activities may concentrate on employability skills, community skills, mobility, and vocational training. Home and neighborhood activities may concentrate on personal responsibility and daily chores. Community-based activities may focus on part-time work after school and in the summer, cooperative education or work-study, individualized vocational training, and volunteer work.

d) **Daily Living Skills** – This segment of the transition plan is also important although not essential to the IEP. Living away from home can be an enormous undertaking for people with disabilities. Numerous skills are needed to live and function as an adult. In order to live as independently as possible, a person should have an income, know how to cook, clean, shop, pay bills, get to a job, and have a social life. Some living situations may entail independent living, shared living with a roommate, or supported living or group homes. Areas that may need to be looked into include: personal and social skills; living options; income and finances; medical needs; and community resources and transportation.

Skill 5.07   Use assessment data and information to plan appropriate individual programs for all students with disabilities, including those from culturally and/or linguistically diverse backgrounds.

Assessment data and information is one resource for the special educator who is writing an IEP. Such data can provide some information on the student's current level of functioning in social skills, speech, language, academics, cognitive skills, and fine and gross motor skills. (It is important to note that the student's classroom performance should also be taken into account when writing current level of performance.)

Assessment data can also generate areas of delay that should be included in the student's IEP goals and objectives. For example, a student who has tested as having a delay in rote memory skills may have an IEP objective to rote count to 25 or to recite the alphabet. A student who demonstrates a reading delay of two years may have IEP goals and objectives that reflect that he will demonstrate comprehension skills with material at that grade level.

Usually if there is a year or more delay in an area, the student will be eligible for special education services. (However, according to IDEA 2004, such a determination no longer must solely depend on a discrepancy in areas of achievement but may also be the result of how the student in doing in class.)This data (again, with classroom performance) can also help determine which subjects might be considered for inclusion.
The need for programming in specific therapies may also be the result of formal assessment. Such therapies might include: speech and language, physical therapy, occupational therapy, vision therapy, or music therapy.

Formal assessment and school behaviors may result in the writing of a functional behavioral plan as a part of the IEP.

The special education student with a culturally- or linguistically-diverse background will need additional considerations. Although special education must not be determined as needed because of a cultural or linguistic diversity, certainly some students qualify for special education services and come from a diverse background.

In the case of the ELL special education student, materials and activities must be at the student's developmental level and must, as needed, parallel skills in the child's first language and then in English. The Special Education Teacher is also reminded to foster an appreciation and respect for the student's cultural and linguistic background.

Skill 5.08   Demonstrating understanding of requirements for creating and maintaining records and preserving confidentiality

One of the most important professional practices a teacher must maintain is student confidentiality. This extends far beyond paper records and goes into the realm of oral discussions. Teachers are expected not to mention the names of students, and often the specifics of their character, in conversations with those who are not directly involved with them, inside and outside of school.

In the school environment, teacher record keeping comes in three main formats with specific confidentiality rules. All of the records stated below should be kept in a locked place within the classroom or an office within the school:

Learn more about Confidentiality and the Law:
http://www.wrightslaw.com/info/ferpa.index.htm

1) *Teacher's personal notes on a student.*
When a teacher takes notes on a student's actions, including behaviors and/or grade performance that are not intended to be placed in a school recorded format, such as a report card, the teacher may keep this information private and confidential to his/her own files. Teachers may elect to share this information or not.

2) *Teacher daily recorded grades and attendance of the student.*
Teachers' grade books and attendance records are to be open to the parent/guardian of that child who wishes to check on his/her child. Only that child's information may be shared, not that of others.

3) *Teacher recorded/notation on records that appear in the student's cumulative file.*
There are specific rules regarding the sharing of the Cumulative Records of students.

   a) Cumulative files will follow a student that transfers within the school district, from school to school.
   b) All information placed in a cumulative file may be examined by a parent at any time it is requested. If parents show up to review their child's cumulative file, the file should be shown as it is in its current state. (This includes IEPs.)
   c) When information from a cumulative file is requested by another person/entity outside of the parent/guardian, the information may not be released without the express written consent of the parent/guardian. The parental consent must specify which records may be shared with the other party of interest.
   d) A school in which a student may intend to enroll may receive the student's educational record without parental consent. However, the school sending that information must make a reasonable attempt to notify the parent/guardian of the request. (FERPA)

Today's world is quickly becoming a digital environment. Teacher's now communicate often with email and are keeping records in digital formats, often within a district-mandated program. Teachers should keep in mind that emails and other electronic formats can be forwarded and are as "indelible" as permanent ink, so teachers should maintain a professional decorum, just as when they are writing their own records that will be seen outside of their personal notations.

SUBAREA II.   **PROMOTING STUDENT LEARNING AND DEVELOPMENT IN A COLLABORATIVE LEARNING COMMUNITY**

COMPETENCY 0006   **UNDERSTAND METHODS OF PLANNING AND MANAGING TEACHING AND LEARNING ENVIRONMENTS FOR INDIVIDUALS WITH DISABILITIES.**

Skill 6.01   **Demonstrating knowledge of basic principles of classroom management and research-based best practices for managing learning environments for students with disabilities**

Classroom Management Techniques

Classroom management plans should be in place when the school year begins. Developing a management plan takes a proactive approach—that is, deciding what behaviors will be expected of the class as a whole, anticipating possible problems, and teaching the behaviors early in the school year.

Behavior management techniques should focus on positive procedures that can be used at home as well as at school. Involving the students in the development of the classroom rules lets the students know the rationale for the rules and allows them to assume responsibility for the rules because they had a part in developing them. When students get involved in helping establish the rules, they will be more likely to assume responsibility for following them. Once the rules are established, enforcement and reinforcement for following the rules should begin immediately.

Consequences should be introduced when the rules are introduced, and they should be clearly stated, and understood by all of the students. The severity of the consequence should match the severity of the offense and must be enforceable. The teacher must apply the consequence consistently and fairly, so the students will know what to expect when they choose to break a rule.

Like consequences, students should understand what rewards to expect for following the rules. The teacher should never promise a reward that cannot be delivered and should always follow through with the reward as soon as possible. Consistency and fairness are also necessary for rewards to be effective. Students will become frustrated and give up if they see that rewards and consequences are not delivered timely and fairly.

About four to six classroom rules should be posted where students can easily see and read them. These rules should be stated positively and describe specific behaviors, so they are easy to understand. Certain rules may also be tailored to meet target goals and IEP requirements of individual students. (For example, a new student who has had problems with leaving the classroom may need an individual behavior contract to assist him or her with adjusting to the class rule about remaining in the assigned area.) As the students demonstrate the behaviors, the teacher should provide reinforcement and corrective feedback. Periodic "refresher" practice can be done as needed, for example, after a long holiday or if students begin to "slack off". A copy of the classroom plan should be readily available for substitute use, and the classroom aide should also be familiar with the plan and procedures.

The teacher should clarify and model the expected behavior for the students. In addition to the classroom management plan, a management plan should be developed for special situations, (i.e., fire drills) and transitions (i.e., going to and from the cafeteria). Periodic review of the rules, as well as modeling and practice, may be conducted as needed, such as after an extended school holiday.

Procedures that use social humiliation, withholding of basic needs, pain, or extreme discomfort should never be used in a behavior management plan. Emergency intervention procedures used when the student is a danger to himself or others are not considered behavior management procedures. Throughout the year, the teacher should periodically review the types of interventions being used, assess the effectiveness of the interventions used in the management plan, and make revisions as needed for the best interests of the child.

Motivation

Before the teacher begins instruction, he or she should choose activities that are at the appropriate level of student difficulty, are meaningful, and relevant. Teacher behaviors that motivate students include:

- Maintain success expectations through teaching, goal setting, establishing connections between effort and outcome, and self-appraisal and reinforcement.
- Have a supply of intrinsic incentives, such as rewards, appropriate competition between students, and the value of the academic activities.
- Focus on students' intrinsic motivation through adapting the tasks to students' interests, providing opportunities for active response, including a variety of tasks, providing rapid feedback, incorporating games into the lesson, and allowing students the opportunity to make choices, create, and interact with peers.

- Stimulate students' learning by modeling positive expectations and attributions. Project enthusiasm, and personalize abstract concepts. Students will be better motivated if they know what they will be learning about. The teacher should also model problem-solving and task-related thinking so students can see how the process is done.

For adolescents, motivation strategies are usually aimed at getting the student actively involved in the learning process. Since the adolescent has the opportunity to get involved in a wider range of activities outside the classroom (job, car, being with friends), stimulating motivation may be the focus even more than academics.

Motivation may be achieved through extrinsic reinforcers or intrinsic reinforcers. This is accomplished by allowing the student a degree of choice in what is being taught or how it will be taught. The teacher will, if possible, obtain a commitment either through a verbal or written contract between the student and the teacher. Adolescents also respond to regular feedback, especially when that feedback shows that they are making progress.

Rewards for adolescents often include free time for listening to music, for recreation or for games. They may like extra time for a break or exemption from a homework assignment. They may receive rewards at home for satisfactory performance at school. Other rewards include self-charting progress, and tangible reinforcers. In summary, motivational activities may be used for goal setting, self-recording of academic progress, self-evaluation, and self-reinforcement.

Classroom Interventions

Classroom interventions anticipate student disruptions and nullify potential discipline problems. Every student is different, and each situation is unique; therefore, student behavior cannot be matched to specific interventions. Good classroom management requires the ability to select appropriate intervention strategies from an array of alternatives. The following non-verbal and verbal interventions were explained in Henley, Ramsey, and Algonzzine (1993).

| **Helpful Hints on classroom interventions:** |
| http://www.behavioradvisor.com/RememberYourGoal.html |

Nonverbal Interventions - The use of nonverbal interventions allows classroom activities to proceed without interruption. These interventions also enable teachers to avoid "power struggles" with students.

Body Language - Teachers can convey authority and command respect through body language. Posture, eye contact, facial expressions, and gestures are examples of body components that signal leadership to students.

Planned Ignoring - Many minor classroom disturbances are best handled through planned ignoring. When teachers ignore attention-seeking behaviors, often students do likewise.

Signal Interference - There are numerous non-verbal signals that teachers can use to quiet a class. Some of these are eye contact, snapping fingers, a frown, shaking the head, or making a quieting gesture with the hand. A few teachers present signs like flicking the lights, putting her finger over her lips, or winking at a selective student.

Proximity Control - Teachers who move around the room often merely need to stand near a student or small group of students or gently place a hand on a student's shoulder to stop a disturbing behavior. Teachers who stand or sit as if rooted are compelled to issue verbal directions in order to deal with student disruptions.

Removal of Seductive Objects - Some students become distracted by objects. Removing seductive objects eliminates the need some students have to handle, grab, or touch objects that distract their attention. One of the best ways to accomplish this is to "Fall in Love" with the object and express a concern to place it somewhere safe, like on your desk.

Verbal Interventions - Because non-verbal interventions are the least intrusive, they are generally preferred. Verbal Interventions are useful after it is clear that non-verbal interventions have been unsuccessful in preventing or stopping disruptive behavior.

Humor - Some teachers have been successful in dispelling discipline problems with a quip or an easy comment that produces smiles or gentle laughter from students. This does not include sarcasm, cynicism, or teasing, which increase tension and often create resentment.

Sane Messages - Sane messages are descriptive and model appropriate behavior. They help students understand how their behavior affects others. "Karol, when you talk during silent reading, you disturb everyone in your group," is an example of a sane message.

Restructuring - When confronted with student disinterest, the teacher makes the decision to change activities. This is an example of an occasion when restructuring could be used by the teacher to regenerate student interest.

Hypodermic Affection - Sometimes students get frustrated, discouraged, and anxious in school. Hypodermic affection lets students know they are valued. Saying a kind word, giving a smile, or just showing interest in a child give the encouragement that is needed.

Praise and Encouragement - Effective praise is directed at student behavior rather than at the student personally. "Catching a child being good," is an example of an effective use of praise that reinforces positive classroom behavior. Comments like, "You are really trying hard," encourage student effort.

Alerting - Making abrupt changes from one activity to another can bring on behavior problems. Alerting helps students to make smooth transitions by giving them time to make emotional adjustments to change.

Accepting Student Feelings - Providing opportunities for students to express their feelings, even those that are distressful, helps them to learn to do so in appropriate ways. Role playing, class meetings or discussions, life space interviews, journal writings, and other creative modes help students to channel difficult feelings into constructive outlets.

Transfer Between Classes And Subjects

Effective teachers use class time efficiently. This results in higher student subject engagement and will likely result in more subject matter retention. One way teachers use class time efficiently is through a smooth transition from one activity to another; this activity is also known as "management transition." Management transition is defined as, "Teacher shifts from one activity to another in a systemic, academically-oriented way." One factor that contributes to efficient management transition is the teacher's management of instructional material. Effective teachers gather their materials during the planning stage of instruction. By doing this, a teacher avoids flipping through things looking for the items necessary for the current lesson. Momentum is lost and student concentration is broken when this occurs.

Additionally, teachers who keep students informed of the sequencing of instructional activities maintain systematic transitions because the students are prepared to move on to the next activity. For example, the teacher says, "When we finish with this guided practice together, we will turn to page twenty-three, and each student will do the exercises. I will then circulate throughout the classroom, helping on an individual basis. Okay, let's begin." Following an example such as this will lead to systematic, smooth transitions between activities because the students will be turning to page twenty-three when the class finishes the practice without a break in concentration.

Another method that leads to smooth transitions is to move students in groups and clusters rather than one by one. This is called "group fragmentation." For example, if some students do seat work while other students gather for a reading group, the teacher moves the students in pre-determined groups. Instead of calling the individual names of the reading group, which would be time consuming and laborious, the teacher simply says, "Will the blue reading group please assemble at the reading station. The red and yellow groups will quietly do the vocabulary assignment I am now passing out." As a result of this activity, the classroom is ready to move on in a matter of seconds rather than minutes.

Additionally, the teacher may employ academic transition signals, defined as academic transition signals— "teacher utterance that indicate[s] movement of the lesson from one topic or activity to another by indicating where the lesson is and where it is going." For example, the teacher may say, "That completes our description of clouds; now we will examine weather fronts." Like the sequencing of instructional materials, this keeps the student informed on what is coming next, so they will move to the next activity with little or no break in concentration.

Therefore, effective teachers manage transitions from one activity to another in a systematically-oriented way through efficient management of instructional matter, sequencing of instructional activities, moving students in groups, and by employing academic transition signals. Through an efficient use of class time, achievement is increased because students spend more class time engaged in on-task behavior.

Transition refers to changes in class activities that involve movement. Examples are:
   (a) Breaking up from large-group instruction into small groups for learning centers and small-group instructions
   (b) Classroom to lunch, to the playground, or to elective classes
   (c) Finishing reading at the end of one period and getting ready for math the next period
   (d) Emergency situations, such as fire drills

Successful transitions are achieved by using proactive strategies. Early in the year, the teacher pinpoints the transition periods in the day and anticipates possible behavior problems, such as students habitually returning late from lunch. After identifying possible problems with the environment or the schedule, the teacher plans proactive strategies to minimize or eliminate those problems. Proactive planning also gives the teacher the advantage of being prepared, addressing behaviors before they become problems, and incorporating strategies into the classroom management plan right away. Transition plans can be developed for each type of transition and the expected behaviors for each situation taught directly to the students.

Please refer to skill 15.1 for more classroom management techniques that affect student behavior.)

Skill 6.02 **Demonstrating an understanding of the roles of the special educator, general educator, and other professionals in creating a learning environment that promotes students' achievement of goals and objectives**

The role of the Special Education Teacher and the general education teacher is to work together to ensure that students with disabilities are able to attain their educational objectives in the least restrictive environment. Some students are best served in the general education setting with additional accommodations, while other students may be best served in the special education setting. The educators must work together to decide what educational program is best suited for the student and where the student can best meet his goals and objectives.

These decisions should be made during the student's CSE meeting. It is important that the Special Education Teacher, the general education teacher, and other interested professionals, such as the speech teacher, are in attendance at the meeting so they can discuss and collaborate on their role in helping the student.

Students with disabilities often experience insufficient access to and a lack of success in the general education curriculum. To promote improved access to the general curriculum for all learners, information should be presented in various formats using a variety of media forms; students should be given numerous methods to express and demonstrate what they have learned; and students should be provided with multiple entry points to engage their interest and motivate their learning.

Printed reading materials can be challenging to individuals with disabilities. Technology can help alleviate some of these difficulties by providing a change from printed text to electronic text that can be modified, enhanced, programmed, linked, and searched.

Text styles and font sizes can be changed, as required, by readers with visual disabilities. Text can be read aloud with computer-based text-to-speech translators and combined with illustrations, videos, and audio. Electronic text provides alternative formats for reading materials that can be tailored to match learner needs and be structured in ways that enhance the learning process and expand both physical and cognitive access.

Skill 6.03 Applying techniques of collaborative planning with general educators and other professionals

Lesson Plan Collaboration

According to Walther-Thomas et al (2000), *Collaboration for Inclusive Education*, ongoing professional development that provides teachers with opportunities to create effective instructional practice is vital and necessary. "A comprehensive approach to professional development is perhaps the most critical dimension of sustained support for successful program implementation." The inclusive approach incorporates learning programs that include all stakeholders in defining and developing high quality programs for students. Figure 1 below shows how an integrated approach of stakeholders can provide the optimal learning opportunity for all students.

Figure 1-Integrated Approach to Learning

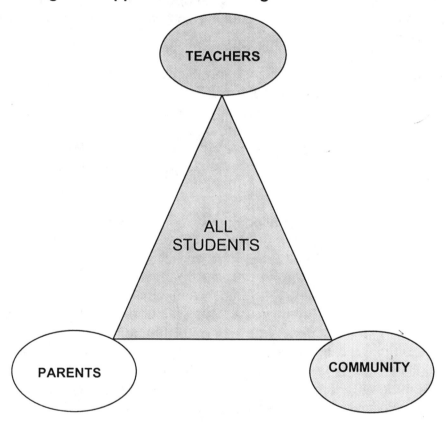

In the integrated approach to learning, teachers, parents, and community support become the integral apexes to student learning. The focus and central core of the school community is triangular as a representation of how effective collaboration can work in creating success for student learners. The goal of student learning and achievement now become the heart of the school community. The direction of teacher professional development in constructing effective instruction is clearly articulated in a greater understanding of facilitating learning strategies that develop skills and education equity for students.

Teachers need diversity in their instructional toolkits, which can provide students with clear instruction, mentoring, inquiry, challenge, performance-based assessment, and journal reflections on their learning processes. For teachers, having a collaborative approach to instruction fosters for students a deeper appreciation of learning, subject matter, and knowledge acquisition. Implementing a consistent approach to learning from all stakeholders will create equitable educational opportunities for all learners.

Research has shown that educators who collaborate become more diversified and effective in implementation of curriculum and assessment of effective instructional practices. The ability to gain additional insight into how students learn and modalities of differing learning styles can increase a teacher's capacity to develop proactive instructional methods. Teachers who team teach or have daily networking opportunities can create a portfolio of curriculum articulation and inclusion for students.

People in business are always encouraged to network in order to further their careers. The same can be said for teaching. If English teachers get together and discuss what is going on in their classrooms, those discussions make the "whole" much stronger than the parts. Even if there are not formal opportunities for such networking, it is wise for schools, or even individual teachers, to develop them and seek them out.

Skill 6.04 **Demonstrating familiarity with factors involved in creating a learning environment that is safe, positive, and supportive, in which diversity is celebrated, and that encourages active participation by learners in a variety of individual and group settings**

Learning styles refer to the ways in which individuals learn best. Physical settings, instructional arrangements, materials available, techniques, and individual preferences are all factors in the teacher's choice of instructional strategies and materials. Information about the student's preference can be done through a direct interview or a Likert-style checklist where the student rates his preferences.

Physical Environment (Spatial Arrangements)

The physical setting of the classroom contributes a great deal toward the propensity for students to learn. An adequate, well-built, and well-equipped classroom will invite students to learn. This has been called "invitational learning." Among the important factors to consider in the physical setting of the classroom are the following:

    a)   adequate physical space
    b)   repair status
    c)   lighting adequacy
    d)   adequate entry/exit access (including handicap accessibility)
    e)   ventilation/climate control
    f)   coloration

A classroom must have adequate physical space so students can conduct themselves comfortably. Some students are distracted by windows, pencil sharpeners, doors, etc. Some students prefer the front, middle, or back rows.

Learn more about how to create a physical environment that stimulates learning: http://behavioradvisor.com/ClassroomDesign.html

The teacher has the responsibility to report any items of classroom disrepair to maintenance staff. Broken windows, falling plaster, exposed sharp surfaces, leaks in ceiling or walls, and other items of disrepair present hazards to students.

Another factor which must be considered is adequate lighting. Report any inadequacies in classroom illumination. Florescent lights placed at acute angles often burn out faster. A healthy supply of spare tubes is a sound investment.

Local fire and safety codes dictate entry and exit standards. In addition, all corridors and classrooms should be wheelchair accessible for students and others who use them. Older schools may not have this accessibility.

Another consideration is adequate ventilation and climate control. Some classrooms in some states use air conditioning extensively. Sometimes it is so cold as to be considered a distraction. Specialty classes, such as science, require specialized hoods for ventilation. Physical education classes have the added responsibility for shower areas and specialized environments that must be heated, such as pool or athletic training rooms.

Classrooms with warmer subdued colors contribute to students' concentration on task items. Neutral hues for coloration of walls, ceiling, and carpet or tile are generally used in classrooms so distraction due to classroom coloration may be minimized.

> **Helpful tips on how to organize your classroom environment:**
> http://www.cyc-net.org/cyc-online/cycol-0403-hewitt.html

In the modern classroom, there is a great deal of furniture, equipment, supplies, appliances, and learning aids to help the teacher teach and students learn. The classroom should be provided with furnishings that fit the purpose of the classroom. The kindergarten classroom may have a reading center, a playhouse, a puzzle table, student work desks/tables, a sandbox, and any other relevant learning/interest areas.

Whatever the arrangement of furniture and equipment may be, the teacher must provide for adequate traffic flow. Rows of desks must have adequate space between them for students to move and for the teacher to circulate. All areas must be open to line-of-sight supervision by the teacher.

In all cases, proper care must be taken to ensure student safety. Furniture and equipment should be situated safely at all times. No equipment, materials, boxes, etc. should be placed where there is danger of falling over. Doors must have entry and exit accessibility at all times.

Noise level should also be considered as part of the physical environment. Students vary in the degree of quiet that they need and the amount of background noise or talking that they can tolerate without getting distracted or frustrated. So a teacher must maintain an environment that is conducive to the learning of each child.

The major emergency responses include two categories for student movement: tornado warning response; and building evacuation, which includes most other emergencies (fire, bomb threat, etc.). For tornadoes, the prescribed response is to evacuate all students and personnel to the first floor of multi-story buildings and to place students along walls away from windows. All persons, including the teacher, should then crouch on the floor and cover their heads with their hands. These are standard procedures for severe weather, particularly tornadoes.

Most other emergency situations require evacuation of the school building. Teachers should be thoroughly familiar with evacuation routes established for each classroom in which they teach. Teachers should accompany and supervise students throughout the evacuation procedure and check to see that all students under their supervision are accounted for. Teachers should then continue to supervise students until the building may be reoccupied (upon proper school or community authority) or until other procedures are followed for students to officially leave the school area and cease to be the supervisory responsibility of the school. Elementary students evacuated to another school can wear nametags, and parents or guardians should sign them out at a central location.

Instructional Arrangements

Some students work well in large groups; others prefer small groups or one-to-one instruction with the teacher, aide, or volunteer. Instructional arrangements also involve peer-tutoring situations with the student as tutor or tutee. The teacher also needs to consider how well the student works independently with seatwork.

Skill 6.05   Recognizing instructional management techniques that encourage self-advocacy and increased independence

Learning about one's self involves the identification of learning styles, strengths and weakness, interests, and preferences. For students with mild disabilities, developing an awareness of the accommodations they need will help them ask for necessary accommodations on a job and in postsecondary education. Students can also help identify alternative ways they can learn.

Self-advocacy involves the ability to effectively communicate one's own rights, needs, and desires and to take responsibility for making decisions that impact one's life.

There are many elements in developing self-advocacy skills in students who are involved in the transition process. Helping the student to identify future goals or desired outcomes in transition planning areas is a good place to start. Self-knowledge is critical for the student in determining the direction that transition planning will take.

> **Learn more about How to teach self-advocacy:**
> http://www.pacer.org/parent/php/PHP-c95.pdf

The role of the teacher in promoting self-advocacy should include encouraging students to participate in the IEP process, as well as other key parts of their educational development.   Self-advocacy issues and lessons are effective when they are incorporated into the student's daily life. Teachers should listen to the student's problems and ask the student for input on possible changes that he may need. The teacher should talk with the student about possible solutions, discussing the pros and cons of doing something. A student who self-advocates should feel supported and encouraged. Good self-advocates know how to ask questions and get help from other people. They do not let other people do everything for them.

> **Helpful lesson plans on creating self-advocacy in your students:**
> http://www.intel.com/ca/education/unitplans/Speaking_Out/

Students need to practice newly acquired self-advocacy skills. Teachers should have students role play various situations, such as setting up a class schedule, moving out of the home, and asking for accommodations needed for a course.

The impact of transition planning on a student with a disability is very great. The student should be an active member of the transition team, as well as the focus of all activities. Students often think that being passive and relying on others to take care of them is the way to get things done. Students should be encouraged to express their opinions throughout the transition process. They need to learn how to express themselves so that others listen and take them seriously. These skills should be practiced within a supportive and caring environment.

Skill 6.06   Demonstrating an understanding of effective collaboration among teachers and other professionals to design and manage daily routines, including transition time that promote students' success in a variety of instructional settings

Effective collaboration among teachers and other professionals allows them to feel supported by other teachers in their mission to better meet the needs of their students. When collaboration is done successfully, teachers feel comfortable admitting what they do not know without feeling embarrassed, as it is assumed that everyone is faced with challenges and has knowledge to bring to the situation. When teachers are able to share challenges and difficulties, as well as successful teaching strategies, teachers can effectively evaluate teaching practices in school and provide a variety of resources for teachers to use in their classroom.

> **Learn more how to collaborate effectively with the general education teacher:** http://www.teachervision.fen.com/teaching-methods/resource/29

In collaborating, teachers can discuss effective techniques in dealing with transition time so that what is done effectively in one class can be shared and tried in other settings.

When teachers are sharing ideas for successful teaching practices with one another, they will have a wider base of knowledge to bring to the classroom. A variety of pedagogical approaches will be available, and the teachers will have a resource to rely on when they need additional input or advice in effectively teaching students. Additionally, if a teacher is part of a community of sharing, that teacher is more likely to value the benefits of the support and knowledge that is created in such a community. Teachers who place importance on collaboration, sharing, and peer-oriented learning will attempt to create similar communities in their classes. A community of sharing within the classroom permits students to feel safe sharing ideas, challenges, and achievements with peers.

Depending on a student's disability and the school setting, Special Education Teachers need to work with speech pathologists, school Psychologists, Occupational Therapists, Social Workers, general education teachers, and community workers to plan the optimal education program for each student. Special Education Teachers who work in inclusive settings or who co-teach or team-teach with general education teachers must spend enough time to sufficiently plan, develop, and put into practice an educational situation that is stimulating and suitable for all the students in the class.

Parents are also a significant part of the collaboration team. They are the experts on their child. Both parents and teachers have a lot to give in the educational planning for students with disabilities. If they work together, they can be a strong team.

Collaboration and working together requires time, which is in short supply in the educational setting. Educators never have enough time to do everything that they want to do. In order to work effectively, Special Education Teachers need the time to work and plan with parents and other professionals.

Skill 6.07   Demonstrating familiarity with techniques for supporting the functional integration of students with disabilities in various settings, including general education settings

Review of Student Needs with Inclusion Teacher and Support Staff

It may be determined at a student's IEP meeting that some time in the general education setting is appropriate. The activities and classes listed for inclusion may be field trips, lunch, recess, physical education, music, library, art, computers, math, science, social studies, spelling, reading, and/or English. The IEP will specify which classes and activities and the amount of time that the student will be with general education peers. The IEP will also list any modifications or accommodations that will be needed.

Modifications which may be considered for the general education classroom include the amount of work or type of task required. Modifications for a student with a learning disability might include a reduced number of spelling words or writing the vocabulary word that goes with a given definition instead of writing the definition that goes with a given word.

Accommodations are changes to the school environment or the use of necessary equipment to overcome a disability. An accommodation for a student with a hearing impairment might include the use of an auditory trainer or asking another student to serve as a note taker.

Prior to the student starting in a general education placement (regardless of the minutes on the IEP), the general education teacher and support staff (if any) should be inserviced on the student's disability and his needs according to his IEP. Sometimes this inservicing happens as the student's IEP is developed. Other times, it is done at a later date.

Student Expectations in the Inclusion Setting

The student with a disability should be well aware of his responsibilities in the general education setting ahead of time. These expectations should be a combination of behavior and task performance. Although the student should be aware of needed accommodations and modifications and should be a self-advocate for such, he should not use his disability as an excuse for not fulfilling the expectations.

Students may benefit from previewing material, using a checklist to keep track of materials and assignments, keeping an assignment notebook, reviewing materials after the lesson, and using study aids such as flashcards. Sometimes a behavior tracking chart may also be used.

Monitoring Student Progress in the Inclusion Setting

Once the student is in the general education setting for the time and activities listed on the IEP, the Special Education Teacher will need to monitor student progress. This can be done through verbal follow up with the general education teacher or by asking her to complete a progress form periodically. Of course, grades and the student's ability to restate learned information or answer questions are also indicators.

Evaluation of Student's Future Placement in the Inclusion Setting

If the student is successful in the general education activities and classes listed on the IEP, the Special Education Teacher may consider easing back on modifications and accommodations on the next IEP. She may also consider adding minutes or classes for the student's general education inclusion.

If the student had difficulty, the special educator may consider adding more modifications or accommodations on the next IEP. If the student had significant difficulty, he may need to receive more services in the special education classroom.

Skill 6.08 **Recognizing appropriate collaborative techniques for ensuring the positive and effective functioning of classroom paraprofessionals, aides, and volunteers**

This section will specifically address the working relationship teachers should have with those they work with in their classroom environment. There are 6 basic steps to having a rewarding collaborative relationship with those whom you share a working environment, whether they are paraprofessionals, aides or volunteers.

While it is understood that there are many titles to those who may be assisting in your room, this section will summarize their titles as "Classroom Assistants."

> **Learn more about Creating a Classroom Team:**
> http://www.aft.org/pubs-reports/psrp/classroom_team.pdf

1) *Get to know each other.*
   The best way to start a relationship with anyone is to find time alone to get to know each other. Give your new classroom assistant the utmost respect, and look at this as an opportunity to share your talents and learn those of your co-worker. Remember that this is your opportunity to find places you agree and disagree, which can help maintain and build your working relationship. Good working relationships require the knowledge of where each other's strengths and weaknesses are. So share what your strengths and weaknesses are, and listen to theirs. This knowledge may create one of one of the best working relationships you have ever had.

2) *Remember communication is a two-way street.*
   As a professional educator, it is important to remember that you must actively communicate with others. This is especially important with your classroom assistant. Let them see you listening. Pay attention and make sure that your classroom assistant sees that you care what he/she thinks. Encourage them to engage you in conversation by asking for more information. When you ask

> **Learn more about working together collaboratively with your classroom assistant:**
> http://www.aft.org/pubs-reports/psrp/classroom_team.pdf

for clarification of what a student said, you are also displaying interest and active listening. Remember also that asking your classroom assistant for details and insights may help you further meet the needs of your students.

2) It is also your responsibility to remove and prevent communication barriers in your working relationship. You are the professional! You must be the one to avoid giving negative criticism or put downs. Do not "read" motivations into the actions of your classroom assistant. Learn about them through communicating openly.

3) *Establish clear roles and responsibilities.*
The Access Center for Improving Outcomes of All Students K-8 has defined these roles in the graph on the next page.

	Teacher Role	Classroom Assistant Role	Areas of Communication
Instruction	▪ Plan all instruction, including what goals/objectives you expect in your small groups. ▪ Provide instruction in whole-class settings.	▪ Work with small groups of students on specific tasks, including review or re-teaching of content ▪ Work with one student at a time to provide intensive instruction or remediation on a concept or skill	▪ Teachers provide specific content and guidance about curriculum, students, and instructional materials ▪ Classroom Assistants note student progress and give feedback to teachers
Curriculum & Lesson Plan Development	▪ Develop all lesson plans and instructional materials ▪ Ensure alignment with standards, student needs, and IEPs	▪ Provide assistance in development of classroom activities, retrieval of materials, and coordination of activities	▪ Mutual review of lesson plan components prior to class ▪ Teachers provide guidance about specific instructional methods
Classroom Management	▪ Develop and guide class-wide management plans for behavior and classroom structures ▪ Develop and monitor individual behavior management plans	▪ Assist with the implementation of class-wide and individual behavior management plans ▪ Monitor hallways, study hall, & other activities outside normal class	▪ Teachers provide guidance about specific behavior management strategies & student characteristics ▪ Classroom Assistants note student progress & activities and give feedback to teachers

(*Working Together: Teacher-Paraeducator Collaboration*, The Access Center for Improving Outcomes of All Students K-8, http://www.k8accesscenter.org/documents/RESOURCELIST3-1.doc)

While the graph is nice and understandable by both parties, it is often helpful to write out what roles and expectations you have for your classroom assistant together in a contract-type fashion.

4) *Plan together.*
Planning together lets your paraprofessionals know you consider them valuable and provides a timeline of expectations that will aide both of you in your classroom delivery to your students. This also gives the impression to your students that you are on the same page and that you both know what is going to happen next.

Show a united front.
It is essential to let your students know that both adults in the room deserve the same amount of respect. Have a plan in place on how you should address negative behaviors individually and together. DO NOT make a statement in front of your students that your classroom assistant is wrong. Take time to address issues you may have regarding class time privately, not in front of the class.

5) Reevaluate your relationship.
Feedback is wonderful! Stop every now and then and discuss how you are working as a team. Be willing to listen to suggestions. Taking this time may be your opportunity to improve your working relationship.

COMPETENCY 0007   UNDERSTAND PRINCIPLES OF CURRICULUM
                   DEVELOPMENT AND INSTRUCTIONAL PLANNING
                   FOR STUDENTS WITH DISABILITIES.

Skill 7.01   Demonstrating knowledge of instructional planning for a
              variety of inclusive models (e.g., co-teaching, push-in,
              consultant teaching [CT])

According to IDEA 2004, students with disabilities are to participate in the
general education program to the extent that it is beneficial for them. As these
students are included into a variety of general education activities and classes,
the need for collaboration among teachers grows.

Co-Teaching

One model that is used for general education and Special Education Teachers to
collaborate is co-teaching. In this model, both teachers actively teach in the
general education classroom. Perhaps both teachers will conduct a small science
experiment group at the same time, switching groups at some point in the lesson.
Perhaps in social studies, one teacher will lecture while the other teacher writes
notes on the board or points out information on a map.

In the co-teaching model, the general education teacher and special educator
often switch roles back and forth within a class period or perhaps at the end of a
chapter or unit.

Push-in Teaching

In the push-in teaching model, the special educator is teaching parallel material
in the general education classroom. When the regular education teacher is
teaching word problems in math, for example, the special educator may be
working with some students on setting up the initial problems and then having
them complete the computation. Another example would be in science when the
general education teacher is asking review questions for a test, and the special
educator is working with a student who has a review study sheet to show the
answer from a group of choices.

In the push-in teaching model, it may appear that two versions of the same
lesson are being taught or two types of student responses/activities are being
monitored on the same material. The push-in teaching model would be
considered one type of differentiated instruction in which two teachers are
teaching simultaneously.

Consultant Teaching

In the consultant teaching model, the general education teacher conducts the class after planning with the special educator about how to differentiate activities so that the needs of the student with a disability are met.

In a social studies classroom using the consultant teaching model, both teachers may discuss what the expectations will be for a student with a learning disability and fine motor difficulty when the class does reports on states. They may decide that doing a state report is appropriate for the student; however, he may use the computer to write his report so that he can utilize the spell check feature and so that his work is legible.

Skill 7.02 Demonstrating knowledge of instructional methods, techniques, and curricula, including assistive and instructional technologies, used with students to accommodate specific disabilities

No two students are alike. It follows, then, that no students *learn* alike. To apply a one-dimensional instructional approach and a strict tunnel-vision perspective of testing is to impose learning limits on students. All students have the right to an education, but there cannot be a singular path to that education. A teacher must acknowledge the variety of learning styles and abilities among students within a class (and, indeed, the varieties from class to class) and apply multiple instructional and assessment processes to ensure that every child has appropriate opportunities to master the subject matter, demonstrate such mastery, and improve and enhance learning skills with each lesson.

It has been traditionally assumed that a teacher will use direct instruction in the classroom. The amount of time devoted to it will vary according to the age of the class, as well as other factors. Lecturing can be very valuable because it is the quickest way for transferring knowledge to students, and they can also learn note-taking and information-organizing skills in this way. However, having said that, there are many cautions to using an excessive amount of lecturing in a class of any age. In the first place, attention spans, even of senior high-school students, are short when they are using only one sense—the sense of hearing. Teachers should limit how much lecture they do as compared to other methods and how long the lectures last.

- Break up the presentation with different rates of speaking, giving students a "stretch" break", varying voice volume, etc...
- Establish rules of conduct for large groups, and praise students who follow the rules.

B. **Small-Group Instruction**

Small-group instruction usually includes 5 to 7 students and is recommended for teaching basic academic skills, such as math facts or reading. This model is especially effective for students with learning problems. Composition of the groups should be flexible to accommodate different rates of progress through instruction. The advantages of teaching in small groups is that the teacher is better able to provide feedback, monitor student progress, and give more instruction, praise, and feedback. With small groups, the teacher will need make sure to provide a steady pace for the lesson, provide questions and activities that allow all to participate, and include lots of positive praise.

C. **One Student with Teacher**

One-to-one tutorial teaching can be used to provide extra assistance to individual students. Such tutoring may be scheduled at set times during the day or provided as the need arises. The tutoring model is typically found more in elementary and resource classrooms than in secondary settings.

D. Peer Tutoring

In an effective peer tutoring arrangement, the teacher trains the peer tutors and matches them with students who need extra practice and assistance. In addition to academic skills, the arrangement can help both students work on social skills, such as cooperation and self-esteem. Both students may be working on the same material, or the tutee may be working to strengthen areas of weakness. The teacher determines the target goals, selects the material, sets up the guidelines, trains the student tutors in the rules and methods of the sessions, and monitors and evaluates the sessions.

E. **Cooperative Learning**

Cooperative learning differs from peer tutoring in that students are grouped in teams or small groups, and the methods are based on teamwork, individual accountability, and team reward. Individual students are responsible for their own learning and share of the work, as well as the group's success. As with peer tutoring, the goals, target skills, materials, and guidelines are developed by the teacher. Teamwork skills may also need to be taught. By focusing on team goals, all members of the team are encouraged to help each other as well as improve their individual performance.

Curriculum Design

Effective curriculum design assists the teacher from teacher demonstration to independent practice. Components of curriculum design include:

- quizzes or reviews of the previous lesson
- step-by-step presentations with multiple examples
- guided practice and feedback
- independent practice that requires the student to produce faster responses

The chosen curriculum should introduce information in a cumulative sequence and not introduce too much new information at one time. Review difficult material and practice to aid retention. New vocabulary and symbols should be introduced one at a time, and the relationships of components to the whole should be stressed. Students' background information should be recalled to connect new information to the old. Finally, teach strategies or algorithms first, and then move on to tasks that are more difficult.

Course objectives may be obtained from the department head at the local school. The ESE coordinator may have copies of objectives for functional courses or applied ESE courses. District program specialists also have lists of objectives for each course provided in the local school system. Additionally, publishers of textbooks will have scope and sequence lists in the teacher's manual.

Addressing Students' Needs

There are a number of procedures teachers can use to address the varying needs of the students. Some of the more common procedures are:

1. Varied assignments
A variety of assignments on the same content allows students to match learning styles and preferences with the assignment. If all assignments are writing assignments, for example, students who are hands-on or visual learners are at a disadvantage unrelated to the content base itself.

2. Cooperative learning
Cooperative learning activities allow students to share ideas, expertise, and insight with a non-threatening setting. The focus tends to remain on positive learning rather than on competition.

3. Structured environment
Some students need and benefit from clear structure that defines the expectations and goals of the teacher. The student knows what is expected and when and can work and plan accordingly.

4. Clearly-stated assignments

Assignments should be clearly stated, along with the expectation and criteria for completion. Reinforcement and practice activities should not be a guessing game for the students. The exception to this is, of course, those situations in which a discovery method is used.

5. Independent practice

Independent practice involving application and repetition is necessary for thorough learning. Students learn to be independent learners through practicing independent learning. These activities should always be within the students' abilities to perform successfully without assistance.

6. Repetition

Very little learning is successful with a single exposure. Learners generally require multiple exposures to the same information for learning to take place. However, this repetition does not have to be dull and monotonous. In conjunction with #1 above, varied assignments can provide repetition of content or skills practiced without repetition of specific activities. This helps keep learning fresh and exciting for the student.

7. Overlearning

As a principle of effective learning, overlearning recommends that students continue to study and review after they have achieved initial mastery. The use of repetition in the context of varied assignments offers the means to help students pursue and achieve overlearning.

(Refer to Skill 8.05 to learn about assistive and instructional technology.)

Skill 7.03 Demonstrating understanding of the connection between curriculum and IEP goals and objectives

No Child Left Behind, Public Law 107-110, was signed on January 8, 2002. It addresses accountability of school personnel for student achievement, with the expectation that every child will demonstrate proficiency in reading, math, and science. For example, all students should know how to read by grade three.

General education curriculum should reflect state learning standards. Because special educators are responsible for teaching students to a level of comparable proficiency as their non-disabled peers, this curriculum should also be followed closely in the special education program.

Naturally, certain modifications and accommodations will be necessary to meet learning standards. IEP goals and objectives are based on the unique needs of the child with a disability in meeting the curriculum expectations of the school (and the state/nation). Consider some of the following hypothetical cases.

Teachers in grades K-3 are mandated to teach reading to all students using scientifically-based methods with measurable outcomes. Some students (including some with disabilities) will not learn to read successfully unless taught with a phonics approach. It is the responsibility of the general education teacher and Special Education Teacher to incorporate phonics into the reading program.

Students are expected to learn mathematics. While some students will quickly grasp the mathematical concept of groupings of tens (and further skills of adding and subtracting large numbers), others will need additional practice. Research shows that many students with disabilities need a hands-on approach. Perhaps those students will need additional instruction and practice using snap-together cubes to grasp the grouping-by-tens concept.

School districts, individual general education classrooms, and special education classrooms are no longer functioning independently. Learning standards set forth by the government now holds all education to the same bar and is evidenced in curriculum and related IEP goals and objectives.

Skill 7.04 Demonstrating an understanding of effective collaboration among teachers and other professionals to develop and implement appropriate curricula for students with disabilities

The Individuals with Disabilities Education Act (1997) requires the collaboration of educational professionals in order to provide equitable opportunities for students with disabilities.

Collaboration in a school environment can take place between a variety of advocates for the students, including general educators, Special Education Teachers, school Psychologists, speech and language pathologists, interpreters, administrators, parents, and other professionals serving students with special needs. Sporadic communication between mainstream educators and other educational professionals damages the educational experience given to students.

Students with disabilities develop greater self-images and recognize their own academic and social strengths when they are included in the mainstream classroom and are serviced by teams of educational professionals. The staff report professional growth, personal support, and enhanced teaching motivation. The frequent practice of creating teacher assistance teams in order to provide intervention support to the general educator often fail due to time constraints and the lack of commitment given to collaboration.

Every member of a collaborative team has precise knowledge of his or her discipline, and transdisciplinary teams integrate these areas. For example, an ESL teacher can provide knowledge regarding the development of language skills and language instruction methodology. Counselors and Psychologists can impart knowledge as human development specialists and show their expertise in conducting small-group counseling and large-group interventions. School staff and instructors can benefit from what mainstream teachers can add in the area of performance information and knowledge of measures and benchmarks. Special Education Teachers can provide insight into designing and implementing behavior management programs and strategies for effective instruction to students with special needs. Speech pathologists can contribute their knowledge of speech and language development and provide insight into the identification of learning disabilities in language-minority students. Transdisciplinary teaming requires team members to build on the strengths and the needs of their particular populations. Therefore, each professional can contribute when it comes to developing and implementing appropriate curricula.

Skill 7.05 Demonstrate familiarity with strategies for integrating affective, social, and career/vocational skills with academic curricula.

A major focus of special education is to prepare students to become working, independent members of society. IDEA 2004 (Individuals with Disabilities Education Act) also includes preparing students for *further education*. Certain skills beyond academics are needed to attain this level of functioning.

Affective and Social Skills transcend all areas of life. When an individual is unable to acquire information on expectations and reactions of others or misinterprets those cues, he is missing an important element needed for success as an adult in the workplace and in the community in general.

Special education should incorporate a level of instruction in the affective/social area, as many students will not develop these skills without instruction, modeling, practice, and feedback.

Affective and social skills taught throughout the school setting might include: social greetings; eye contact with a speaker; interpretation of facial expression, body language, and personal space; ability to put feelings and questions into words; and use of words to acquire additional information as needed.

Career/Vocational Skills of responsibility for actions, a good work ethic, and independence should be incorporated into the academic setting. If students are able to regulate their overall work habits with school tasks, it is likely that the same skills will carry over into the work force. The Special Education Teacher may assess the student's level of career/vocational readiness by using the following list.

- Being prepared by showing responsibility for materials/school tools, such as books, assignments, study packets, pencils, pens, and assignment notebook.
- Knowing expectations by keeping an assignment notebook completed and asking questions when unsure of the expectations.
- Use of additional checklists as needed.
- Use of needed assistive devices.
- Completing assignments on time to the best of his ability.

An additional responsibility of the special educator when teaching career/vocational skills is recognition that a variety of vocations and skills are present in the community. If academics, per se, are not an area in which students excel, other exploratory or training opportunities should be provided. Such opportunities might include art, music, culinary arts, childcare, technical, or building instruction. These skills can often be included (although not to the exclusion of additional programs) within the academic setting. For example, a student with a strong vocation interest in art may be asked to create a poster to show learned information in a science or social studies unit. While addressing a career/vocational interest and skill this way, the teacher would also be establishing a program of differentiated instruction.

Skill 7.06 Recognizing strategies and techniques for ensuring the efficient and effective use of instructional time

Schedule development depends upon the type of class (elementary or secondary) and the setting (regular classroom or resource room). There are, however, general rules of thumb that apply to both types and settings:

1. Allow time for transitions, planning, and setups.
2. Aim for maximum instructional time by pacing the instruction quickly and allotting time for practice of the new skills.
3. Proceed from short assignments to long ones, breaking up long lessons or complex tasks into short sessions or step-by-step instruction.
4. Follow a less-preferred academic or activity with a highly-preferred academic or activity.
5. In settings where students are working on individualized plans, do not schedule all the students at once in activities that require a great deal of teacher assistance. For example, have some students work on math or spelling while the teacher works with the students in reading, which usually requires more teacher involvement.
6. Break up a longer segment into several smaller segments with a variety of activities.

Special Considerations for Elementary Classrooms

1. Determine the amount of time that is needed for activities such as P.E., lunch, or recess.
2. Allow about 15 to 20 minutes each for opening and closing exercises. Spend this time for "housekeeping" activities, such as collecting lunch money, going over the schedule, cleaning up, reviewing the day's activities, and getting ready to go home.
3. Schedule academics for periods when the students are more alert and motivated, usually in the afternoon.
4. Build in time for slower students to finish their work; others may work at learning centers or other activities of interest. Allowing extra time gives the teacher time to give more attention where it is needed, conduct assessments, or for students to complete or correct work.

Special Considerations for Secondary Classes

Secondary school days are usually divided into five, six, or seven periods of about 50 minutes, with time for homeroom and lunch. Students cannot stay behind and finish their work since they have to leave for a different room. Resource room time should be scheduled so that the student does not miss academic instruction in his classroom or miss desirable nonacademic activities. In schools where ESE teachers also co-teach or work with students in the regular classroom, the regular teacher will have to coordinate lesson plans with those of the Special Education Teacher. Consultation time will also have to be budgeted into the schedule.

(Please see skill 6.01 for more time management strategies.)

Skill 7.07 Demonstrating knowledge of methods for preparing and organizing materials to implement daily lesson plans

It is essential to use the school system's course of study and the student's IEP to prepare and organize materials to implement daily lesson plans. IEPs have to demonstrate that the student is working on goals as close to their general education peers as possible. Therefore, the school system's course of study should be a document used to create the annual goals of the IEP. The materials gathered should be adapted to fit the needs of each student, or specially-designed materials should be purchased.

(Please refer to skill 8.03 to review ways to adapt materials.)

The IEP must also include any assistive technology that may be needed for the student to be successful. The teacher must gather the necessary technology before planning a lesson. Please refer to skill 8.06 to learn about different kinds of assistive technology.

The organization of materials should be based on the lessons plans. Assistive technology will usually be used all year long. Therefore, if it needs to be purchased, it should be purchased as early in the year as possible. Other materials may be gathered and prepared a few days in advance, ensuring classroom time will not be wasted while gathering materials.

Skill 7.08 Demonstrating understanding of language diversity and various communication styles and modes in planning effective instruction for students with disabilities

The average classroom today is composed of several different cultures. Your understanding of your students' actions and the manner in which you communicate with them now requires your foresight into what cultural influences your students bring with them to the classroom. Knowledge of these areas will help you to serve as both an advocate and interpreter for the student who may appear "odd" when he/she is only doing what is expected in his/her culture. This is especially true for those who are new to the country or are in the elementary level.

It is possible that the next students in your classroom may be Vietnamese, and you may begin to think they are polite, but slow learners, because they are quiet and do not take part in classroom discussions. Your impression would be different if you had learned that children in Vietnam believe their teachers are never wrong; they are taught through rote memorization, and classroom discussion/open participation is a foreign concept to them.

Unfortunately, some teachers may think that students of a certain culture learn slower in one area, while misunderstanding the fact that they may learn differently. Therefore, it may be important to compliment your instruction with peer tutoring so sharing of their different cultural strengths may build a unique opportunity for both cultures to grow side by side.

Recognition of cultural differences allows the teacher to build on different cultural strengths at opportune times. This may also give culturally-aware teachers the ability to soar above others in their teaching environment.

COMPETENCY 0008 UNDERSTAND PRINCIPLES AND METHODS INVOLVED IN INDIVIDUALIZING INSTRUCTION FOR STUDENTS WITH DISABILITIES.

Skill 8.01 Demonstrating an understanding of effective collaboration among teachers and other professionals to individualize instruction in a variety of inclusive models (e.g., co-teaching, push-in, consultant teaching [CT]

(Please refer to Skill 7.01.)

Skill 8.02 Applying techniques for planning, adapting, and sequencing instruction to meet IEP goals and objectives

In order to assist students in meeting their IEP goals and objectives, teachers must organize effective learning environments by creating and utilizing appropriate techniques for designing physical environments to meet individual needs and provide instruction of IEP objectives within natural occurring routines.

Teachers must plan instruction with the ultimate goal in mind of having their students master their IEP goals and objectives. It is important that the curriculum is modified in such a manner that individual IEP goals can be taught and that students with similar abilities are grouped together so that they can be taught the same material if their IEP goals are similar.

The instruction should be given in a sequential manner so that specific skills that must be mastered first are taught first.

The goals and objectives in the student's IEP should focus on the skills and behaviors the student needs to learn in order to be involved in and progress in the general curriculum. The goals and objectives should reflect special education. For students who are at transition age, goals and objectives should reflect skills that the student is lacking in. The goals in the IEP are statements that describe what the student can reasonably be expected to accomplish within a 12-month period of time. The components of a goal statement should include the skill or behavior that needs to be changed, the direction of the change, and the anticipated annual ending level of performance.

Skill 8.03 Demonstrating knowledge of instructional and remedial methods, techniques, and materials used to address individual students' learning styles, strengths, and needs

(Please refer to **Skill 5.03** to read about remedial methods and materials used to address individual students' learning styles, strengths, and needs. Please refer to **Skill 7.02** to read about instructional techniques used to address individual students' learning styles, strengths, and needs. **Skill 4.05** would also be a helpful skill to read.)

Skill 8.04 **Recognizing how cultural perspectives influence the relationship among families, schools, and communities, as related to effective instruction for students with disabilities**

The teacher should be familiar with the effects of cultural stereotypes and racism on the development of students with disabilities. The teacher should know that variations in beliefs, traditions, and values exist across and within cultures. Teachers should also be familiar with the characteristics and biases of their own cultures and how these biases can impact their teaching, behavior, and communication.

The teacher should include multicultural perspectives in his lessons and convey to students how knowledge is developed from the vantage point of a particular culture.

Educators need to ensure they demonstrate positive regard for the culture, religion, gender, and varying abilities of students and their families. This should include showing sensitivity to students with different cultural and ethnic backgrounds when designing the curriculum.

Teachers who use themes with a multicultural perspective should ensure that they are not teaching material that could be considered culturally insensitive or offensive.

For professional development training programs to be successful, it is crucial that teachers develop an in-depth understanding of the influence of culture and language on students' academic performance to differentiate between genuine learning problems and cultural differences.

Culturally-sensitive teaching creates a helpful, receptive, and enriched educational setting that permits each student to feel comfortable as they look at their attitudes and share their thoughts.

As members of a culturally-pluralistic society, students and educators must develop healthy and open-minded attitudes and interpersonal skills to communicate and collaborate across cultures and to function successfully in many situations.

Multiculturalism is for all students and teachers because in unbiased classrooms, students hear the voices of a variety of different cultural groups. This enables students to be able to understand the world from multiple ethnic and cultural perspectives, instead of just agreeing with the point of view of the mainstream culture.

Skill 8.05   Recognizing effective strategies for involving the individual and family in setting instructional goals and charting progress

Involving the special education student (when appropriate) and his family in setting instructional goals is necessary to develop a well-rounded IEP. When families help set goals for things that are important to the special education student, subsequent increased family cooperation and involvement are usually evident. Typically, the parent of the child knows the child best, so meshing the school goals and those of the family will provide a program that is most thorough in meeting the student's needs.

Progress on these mutually-accepted goals, as well as those initiated by the school, can be charted or measured in a variety of ways. The methods used to track the goals should be those indicated in the goals and objectives section of the IEP.

Charting is a formal tracking method of student behavior and progress. Often based on a functional behavioral assessment portion of the IEP, the chart will include behaviors (positive or negative), the time covered, and frequency of the behavior, which is often shown with tally marks.

Anecdotal Records are a journaling of behaviors observed in the home or classroom. Such records may be notes kept by the classroom teacher or therapist or notes from the parent (often literally in the form of paper notes, passbook entries, or emails) regarding student success and challenges.

Observations are a more focused form of anecdotal records when a specific activity, class, or time period is observed, and the behaviors and skills of the individual student are recorded. Often, a comparison of student behavior in various settings gives information needed to write appropriate IEP goals.

Rating Scales are frequently used to assess a student's behavior or level of functioning in a particular environment (home, classroom, or playground). Often, these scales are given to more than one person (parent, teacher, and therapist) to complete so that a more comprehensive picture of the student is obtained.

Commonly used rating scales containing a component for professionals and parents include the Conners' Rating Scale, the Vineland Adaptive Behavior Scale, and the Child Development Inventory.

Informal Tests are ways of tracking a student's behaviors through the use of classroom tests and assignments in various subject areas.

Formal Tests may include standardized tests that are administered to all students at the local and state levels, alternative assessments as indicated on the child's IEP, and tests used by a Psychologist or therapist to assess skills and deficiencies. Formal testing results give measurable data, which can be used in school-parent discussions for planning IEP goals and objectives.

Skill 8.06   Demonstrating knowledge of assistive and instructional technologies for students with disabilities (e.g., alternative input and output devices)

Assistive Devices

Sensory Impairments: Vision and Hearing

The use of electronic devices is nothing new to persons with vision and hearing impairments. For many years, people with sensory impairments have utilized various kinds of technologies to help them learn and function in society (Smith & Luckasson, 1992).

Other technology users who have and continue to benefit from modern scientific advances are those with physical and health impairments and speech/communication disorders. Though the assistive devices are presented in categories, overlap occurs. For example, communication boards can be used to facilitate sound and communication, physical conditions, and when in raised symbols, can also facilitate visually-impaired persons. Computers and television screens can be adapted to assist persons with visual, auditory, physical, and speech/communication problems.

Visual Impairments

Visual Aids. For those with visual disorders, the Laser Cane and Sonicguide are two examples of electronic devices that have been in use for some time. These devices operate on the principle that people can learn to locate objects by hearing their echoes. For instance, the Laser Cane emits three beams of infrared light (one up, one down, and one straight ahead) that are converted into sound when they strike objects in the path of the person. The Sonicguide functions as an ultrasonic aid that helps youngsters born blind to gain an awareness of their environment and the objects in it. The device is worn on the head, emits ultrasound, and converts reflections from objects into audible sounds.

A newly developed machine, the Personal Companion, can respond to human voice and answer with synthesized voice. It can look up someone's telephone number from an internal directory and dial the telephone. Even though it cannot write a check, it can balance someone's checkbook. The Personal Companion can "read" aloud sections from a morning newspaper delivered through telecommunications over telephone lines. This machine can maintain a daily appointment book and turn on and off appliances such as radio or lights.

Advances in computer technology are providing access to printed information for many people with visual impairments. Books are available on computer disks, allowing for a variety of outputs: voice, enlarged print, and Braille.

Organizations, such as the Visually Impaired and Blind User Group (VIBUG) of the Boston Computer Society are exchanging information to expand computer literacy among persons with visual impairments (Smith & Luckasson, 1992). Personal computers with special printers can transform print to Braille. By attaching a specially-designed Braille printer to a computer, standard text can be converted into Braille, allowing teachers to produce copies of handouts, worksheets, tests, maps, charts, and other class materials in Braille.

Closed-Circuit Television (CCTV) can be used to enlarge the print found in printed texts and books. By using a small television camera with a zoom lens and a sliding reading stand upon which the printed materials are placed, the greatly enlarged printed material can be viewed on a television monitor. All types of printed materials can be enlarged, such as magazines, textbooks, and photocopied handouts.

Computers with special word processing programs can produce large print displays that enable persons to adjust the size of the print with their visual capabilities. Not only can different size print be selected for individual students on the viewing monitor, but hard copy printouts can be printed in different sizes for individual uses.

Computers are also useful for Braille conversion to print. Students can type in Braille and the computer will convert the Braille into English print for the teachers, etc. who interact with the student. PCs not Macs are the chosen style of computers as PCs allow for more than one key to work as a function. At times 6 keys at a time need to be used for a function.

Audio Aids. Talking books have been available through the Library of Congress since 1934, using specially designed record players and tape cassette machines developed by the American Printing House for the Blind. Regional resource and materials centers disseminate these records, tapes, and machines. Audiotape versions of many classic books and current best-sellers are available in most bookstores.

Newly devised systems that allow printed materials to be synthesized into speech are available. They can be purchased at a much lower cost and with higher quality sound than older devices such as the Kurzwell Reader. One of these newer systems uses a small sensor attached to a computer. When the sensor is moved along a line of type, information is passed to the computer, which in turn translates the print to speech. The person listening can select how fast he/she wants the speech to be delivered (rate), the pitch, and the gender of the voice/sound the computer generates. This enables students with visual impairments to use the same books and materials as their regular classmates. They do not have to wait for orders to be prepared or mailed to them.
For those who listen to television but cannot see what is happening, new technology is being piloted at the present time which adds a soundtrack. By using the added soundtrack available in stereo televisions, descriptive videos tell the listener the nonverbal messages others see on the screen.

Hearing Impairments

Visual Aids. Telecommunications and alerting devices are two types of assistive devices that use sight and touch. Captions are like subtitles that appear at the bottom of a television screen that can be read. Open captions appear on the screen for all viewers to see (e.g., foreign films translations) and have been available for some time. Closed captions are relatively new and are somewhat expensive. In this system, captions can be seen on the screen only if a decoder is accessible.

The Telecommunication Device for the Deaf (TDD) enables persons who have hearing impairments to make and receive telephone calls. A teletypewriter connected to the telephone prints out a voice message. The teletypewriter can also print out messages, but the receiver must have a teletypewriter as well in order to do this. A TDD can be used in a relay system, where the operator places the call on a voice line and reads the typed message to the non-TDD user. A full conversation can be made using a relay system (Smith & Luckasson, 1992).

DeafNet and Disabilities Forum are computer networks that provide electronic mail for persons with hearing impairments. These network systems function like other kinds of electronic mail where individuals or groups can subscribe to a communication system that transfers printed messages to subscribers. Electronic mail enables individuals and groups with common interests to communicate by using computers and information sent by telephone lines.

Audio Aids. Hearing aids and other equipment that help people make better use of their residual hearing are referred to as assistive listening devices (ALDs). For those with hearing impairments, the hearing aid is the most commonly used electronic device. Other types of ALDs help individuals with hearing impairments use their residual hearing.

Hearing aids differ in size, cost, and efficiency. Types range from wearable hearing aids to group auditory training units that can be used by several children at the same time. Wearable hearing aids can be inserted into the external auditory canal, built into glasses, and worn behind glasses, behind the ear, and on clothing.

FM (frequency-modulated) transmission devices (auditory trainers) are used in some classrooms by teachers and students. To use an auditory trainer, the teacher speaks into a microphone, and the sound is received directly by each student's receiver or hearing aid. This system reduces background noise, allows teachers to move freely around the room, and helps students benefit more from lectures.

The audio loop is an ALD that directs sound from its source directly to the listener's ear through a specially-equipped hearing aid or earphone. Sound travels through a wire connection or by radio waves. Audio loops can be built into the walls of a classroom or some smaller area like a conference room.

Physical and Health Impairments

Technology has helped individuals with physical and health impairments to gain access to and control the environment around them, communicate with others, and take advantage of health care. There are high-tech devices, such as computers, but also low-tech devices like built-up spoons and crutches. Electric typewriters, computer keyboards, and automated language boards provide means for communication to occur.

Mobility has been assisted by use of lightweight or electric specialized wheelchairs. These include motorized chairs, computerized chairs, chairs in which it is possible to rise, wilderness sports chairs, and racing chairs (Smith & Luckasson, 1992). Electronic switches allow persons with only partial movement (e.g., head, neck, fingers, toes) to be more mobile. Even driving a car is possible.

Mobility is also enhanced by use of artificial limbs, personalized equipped vans, and electrical walking machines. Myoelectric (or bionic) limbs contain a sensor that picks up electric signals transmitted from the person's brain through the limb. Robotic arms can manipulate objects by at least three directional movements: extension/retraction, swinging/rotating, and elevation/depression. Manipulator robots can assist by dialing a telephone, turning book pages, and drinking from a cup.

Speech/Communication

A communication board is a flat surface on which words, pictures, or both can be placed. The student is encouraged to point to the symbols of what he or she wants to communicate. Simple boards can be made from magazine or newspaper pictures. Others can be written on to display messages. More sophisticated boards incorporate an attachment that synthesizes a "voice." Communication books function like a board and assist communication.

Media Equipment

Many types of media equipment are available for use in the classroom. Multidimensional teaching approaches are possible with machines that provide instruction through various sensory modality channels. Individual receptive strengths can be matched with equipment directing learning through visual, auditory, haptic, or multidimensional input channels.

The <u>CD Player</u> is particularly of benefit to students who learn best by auditory input. Both frequently accompany commercial instructional programs (e.g., reading kits, programmed workbooks) and can be operated by students trained to do so. Both can accommodate earphones or headsets for single or group listening opportunities.

CD players offer the additional benefit of being lightweight for transporting relatively inexpensive, and adaptable for recording information or responses by teachers or students. Teacher recorded CDs offer the opportunity for students to read along with or follow story sequences with accompanying pictures, listen to stories for pleasure, practice spelling words, and learn to follow instructions. They can also be used to answer comprehension questions, discriminate auditory sounds, perform word study exercises, and in general, maintain and motivate student interest.

Media such as <u>VCRs. DVDs, and Television </u>provide unlimited opportunities for visual and auditory input. Equipment of this type offer the capability of presenting instructional content to individuals or groups of students in a format that readers and nonreaders alike can understand. Special effects (e.g., flashbacks, fades, close-ups, quick and slow pans) can be obtained by use of videocassettes. Selected pauses and review of material are easily achieved by means of filmstrips and videocassettes.

CCTV, a special television programs, and VHS and DVDs are often used to supplement and to enhance instructional material already introduced. On occasion, instructional material is introduced by these means. Reinforcement may also be delivered through the showing of entertaining visual material.

Dependent on your schools policies, students may be allowed to go to a media center and view a video for pleasure. Another alternative is to show a part of a selected video and ask students to hypothesize what preceded the viewed portion, or what followed the action they saw. Students can be asked to write a narrative for a film which they have only seen in silence. A videocassette dealing with a social problem can be stopped before the solutions are offered; students may offer their own solutions. A videocassette portraying a dramatic story can be ended prematurely. Students are directed to write endings and act them out.

The Overhead Projector (OVH) is an easy-to-use and maintain visual communication device. A bright lamp source transmits light through the translucent material to a screen close to the machine. Transparencies can be purchased commercially or made from clear photocopies of materials.

Computers and Software

PCs and Macs are valuable teaching tools. Software programs and adaptations enable learners with disabilities (i.e., physical, cognitive, and sensory) to profit from instruction in the classroom which they might not be able to receive otherwise. For example, tutorial programs simulate the teaching function of presentations, questions, and feedback. By this means, children are provided learning exercises on an appropriate level of difficulty, and in an interesting manner. Other programs can be used which allow drill and practice (with correct answers shown) over previously learned material. Games are effective as motivators and reinforcers. In addition, use of computer software provides a way of testing students that is more appealing to many than a written test.

Teachers can acquire the skills needed to program the computer so that tasks provided by software correspond with students' individualized education programs. Teaching students to program will develop problem-solving and discovery skills, and also foster reasoning comprehension skills.

Stages of Learning

Suggestions about selecting and using software were given by Male (1994). First, make sure there is a curriculum correspondence between what students are working on at their desks and what they do at the computers. This should follow what he calls stages of learning. Then, make certain the students proceed through the five stages of learning. Software should be selected with these stages in mind:

1. Acquisition: Introduction of a new skill.
2. Proficiency: Practice under supervision to achieve accuracy and speed.
3. Maintenance: Continued practice without further instruction.
4. Generalization: Application of the new skills in new settings and situations.

5. <u>Adaptation</u>: Modifications of the task to meet new needs and demands of varying situations.

Computer-Assisted Instruction

Computers are used to provide a safe, stimulating learning environment for many youth. The computer does not evaluate or offer subjective opinions about the student's work. It merely provides feedback about the correctness or incorrectness of each answer in a series. The computer is like an effective teacher by the way in which it:

1. Provides immediate attention and feedback.
2. Individualizes to the particular skill level.
3. Allows students to work at their own pace.
4. Makes corrections quickly.
5. Produces a professional looking product.
6. Keeps accurate records on correct and error rates.
7. Ignores inappropriate behavior.
8. Focuses on the particular response.
9. Is nonjudgmental. (Smith & Luckasson, 1992)

Computers are useful in helping to teach traditional academic subjects like math, reading, spelling, geography, and science. Effective teachers allow for drill and practice on the computer, monitor student progress, and reinforce appropriately. When students have mastered a particular level, these teachers help them to progress to another level. Reasoning and problem-solving are other skill areas which teachers have discovered can be taught using computers.

Today teachers utilize the Internet as a mode for students to research topics. Providing students opportunities to learn by doing research and creating a PowerPoint to share what they learned can take away some of the fear students have with presenting in front of a crowd. When students are given assignments like this it is best to provide them with a list of sites on a sheet of paper, or by Social Bookmarking that will keep them on task.

Teachers are also placing class work and homework assignments Online. EdVideo.com is just one of many sources that exist to provide a medium for teachers to create online class work. NYLearns is another resource teachers are using to post class work and homework assignments.

Computer games can enhance learning skills and provide a highly-desired reinforcement opportunity. When played alone, the games serve as leisure activities for the individual. When played with classmates, the games can help develop interpersonal relationships. This is particularly applicable to youngsters with behavioral disorders, and with learning and intellectual disabilities, as well as those without any identified disability.

Word Processors

Word processors are used to assist students with written composition. Students with learning disabilities often have difficulty organizing thoughts. Problems with writing are compounded by handwriting difficulties. Many teachers report that use of a word processor has enabled them to motivate students to write. Most are less resistant to rewriting texts when they can do it on a word processing program that erases and replaces text quickly. Printed texts in typewritten form are easier to read. Spelling checkers, built into many word processing programs, assist those who may not be able to spell words correctly. Another option is a thesaurus, which provides synonyms, and in so doing, helps to build vocabulary. The overall quantity and quality of written work improves when word processing programs are used in conjunction with computers.

When working on the word processor, each student needs a data disk so that his work can be evaluated over time and stored electronically. Having a portfolio of printouts enables students to take work home to show parents.

Process Approach

The process approach to writing is encouraged, especially when using a word processor (Male, 1994). These stages include planning/prewriting, drafting, revising/editing, and sharing/publication. Progressing through these stages is particularly helpful to developing writers.

The planning stage is characterized by written outlines, brainstorming, clustering or mind mapping, and lists of ideas, themes, or key words. These activities are ideally suited to a classroom that has a large television monitor or a computer projection device that will allow the teacher to list, group, revise, and expand ideas as students share them. Printed copies of what was generated by the group can be distributed at the end of the class session.

In the **drafting stage**, individuals can do draft work at a computer by themselves, or they can collaborate as a group on the work. Some students may choose to use pencil and paper to do initial draft work, or they may want to dictate stories to the teacher or another student who writes them down for them.

Students share their work during the **revising/editing stage**. Students read their stories aloud to a partner, a small group, or the whole class. Classmates are instructed to ask questions and give feedback that will help the writer make revisions to his work. After the story has been completed content wise, attention is given to mechanics and writing conventions.

The **sharing/publication stage** enables students to experience being authors responding to an audience. Students are encouraged to share their work by reading it aloud and in printed form. They can do this with or without graphics or illustrations.

Skill 8.07 **Demonstrating an understanding of effective collaboration among teachers and other professionals to facilitate students' use and independent management of assistive technologies in various settings**

Determination of Student Need for Assistive Technology

Often, the special educator will identify the need for consultation or testing in an area that a student is having difficulty. Testing, or other professional evaluation, may result in the trial or ongoing use of some form of assistive technology as listed on the student's IEP.

Development of Student Skill Using Specific Assistive Technology

Students who have been identified as needing assistive technology require training in the use of the equipment. Sometimes a therapist or consultant will "push in" to the classroom, providing training for the student in the classroom setting. Other times, the student will practice using the assistive technology in a separate setting until a level of experience/expertise is reached. Then the assistive technology may be used in the special education or inclusion classroom.

Learn more about available Assistive Technologies: http://www.abilityhub.com

Communication of Expected Skill Level in the Classroom

As students begin to use assistive technology in the classroom, the desired use (including activity, location, and time) should be outlined for the special educator so that misunderstanding does not result in a student misusing or under using the technology. The student, then, will have a level of accountability and be functioning to the best of his abilities.

Training of School Personnel on Use of Assistive Technology

Although special educators are often trained in using a variety of assistive devices, advances in technology make it necessary for professionals to participate in ongoing training for new or unfamiliar equipment. This training may be conducted by a knowledgeable therapist or consultant in the school district, or school personnel may need to attend a workshop off campus.

Evaluation of Student Independent Management of Assistive Technology in Various Settings

Ongoing evaluation of the student's use of the equipment is vital. This may be monitored through observation by the therapist or consultant, anecdotal records of the special educator, or some type of checklist. Often, an IEP goal will address how the use and evaluation of the student's performance with the equipment will be implemented.

COMPETENCY 0009 UNDERSTAND STRATEGIES AND TECHNIQUES USED TO PROMOTE STUDENTS' LANGUAGE ARTS SKILLS IN A VARIETY OF SETTINGS.

Skill 9.01 Identify types and characteristics of language arts difficulties associated with various disabilities.

Written expression is one of the highest forms of communication. It reflects a person's level of comprehension, concept development, and abstraction (Mercer & Mercer, 1993). Handwriting is primarily a visual-motor process that includes the writing or copying of word forms, whereas written expression reflects a person's cognitive abilities.

Prerequisite to developing skills in written expression is the need for experiences in listening, reading, spelling, handwriting, and oral expression. Activities in written expression should begin as early as kindergarten and first grade, with skills developed concurrently with prerequisite experiences. Typically, problems in written expression are not identified until the upper elementary grade levels, when the student is required to use language arts skills in written composition.

Problems in written expression can be diagnosed by the teacher through formal and informal means. Written expression produces a tangible product that may be evaluated by the teacher using a criterion-referenced tool. Students with deficits in reading and spelling typically exhibit difficulties in written expression. Particular areas of difficulty include limited vocabulary, immature topic selections, spelling errors, inaccurate syntax, poor organization of thoughts, and obvious stylistic errors. Inadequate cognitive abilities and grammatical inaccuracies may be detected. Children who are lacking in the development of comprehension skills may be unable to reflect upon the subject and use reasoning skills in the development of content. Likewise, children with hyperactive or impulsive traits are often unable to focus upon details of content and subdivide materials. Deficits may be identified at any point where visual, motor, and cognitive abilities come into play in the production of written expression.

Instruction in written expression should culminate in independently-written prose by students. Teacher prompting and feedback will vary, based on the degree of dependency individual students exhibit. For example, the language experience approach, largely a teacher-directed group (although sometimes individual) activity, is typically used as a form of initial instruction in written expression. The benefit of this activity is in the development of a topic of high interest, the use of students' thoughts and the students' speaking vocabularies, and, of course, the immediate prompting and feedback of an encouraging and motivating nature from the teacher.

Skill 9.02 Demonstrating familiarity with a range of approaches to language arts instruction that meet the needs of students with disabilities

Beginning Reading Approaches

Methods of teaching beginning reading skills may be divided into two major approaches—code emphasis and meaning emphasis. Both approaches have their supporters and their critics. Advocates of code emphasis instruction point out that reading fluency depends on accurate and automatic decoding skills, while advocates of meaning emphasis favor this approach for reading comprehension. Teachers may decide to blend aspects of both approaches to meet the individual needs of their students.

Bottom-up or Code-Emphasis Approach
- Letter-sound regularity is stressed.
- Reading instruction begins with words that consist of letter or letter combinations that have the same sound in different words. Component letter-sound relationships are taught and mastered before introducing new words.
- Examples—phonics, linguistic, modified alphabet, and programmed reading series, such as the Merrill Linguistic Reading Program and DISTAR Reading.

Top-down or Meaning-Emphasis Model
- Reading for meaning is emphasized from the first stages of instruction.
- Programs begin with words that appear frequently, which are assumed to be familiar and easy to learn. Words are identified by examining meaning and position in context and are decoded by techniques such as context, pictures, initial letters and word configurations. Thus, a letter may not necessarily have the same sound in different words throughout the passage.
- Examples: Whole language, language experience, and individualized reading programs.

Other approaches that follow beginning reading instruction are available to help teachers design reading programs. Choice of approach will depend on the students' strengths and weaknesses. No matter what approach or combination of approaches is used, the teacher should encourage independent reading and build activities into the reading program that stimulate students to practice their skills through independent reading.

Developmental Reading Approaches

Developmental reading programs emphasize daily, sequential instruction. Instructional materials usually feature a series of books, often basal readers, as the core of the program.

Basal Reading

Basal reader series form the core of many widely-used reading programs from pre-primers to eighth grade. Depending on the series, basal readers may be meaning-emphasis or code-emphasis. Teacher manuals provide a highly-structured and comprehensive scope and sequence, lesson plans, and objectives. Vocabulary is controlled from level to level, and reading skills cover word recognition, word attack, and comprehension.

Advantages of basal readers are the structured, sequential manner in which reading is taught. The teacher manuals have teaching strategies, controlled vocabulary, assessment materials, and objectives. Reading instruction is in a systematic, sequential, and comprehension-oriented manner.

Many basal reading programs recommend the directed reading activity procedure for lesson presentation. Students proceed through the steps of motivation preparation for the new concepts and vocabulary, guided reading, and answering questions that give a purpose or goal for the reading, development of strengths through drills or workbooks, application of skills, and evaluation.

A variation of the directed reading method is direct reading-thinking, where the student must generate the purposes for reading the selection, form questions, and read the selection. After reading, the teacher asks questions designed to get the group to think of answers and to justify their answers.

A disadvantage of basal readers is the emphasis on teaching to a group rather than to the individual. Critics of basal readers also claim that the structure may limit creativity and not provide enough instruction on organizational skills and reading for secondary content levels. Basal readers, however, offer the advantage of a prepared comprehensive program and may be supplemented with other materials to meet individual needs.

Phonics Approach

Word recognition is taught through grapheme-phoneme associations, with the goal of teaching the student to independently apply these skills to new words. Phonics instruction may be synthetic or analytic. In the synthetic method, letter sounds are learned before the student goes on to blend the sounds to form words. The analytic method teaches letter sounds as integral parts of words. The sounds are usually taught in the sequence: vowels, consonants, consonant blends at the beginning of words (e.g., bl and dr), and consonant blends at the end of words (e.g., ld and mp), consonant and vowel digraphs (e.g., ch and sh) and diphthongs (e.g., au and oy).

Critics of the phonics approach point out that the emphasis on pronunciation may lead to the student focusing more on decoding than comprehension. Some students may have trouble blending sounds to form words, and others may become confused with words that do not conform to the phonetic "rules".

However, advocates of phonics say that the programs are useful with remedial reading and developmental reading. Examples of phonics series are *Science Research Associates, Merrill Phonics,* and DML's *Cove School Reading Program.*

Linguistics Approach

In many programs, the whole-word approach is used. This means that words are taught in families as a whole (e.g., cat, hat, pat, and rat). The focus is on words instead of isolated sounds. Words are chosen on the basis of similar spelling patterns, and irregular spelling words are taught as sight words. Examples of programs using this approach are *SRA Basic Reading Series* and *Miami Linguistic Readers* by D.C. Heath.

Some advantages of this approach are that the student learns that reading is talk written down and develops a sense of sentence structure. The consistent visual patterns of the lessons guide students from familiar words to less familiar words to irregular words. Reading is taught by associating with the student's natural knowledge of his own language. Disadvantages are extremely controlled vocabulary, in which word-by-word reading is encouraged. Others criticize the programs for the emphasis on auditory memory skills and the use of nonsense words in the practice exercises.

Whole Language Approach

In the whole language approach, reading is taught as a holistic, meaning-oriented activity and is not broken down into a collection of skills. This approach relies heavily on literature or printed matter selected for a particular purpose. Reading is taught as part of a total language arts program, and the curriculum seeks to develop instruction in real problems and ideas. Two examples of whole language programs are *Learning Through Literature* (Dodds and Goodfellow) and *Victory!* (Brigance). Phonics is not taught in a structured, systematic way. Students are assumed to develop their phonetic awareness through exposure to print. Writing is taught as a complement to reading. Writing centers are often part of this program, as students learn to write their own stories and read them back or follow along with an audiotape of a book while reading along with it.

While the integration of reading with writing is an advantage of the whole language approach, the approach has been criticized for the lack of direct instruction in specific skill strategies. When working with students with learning problems, instruction that is more direct may be needed to learn the word-recognition skills necessary for achieving comprehension of the text.

Language Experience Approach

The language experience approach is similar to whole language in that reading is considered as a personal act, literature is emphasized, and students are encouraged to write about their own life experiences. The major difference is that written language is considered a secondary system to oral language, while whole language treats the two as parts of the same structure. The language experience approach is used primarily for use with beginner readers but can also be used for corrective instruction with older elementary and with other older students. Reading skills are developed, along with listening, speaking and writing skills. The materials consist, for the most part, of the student's skills. The philosophy of language experience includes:

- What students think about, they can talk about.
- What students say, they can write or have someone write.
- What students write or have someone write for them, they can read.

Students dictate a story to a teacher as a group activity. Ideas for stories can originate from student artwork, news items, or personal experiences, or they may be creative. Topic lists, word cards, or idea lists can also be used to generate topics or ideas for a class story. The teacher writes down the stories in a first draft, and the students read them back. The language patterns come from the students, and they read their own written thoughts. The teacher provides guidance on word choice, sentence structure, and the sounds of the letters and words. The students edit and revise the story on an experience chart. The teacher provides specific instruction in grammar, sentence structure, and spelling, if the need arises, rather than using a specified schedule. As the students progress, they create their individual storybooks, adding illustrations if they wish. The storybooks are placed in folders to share with others. Progress is evaluated in terms of the changes in the oral and written expression, as well as in mechanics. There is no set method of evaluating student progress. That is one disadvantage of the language experience approach. However, the emphasis on student experience and creativity stimulates interest and motivates the students.

Individualized Reading Approach

Students select their own reading materials from a variety, according to interest and ability, and they are more able to progress at their own individual rates. Word recognition and comprehension are taught as the student needs them. The teacher's role is to diagnose errors and prescribe materials although the final choice is made by the students. Individual work may be supplemented by group activities with basal readers and workbooks for specific reading skills. The lack of systematic checks and developmental skills and emphasis on self-learning may be a disadvantage for students with learning problems.

Skill 9.03 **Demonstrate knowledge of principles of and methods for assessing and developing students' reading and other language arts skills.**

Most reading programs conceptually separate the reading process into three major categories: sight word vocabulary, word attack skills, and comprehension. These three areas constitute the basic questions that should be asked by a teacher when assessing a student's current level of functioning. From answers obtained, the pertinent questions are:

1. How large is the student's sight word vocabulary?
2. What kinds of word attack skills does the student employ?
3. How well developed are the student's comprehension skills?

Sight words are printed words that are easily identified by the learner. The selection of words to be learned will rely to some extent on the age and abilities of the student. Primary age students will use word lists composed of high-frequency words like basal readers and Dolch Word Lists.

Word attack skills are those techniques that enable a student to decode an unknown word, so he can pronounce and understand it in the right context. Word attack skills are included in the areas of phonics, structural analysis, contextual and configuration clues, and decoding.

Comprehension skills are categorized into levels of difficulty. The teacher should consider the following factors when analyzing a student's reading comprehension level (Schloss & Sedlak, 1986):

1. The past experience of the reader.
2. The content of the written passage.
3. The syntax of the written passage.
4. The vocabulary used in the written passage.
5. The oral language comprehension of the student.
6. The questions being asked to assess comprehension.

The major categories of reading skills, basic reading skills within these categories, and strategies for the development of each are listed. Suggestions for assisting the reader in improving silent and oral reading skills are given. Some skills overlap categories.

Comprehension involves understanding what is read regardless of the purpose or thinking skills employed. Comprehension can be delineated into categories of differentiated skills. Benjamin Bloom's taxonomy includes: knowledge, comprehension, application, analysis, synthesis, and evaluation. Thomas Barrett suggests that comprehension categories be classified as: literal meaning, reorganization, inference, evaluation, and appreciation. An overview of comprehension skills is presented in Skill 4 in this section. Strategies that might prove beneficial in strengthening a student's comprehension involve:

1. Asking questions of the student before he reads a passage. This type of directed reading activity assists the student in focusing attention on the information in the text that will help him to answer the questions.
2. Using teacher questions to assist the student in developing self-questioning skills covering all levels of comprehension.

Silent and Oral Reading Skills

Silent reading refers to the inaudible reading of words or passages. Since the reading act is one on a covert basis, the accuracy of the reading process can only be inferred through questions or activities required of the student following his reading. What may be observed is attention given to the printed material, the eye movements, an indication of relative pace, and body language signifying frustration or ease of reading. Strategies that might assist the child in reading silently are:

1. Preparing activities or questions pertaining to the printed passage. Vary the activities so that some are asking specific comprehension questions while others are geared toward creative expression like art and written composition.
2. Allowing time for pleasurable reading, such as through an activity like sustained silent reading.

(Please refer to **previous skills** for more information.)

Skill 9.04   Recognize strategies for promoting students' enjoyment and independent involvement in reading and writing.

Students' Enjoyment and Independent Involvement in Reading

When students are able to independently use reading skills for enjoyment, a key goal of literacy development has been attained. Initially, Special Education Teachers choose books with a high correlation between text and pictures that have been read in class. These may be displayed in a classroom reading area for students to read independently. Note that the emergent reader may, at first, be paraphrasing the story or reciting the words from memory instead of actually reading the words.

Special Education Teachers may also select a set of books from which to choose during library time.

As students progress in reading skills, the special educator changes the materials that are available for the students to read. Typically, material read for enjoyment is at a reading level that is easy for the student so that he maintains interest and effort. Books such as hi/lo (high interest/low reading level) books are often good choices for the student with significant reading delays.

After a certain level of reading is reached, special education students may enjoy participating in reading reward programs such as Accelerated Reader, Reading Counts, Book It, or others through which the child can acquire prizes, fast food coupons, or tickets for theme parks and sporting events. It is the role of the special educator to evaluate if the amount of required reading is realistic for the student with disabilities or if it should be modified per individual needs.

Students with disabilities who also come from diverse cultural or linguistic backgrounds will need materials that are even more specific to their needs. Many publishers now print books with the bilingual child in mind.

In addition to traditional print books, students may be motivated to read classroom magazines or graphic novels independently because of the engaging illustrations and topics. Students with disabilities often enjoy reading text or directions for games and activities on the computer. The typical shortened text for computer materials, graphics, audio components, and interactive features of computer materials appeal to many students with disabilities. Another consideration is box or board games that incorporate reading skills, such Scrabble Jr. and Boggle, Jr.

Schloss, Marriman, and Pfiefer (cited in Schloss & Sedlack, 1986), describe a procedure that systematically and sequentially reduces teacher involvement in written production by students. The procedure calls for these actions by the teacher during the instruction:

1. Present a topic or elicit one from the student.
2. Say each sentence before writing it.
3. Inform the student that spelling assistance will be given if needed.
4. Give the student at least 20 seconds to self-initiate a sentence.
5. Provide a motivational prompt if after 20 seconds a sentence has not been vocalized, such as, "Just try to do your best."
6. Provide a content prompt if after another 20 seconds a sentence has not been vocalized, like, "Write about what the cat did to the dog."
7. Provide a literal prompt if after a third 20-second interval a sentence has not been produced, such as, "Write 'the dog chased the cat up the tree.'"

8. After the student writes a sentence, return to step 4, and repeat the sequence, as needed, while the student is writing the composition.
9. Upon completion of the activity, discuss with the student the number of sentences that were produced at each level.
10. Reinforce the student for producing larger numbers of sentences at levels indicative of greater student independence.

Identify the Sequence of Development of Written Expression Skills

Composition should be taught as a process rather than a product. The first step in learning composition is having access to literature and writing materials. When adults read aloud to children, the children learn about styles of literature and the function of print and pictures in a book. Having access to paper and writing materials gives children opportunities to experiment with drawing and writing. When children enter school, they can learn to write notes, label pictures, and keep journals.

Most of the writing children do at school is business related or transactional writing. Transactional writing includes expository (explaining subjects or procedures), descriptive (helps the reader visualize the topic), or persuasive (explaining a point of view). Students may also do expressive writing or poetic writing, which requires knowledge of formal literary style. Initially, students may be resistant to writing, especially expressive writing, because they may be afraid to show their feelings or make mistakes. Journals are especially helpful to encourage students to practice expressive writing.

Writing should be taught as a process, not a product. Free writing will help reduce writing anxiety. Having children participate in journals and free writing will help build confidence. Writing should be integrated in all subject areas, and the atmosphere should be positive. Writing should be fun and include a variety of types of writing. Children's writing should be shared with others for feedback and enjoyment.

Each phase of the writing process has strategies that help the student develop metacognitive skills and proficiency. Instruction should not just focus on the mechanics (grammar, punctuation, spelling) of writing, but also on developing fluency and positive feelings about the process.

Prewriting: the planning phase. During preplanning, the student must decide on a purpose, find a topic, establish an audience, decide how the paper will be organized, and experiment with ideas. Strategies for generating ideas can be done individually or as a group activity and include:

- Listing
- Brainstorming—gathering ideas about the topic
- Interest inventories
- Free writing

Organizing Content: includes graphic approaches that represent the relationships of ideas visually.
- Mapping
- Webbing
- Clustering

Drafting: In this phase, ideas are developed, and the writer makes connections between the ideas. During this phase, mechanics should not be considered, and the student should not spend too much time in this phase. Learner activities include:
- Focus on the ideas, not the content.
- Consult the teacher or peer about the content.
- Read the piece or a portion to defocus and generate new ideas.

Revising: After the drafts have been written, the student may reorganize ideas, select ideas for further development, and edit the paper for mistakes in grammar and spelling. Sections of the paper may be removed or reorganized. Strategies include:
- Putting the paper aside for a day or two
- Asking the teacher or a peer for feedback
- Using scissors and tape to reorganize sections of the paper
- Using the computer to aid in revision

Final Draft: The write gives the paper a final editing, reads the paper to see that everything makes sense, and makes last corrections before turning the paper in. Some of the things that a student can do to prepare the final draft are:
- Use a checklist to check the final copy for errors.
- Read the story into a tape recorder and play it back with a written copy to listen for grammatical errors and pauses where punctuation marks should be.
- Read the paper one sentence at a time to identify sentence fragments.

(Please refer to skill 6.01 to read about how to employ motivational strategies.)

Skill 9.05 **Apply strategies for promoting students' use of critical-thinking and problem-solving skills in language arts.**

Most educators recognize that comprehension covers a wide continuum of lower-to-higher level thinking skills. The following is one way of displaying the continuum, beginning on the low side of the spectrum:

1. **Literal** indicates an understanding of the primary, direct (literal) meaning of words, sentences, or passages.
2. **Inferential** involves an understanding of the deeper meanings that are not literally stated in a phrase, sentence, or passage.
3. **Evaluation** signifies a judgment made by comparing ideas or information presented in the written passage with other experiences, knowledge, or values.
4. **Appreciation** involves an emotional response to the written selection.

Using Barrett's <u>Taxonomy of Cognitive and Affective Dimensions of Reading Comprehension</u>[1], the teacher can determine the student's level of comprehension and stimulate thinking across a continuum of comprehension levels by asking questions similar to these about the story of *The Three Bears*.

I.   **Literal Comprehension** focuses on ideas and information that are explicitly stated in the selection.

  A. <u>Recognition</u> requires the student to locate or identify ideas or information explicitly stated in the reading selection.

   1. Recognition of details. Where did the three bears live?
   2. Recognition of main ideas. Why did the three bears go out for a walk?
   3. Recognition of sequence. Whose porridge was too hot? Whose porridge did Goldilocks taste first?
   4. Recognition of comparisons. Whose porridge was too hot? Too cold? Just right?
   5. Recognition of cause-and-effect relationships. Why didn't Papa Bear's and Mama Bear's chairs break into pieces like Baby Bear's chair?
   6. Recognition of character traits. Which words can you find to describe Goldilocks?

  In any of the above cases, the teacher may provide the answers herself, or she may state the answer without the question and have the child show her in the pictures, or read in the text, the part of the story pertaining to her statement. The objective is to test the child's literal comprehension and not his memory.

B. Recall requires the student to produce from memory ideas and information explicitly stated in the reading selection.

1. Recall of details. What were the names of the three bears?
2. Recall of main ideas. Why did Goldilocks go into the bears' house?
3. Recall of a sequence. In order, name the things belonging to the three bears that Goldilocks tried.
4. Recall of comparisons. Whose bed was too hard? Too soft? Just right?
5. Recall of cause-and-effect relationships. Why did Goldilocks go to sleep in Baby Bear's bed?
6. Recall of character traits. What words in the story describe each of the three bears?

In the above cases, the teacher does not give the answer unless the student cannot provide it himself. The purpose is to test the child's recall of stated facts.

II. **Reorganization** requires the student to analyze, synthesize, and/or organize ideas or information explicitly stated in the selection.

A. Classifying: List the things Goldilocks discovered to be "just right" in the story.
B. Outlining: Outline each thing Goldilocks tried, whether it was just right or did not suit her.
C. Summarizing: Tell me in just a few sentences what happened in the story.
D. Synthesizing: Predict what other things Goldilocks might have tried if the bears had had a daughter.

III. **Inferential comprehension** is demonstrated by the student when he "uses the ideas and information explicitly stated in the selection, his intuition, and his personal experiences as a basis for conjectures and hypotheses," according to Barrett (cited in Ekwall & Shanker, 1983, p. 67).

A. Inferring supporting details. Why do you think Goldilocks found Baby Bear's things to be just right?
B. Inferring main ideas. What did the bear family learn about leaving their house unlocked?
C. Inferring sequence. At what point did the bears discover that someone was in their house?
D. Inferring comparisons. Compare the furniture mentioned in the story. Which was adult size and which was a child's size?

E. Inferring cause-and-effect relationships. What made the bears suspect that someone was in their house?

F. Inferring character traits. Which of the bears was the most irritated by Goldilock's intrusion?

G. Predicting outcomes. Do you think Goldilocks ever went back to visit the bears' house again?

H. Interpreting figurative language. What did the author mean when he wrote, "The tress in the deep forest howled a sad song in the wind?"

IV. **Evaluation** requires the student to make a judgment by comparing ideas presented in the selection with external criteria provided by the teacher, or by some other external source, or with internal criteria provided by the student himself.

A. Judgment of reality or fantasy. Do you suppose that the story of *The Three Bears* really happened? Why or why not?

B. Judgment of fact or opinion. Judge whether Baby Bear's furniture really was just right for Goldilocks. Why or why not?

C. Judgment of adequacy and validity. Give your opinion as to whether it was a good idea for the bears to take a walk while their porridge cooled.

D. Judgment of appropriateness. Do you think it was safe for Goldilocks to enter an empty house?

E. Judgment of worth, desirability, and acceptability. Was Goldilocks a guest or an intruder in the bears' home?

V. **Appreciation** deals with the psychological and aesthetic impact of the selection on the reader.

A. Emotional response to the content. How did you feel when the three bears found Goldilocks asleep in Baby Bear's bed?

B. Identification with characters or incidents. How do you suppose Goldilocks felt when she awakened and saw the three bears?

C. Reaction to the author's use of language. Why do you think the author called the bears Papa, Mama, and Baby instead of Mr. Bear, Mrs. Bear, and Jimmy Bear?

D. Imagery. What is meant by, "His bed is as hard as a rock"?

Skill 9.06   Demonstrate knowledge of strategies for integrating language arts skills across the content areas.

Traditionally, language arts are considered to cover the skills of reading, writing, speaking, listening, and study of literature. Although the language arts areas of reading (literature), speech, and English are subjects in their own rights, language arts skills may be incorporated into every content area subject.

Reading Students read a variety of materials for enjoyment and to gain new information. In the content areas of science and social studies, students may read a textbook or read information from other print and electronic sources.

In particular, the reading strategies of summarization, question answering, question generating, use of graphic organizers, use of text structure and marking, comprehension monitoring, and discussion are useful in science, mathematics, and social studies.

Writing Students may be asked to answer questions with short or extended response, write notes during teaching, or write reports to demonstrate understanding of the material being taught.

Speaking Students use the language arts skills of speaking when they give oral presentations or participate in discussions.

Listening Students also use listening skills when attending to the oral presentations of other students, their teachers, or guest speakers. Listening is also important during classroom discussions.

The study of literature transcends basic reading skills to a source for gathering information about a time in history, a culture, a geographic area, a vocation or career, etc.

To integrate language arts skills across content areas for the student with special needs when the special education or inclusion classroom has students with a variety of ability levels, different assignments (appropriate for the individual student) may be given.

Oral presentations or verbally answering the questions on a test may offer a more appropriate way of demonstrated learning for some learning disabled students.

Special education students who have significant delays in reading skills may be able to listen to a literature selection to gain information about something like a certain weather type. An example of this would be Betsy Byars' book *Tornado.*

Additionally, as special education students use knowledge of text structures, for example, they are better able to approach text which may be at a difficult reading level for them and find needed answered for class assignments.

Special education students may use a graphic organizer to show learned information or to set up information from research which may later be used in report writing.

Using a combination of language arts activities across content areas can provide differentiated instruction for students with special needs.

COMPETENCY 0010   UNDERSTAND STRATEGIES AND TECHNIQUES USED TO PROMOTE STUDENTS' MATHEMATICS SKILLS IN A VARIETY OF SETTINGS.

Skill 10.01   Identify types and characteristics of reasoning and calculation difficulties typically observed in students with disabilities.

Reid, 1985, describes four processes that are directly related to an understanding of numbers. Children typically begin learning these processes in early childhood through the opportunities provided by their caretakers. Children who do not get these opportunities have difficulties when they enter school.

- Describing: characterizing objects, sets, or events in terms of their attributes, such as calling all cats "kitties" whether they are tigers or house cats.
- Classifying: sorting objects, sets, or events in terms of one or more criterion, such as color, size or shape, i.e., black cats versus white cats versus tabby cats.
- Comparing: determining whether two objects, sets, or events are similar or different on the basis of a specified attribute, such as differentiating quadrilaterals from triangles on the basis of the number of sides.
- Ordering: comparing two or more objects, sets, or events, such as ordering children in a family on the basis of age or on the basis of height.

Children usually begin learning these concepts during early childhood:

Equalizing—Making two or more objects or sets alike on an attribute, such as putting more milk into a glass so that it matches the amount of milk in another glass.
Joining—Putting together two or more sets with a common attribute to make one set, such as buying packets of X-Men trading cards to create a complete series.
Separating—Dividing an object or set into two or more sets, such as passing out cookies from a bag to a group of children so that each child gets three cookies.
Measuring—Attaching a number to an attribute, such as three cups of flour or ten gallons of gas.
Patterns—Recognizing, developing, and repeating patterns, such as secret code messages or designs in a carpet or tile floor.

However, most children are not developmentally ready to understand these concepts before they enter school:

- Understanding and working with numbers larger than ten: They may be able to recite larger numbers but are not able to compare or add them, for example.
- Part-whole concept: The idea of one number as being a part of another number.
- Numerical notation: Place value, additive system, and zero symbol.

Children with learning problems often have difficulty with these concepts after they enter public school because they have either not had many experiences with developing these concepts, or they are not developmentally ready to understand such concepts as part-whole, for example.

Sequence of Mathematics Understanding

The understanding of mathematical concepts proceeds in a developmental context from concrete to semi-concrete to abstract. Children with learning difficulties may still be at the semi-concrete level when their peers are ready to work at the abstract level. This developmental sequence has implications for instruction because the teacher will need to incorporate concrete and/or semi-concrete into lessons for students who did not master these stages of development in their mathematics backgrounds. These levels may be explained as follows:

- Concrete: An example of this would be demonstrating 3 + 4 = 7 by counting out three buttons and four buttons to equal seven buttons.
- Semi-concrete: An example would be using pictures of three buttons and four buttons to illustrate 3 + 4 = 7.
- Abstract: The student solves 3 + 4 = 7 without using manipulatives or pictures.

In summary, the levels of mathematics content involve:

- Concepts, such as the understanding of numbers and terms
- Development of mathematical relationships
- Development of mathematical skills, such as computation and measuring
- Development of problem-solving ability not only in books, but also in the environment

Skill 10.02 Demonstrating knowledge of principles and methods for improving students' computation and reasoning skills

The National Council of Teachers of Mathematics, in its *Principles and Standards for School Mathematics* (2000), notes that math is a "highly interconnected and cumulative subject." Accordingly, teachers should begin by steeping classrooms in mathematics awareness, examining their own attitudes and aptitudes in math, and preparing themselves to be the best help they can to students. The teacher's deep understanding of math at the concrete, representational, and abstract levels is important to helping students to perceive the presence of math across the curriculum and in everyday activities.

David Allsopp, Ph.D., associate professor at University of South Florida, has done substantive research on best classroom practices for special needs mathematics students. He suggests that for special needs students:

- Direct instruction with significant guided practice, repetition, and support from teachers is actually more effective than student-centered instruction.

- Teaching problem-solving strategies is more effective than exclusively using rote practice.

- Concrete instruction, persistently applied throughout the levels of mathematics curriculum, is more effective in helping students develop computation and problem-solving skills and to prepare for abstract mathematics work.

- Ongoing assessment of students' performance and sharing and discussing their progress and successes with them improves learning outcomes.

- Engaging students as active participants in their learning by encouraging and teaching metacognitive behaviors like goal setting, self-monitoring, and self-talk, and showing them how to apply these skills not only to their mathematics work but to general problem solving, boosts math proficiency.

- Well-planned cooperative learning activities, such as peer tutoring and work groups, can offer students opportunities for meaningful practice and skill enhancement.

Skilled teachers can apply these special needs principles to a variety of engaging approaches to instruction, which may include instructional games, use of technology, daily living activities, journaling, integration with science or literature, and cross-curricular applications in subjects such as physical education and art.

Skill 10.03 Applying strategies for promoting students' use of critical-thinking and problem-solving skills in mathematics

Problem Solving

The skills of analysis and interpretation are necessary for problem solving. Students with learning disabilities find problem solving difficult, with the result that they avoid problem solving activities. Skills necessary for problem solving include:

1) *Identification of the main idea*: What is the problem about?
2) *Main question of the problem:* What is the problem asking for?

3) *Identifying important facts:* What information is necessary to solve the problem?
4) *Choose a strategy and an operation:* How will the student solve the problem and with what operation?
5) *Solve the problem:* Perform the computation.
6) *Check accuracy of computation and compare the answer to the main question:* Does it sound reasonable?
7) *If solution is correct:Repeat the steps.*

Identify Effective Teaching Methods for Developing the Use of Math Skills in Problem-Solving

One of the main reasons for studying mathematics is to acquire the ability to perform problem-solving skills. Problem solving is the process of applying previously-acquired knowledge to new and novel situations. Mathematical problem solving is generally thought of as solving word problems; however, there are more skills involved in problem solving than merely reading word problems, deciding on correct conceptual procedures, and performing the computations. Problem-solving skills involve posing questions; analyzing situations; hypothesizing, translating, and illustrating results; drawing diagrams; and using trial and error. When solving mathematical problems, students need to be able to apply logic, and thus, determine which facts are relevant. Table 7-1 demonstrates this process.

Problem solving has proven to be the primary area of mathematical difficulty for students. The following methods for developing problem-solving skills have been recommended.

1. Allot time for the development of successful problem-solving skills. It is a complex process and needs to be taught in a systematic way.
2. Be sure prerequisite skills have been adequately developed. The ability to perform the operations of addition, subtraction, multiplication, and division are necessary sub-skills.
3. Use error analysis to diagnose areas of difficulty. One error in procedure or choice of mathematical operation, once corrected, will eliminate subsequent mistakes following the initial error like the domino effect. Look for patterns of similar mistakes to prevent a series of identical errors. Instruct children on the usage of error analysis to perform self-appraisal of their own work.
4. Teach students appropriate terminology. Many words have a different meaning when used in a mathematical context rather than in every day life. For example, "set" in mathematics refers to a grouping of objects, but it may be used as a verb, such as in "set the table." Other words that should be defined include "order," "base," "power," and "root."

5. Have students estimate answers. Teach them how to check their computed answer to determine how reasonable it is. For example, Teddy is asked how many hours he spent doing his homework. If he worked on it two hours before dinner and one hour after dinner, and his answer came out to be 21, Teddy should be able to conclude that 21 hours is the greater part of a day and is far too large to be reasonable.

6. Remember that development of math readiness skills enables students to acquire prerequisite concepts and to build cognitive structures. These prerequisite skills appear to be related to problem-solving performance.

Skill 10.04 Demonstrating familiarity with techniques for encouraging students' application of mathematics skills in a variety of contexts, including practical daily living situations

In a paper published by the ERIC Clearinghouse on Disabilities and Gifted Education, author Cynthia Warger writes, "...for students with disabilities to do better in math, math must be meaningful for them. Both knowing and doing mathematics must be emphasized to enhance the quality of mathematics instruction and learning for students with disabilities." (Warger, 2002)

Real-world applications of mathematics abound and offer highly-motivating opportunities for computational practice and the development of number sense and mathematical reasoning and can give students confidence in their mathematical abilities. Finding the mathematical connections in outdoor games, planning for the purchase of lunch, comparing heights among classmates, calculating the time until recess, and figuring out which sports team is headed for the playoffs are just a few examples.

The Special Connections Project at the University of Kansas suggests a number of strategies in a paper called *Creating Authentic Mathematics Learning Contexts*:

- Begin where the students are. Their ages, interests, and experiences are excellent clues to the kinds of contexts that will offer the most compelling learning opportunities, whether school-, family-, or community-related.

- Document interests. Comparing and contrasting them can help identify patterns and differences and assist with lesson and activity planning. Documenting and reviewing this information (student names, hobbies, interests, family activities, etc.) could be an activity you share with your students.

- Model the desired concept, skill, or strategy explicitly and within the real-world context. Observing your problem-solving approach and its outcome helps ground students in the math and begins to strengthen associations between mathematics concepts and real-life situations.

- Reinforce the associations by demonstrating the relevance of the concept, skill, or strategy being taught to the "authentic context".

- Offer opportunities for guided, supported practice of the concept, skill or strategy; this includes feedback, redirection, remodeling, if needed, and acknowledgement of progress and successes.

Skill 10.05   Evaluating, selecting, and adapting instructional strategies, materials, and resources to individualize instruction and facilitate student achievement in mathematics

Etiologies of the learning challenges some students face can be diverse, as can their outcomes. Teachers of students with special needs are skilled at assessing, observing, implementing, reassessing and making changes to the educational environment, tools, and approaches they are using with students.

To accomplish this with math instruction, teachers must begin by identifying the nature of math as a curricular area, using that information to task-analyze the concepts, skills, and strategies they want to teach. Then, teachers focus on each student's observed and documented strengths and challenges, as well as the relevant information from his/her formal assessments and individualized education plan (IEP). Such analysis may constitute an initial assessment.

In the NCTM journal article, *Planning Strategies for Students with Special Needs* (*Teaching Children Mathematics*, 2004), Brodesky et al. suggest that the next step in deciding on strategies, materials, and resources would be to identify the "barriers" that students' documented and observed would present challenges as they work to meet the goals and objectives of the math curriculum and their IEPs. Data-based assessments are an alternative or adjunct to such observational and record review. This information can help direct teachers' thinking about proactive solutions, including the selection and/or adaptation of the best strategies, materials and resources.

Once teachers have thus developed a clear picture of the goals and needs of their math students with learning differences, they can seek resources for best practices, including school district-based support, the federal and state departments of education, teacher training programs, and education literature. Ultimately, skilled teachers will layer creativity and keen observation with their professional skills to decide how best to individualize instruction and facilitate student achievement. Examples include:

- Varying learning modalities (visual, kinesthetic, tactile, aural)
- Integrating technology (calculators, computers, game consoles)
- Providing tools and manipulatives (Cuisinart rods, beans, protractors)
- Developing a range of engaging activities (games, music, storytelling)
- Using real-world problem solving (fundraising, school-wide projects, shopping, cooking, budgeting)
- Adopting a cross-curricular approach (studying historical events strongly influenced by math, music theory)
- Developing basic skills (guided practice, pencil-and-paper computation, journaling, and discussing problem-solving strategies)
- Adaptations (extended wait time, recorded lessons, concept videos, ergonomic work areas, mixed-ability learning groups)

COMPETENCY 0011 UNDERSTAND STRATEGIES AND TECHNIQUES USED TO PROMOTE STUDENTS' ACQUISITION OF FUNCTIONAL LIVING SKILLS.

Skill 11.01 Demonstrating knowledge of methods for teaching students with disabilities to use problem-solving, decision-making, and other cognitive strategies to meet their own needs

Teachers should have a toolkit of instructional strategies, materials, and technologies to encourage and teach students how to problem solve and think critically about subject content and even living skills. With each curriculum chosen by a district for school implementation, comes an expectation that students must master benchmarks and standards of learning skills. There is an established level of academic performance and proficiency in public schools that students are required to master in today's classrooms. Research of national and state standards indicate that there are additional benchmarks and learning objectives in the subject areas of science, foreign language, English language arts, history, art, health, civics, economics, geography, physical education, mathematics, and social studies that students are required to master in state assessments (Marzano & Kendall, 1996).

A critical-thinking skill is a skill target that teachers help students develop to sustain learning in specific areas that can be applied within other areas. For example, when learning to understand algebraic concepts in solving a math word problem on how much fencing material is needed to build a fence around a backyard area that is 8' x 12", a math student must understand the order of numerical expression in how to simplify algebraic expressions. Teachers can provide instructional strategies that show students how to group the fencing measurements into an algebraic word problem that, with minor addition, subtraction, and multiplication can produce a simple number equal to the amount of fencing materials needed to build the fence.

Students use basic skills to understand things that are read, such as a reading passage or a math word problem or directions for a project. However, students apply additional thinking skills to fully comprehend how what was read could be applied to their own lives or how to make comparatives or choices based on the factual information given. These higher-order thinking skills are called critical-thinking skills, as students think about thinking, and teachers are instrumental in helping students use these skills in everyday activities:

- Analyzing bills for overcharges
- Comparing shopping ads or catalogue deals
- Finding the main idea from readings
- Applying what's been learned to new situations
- Gathering information/data from diverse sources to plan a project
- Following a sequence of directions

- Looking for cause and effect relationships
- Comparing and contrasting information in synthesizing information

Attention to learner needs during planning is foremost and includes identification of that which the students already know or need to know; the matching of learner needs with instructional elements such as content, materials, activities, and goals; and the determination of whether or not students have performed at an acceptable level following instruction.

The ability to create a personal and professional charting of students' academic and emotional growth found within the performance-based assessment of individualized portfolios becomes a toolkit for both students and teachers. Teachers can use semester portfolios to gauge student academic progress and personal growth of students who are constantly changing their self-images and worldviews on a daily basis. When a student is studying to master a math concept and is able to create a visual of the learning that transcends beyond the initial concept to create a bridge connecting a higher level of thinking and application of knowledge, then the teacher can share a moment of enjoyable math comprehension with the student.

The idea of using art concepts as visual imagery in helping students process conceptual learning of reading, math, and science skills creates a mental mind mapping of learning for students processing new information. Using graphic organizers and concept web guides that center around a concept and the applications of the concept is an instructional strategy that teachers can use to guide students into further inquiry of the subject matter. Imagine the research of the German chemist Fredrich August Kekule when he looked into a fire one night and solved the molecular structure of benzene, and you can imagine fostering that same creativity in students. Helping students understand the art of "visualization" and the creativity of discovery may impart a student visualizing the cure for AIDS or cancer or creating reading programs for the next generation of readers.

Helping students become effective note-takers and stimulating a diversity of perspectives for spatial techniques that can be applied to learning is a proactive teacher strategy in creating a visual learning environment where art and visualization become natural art forms for learning. In today's computer environment, students must understand that computers cannot replace the creative thinking and skill application that comes from the greatest computer on record, the human mind.

Skill 11.02   Demonstrate an understanding of effective collaboration among teachers and other professionals to facilitate students' maintenance and generalization of skills across learning environments.

Transfer of Learning

Transfer of learning occurs when experience with one task influences performance on another task. Positive transfer occurs when the required responses are about the same and the stimuli are similar, such as moving from baseball to handball to racquetball, or from field hockey to soccer. Negative transfer occurs when the stimuli remain similar, but the required responses change, such as shifting from soccer to football, tennis to racquetball, and boxing to sports karate. Instructional procedures should stress the similar features between the activities and the dimensions that are transferable. Specific information should emphasize when stimuli in the old and new situations are the same or similar and when responses used in the old situation apply to the new.

To facilitate learning, instructional objectives should be arranged in order according to their patterns of similarity. Objectives involving similar responses should be closely sequenced; thus, the possibility for positive transfer is stressed. Likewise, learning objectives that involve different responses should be programmed within instructional procedures in the most appropriate way possible. For example, students should have little difficulty transferring handwriting instruction to writing in other areas; however, there might be some negative transfer when moving from manuscript to cursive writing. By using transitional methods and focusing upon the similarities between manuscript and cursive writing, negative transfer can be reduced.

Generalization

Generalization is the occurrence of a learned behavior in the presence of a stimulus other than the one that produced the initial response (e.g., novel stimulus). It is the expansion of a student's performance beyond conditions initially anticipated. Students must be able to generalize what is learned to other settings (e.g., reading to math, word problems; resource room to regular classroom).

Generalization training is a procedure in which a behavior is reinforced in each of a series of situations until it generalizes to other members of the same stimulus class. Stimulus generalization occurs when responses, which have been reinforced in the presence of a specific stimulus, the discriminative stimulus (SD), occur in the presence of related stimuli (e.g., bathrooms labeled women, ladies, dames). In fact, the more similar the stimuli, the more likely it is that stimulus generalization will occur. This concept applies to intertask similarity, in that the more one task resembles another, the greater the probability the student will be able to master it. For example, if Johnny has learned the initial consonant sounds of "b" and "d," and he has been taught to read the word "dad," it is likely that when he is shown the word "bad," he will be able to pronounce this formerly unknown word upon presentation. (Refer to Skill 2 in this section).

Generalization may be enhanced by the following:

1. Use many examples in teaching to deepen application of learned skills.
2. Use consistency in initial teaching situations, and later introduce variety in format, procedure, and use of examples.
3. Have the same information presented by different teachers, in different settings, and under varying conditions.
4. Include a continuous reinforcement schedule at first, later changing to delayed and intermittent schedules as instruction progresses.
5. Teach students to record instances of generalization and to reward themselves at that time.
6. Associate naturally-occurring stimuli when possible.

Skill 11.03 Demonstrate familiarity with strategies for linking life skills instruction to employment and independent, community, and personal living.

Adaptive life skills refer to the skills that people need to function independently at home, school, and in the community. Adaptive behavior skills include communication and social skills (intermingling and communicating with other people); independent living skills (shopping, budgeting, and cleaning); personal care skills (eating, dressing, and grooming); employment/work skills (following directions, completing assignments, and being punctual for work); and functional academics (reading, solving math problems, and telling time).

Teaching adaptive behavior skills is part of the special education program for students with disabilities. Parent input is a critical part of the adaptive behavior assessment process since there are many daily living skills that are observed primarily at home and are not prevalent in the educational setting.

The measurement of adaptive behavior should consist of surveys of the child's behavior and skills in a diverse number of settings, including his class, school, home, neighborhood, or community. Since it is not possible for one person to observe a child in all of the primary environments, measurement of adaptive behavior depends on the feedback from a number of people. Because parents have many opportunities to observe their child in an assortment of settings, they are normally the best source of information about adaptive behavior. The most prevalent method for collecting information about a child's adaptive behavior skills in the home environment is to have a school Social Worker, school Psychologist, or guidance counselor interview the parents using a formal adaptive behavior assessment rating scale. These individuals may interview the parents at home or hold a meeting at the school to talk with the parents about their child's behavior. Adaptive behavior information is also procured from school personnel who work with the student in order to understand how the child functions in the school environment.

There are a variety of strategies for teaching adaptive life skills, including incorporating choice, which entails allowing students to select the assignment, and allowing students to select the order that they complete tasks. In addition, priming or pre-practice is an effective classroom intervention for students with disabilities. Priming entails previewing information or activities that a student is likely to have problems with before he/she begins working on that activity. Partial participation or multi-level instruction is another strategy, and it entails allowing a student with a disability to take part in the same projects as the rest of their class, with specific adaptations to the activities so that they suit a student's specific abilities and requirements. Additional instructional practices include self-management, which entails teaching the student to function independently without relying on a teacher or a one-on-one aid. This strategy allows the student to become more involved in the intervention process, and it improves autonomy.

Cooperative groups are an effective instructional technique for teaching social skills. They have been known to result in increased frequency, duration, and quality of social interactions. Peer tutoring entails two students working together on an activity, with one student giving assistance, instruction, and feedback to the other.

Understand the Need for a Functional Curriculum

A functional curriculum approach focuses upon what students need to learn that will be useful to them and to prepare them for functioning in society as adults. With this approach, concepts and skills needed for personal-social, daily living, and occupational readiness are taught to students. The specific curriculum content needs to be identified in a student's individualized educational program (IEP) and be considered appropriate for his chronological age and current intellectual, academic, or behavioral performance levels (Clark, 1994).

The need for a functional curriculum has been heightened by the current focus upon transition, movement from one level to another, until the individual is prepared to live a life in a self-sufficient manner. The simplest form includes movement from school to the world of work. But like career education, life preparation includes not only occupational readiness, but also personal-social and daily living skills.

Halpern (1992) contends that special education curriculum tends to focus too much on remedial academics and not enough on functional skills.

A functional curriculum includes life skills and teaches them in the classroom and in the community. When using this approach, basic academic skills are reinforced in an applied manner. For instance, math skills may be taught in budgeting, balancing checkbooks, and/or computing interest payments for major purchases.

The Adult Performance Level (APL) has been adapted for secondary level students in special education in a number of school districts in Texas and Louisiana. The APL serves as a core curriculum blending practical academic development with applications to the various demands of community living in adulthood.

Functional competence, as addressed in APL, is conceptualized as two-dimensional. Major skill areas are integrated into general content/knowledge domains. The major skills that have been identified by this curriculum model as requisite for success are reading, writing, speaking, listening, viewing, problem solving, interpersonal relations, and computation.

Skill 11.04 **Demonstrating knowledge of methods, including collaboration among professionals in a variety of settings, for promoting students' development of independence to the fullest extent possible**

(Please refer to skill 6.05 and 6.06.)

Skill 11.05 **Recognizing that cultural, linguistic, and gender differences need to be taken into account when developing instructional content, materials, resources, and strategies for promoting students' functional living skills**

Writing functional living skills curriculum for a student requires understanding that it is not just the IQ that defines the label/diagnosis of mental retardation. The American Association on Mental Retardation reminds us of the impact culture has on everyone's development by adding two assumptions to the validating of the diagnosis of mental retardation.

1) Limitations in present functioning must be considered within the context of community environments typical of the individual's age peers and *culture*.

2) Valid assessment considers *cultural and linguistic* diversity, as well as differences in communication, sensory, motor, and behavioral factors.

Teachers must recognize these facts in relation to everyday life for their students. Interviewing parents is a way of including them in the development of a functional skills program and allows the teacher to learn what is considered a cultural norm in his/her student's home life. The planned method of instruction may also be considered culturally insensitive and must be examined for this possibility.

Materials and resources also must be considered as possibly offensive to some cultures. The provision of a check before implementation of a functional living skills program can negate this issue.

Instructional methods of functional skills can best avoid cultural conflict when utilizing the following methods:

1. Use the think aloud process: Teachers state simple questions and answer them as part of the thought process while demonstrating a specific skill and also allow for group discussions and questions to be offered on the specific skill being addressed.
2. Create opportunities for students to ask open-ended questions regarding the skill to be completed.
3. Provide multiple examples of how to attain a skill.
4. Include the use of student designed art to show how a skill must be completed.
5. Scaffolding allows for a skill to be taught through small steps. Reach a small objective and build upon each one to reach a selected skill.

Skill 11.06 **Demonstrate understanding of the development and use of a task analysis.**

A teacher can use the set of behavioral specifications that are the result of the task analysis to prepare tests that will measure the student's ability to meet those specifications. These tests are referred to as criterion measurements. If task analysis identifies which skills will be needed to perform a task successfully, then the criterion measurements will further identify whether the student possesses the necessary skills or knowledge for that task. The level of performance that is acceptable is the "criterion level."

Criterion measurements must be developed along certain guidelines if they are to accurately measure a task and its sub-skills. Johnson and Morasky (1977) give the following guidelines for establishing criterion measurement:

1. Criterion measurement must directly evaluate a student's ability to perform a task.
2. Criterion measurements should cover the range of possible situations in order to be considered an adequate measure.
3. Criterion measurements should measure whether or not a student can perform the task without additional or outside assistance. They should not give any information that the student is expected to possess.
4. All responses in the criterion measurement should be relevant to the task being measured.

Behavioral objectives offer descriptive statements defining the task that the student will perform, stating the conditions under which the task will occur, and showing the criterion measurement required for mastery. The criterion measurement is the process for evaluating what the student can do. For the instruction to be meaningful, there must be a precise correspondence between the capabilities determined in a criterion measurement and the behavioral demands of the objective.

Skill 11.07   Demonstrating knowledge of instructional techniques and strategies that promote successful transitions (e.g., from home to school; preschool to grade school; classroom to classroom; school to school; school to adult life roles, employment, or post-secondary education or training)

(For transitional techniques related to the classroom please refer to skill 5.07.)

School to Adult Life Roles

IDEA 2004 requires those receiving special education services to have transition plans. Planning for transition into the world after school needs the input of the student, parents, teacher and others involved in delivering services. It should be based on the student's individual strengths, preferences and interests. The goals of the students are often referred to as post-school outcomes. Ideally post-school outcomes/objectives of the students seek realistic goals. Unfortunately this is not always true and some guidance towards "alternatives" for the future should be provided.

Transition planning must look into providing instruction/training in vocational programming when possible and where related services outside the school environment can be tied into making a student's transition successful. It is also possible that transition planning could provide job opportunities that may lead beyond the school years, and possibly to the ability to achieve what may be considered "normal" independence.

School districts New York State often refer those students finishing their school careers to their established departments for Vocational and Educational Services for Individuals with Disabilities (VESID) which will coordinate the delivery of additionally needed services beyond secondary level of education. State departments such as these offer continued support in college environments, training schools and assist those with disabilities to find jobs.

Other community resources should be pointed out to the student and parent that can assist with the transition to the "real world" environment to provide some continuity as the emerging adult leaves the protective school environment.

COMPETENCY 0012 UNDERSTAND STRATEGIES AND TECHNIQUES USED TO IMPROVE THE SOCIAL COMPETENCE OF STUDENTS WITH DISABILITIES.

Skill 12.01 Identify social skills needed for various educational and functional living environments, as well as for personal and social behavior in various settings.

Many youngsters with disabilities have difficulty in developing social behavior that follows accepted norms. While non-disabled children learn most social behaviors from family and peers, children with disabilities are the product of a wide, complex range of different social experiences. When coupled with one or more of the disabilities, this experience adds up to a collective deficit in interpersonal relationships.

There is an irreducible philosophical issue underlying the realm of social behavior among children with disabilities. To some extent, the disability itself causes maladaptive behaviors to develop. Regardless of whether social skill deficits are seminal or secondary among youth with disabilities, it is the task of the special education professional to help each child develop as normally as possible in the social-interpersonal realm.

Children with disabilities can be taught social-interpersonal skills through developing sensitivity to other people, through making behavioral choices in social situations, and through developing social maturity.

Sensitivity to Others

Central to the human communication process is the nonverbal domain. Children with disabilities may perceive facial expressions and gestures differently than their non-disabled peers due to their impairment. There are several kinds of activities to use in developing a child's sensitivity to other people. Examples of these activities follow.

1. Offer a selection of pictures with many kinds of faces to the child. Ask the child to identify or classify the faces according to the emotion that appears in the picture. Allow the child to compare his reactions to those of the other students.
2. Compare common gestures through a mixture of acting and discussion. The teacher can demonstrate shaking her head in the negative, and then ask the students for the meaning of the gesture. Reactions can be compared, and then a game can be started in which each student performs a gesture while others tell what it means.

3. Filmstrips, videotapes, and movies are available in which famous people and cartoon characters utilize gestures. Children can be asked what a particular gesture means.
4. Tape recording with playback can be used to present social sounds. Again, a game is possible here, and the activity focuses the student's attention on one narrow issue—the sound and its precise social meaning.
5. Pairs of students can be formed for exercises in reading each other's gestures and nonverbal communications. Friendships of a lasting nature are encouraged by this activity.

Social Situations

Inherent differences in appearances and motions among children with disabilities cause some of them to develop behavior problems in social situations. It is necessary to remediate this situation in order to provide as normal a life as possible in order to sustain as normal an adulthood as possible.

Below are some activities that strengthen a child's skills in social situations.

1. Anticipate the consequences of social actions. Have the students act out roles, tell stories, and discuss the consequences that flow from their actions.
2. Gain appropriate independence. Students can be given exercises in going places alone. For the very young, and for those with development issues, this might consist of finding a location within the room. Go on a field trip into the city. Allow older students to make purchases on their own. Using play money in the classroom for younger children would be beneficial.
3. Make ethical and/or moral judgments. The unfinished story, requiring the pupil to finish it at the point where a judgment is required, makes an independent critique of the choices made by the characters in the play.
4. Plan and execute. Children with disabilities can be allowed to plan an outing, a game, a party, or an exercise.

Having the teacher set an example is always a good way to teach social maturation. If the classroom is orderly, free of an oppressive atmosphere, and full of visibly rational judgments about what is going on, the students absorb the climate of doing things in a mature manner.

Skill 12.02   Demonstrate knowledge of effective social skills instruction and reinforcement by educators and other professionals across a variety of educational settings.

In an effective peer tutoring arrangement, the teacher trains the peer tutors and matches them with students who need extra practice and assistance. In addition to academic skills, the arrangement can help both students work on social skills, such as cooperation and self-esteem. Both students may be working on the same material, or the tutee may be working to strengthen areas of weakness. The teacher determines the target goals, selects the material, sets up the guidelines, trains the student tutors in the rules and methods of the sessions, and monitors and evaluates the sessions.

Adaptive life skills refer to the skills that people need to function independently at home, school, and in the community. Adaptive behavior skills include communication and social skills (intermingling and communicating with other people); independent living skills (shopping, budgeting, and cleaning); personal care skills (eating, dressing, and grooming); employment/work skills (following directions, completing assignments, and being punctual for work); and functional academics (reading, solving math problems, and telling time).

Teaching adaptive behavior skills is part of the special education program for students with disabilities. Parent input is a critical part of the adaptive behavior assessment process since there are many daily living skills that are observed primarily at home and are not prevalent in the educational setting.

The measurement of adaptive behavior should consist of surveys of the child's behavior and skills in a diverse number of settings, including his class, school, home, neighborhood, or community. Since it is not possible for one person to observe a child in all of the primary environments, measurement of adaptive behavior depends on the feedback from a number of people. Because parents have many opportunities to observe their child in an assortment of settings, they are normally the best source of information about adaptive behavior. The most prevalent method for collecting information about a child's adaptive behavior skills in the home environment is to have a school Social Worker, school Psychologist, or guidance counselor interview the parents using a formal adaptive behavior assessment rating scale. These individuals may interview the parents at home or hold a meeting at the school to talk with the parents about their child's behavior. Adaptive behavior information is also procured from school personnel who work with the student in order to understand how the child functions in the school environment.

There are a variety of strategies for teaching adaptive life skills, including incorporating choice, which entails allowing students to select the assignment, and allowing students to select the order that they complete tasks. In addition, priming or pre-practice is an effective classroom intervention for students with disabilities. Priming entails previewing information or activities that a student is likely to have problems with before he/she begin working on that activity. Partial participation or multi-level instruction is another strategy, and it entails allowing a student with a disability to take part in the same projects as the rest of his/her class, with specific adaptations to the activity so that it suits a student's specific abilities and requirements. Additional instructional practices include self-management, which entails teaching the student to function independently without relying on a teacher or a one-on-one aid. This strategy allows the student to become more involved in the intervention process, and it improves autonomy.

Cooperative groups are an effective instructional technique for teaching social skills. It has been known to result in increased frequency, duration, and quality of social interactions. Peer tutoring entails two students working together on an activity, with one student giving assistance, instruction, and feedback to the other.

Skill 12.03 Demonstrate familiarity with instructional techniques that promote the student's self-awareness, self-control, self-reliance, self-esteem, and personal empowerment.

Self-Concept

Self-concept may be defined as the collective attitudes or feelings that one holds about oneself. Children with disabilities perceive, early in life, that they are deficient in skills that seem easier for their peers without disabilities. They also receive expressions of surprise or even disgust from both adults and children in response to their differing appearance and actions, again resulting in damage to the self-concept. The Special Education Teacher, for these reasons, will want to direct special and continuing effort to bettering each child's own perception of himself.

1. The poor self-concept of a child with disabilities causes that student, at times, to exhibit aggression or rage over inappropriate things. The teacher can ignore this behavior unless it is dangerous to others or too distracting to the total group, thereby reducing the amount of negative conditioning in the child's life. Further, the teacher can praise this child, quickly and frequently, for the correct responses he makes, remembering that these responses may require special effort on the student's part to produce. Further, correction, when needed, can be done tactfully, in private.

2 The child whose poor self-concept manifests itself in withdrawn behavior should be pulled gently into as many social situations as possible by the teacher. This child must be encouraged to share experiences with the class, to serve as teacher helper for projects, and to be part of small groups for tasks. Again, praise for performing these group and public acts is most effective if done immediately.

3. The teacher can plan, in advance, to structure the classroom experiences so that aversive situations will be avoided. Thus, settings that stimulate the aggressive child to act out can be redesigned, and situations that stimulate group participation can be set up in advance for the child who acts in a withdrawn manner.

Frequent, positive, and immediate are the best terms to describe the teacher feedback required by children with disabilities. Praise for very small correct acts should be given immediately and repeated when each correct act is repeated. Criticism or outright scolding should be done, whenever possible, in private. The teacher should first check the total day's interactions with students to ensure that the number and qualitative content of verbal stimuli is heavily on the positive side. While this trait is desirable in all good teaching, it is fundamental and utterly necessary to build the fragile self-concept of youngsters with disabilities.

4. The teacher must have a strategy for use with the child who persists in negative behavior outbursts. One system is to intervene immediately and break the situation down into three components. First, the teacher requires the child to identify the worst possible outcome from the situation, the thing that he fears. To do this task, the child must be required to state the situation in the most factual way he can. Second, he is required to state what would really happen if this worst possible outcome happened and to evaluate the likelihood of it happening. Third, he is asked to state an action or attitude that he can take after examining the consequences in a new light. This process has been termed <u>rational emotive therapy</u>.

(Please refer to skills 6.05 and 6.06.)

Skill 12.04   Recognizing effective strategies across a range of educational settings for preparing students to live harmoniously and productively in a diverse society

Effective teaching and learning for students begins with teachers who can demonstrate sensitivity for diversity in teaching and relationships within school communities. Student portfolios include work that has a multicultural perspective and inclusion where students share cultural and ethnic life experiences in their learning. Teachers are responsive to including cultural and diverse resources in their curriculum and instructional practices. Exposing students to culturally-sensitive room decorations and posters that show positive and inclusive messages is one way to demonstrate inclusion of multiple cultures. Teachers should also continuously make cultural connections that are relevant and empowering for all students and communicate academic and behavioral expectations. Cultural sensitivity is communicated beyond the classroom with parents and community members to establish and maintain relationships.

Diversity can be further defined as the following:

- Differences among learners, classroom settings, and academic outcomes
- Biological, sociological, ethnicity, socioeconomic status, psychological needs, learning modalities and styles among learners
- Differences in classroom settings that promote learning opportunities, such as collaborative, participatory, and individualized learning groupings
- Expected learning outcomes that are theoretical, affective, and cognitive for students

Teachers establish a classroom climate that is culturally respectful and engaging for students. In a culturally-sensitive classroom, teachers maintain equity and fairness in student interactions and curriculum implementation. Assessments include cultural responses and perspectives that become further learning opportunities for students. Other artifacts that could reflect teacher/student sensitivity to diversity might consist of the following:

- Student portfolios reflecting multicultural/multiethnic perspectives
- Journals and reflections from field trips/guest speakers from diverse cultural backgrounds
- Printed materials and wall displays from multicultural perspectives
- Parent/guardian letters in a variety of languages reflecting cultural diversity
- Projects that include cultural history and diverse inclusions
- Disaggregated student data reflecting cultural groups
- Classroom climate of professionalism that fosters diversity and cultural inclusion

The target of diversity allows teachers a variety of opportunities to expand their experiences with students, staff, community members, and parents from culturally-diverse backgrounds so that their experiences can be proactively applied in promoting cultural diversity inclusion in the classroom. Teachers are able to engage and challenge students to develop and incorporate their own diversity skills in building character and relationships with cultures beyond their own. In changing the thinking patterns of students to become more culturally inclusive in the 21st century, teachers are addressing the globalization of our world.

Skill 12.05 Demonstrating knowledge of strategies for integrating social skills across curricula.

After a student has been taught appropriate social skills and interpersonal skills, there are a variety of ways to evaluate and document their process.

Some methods are as follows:

Communication Notebook

A communication notebook is a notebook passed from teacher to parent or other person involved with the student to discuss the student's behavior. This ensures the generalization of skills. It can also be used to discuss the individual's social and interpersonal skills across settings.

Direct Observation

Direct observation is another way of evaluating and documenting interpersonal interactions. Direct observation occurs when the recorder is making note of the behavior as it is occurring.

COMPETENCY 0013   UNDERSTAND THE DEVELOPMENT AND IMPLEMENTATION OF BEHAVIOR INTERVENTIONS.

Skill 13.01   Demonstrating familiarity with a variety of effective behavior management techniques appropriate to the needs of students with disabilities, based on the individual's IEP

Discipline Approaches Traditionally Used with Students with Behavior Disorders

Several approaches to student discipline are offered in this review. Examples are given to demonstrate principles of each. Teachers need to be familiar with these well-known approaches so that they can be used selectively when particular student behaviors and situations occur.

Life-Space Interview (Redl)

The life-space interview is a here-and-now intervention built around the child's life experience. It is applied in an effort towards increasing conscious awareness of distorted perceptions. These perceptions may be directed toward how one reacts to the behaviors and pressures of other persons. It is sometimes referred to as emotional first aide.

Example:

Jack, a 10-year old fifth grader, is enrolled in Mr. Bird's resource room for students with behavior disorders. Jack's social behavior is creating difficulties for him, his classmates, and his teachers. Jack's unacceptable social behaviors have caused him to be ignored by some students, overly rejected by others, and used as a scapegoat by a few.

Essentially, Jack believes he is unacceptable to his peers. He feels that others are making fun of him or rejecting him, even when they are being friendly. When Jack feels he is being rejected, he immediately attempts to escape his discomfort. He tries to isolate himself by placing his backpack over his head, walking the hallways sideways with his face to the wall, and so on.

Mr. Bird recognizes that eventually this behavior will affect all facets of Jack's functioning, including his academics. Involved staff discussed and agreed that life-space interviewing was an appropriate intervention in Jack's case. Each time Jack engaged in the behavior, he was immediately removed by a supportive adult from the setting in which the behavior occurred.

The incident was reconstructed and discussed, and a plan for a more acceptable response by Jack to a classmate's smile, wave, and so on, was agreed on by Jack and the supportive adult. Jack returned to the setting in which the behavior occurred and continued his daily schedule.

Over time, and after many life-space interviews, Jack increased his capacity to differentiate between social acceptance and rejection.

Interview Guidelines:

1. Be polite to the individual. If you don't have control of your emotions, do not begin the interview.
2. Sit, kneel, or stand to establish eye contact. Talk with, never at, the individual being interviewed.
3. When you are unsure about the history of the incident, investigate. *Do not conduct an interview on the basis of second-or third-hand information or rumors.*
4. *Ask appropriate questions* to obtain a knowledgeable grasp of the incident. However, do not probe areas of unconscious motivation; limit the use of "why" questions.
5. *Listen to the individual* and attempt to comprehend his/her perception of the incident.
6. *Encourage the individual to ask questions.* Respond to the child's questions appropriately.
7. When the individual is suffering from apparent shame and/or guilt because of the incident, *attempt to reduce and minimize these feelings.*
8. *Facilitate the individual's efforts to communicate* what he/she wishes today.
9. Work carefully and patiently with the individual to develop a mutually-acceptable plan of action for immediate or future implementation.

Reality Therapy

In reality therapy, the therapist or teacher takes present behavior and confronts students about whether their behavior is helping them or hurting them. Confrontational questions assist the individual in taking responsibility for his or her behavior. Responsibility is seen as the ability to fulfill one's personal needs in a manner that does not deprive other individuals of their ability to fulfill their needs. The teacher acts as a facilitator as he or she assists the individual in developing a plan by which to resolve troublesome behavior. The student generally feels more responsible for enacting the plan if it is written and signed. In summary, reality therapy is the process of teaching an individual to face existing reality, to function responsibly, and, as a result, to fulfill personal needs.

Example:

Kyle, a tenth-grade student at Greenwood High School, had superior academic potential. However, he was flunking several subjects. It became evident that Kyle's future relative to graduation and college was being affected by his behavior.

Mr. Scott, Kyle's favorite teacher, decided he needed to help the boy. He did not want Kyle to jeopardize his future. Mr. Scott decided to use the reality therapy approach with Kyle. After all, he and Kyle were friends; he cared about the boy, and he knew Kyle could improve with help.

In their first session, Mr. Scott confronted Kyle with questions like, "What are you doing?"; "Is it helping you?"; "If not, what else could you do to help yourself?" It was found that Kyle would not work in any subject area if he did not like the teacher. If the teacher was too demanding, unfriendly, and so on, Kyle just gave up and refused to study.

Kyle recognized that his behavior was only harmful to himself. He and Mr. Scott developed a plan of action. During the next few months, they met regularly to monitor Kyle's progress and to write and revise the plan as needed. Kyle learned to accept responsibility for his behavior. His grades improved dramatically.

Guidelines for teachers engaged in the interview:

1. *Be personal.* Demonstrate to the individual that you are a friend who cares about the individual and who is interested in his or her welfare.

2. *Focus the therapeutic process on the individual's present behavior,* not his past behavior. Accept the individual's expressed feelings, but do not probe into unconscious motivators. Confront by asking what, how, and who questions. Limit asking why questions.

3. *Do not preach, moralize, or make value judgments* about the individual's behavior.

4. *Help the individual formulate a practical plan* to increase responsible behavior.

5. *Encourage the individual to overtly make a commitment* to the mutually-agreed plan.

6. *Do not accept the individual's excuses* for irresponsible behavior. When a plan fails or cannot be implemented, develop another.

7. *Do not punish* the individual for irresponsible behavior. As a general principle, allow the individual to realize the logical consequences of irresponsible behavior unless the consequences are unreasonably harmful.

Transactional Analysis (Berne & Harris)

Transactional analysis is considered to be a rational approach to understanding human behavior. It is based on the assumption that individuals can learn to have trust in themselves, think for themselves, make their own decisions, and express personal feelings. According to this approach, there are different persons within us. Our day-to-day experiences serve as stimuli that evoke memories of past situations and cause a person to relive the events with recorded images and feelings.

This behavioral intervention provides the teacher with a framework for viewing what is said to and by students. The principles of this intervention can be applied on the job, in the home, in the classroom, and in the neighborhood—wherever people deal with people. Although transactional analysis procedures are primarily intellectual or cognitive, the person using them gains emotional, as well as intellectual, insight into self and others.

The personality is composed of three ego states: (1) the parent, (2) the child, and (3) the adult. Individuals are in the parent state when acting, thinking, and feeling as they observed their parents doing. Individuals are in the adult ego state when dealing with current reality, gathering facts, and computing objectively. Individuals are in the child ego state when they are feeling and acting as they did when they were children.

Ego states are most evident and observable in an individual's transactions (interactions, exchanges) with others. The process of transactional analysis is primarily the examination of exchanges between the individual and others in the environment.

Although there are many specific types of transactions, there are three major ones:

1. Complementary transactions: These are predictable reactions received from a person in response to an act. For example, the usual response of a child to a parent requesting him or her to clean his room is that the child grumbles a little but does it.
2. Cross - transactions: These transactions occur when an individual receives an unpredictable response from another individual. For example, an unexpected response from a child who usually cleans his room might be: "No way, I wont' do it. You're the mother, and it's your job." An unexpected response from a colleague who is usually helpful in emergencies when requested to substitute might be: "Forget it. I have enough to do. It's your emergency, your class, and your problem, not mine."

3. <u>Ulterior transactions</u>: These transactions have a hidden message in which what is stated is not the real message being sent. For example, a man who is both a husband and a father is painting his large family house. He would like and needs help. Instead of saying, "Hey, people, I need help," he complains about the work, his tiredness and muscle aches, his age, the size of the house, and so on. His purpose is really to obtain help, not sympathy.

All humans have a personality composed of the three ego states, which are found to be a result of our reactions to stimulation from others in the environment. This reaction is a result of reinforcement, or strokes, from others in the environment. A stroke is a form of recognition, or attending to, that is necessary for all human beings. Strokes may be verbal or physical, positive or negative.

Four life positions that predominate in a person's personality are:

1. I'm not okay; you're okay.
2. I'm not okay; you're not okay.
3. I'm okay; you're not okay.
4. I'm okay; you're okay.

The fourth position - we are both okay - is only entered because of a conscious and verbal decision. Transactional analysis is designed to help the individual attain this position.

Role-playing and Psychodrama (Moreno & Raths)

Psychodrama was originally developed for therapeutic purposes. Role playing can help an individual clarify feelings and emotions as they relate to existing reality in three ways.

1. It can focus on real occurrences. An incident may be reenacted and the participants told to attend to the feelings aroused, or an incident may be reenacted with the participants changing roles and attending the feelings of the aroused by these new roles. An individual may be directed to deliver a soliloquy (monologue) to recreate an emotionally-loaded event. Emphasis here is on expressing feelings that were hidden or held back when the event first occurred.
2. It can focus on significant others. The individual may portray a significant person in his or her life about whom a great amount of conflict is felt.

3. It can focus on processes and feelings occurring in new situations. Directions for this type of role playing may be very specific, with the participants provided with special characters and actions, or directions may be vague, allowing the participants to form their own characters.

Role playing and psychodrama techniques have been incorporated into several affective education programs concerned specifically with clarification of values and standards.

Example:

George, a 13-year-old eighth grader, was shorter than the other boys in his grade. First the girls, and then the boys, grew several inches while George's height seemed to stay the same. His classmates were constantly making fun of his size. They called him "runt," "shorty," "midget," and "dwarf." Each day, someone came up with a new name to call him.

George was a sensitive person, and whenever he was called a name, he withdrew. More and more, the teacher began seeing George sitting alone while the others played. Mrs. Wright was very concerned about George's mental well-being and his classmate's lack of consideration and empathy for George and the other children who were different. She believed that role playing might be a method of helping the whole class, including George, gain insight into their behavior.

As the students began to empathize with the feelings of the characters they were role playing, George became more accepted and less a target of their hurtful behavior. George began playing with the others more readily during free time.

The Principle of Contingency Management in the Classroom

The term contingency refers to the planned, systematic relationship that is established between a behavior and a consequence. Thus, contingency management is an approach that teachers attempt to modify behavior by managing the contingencies, or consequences, for those behaviors. Contingency management incorporates the systematic use of reinforcement and punishment to develop, maintain, or change behavior. The following guidelines may be used in developing a contingency management plan:

1. Decide what to measure: A desired target behavior is specified and defined.
2. Select a measurement strategy: The behavior must be observable and measurable, as in frequency and duration.
3. Establish a baseline: The level of the behavior prior to implementing a treatment plan or an intervention must be established.

4. <u>Design a contingency plan</u>: Reinforcers or punishers are selected that correspond with behavioral consequences.
5. <u>Implement the contingency plan</u>: Collect data, provide reinforcement or punishment for the behavioral occurrences in accordance with the schedule selected for use, and record behavioral measurements on a graph.
6. <u>Evaluate the program</u>: Modify the contingency management plan as needed. Modifications can be achieved by (1) a reversal to baseline to determine effects of treatment on behavior, (2) changing the reinforcer or punisher if needed, or (3) implementing a new treatment.

A contingency management plan can be very useful in the classroom setting. In most classrooms, teachers specify what behaviors are expected and the contingencies for performing those behaviors. Contingencies are stated in the form of "If…then…" statements. Contingency management may take the form of various treatment techniques, such as token economies, contingency contracting, and precision teaching.

Students may be involved in the process of designing, implementing, and evaluating a contingency management plan. They can decide on behaviors that are in need of modification, select their reinforcers, assist in data collection, record the data on graphs, and evaluate the effectiveness of the contingency or treatment plan. The ultimate goal in allowing students to participate in contingency management is to encourage their use of the procedures that they have been taught to manage their own behavior. As with self-recording, the transition from teacher-managed to student-managed programs must be gradual, and students should be explicitly taught how to use self-reinforcement or self-punishment.

The Methodology of Backward Chaining and Applicable Situations

Behavioral chaining is a procedure where individual responses are reinforced for occurring in sequence to form a complex behavior. Each link is subsequently paired with its preceding one; thus, each link serves as a conditioned reinforcer for the link immediately preceding it. Behavior chains can be acquired by having each step in the chain verbally prompted or demonstrated. The prompts can then be faded and the links combined, with reinforcement, occurring after the last link has been performed.

In backward chaining, the components of the chain are acquired by reversing the order of the steps like sub-skills necessary to successfully complete the target task. The task is modeled in correct order by the teacher, and then each sub-skill is modeled in reverse order from beginning to end. The student practices the modeled sub-skill, and upon mastery of it, reverses back to the correct order until the task is completed. In this way, the final link or target behavior is consistently reinforced, and preceding links are built on, one at a time.

An example of backward chaining would be teaching a child to dress himself. The child is given the instruction, "Jimmy, take your jacket off," and his jacket is unzipped and lifted off the shoulders and down the arms until only the cuffs remain on Jimmy's wrists. If he does not pull the jacket the rest of the way off, he is physically guided to do so. He is given a reinforcer following removal of the garment. During the next session, the procedure is repeated, but the sleeve is left on his arms. In subsequent sessions, both arms are left in the sleeves, and then the jacket is left zipped. The instruction, "Jimmy, take your jacket off" is always presented, and a reinforcer is given only when the task is completed. The removal of each garment is taught in this manner, and the component steps are combined until instruction like, "Jimmy, take your jacket off" has acquired stimulus.

Backward chaining may be used to teach other self-help skills, such as toileting, grooming, and eating. Many academic and preacademic readiness skills could be effectively taught using this procedure as well. Steps until the final one are provided, with prompting occurring on the last step, and reinforcements delivered following the behavior. Each step in the program is prompted until the student can perform the entire sequence by himself. The backward chaining procedure may be of greatest assistance when a student experiences limited receptive abilities or imitative behavior.

Skill 13.02 **Demonstrating an understanding of effective collaboration among teachers and other professionals to identify appropriate modifications to the learning environment (i.e., schedule and physical arrangement) to manage inappropriate behaviors**

Teachers of exceptional students are expected to manage many roles and responsibilities, not only concerning their students, but also with respect to students' caregivers and other involved educational, medical, therapeutic, and administrative professionals. Because the needs of exceptional students are by definition multidisciplinary, a teacher of exceptional children often serves as the hub of a many-pronged wheel while communicating, consulting, and collaborating with the various stakeholders in a child's educational life. Managing these relationships effectively can be a challenge, but it is central to successful work in exceptional education.

Collaboration

- Special educators are part of the instructional or planning team.
- Teaming approaches are used for problem solving and program implementation.
- Regular teachers, Special Education Teachers, and other specialists collaborate (e.g., co-teach, team teach, work together on teacher assistance teams).

To ensure the greatest possibility of the child's educational success, all concerned parties must collaborate to discuss appropriate modifications to the learning environment. Each professional will bring forth information from his/her area of expertise and share it with the remainder of the team. Members should also share their knowledge of the child from previous interactions with the child. For example, the child's previous teacher may be able to offer some suggestions about modifications that were previously successful. The team discusses the best accommodations for the child based on the child's exceptionality and strengths and weaknesses. The team should communicate often to verify the success or failure of the modifications and to adjust or add modifications as needed.

Scheduling

Scheduling is a very important area to discuss thoroughly for each student. Not only is it important to ensure the child is receiving the necessary classes and extra assistance, but what time of the day each subject should be taught is extremely important also. For example, if the student is more alert and focused in the afternoon, he may need to take his weakest academic courses in the afternoon. Also, the Nurse may know that the child takes medication after lunch that makes him drowsy or not as alert; therefore, that child may need to take his weakest academic courses in the morning.

Physical Arrangement

Physical arrangement is another important area to discuss with other professionals. The Special Education Teacher and the previous teacher may offer suggestions based on their prior knowledge of the child. The child may function better in the front of the class or away from windows. A physical therapist may suggest the child is seated near the door. So it is essential that the team collaborates to discuss potential modifications of the child's learning environment to address the needs of the whole child.

Skill 13.03 **Understanding the importance of ongoing communication about behavior interventions among the student, the student's teachers, and the student's parents/guardians**

When implementing a behavior intervention plan, it is important that the plan is put into place with input from all the people who work with the student. This should include the student's parents, teachers, support teachers, and other interested parties. This is important so that all parties involved can agree on expectations, as well as rewards or consequences.

If a reward or punishment is established in the school, then it must be reinforced in the home setting so the student sees consistency and so the behavior plan can flow between settings.

It is important that all parties ensure ongoing communication on a daily, if not weekly, basis to ensure that proper feedback and follow-up is taking place. The behavior intervention plan should define behaviors and consequences, and it should be adaptable to different places, such as the classroom, playground, after-school program, daycare, etc. In order for consistency to take place, proper communication will have to take place on an ongoing basis. Consistency will help the students learn what is expected of them.

The Behavior Intervention Plan (BIP) should be evaluated to make sure that it is being followed and to make sure that it is working effectively. The plan should be reviewed at least annually, but can be reviewed whenever any member of the team feels that a review is necessary.
At intervals scheduled by the IEP team, the behavioral intervention case manager, parents/guardians, and others, as appropriate, shall evaluate the effectiveness of the behavioral intervention plan.

If the IEP team determines that major changes in the behavioral intervention plan are necessary, the teacher and behavioral intervention case manager shall conduct additional functional analysis assessment and propose changes.

The parent/guardian and the behavioral intervention case manager or qualified designee may make minor modifications in accordance with law without an CSE meeting. The IEP team also may include in the plan contingency schedules for altering specified procedures, their frequency or their duration, without reconvening the IEP team.

Skill 13.04   Recognizing that teacher attitudes and behaviors positively or negatively influence the behavior of students with disabilities

Influence of Teacher Attitudes

The attitude of the teacher can have both a positive or negative impact on student performance. A teacher's attitude can impact the expectations that the teacher may have toward the student's potential performance, as well as how the teacher behaves toward the student. This attitude, combined with expectations, can impact the students' self image, as well as their academic performance.

Negative teacher attitudes toward students with disabilities are detrimental to the handicapped students mainstreamed in general education classrooms. The phenomenon of a self-fulfilling prophecy is based on the attitude of the teacher. A self-fulfilling prophecy means that what we expect to happen is usually what ends up happening. In the context of education, this can mean that the predictions of a teacher about the ability of a student to achieve or not to achieve educational objectives are always proven to be correct.

In subtle ways, teachers communicate their expectations of individual students. In turn, the students may adjust their behaviors to match the teacher's expectations. Based on this, the teacher's expectations of what will happen comes true, which is a self-fulfilling prophecy.

Researchers in psychology and education have investigated this occurrence and discovered that many people are sensitive to verbal and nonverbal cues from others regarding how they expect to be treated. As a result, they may consciously and subconsciously change their behavior and attitudes to conform to another person's hopes. Depending on the expectation, this can be either advantageous or detrimental.

The teacher's attitude toward a student can be shaped by a number of variables, including race, ethnicity, disability, behavior, appearance, and social class. All of these variables can impact the teacher's attitude toward the student and how the student will achieve academically.

The premise of the self-fulfilling prophecy is the prediction and expectation of a teacher, which in turn impacts on the attitude of the teacher towards that student.

Researchers question whether the fact that a teacher believes the prediction to be correct means that the teacher will behave in a certain manner towards that student. The teacher has a responsibility to not allow her negative attitudes toward the student to impact how she perceives the student or interacts with him. If the teacher is able to communicate to all of her students that they all have great potential, and is optimistic regarding this, then the student should excel in some aspect of his educational endeavors, as long as the teacher is able to make the student believe in himself.

It can be hard for teachers to maintain a positive attitude at all times with all students, but it is important to be encouraging to all students at all times, as every student has the potential to be successful in school. Consistent encouragement can help turn a "C" student into a "B" or even "A" student while negative feedback can lead to failure and loss of self esteem.

Teachers should utilize their verbal communication skills to ensure that the things they communicate to students are said in the most positive manner possible. For example, instead of saying, "You talk to much," it would be more positive to state, "You have excellent verbal communication skills and are very sociable."

Teachers have a major influence on what happens in the classrooms because they are the primary decision makers, and they set the tone for how the information they distribute is absorbed.

For teachers to rise above their prejudices and preset attitudes, it is important that teachers are given training and support services to enable them to deal with students who come from challenging backgrounds or present challenging behaviors.

Skill 13.05   Identifying effective strategies for crisis prevention and intervention

According to the Center for Effective Collaboration and Practice, most schools are safe, but the violence from the surrounding communities have begun to make their way into the schools. Fortunately, there are ways to intervene and prevent crisis in our schools.

First, administrators, teachers, families, students, support staff, and community leaders must be trained and/or informed on early warning signs. It should also be emphasized not to use these warning signs to inappropriately label or stigmatize individual students because they may display some of the following warning signs.

Some early warning signs are as follows:

- Social withdrawal
- Excessive feelings of isolation and being alone
- Excessive feelings of rejection
- Being a victim of violence
- Feelings of being picked on and persecuted
- Low school interest and poor academic performance
- Expression of violence in writings and drawings
- Uncontrolled anger
- Patterns of impulsive and chronic hitting, intimidating, and bullying
- History of discipline problems
- Past history of violent and aggressive behavior
- Intolerance for differences and prejudicial attitudes
- Drug use and alcohol use
- Affiliation with gangs
- Inappropriate access to, possession of, and use of firearms
- Serious threats of violence

Imminent Warning Signs

Early warning signs and imminent warning signs differ because imminent warning signs require an immediate response. Imminent warning signs indicate that a student is very close to behaving in a way that is potentially dangerous to self and/or to others.

Imminent warning signs may include:

- Serious physical fighting with peers or family members
- Severe destruction of property
- Severe rage for seemingly minor reasons
- Detailed threats of lethal violence
- Possession and/or use of firearms and other weapons
- Other self-injurious behaviors or threats of suicide

When imminent signs are seen, school staff must follow the school board policies in place, which typically include reporting it to a designated person or persons before handling anything on your own.

Intervention and Prevention Plan

Every school system's plan may be different, but the plan should be derived from some of the following suggestions:

Share responsibility by establishing a partnership with the child, school, home, and community. Schools should collaborate with community agencies to coordinate the plan, in addition to rendering services to students who made need assistance. The community involvement should include child and family service agencies, law enforcement and juvenile justice systems, mental health agencies, businesses, faith and ethnic leaders, and other community agencies.

Inform parents and listen to them when early warning signs are observed. Effective and safe schools make persistent efforts to involve parents by: informing them routinely about school discipline policies, procedures, and rules, and about their children's behavior (both good and bad); involving them in making decisions concerning school-wide disciplinary policies and procedures; and encouraging them to participate in prevention.

Maintain confidentiality and parents' rights to privacy. Parental involvement and consent is required before personally identifiable information is shared with other agencies, except in the case of emergencies or suspicion of abuse.

Develop the capacity of staff, students, and families to intervene. Schools should provide the entire school community—teachers, students, parents, and support staff—with training and support in responding to imminent warning signs, preventing violence, and intervening safely and effectively. Interventions must be monitored by professionals who are competent in the approach.

Support students in being responsible for their actions. Schools and members of the community should encourage students to see themselves as responsible for their actions and actively engage them in planning, implementing, and evaluating violence prevention initiatives.

Simplify staff requests for urgent assistance. Many school systems and community agencies have complex legalistic referral systems with timelines and waiting lists. This should be a simple process that does not prevent someone from requesting assistance.

Drill and Practice

Most schools are required to have drills and to provide practice to ensure that everyone is informed of proper procedures to follow if emergencies occur. In addition to violence caused by a student, the emergency can also be an intruder in the building, a bomb threat, or a fire.

Skill 13.06 **Demonstrating an understanding of ethical considerations, laws, rules and regulations, and procedural safeguards regarding behavior interventions, including the concept of least restrictive intervention consistent with the needs of the individuals with disabilities**

1. **Free Appropriate Public Education (FAPE)** Special education and related services which: (1) are provided at public expense; (2) meet the standards of the state educational agency; (3) include preschool, elementary, and/or secondary education in the state involved, (4) are provided in conformity with each student's individualized education program, if the program is developed to meet requirements of the law.

2. **Notification and procedural rights for parents**. These include:
   - Right to examine records and obtain independent evaluations
   - Right to receive a clearly-written notice that states the results of the school's evaluation of their child and whether the child meets eligibility requirements for placement or continuation of special services
   - Parents who disagree with the school's decision may request a **due process** hearing and a **judicial hearing** if they do not receive satisfaction through due process.

3. **Identification and services to all children**: States must conduct public outreach programs to seek out and identify children who may need services.

4. **Necessary related services**: Developmental, corrective, and other support services that make it possible for a student to benefit from special education services must be provided. These may include speech, recreation, or physical therapy.

5. **Individualized assessments**: Evaluations and tests must be nondiscriminatory and individualized.

6. **Individualized Education Plans**: Each student receiving special education services must have an **individualized education plan** developed at a meeting that is attended by a qualified representative of the local education agency (LEA). Others who should attend would be the proposed Special Education Teachers, mainstream teachers, parents, and, when appropriate, the student.

7. **Least restrictive Environment (LRE)**: There is no simple definition of LRE. LRE differs with the child's needs. LRE means that the student is placed in an environment that is not dangerous or overly controlling or intrusive. The student should be given opportunities to experience what other peers of similar mental or chronological age are doing. Finally, LRE should be the environment that is the most integrated and normalized for the student's strengths and weaknesses. LRE for one child may be a regular classroom with support services, while LRE for another may be a self-contained classroom in a special school.

(Please refer to skill 4.)

A continuum of educational services must be made available by the LEA. Children must be placed in their least restrictive environment, and, insofar as possible, with regular classmates.

(Please refer to skill 4.01 for the Cascade of Special Education Services.)

Skill 13.07 Demonstrating an understanding of how to develop, implement, and evaluate a Functional Behavior Assessment (FBA)

A Functional Behavior Assessment (FBA) is a method of gathering information. The information that is collected is utilized to assess why problem behaviors occur. The data will also help pinpoint things to do that will help alleviate the behaviors. The data from a functional behavioral assessment is used to create a positive behavioral intervention plan.

The Individuals with Disabilities Education Act (IDEA) specifically calls for a functional behavior assessment when a child with a disability has his/her present placement modified for disciplinary reasons. IDEA 2004 states that the FBA must be written by a team. Not an individual. However, it does not elaborate on how a FBA should be specifically written, as the procedures may vary dependent on the specific child. Even so, there are several specific elements that should be a part of any functional behavior assessment.

The first step is to identify the particular behavior that must be modified. If the child has numerous problem behaviors, then it is important to assess which behaviors are the primary ones that should be addressed. This should be narrowed down to one or two primary behaviors. The primary behavior is then described so that everyone is clear as to what the behaviors consist of. The most typical order of procedures is as follows:

Identify and come to an agreement about the behaviors that need to be modified. Find out where the behaviors are most likely to happen and where they are not likely to happen. Identify what may trigger the behavior to occur.

The team will ask these types of questions: What is unique about the surroundings where behaviors are not an issue? What is different in the locations where the problem conduct occurs? Could they be linked to how the child and teacher get along? Does the amount of other students or the work a child is requested to do trigger the difficulty? Could the time of day or a child's frame of mind affect the behaviors? Was there a bus problem or an argument in the hallway? Are the behaviors likely to happen in a precise set of conditions or a specific location? What events seem to encourage the difficult behaviors?

Assemble data on the child's performance from as many resources as feasible. Develop a hypothesis about why difficult behaviors transpire (the function of the behaviors). A hypothesis is an educated deduction based on data. It helps foretell in which location and for what reason problem behaviors are most likely to take place and in which location and for what reason they are least likely to take place. Single out other behaviors that can be taught that will fulfill the same purpose for the child.

Test the hypothesis. The team develops and utilizes positive behavioral interventions that are written into the child's IEP or behavior intervention plan. Assess the success of the interventions. Modify or fine-tune as required.

If children have behaviors that place them or others at risk, they may require a crisis intervention plan. Crisis interventions should be developed before they are required. The team should determine what behaviors are crises and what they (and the child) will do in a crisis. By having a plan that guides actions, teachers can assist children through difficult emotional circumstances.

Essential Elements of a Behavior Intervention Plan

A Behavior Intervention Plan is utilized to reinforce or teach positive behavior skills. It is also known as a behavior support plan or a positive intervention plan. The child's team normally develops the Behavior Intervention Plan. The essential elements of a Behavior Intervention Plan are as follows:

- Skills training to increase the likelihood of appropriate behavior
- Modifications that will be made in classrooms or other environments to decrease or remove problem behaviors
- Strategies to take the place of problem behaviors and institute appropriate behaviors that serve the same function for the child
- Support mechanisms for the child to utilize the most appropriate behaviors

The IEP team determines whether the school discipline procedures need to be modified for a child, or whether the penalties need to be different from those written into the policy. This decision should be based on an assessment and a review of the records, including the discipline records or any manifestation determination review(s) that have been concluded by the school. A child's IEP or Behavior Intervention Plan should concentrate on teaching skills. Sometimes school discipline policies are not successful in rectifying problem behaviors. That is, the child does not learn what the school staff intended through the use of punishments, such as suspension. The child may learn instead that problem behaviors are useful in meeting a need, such as being noticed by peers. When this is true, it is difficult to defend punishment, by itself, as effective in changing problem behaviors. One of the most useful questions parents can ask when they have concerns about the discipline recommendations for their child is, "Where is the data that supports the recommendations?" Special education decisions are based on data. If school staff wants to use a specific discipline procedure, they should check for data that support the use of the procedure.

Skill 13.08   Recognizing the importance of teacher self- assessment reflection in the development and implementation of behavior interventions

While educational literature and studies may suggest best practices in fostering appropriate classroom behavior, teachers must rely on their assessment skills, including observation and data collection, to help them identify the most effective and constructive interventions for their students. Using data they collect through permanent products and observational and anecdotal recording, teachers can document individual and group behaviors and preempt or redirect behavior that might be of concern. Because data collection, by definition, requires tracking information regularly over time, patterns, trends and anomalies are easier to identify and evaluate than through undocumented impressions of behavior.

Teachers may collect information on an individual student, either to establish a baseline or to document areas of interest. For example, it may seem that Susan is constantly kicking the back of her classmate's chair during class, but data collection on Susan's kicking behavior may reveal many more or many fewer such kicks, or that it happens only when Susan has missed breakfast, etc. Data collection that centers on the group may reveal that her classmates don't seem to notice her kicking, or it may show that her kicking, if left unchecked, precipitates disruptive behaviors in others throughout the class period. Teachers can use information revealed through such data analysis to inform their intervention choices.

Before selecting behavioral interventions, teachers should first evaluate the environment and culture in their classrooms. Research conducted by the Northwest Regional Educational Library (Cotton, 1990) agrees that prevention of inappropriate behavior in classrooms is far preferable to remediation but also further suggests that certain baseline practices should be exercised in effective classrooms from the *first day of school*, including:

- Providing a functional and organized learning environment and well-organized instruction;
- Presenting clear rules and routines and supporting students in adhering to them;
- Making plain consequences for inappropriate behavior;
- Ensuring consistent and timely enforcement of those rules; and
- Fostering a sense of personal responsibility in students, and engendering a culture of shared responsibility for classroom management.

Once those fundamental supports are in place, teachers can examine data for clues about adjustments and tools that may help foster appropriate behavior. They then can implement those changes one at a time or in well-considered clusters, keeping in mind that the effects of their interventions should be documented through continued data collection.

So based on the data he'd recorded, Susan's teacher might decide to try adjusting the position of Susan's chair to make it less likely that her swinging leg will hit other students' chairs, *and* to assure that Susan ate breakfast or had access to a snack during morning recess. He might help Susan become more aware of respecting the personal space of other students. He might engage the class in a discussion about things that distract them from their schoolwork and ways classmates can help one another concentrate, which might include keeping feet near one's own desk. Whatever his choices, the teacher's proactive adjustments and interventions will likely be best informed by his analysis of the data collected on Susan and her classmates.

SUBAREA III.   WORKING IN A COLLABORATIVE PROFESSIONAL ENVIRONMENT

COMPETENCY 0014   UNDERSTAND HOW TO ESTABLISH PARTNERSHIPS WITH STUDENTS WITH DISABILITIES AND THEIR FAMILIES TO ENHANCE STUDENTS' ABILITY TO ACHIEVE DESIRED LEARNING OUTCOMES.

Skill 14.01   Identifying effective strategies for collaborating with students with disabilities to promote their development of self-advocacy skills

(Please refer to skills 6.05)

Skill 14.02   Applying strategies for assisting parents/guardians in becoming active participants in the educational team

The best resource a teacher has in reaching a student is having contact with his/her parents/guardians. Good teaching recognizes this fact and seeks to strengthen this bond through communication.

The first contact a teacher has with parents should be before the school year starts. While the teacher may be required to send a letter out stating the required supplies for the class, this does not count as an initial contact.

Parents are used to hearing that their child has done something bad/wrong when they receive a phone call from a teacher. Parents should be contacted whenever possible to give positive feedback. When you call John's mother and say, "John got an 'A' on the test today," you have just encouraged her to maintain open communication lines with you. Try to give 3 positive calls for every negative call you must give.

Parent-Teacher Conferences are scheduled at regular intervals throughout the school year. These provide excellent opportunities to discuss their children's progress, what they are learning, and how it may relate to your future plans for their academic growth. It is not unusual for the parent or teacher to ask for a conference outside of the scheduled Parent-Teacher Conference days. These meetings should be looked at as opportunities to provide assistance to that student's success. Parent-Teacher Conferences require the teacher to appear the consummate professional as a way to encourage parental involvement in their child's education. Using the following strategies will help you before, during and after these meetings.

Before the Conference:
1. Be Prepared! The parents/guardians may be interested in seeing their children's records. This means you should be ready to share your student's portfolios, assessments, and other pertinent information. Make sure your preparation for these meetings allows for you to share grades of the individual child without giving the information of another.
2. Check to see if there are any possible mistakes in your record keeping.
3. Write down at least 3 positive comments you would like to share with the parent, this is a way to declare the positives if you have a need to discuss negatives.
4. Schedule a set amount of time for each conference. Don't overbook your schedule! Remember that some conferences should be allotted more time than others.
5. Anticipating parents' questions will also provide you with the opportunity t appear professional when they are asked.
6. Remember the goal of the conference goes beyond simple communication, it is to forge an alliance to work together for the betterment of their child.
7. Ask your mentor for suggestions in preparing for the conference.

During the Conference:
1. Maintain a professional decorum! Remember the student's needs come first!
2. Remember this is your opportunity to learn about the student from his/her parents. You must show that you value their information.
3. Don't "monopolize" the time. While you may things you consider important to share, parents need opportunities to voice their own concerns.
4. Be an active listener! If you must take notes let the parents know why you have chosen to do this.
5. Remember to ask for suggestions. Get the "inside information" on the strategies that work with the parents. This enables you to show a united front.
6. Closure: Orally summarize the conference at the end. If another conference is needed schedule one.

After the conference:
1. Review your notes. This will help you prepare a course of action.
2. Follow through! If you and the parent agreed upon a strategy or something that needed to be done on your part make sure you follow through!
3. Share any pertinent information with others who work with the student.
4. Commit yourself to maintaining the strength of the parent school connection.
5. Document the time, place and participants for future reference.

Modern technology has opened 2 more venues for communicating with parents. School/Classroom websites are written with the intent of sharing regularly with parents/guardians. Many teachers now post their plans for the marking period and provide extra-credit and homework from these websites. Email is now one of the major modes of communication in the world today. Most parents now have email accounts and are more than willing to give you their email address to be kept appraised of their child's academic progress.

Special events also provide opportunities for parental contact. Poetry readings, science fairs, ice-cream socials, etc. are such events.

Skill 14.03 Demonstrating familiarity with typical concerns of parents/guardians of students with disabilities and with strategies for planning an individualized program that addresses these concerns

All parents share some basic goals for their children. They want their children to grow up to be healthy, happy members of society who lead independent lives with productive employment. Parents of students with disabilities are no different, although the path that their children take may have additional turns and obstacles along the way.

Health: Many children with disabilities have associated health problems or are at risk for health problems. Many also take medication(s) routinely for health or behavioral conditions.

Parents of students with disabilities are concerned with their children's long range health, the cost of health care (as children and later as adults), and the effects of medication on their child's behavior, health, and school work.

It is not uncommon for special education students to take some medication while at school. Providing the school with the needed medication may be a financial strain for the family. Just the fact that others will be aware of the child's health and medications can also be a parental concern.

Parents are often concerned because many of these students have difficulty identifying changes in their health and in communicating possible changes in medication reactions. IEPs often include objectives for the child to communicate changes in his health and effects of medication.

Happiness: The quality of life for more severely disabled children is different than that of the general population. Even students with less severe physical conditions (for example, a learning disability) may have lower self-esteem because they feel "stupid" or "different" because they leave the inclusion classroom for some special education services. Students with disabilities often have difficulty making friends, which can also impact happiness.

Parents of students with disabilities (as all parents) feel the emotional impact of the disability on their children. Parents are anxious to help their children feel good about themselves and fit in to the general population of their peers.

Social goals may be included on the IEP. Some students (particularly those on the autism spectrum) may have a time (per the IEP minutes) to meet with a speech and language pathologist to work on social language. Other students may meet regularly (again, per IEP minutes) with the Social Worker to discuss situations from the classroom or general school setting.

Independence: Initially, parents of students with disabilities may be somewhat overprotective of their child. Soon after, however, parents begin to focus on ways to help their child function independently.

Young children with disabilities may be working on self-care types of independence, such as dressing, feeding, and toilet use. Elementary students may be working on asking for assistance as needed, completing work, and being prepared for class with materials (books, papers, etc.) High school students may be working on driving, future job skills, or preparation for post-secondary education.

Job Training: IDEA 2004 addresses the need for students with a disability to be prepared for a job or post-secondary education in order to be independent, productive members of society.

Job training goals and objectives for the student with a disability may be vocational, such as food service, mechanical, carpentry, etc. Job training goals for other students may include appropriate high school coursework to prepare for a college program.

Productivity: Ultimately, the goal of the parents and the school is for the student to become a productive member of society who can support himself financially and live independently. This type of productivity happens when the student becomes an adult with a measure of good health, positive self-esteem and ability to interact positively with others, independent personal and work skills, and job training.

Particular Stages of Concern: Parents of students with special needs deal with increased concerned at times when the child is going into a new stage of development or age. Some of these times include: when the child is first identified as having a disability, entrance into an early childhood special education program, kindergarten (when it is evident that the disability remains despite services received thus far), third grade (when the student is expected to use more skills independently), junior high school, and entrance into high school.

Additional IEP goals and objectives may be warranted at these times, as the student is expected to use a new set of skills or may be entering a new educational setting.

It should be noted that parents are often more concerned when a younger, non-disabled sibling surpasses the child with the disability in some skill (such as feeding or reading). Previously, the parents may not have fully been aware of what most children can do at a particular age.

Skill 14.04 Recognizing the effects of cultural and environmental influences (e.g., cultural and linguistic diversity, socioeconomic level, abuse, neglect, substance abuse) on students and their families

Hispanic children represent the fastest-growing minority and approximately ¾ of the children designated as Limited English Proficiency (LEP). Additionally, culturally-diverse students may speak a dialect of a language such as Spanish, which has its own system of pronunciation and rules. It should be stressed that speaking a dialect does not in itself mean that the child has a language problem. Certain English sounds and grammar structures may not have equivalents in some languages, and failure to produce these elements may be a function of inexperience with English rather than a language delay.

Learn more about the effects of cultural on special education services: http://www6.semo.edu/southeasttesol/Courses/EN604D/The%20Effects%20of%20Culture%20on%20Special%20Education%20Services.pdf

When minority or culturally-diverse children are being screened for language problems, learning disabilities, or other exceptional student programs, the tests and assessment procedures must be non-discriminatory. Furthermore, testing should be done in the child's native language; however, if school instruction has not been in the native language, there may appear to be a problem because assessments typically measure school language. Even with native English-speaking children, there are differences between the language that is functional at home and in the community and the language requirements of school.

Normality in child behavior is influenced by society's attitudes and cultural beliefs about what is normal for children (e.g., the motto for the Victorian era was, "Children should be seen and not heard"). However, criteria for what is "normal" involves consideration of these factors:

Cultural and societal attitudes towards gender change over time. While attitudes towards younger boys playing with dolls or girls preferring sports to dolls have relaxed, children eventually are expected as adults to conform to the expected behaviors for males and females.

Other factors that influence students with disabilities and their families include abuse, neglect, and substance abuse.

Abuse: Whether abuse to the child or to a parent, the effect transcends the immediate situation to interaction with others in the home, school, and community. If the child with a disability is the one who is abused, he will be distrustful of others. He may also continue the cycle of behavior by acting out in abusive ways towards others.

If a parent of the child with a disability is being abused, the child may feel responsible. He may be actively trying to protect the abused parent. At the least, he will carry emotional, and possibly psychological effects, of living in a home where abuse happens.

A parent who is being abused will be less likely to be able to attend to the needs of the child with a disability. She may be secretive about the fact that the abuse even occurs.

Unfortunately, having a child with a disability puts excessive strain on a marriage. Abusive tendencies may be exaggerated.

Neglect: If a child with a disability is neglected physically or emotionally, he may exhibit a number of behaviors. He will most likely be distrustful of adults in general. He may horde classroom materials, snacks, etc. At the very least, he will be unfocused on school work.

In the instances of abuse and neglect (or suspected instances), the special educator (as all educators) is a mandated reporter to the appropriate agency (such as DCFS – Division of Child and Family Services).

Substance Abuse: If a child with a disability or a parent is involved in substance abuse, that abuse will have a negative effect in the areas of finances, health, productivity, and safety. It is important for the Special Education Teacher to be aware of signs of substance abuse. She should be proactive in teaching drug awareness. She should also know the appropriate school channels for getting help for the student, as well as community agencies that can help parents involved in substance abuse.

Skill 14.05   Demonstrating knowledge of factors that promote effective collaboration in a culturally-responsive program that fosters respectful and beneficial relationships among students, families, and educators

Teachers of exceptional students are expected to manage many roles and responsibilities, not only as concern their students, but also with respect to students' caregivers and other involved educational, medical, therapeutic, and administrative professionals. Because the needs of exceptional students are by definition multidisciplinary, a teacher of exceptional children often serves as the hub of a many-pronged wheel, communicating, consulting, and collaborating with the various stakeholders in a child's educational life. Managing these relationships effectively can be a challenge but is central to successful work in exceptional education.
Students

Useful standards have been developed by the Council for Exceptional Children (2003) that outline best practices in communicating and relating to children and their families. For example, CEC guidelines suggest that effective teachers:

- offer students a safe and supportive learning environment, including clearly-expressed and reasonable expectations for behavior;
- create learning environments that encourage self-advocacy and developmentally-appropriate independence; and
- offer learning environments that promote active participation in independent or group activities.

Such an environment is an excellent foundation for building rapport and trust with students and for communicating a teacher's respect for and expectation that they take a measure of responsibility for their educational development. Ideally, mutual trust and respect will afford teachers opportunities to learn of and engage students' ideas, preferences and abilities.

Parents and Families

Families know students better than almost anyone and are a valuable resource for teachers of exceptional students. Often, an insight or observation from a family member, or his or her reinforcement of school standards or activities, mean the difference between success and frustration in a teacher's work with children. Suggestions for relationship building and collaboration with parents and families include:

> Learn more about Possible Interventions when dealing with difficult cultural influences of disability : http://www.cec.sped.org/AM/Template.cfm?Section=Search&template=/CM/HTMLDisplay.cfm&ContentID=4227

- Using laypersons' terms when communicating with families and making the communication available in the language of the home;
- Searching out and engaging family members' knowledge and skills in providing services, educational and therapeutic, to student;
- Exploring and discussing the concerns of families and helping them find tactics for addressing those concerns;
- Planning collaborative meetings with children and their families and assisting them to become active contributors to their educational team;
- Ensuring that communications with and about families is confidential and conducted with respect for their privacy;
- Offering parents accurate and professionally-presented information about the pedagogical and therapeutic work being done with their child;
- Keeping parents abreast of their rights, of the kinds of practices that might violate them, and of available recourse if needed; and
- Acknowledging and respect cultural differences.

Paraprofessionals and General Education Teachers

Paraprofessionals and general education teachers are also important collaborators with teachers of exceptional students. Although they may have daily exposure to exceptional students, they may not have the theoretical or educational experience to assure their effective interaction with such students. They do bring valuable perspective to, and opportunities for breadth and variety in, an exceptional child's educational experience. General education teachers also offer curriculum and subject matter expertise and a high level of professional support, while paraprofessionals may provide insights born of their particular familiarity with individual students. CEC suggests that teachers can best collaborate with general education teachers and paraprofessionals by:

- Offering information about the characteristics and needs of children with exceptional learning needs
- Discussing and brainstorming ways to integrate children with exceptionalities into various settings within the school community
- Modeling best practices and instructional techniques and accommodations and coaching others in their use
- Keeping communication about children with exceptional learning needs and their families confidential
- Consulting with these colleagues in the assessment of individuals with exceptional learning needs
- Engaging them in group problem-solving and in developing, executing, and assessing collaborative activities
- Offering support to paraprofessionals by observing their work with students and offering feedback and suggestions

Related Service Providers and Administrators

Related service providers and administrators offer specialized skills and abilities that are critical to an exceptional education teacher's ability to advocate for his or her student and meet a school's legal obligations to the student and his or her family. Related service providers—like speech, occupational and language therapists, Psychologists, and physicians—offer expertise and resources unparalleled in meeting a child's developmental needs. Administrators are often experts in the resources available at the school and local education agency levels and the culture and politics of a school system and can be powerful partners in meeting the needs of exceptional education teachers and students. A teacher's most effective approach to collaborating with these professionalS includes:

- Confirming mutual understanding of the accepted goals and objectives of the student with exceptional learning needs as documented in his or her IEP;
- Soliciting input about ways to support related service goals in classroom settings;
- Understanding the needs and motivations of each and acting in support whenever possible;
- Facilitating respectful and beneficial relationships between families and professionals; and
- Regularly and accurately communicating observations and data about the child's progress or challenges.

Skill 14.06 Demonstrating an understanding of how to communicate seffectively and to adapt communication techniques and strategies in response to the characteristics and needs of students and their families

Effective communication strategies are required when dealing with families with student's with disabilities. The communication strategies should be flexible and respond to the individual needs of the families.

Teachers traditionally communicate their educational philosophies to families through parent workshops or newsletters. These methods have their drawbacks, however, as in many cases workshops may have low attendance as parents may have problems with work schedules or with getting outside help to take care of a student with disability.

Newsletters may be thrown away or not read thoroughly; and those that are only written in English distance parents for whom English is not their first language. Family school partnerships are developed when families are encouraged to spend more time in the classroom and when they are offered more information about their child's education. When families are in the classroom, they have a chance to observe teacher-student interactions, ask the teacher questions, and give feedback on curriculum or development. They also have an opportunity to meet other families.

As the structure of families in today's societies continues to change, teachers may need to try different family outreach strategies that target the new family structure, as what was done in the past may not be effective.

Teachers need to have a range of strategies for contacting parents, such as using the telephone, email, letters, newsletters, classroom bulletin boards, and parent-teacher conferences.

Teachers also need to be familiar with the student's home culture and have an appreciation for diversity by planning lessons and activities that are inclusive of the multi-cultural classroom.   Through effective communication, teachers can involve parents as leaders and decision makers in the school. As more students with disabilities are included in the general education curriculum, both special and regular educators will need training that focuses on effectively interacting with parents of children with disabilities to involve them as equal partners in the educational planning and decision-making process for their child.

Effective Communication Skills Between the Sender and the Receiver

Communication occurs when one person sends a message and gets a response from another person. In fact, whenever two people can see or hear each other, they are communicating. The receiver changes roles and becomes the sender once the response is given. The communication process may break down if the receiver's interpretation differs from that of the sender.

Effective teaching depends on communication. By using good sending skills, the teacher has more assurance that she is getting her message across to her students. By being a model of a good listener, a teacher can help her students learn to listen and respond appropriately to others.

Attending Skills

The sender is the person who communicates the message; the receiver is the person who ultimately responds to the message.

Attending skills are used to receive a message. Some task-related attending skills that have been identified include: (1) looking at the teacher when information or instructions are being presented, (2) listening to assignment directions, (3) listening for answers to questions, (4) looking at the chalkboard, and (5) listening to others speak when appropriate.

For some students, special techniques must be employed to gain and hold attention. For example, the teacher might first call the student by name when asking a question to assure attending by that individual, or she may ask the question before calling the name of a student to create greater interest. Selecting students at random to answer questions helps to keep them alert and listening. Being enthusiastic and keeping lessons short and interactive assist in maintaining the attention of those students who have shorter attention spans. Some students may be better able to focus their attention when environmental distractions are eliminated or at least reduced, and non-verbal signals can be used to draw students' attention to the task. Finally, arranging the classroom so that all students can see the teacher helps direct attention to the appropriate location.

Clarity of Expression

Unclear communication between the teacher and special needs students sometimes contributes to problems in academic and behavioral situations. In the learning environment, unclear communication can add to the student's confusion about certain processes or skills he is attempting to master.

There are many ways in which the teacher can improve the clarity of his/her communication. Giving clear, precise directions is one. Verbal directions can be simplified by using shorter sentences, familiar words, and relevant explanations. Asking a student to repeat directions or to demonstrate understanding of them by carrying out the instructions is an effective way of monitoring the clarity of expression. In addition, clarification can be achieved by the use of concrete objects, multidimensional teaching aids, and by modeling or demonstrating what should be done in a practice situation.

Finally, a teacher can clarify her communication by using a variety of vocal inflections. The use of intonation juncture can help make the message clearer, as can pauses at significant points in the communication. For example, verbal praise should be spoken with inflection that communicates sincerity. Pausing before starting key words, or stressing those that convey meanings, helps students learn concepts being taught.

Paraphrasing

Paraphrasing, that is, restating what the student says using one's own words, can improve communication between the teacher and that student. First, in restating what the student has communicated, the teacher is not judging the content—she is simply relating what she understands the message to be. If the message has been interpreted differently from the way intended, the student is asked to clarify. Clarification should continue until both parties are satisfied that the message has been understood.

The act of paraphrasing sends the message that the teacher is trying to better understand the student. Restating the student's message as fairly and accurately as possible assists the teacher in seeing things from the student's perspective.

Paraphrasing is often a simple restatement of what has been said. Lead-ins, such as, "Your position is…" or "It seems to you that…" are helpful in paraphrasing a student's messages. A student's statement, "I am not going to do my math today," might be paraphrased by the teacher as, "Did I understand you to say that you are not going to do your math today?" By mirroring what the student has just said, the teacher has telegraphed a caring attitude for that student and a desire to respond accurately to his message.

To paraphrase effectively a student's message, the teacher should: (1) restate the student's message in her own words; (2) preface her paraphrasing with such remarks as, "You feel…" or "I hear you say that…"; and (3) avoid indicating any approval or disapproval of the student's statements. Johnson (1978) states the following as a rule to remember when paraphrasing: "Before you can reply to a statement, restate what the sender says, feels, and means correctly and to the sender's satisfaction." (p.139)

Descriptive feedback is a factual, objective (i.e., unemotional) recounting of a behavioral situation or message sent by a student. Descriptive feedback has the same effect as paraphrasing, in that: (1) when responding to a student's statement, the teacher restates (i.e., paraphrases) what the student has said or factually describes what she has seen, and (2) it allows the teacher to check her perceptions of the student and his message. A student may do or say something, but because of the teacher's feelings or state of mind, the student's message or behavior might be totally misunderstood. The teacher's descriptive feedback, which Johnson (1972) refers to as "understanding," indicates that the teacher's intent is to respond only to ask the student whether his statement has been understood, how he feels about the problem, and how he perceives the problem. The intent of the teacher is to more clearly "understand" what the student is saying, feeling, or perceiving in relation to a stated message or a behavioral event.

Evaluative feedback is verbalized perception by the teacher that judges, evaluates, approves, or disapproves of the statements made by the student. Evaluative feedback occurs when the student makes a statement, and the teacher responds openly with, "I think you're wrong," "That was a dumb thing to do," or "I agree with you entirely." The tendency to give evaluative responses is heightened in situations where feelings and emotions are deeply involved. The stronger the feelings, the more likely it is that two persons will each evaluate the other's statements solely from his or her own point of view.

Since evaluative feedback intones a judgmental approval or disapproval of the student's remark or behavior, in most instances, it can be a major barrier to mutual understanding and effective communication. It is a necessary mechanism for providing feedback of a quantitative (and sometimes qualitative) instructional nature (e.g., test scores, homework results, classroom performance). In order to be effective, evaluative feedback must be offered in a factual, constructive manner. Descriptive feedback tends to reduce defensiveness and feelings of being threatened because it will most likely communicate that the teacher is interested in the student as a person, has an accurate understanding of the student and what he is saying, and encourages the students to elaborate and further discuss his problems.

To summarize, in the learning environment, as in all situations, effective communication depends upon good sending and receiving skills. Teaching and managing students involves good communication. By using clear, non-threatening feedback, the teacher can provide students with information that helps them to understand themselves better, while at the same time providing a clearer understanding of each student on the teacher's part.

Skill 14.07   Demonstrating knowledge of ethical practices related to communication and collaboration with families, including confidentiality and informed consent

The Family Educational Rights and Privacy Act (1974), also known as the Buckley Amendment, assures confidentiality of student records. Parents are afforded the right to examine, review, request changes in information deemed inaccurate, and stipulate persons who might access their child's records.

Due Process

"Due process is a set of procedures designed to ensure the fairness of educational decisions and the accountability of both professionals and parents in making these decisions" (Kirk and Gallagher, 1986, p. 24). These procedures serve as a mechanism by which the child and his family can voice their opinions or concerns as sometimes dissents. Due process safeguards exist in all matters pertaining to identification, evaluation, and educational placement.

> **Learn more about Due Process and the Law:**
> http://www.wrightslaw.com/info/dp.index.htm

Due process occurs in two realms: substantive and procedural. Substantive due process is the content of the law (e.g., appropriate placement for special education students). Procedural due process is the form through which substantive due process is carried out (e.g., parental permission for testing). Public Law 101-476 contains many items of both substantive and procedural due process.

1. A due process hearing may be initiated by parents of the LEA as an impartial forum for challenging decisions about identification, evaluation, or placement. Either party may present evidence, cross-examine witnesses, obtain a record of the hearing, and be advised by counsel or by individuals having expertise in the education of individuals with disabilities. Findings may be appealed to the state education agency (SEA), and if still dissatisfied, either party may bring civil action in a state of federal district court. Hearing timelines are set by legislation.

2. Parents may obtain an independent evaluation if there is disagreement about the education evaluation performed by the LEA. The results of such an evaluation: (1) must be considered in any decision made with respect to the provision of a free, appropriate public education for the child and (2) may be presented as evidence at a hearing. Further, the parents may request this evaluation at public expense: (1) if a hearing officer requests an independent educational evaluation or (2) if the decision from a due process hearing is that the LEA's evaluation was inappropriate. If the final decision holds that the evaluation performed is appropriate, the parent still has the right to an independent educational evaluation, but not at public expense.

3. Written notice must be provided to parents prior to a proposal or refusal to initiate or make a change in the child's identification, evaluation, or educational placement and must include the following:

    a. a listing of parental due process safeguards
    b. a description and a rationale for the chosen action
    c. a detailed listing of components (e.g., tests, records, reports) which were the basis for the decision
    d. assurance that the language and content of notices were understood by the parents

4. Parental consent must be obtained before evaluation procedures can occur unless there is a state law specifying otherwise.

5. Sometimes parents or guardians cannot be identified to function in the dueprocess role. When this occurs, a suitable person must be assigned to act as a surrogate. This is done by the LEA in full accordance with legislation.

COMPETENCY 0015   UNDERSTAND HOW TO ESTABLISH PARTNERSHIPS WITH EDUCATORS, ADMINISTRATORS, OTHER SCHOOL PROFESSIONALS, AND COMMUNITY MEMBERS TO ENHANCE LEARNING OPPORTUNITIES FOR STUDENTS WITH DISABILITIES.

Skill 15.01   Demonstrate familiarity with a variety of collaborative, inclusive teaching models (e.g., co-teaching, push-in, consultant teaching [CT]) and their implementation.

(Please refer to skill 7.01.)

Special Education Teachers of students with mild to moderate disabilities are moving toward consultative/collaborative models of service delivery. This movement has resulted in more team teaching in the regular classroom and a higher degree of mainstreaming of students. Education of students with more severe disabilities has moved closer in proximity to non-disabled peers. Technology enables a wide range of learners to participate meaningfully in learning and social interaction. Thus, the Special Education Teacher must be able to identify student access needs and match technology resources with appropriate learning activities and curricula.

Composite Scenario of an Inclusive Educational Setting

The following composite scenario, published in the ERIC Clearinghouse Views (1993, p. 66-67), provides a brief description of how regular and special teachers work together to address the individual needs of all of their students.

Jane Smith teaches 3rd grade at Lincoln Elementary School. Three days a week, she co-teaches the class with Lynn Vogei, a Special Education Teacher. Their 25 students include four who have special needs due to disabilities and two others who currently need special help in specific curriculum areas. Each of the students with a disability has an IEP that was developed by a team that included both teachers. The teachers, paraprofessionals, and the school principal believe that these students have a great deal to contribute to the class and that they will achieve their best in the environment of a general education classroom.

All of the school personnel have attended in-service training designed to develop collaborative skills for teaming and problem solving. Mrs. Smith and the two professionals who work in the classroom also received special training on disabilities and how to create an inclusive classroom environment. The school's principal, Ben Parks, had worked in special education many years ago and has received training on the impact of new special education developments and instructional arrangements on school administration. Each year, Mr. Parks works with the building staff to identify areas in which new training is needed. For specific questions that may arise, technical assistance is available through a regional special education cooperative.

Mrs. Smith and Miss Vogel share responsibility for teaching and for supervising their paraprofessional. In addition to the time they spend together in the classroom, they spend two hours each week planning instruction, plus additional planning time with other teachers and support personnel who work with their students.

The teachers use their joint planning time to problem-solve and discuss the use of special instructional techniques for all students who need special assistance. Monitoring and adapting instruction for individual students is an ongoing activity. The teachers use curriculum-based measurement in systematically assessing their students' learning progress. They adapt curricula so that lessons begin at the edge of the students' knowledge, adding new material at the students' pace, and presenting it in a style consistent with the students' learning style. For some students, pre-organizers or chapter previews are used to bring out the most important points of the material to be learned; for other students, new vocabulary words may need to be highlighted, or reduced reading levels may be required . Some students may use special activity worksheets, while others may learn best by using audiocassettes.

In the classroom, the teachers group students differently for different activities. Sometimes, the teachers and paraprofessionals divide the class, each teaching a small group or tutoring individuals. They use cooperative learning projects to help the students learn to work together and form social relationships. Peer tutors provide extra help to students who need it. Students without disabilities are more than willing to help their friends who have disabilities, and vice versa.

While the regular classroom may not be the best learning environment for every child with a disability, it is highly desirable for all who can benefit. It provides contact with age-peers and prepares all students for the diversity of the world beyond the classroom.

Skill 15.02 Demonstrating an understanding of effective communication (e.g., active listening, conflict resolution, building consensus, understanding verbal/nonverbal communication)

Effective communication must occur between teacher and students, as well as among students. Clarity of expression, as well as appropriate feedback, is essential to successful teaching. Thus, the special educator needs to be able to teach students who require varying techniques and approaches. She must be able to recognize specific needs, must possess diagnostic capabilities, and must make the necessary environment and instructional adaptations, all on an individual basis.

Teachers must be able to diagnose individual learning styles because the way in which students learn differs, just as abilities vary. Learning can be affected by environmental elements like sound and room arrangement and physical elements, such as time of day and mobility. Coupled with the concern for learning styles is the use of sensory channels, such as visual, auditory, and haptic. The special needs teacher must identify modality channels through which students process information most proficiently.

Special techniques are needed in order to teach basic skills due to the fact that students vary in their rate of learning, need for routine, ability to memorize or retain what they learn, reasoning skills, and ability to generalize newly-acquired concepts. Students must be able to learn from simple to more complex levels within a task hierarchy in order to experience success and become independent learners to the greatest extent possible.

The teacher may need to respond to feelings as well as words. Not all communication is delivered in a verbal manner. Indeed, words spoken are not always true indicators of what a person means and feels. Non-verbal communication, such as body language, facial expression, tone of voice, and speaking patterns, are all clues to the underlying message the student is attempting to deliver. The teacher demonstrates her willingness to listen by sitting close, leaning forward, making eye contact, and showing understanding by nodding or smiling. By so doing, she is sending the message that she cares, is concerned about the student's feelings, and will take the time necessary to understand what is really being communicated.

To facilitate further communication, the teacher must become an active listener. This involves much more than just restating what the person has said. Her responses must reflect the student's feelings rather than the spoken language. It is essential that the teacher say back what she understands the student's message to mean, as well as the feelings she perceives, and ask for correctness of interpretation. Often, teachers enter into active listening, with body language conveying a willingness to listen, but respond in such a way that judgment or disapproval of the underlying message is conveyed. Evaluative responses from the listener will decrease attempts to communicate. Encouragement towards communicative efforts is enhanced by use of statements rather than questions, spoken in the present tense and with use of personal pronouns, reflective of current feelings about the situation, and offering self-disclosure of similar experiences or feelings if the teacher feels inclined to do so.

Response to the child's feelings is particularly important since his message may not convey what he really feels. For example, a student who has failed a test may feel inadequate and have the need to blame someone else, such as his teacher, for his failure. He might say to her, "You didn't tell me that you were including all the words from the last six weeks on the spelling test." The teacher, if she were to respond solely to the spoken message might say, "I know I told you that you would be tested over the entire unit. You just weren't listening!" The intuitive, sensitive teacher would look beyond the spoken words by saying,

"You're telling me that it feels bad to fail a test." By responding to the child's feelings, the teacher lets him know her understanding of his personal crisis, and the student is encouraged to communicate further.
(Please also refer to skill 14.06.)

Skill 15.03 **Apply collaborative strategies for working with general educators and other professionals in the school to solve problems and build consensus with regard to students with disabilities and the special education program.**

Support And Professional Services

When making eligibility, program, and placement decisions about a student, the Special Education Teacher serves as a member of a multidisciplinary team. Teachers are involved in every aspect regarding the education of individual students; therefore, they need to be knowledgeable not only about teaching and instructional techniques, but also about support services. These services will need to be coordinated, and teachers must be able to work in a collaborative manner.

The concept of mainstreaming special needs students, that is integrating them with their classmates in as many living and learning environments as possible, caught hold about the time that provisions for the Individuals with Disabilities Education Act (IDEA) were formulated in the early- to mid-70s. Even though mainstreaming is not specifically addressed in this legislation, the education of all children and youth with disabilities in their least restrictive environment is mandated. In addition, this important legislation defines special education, identifies related services that may be required if special education is to be effective, and requires the participation of parents and other persons involved in the education of children and youth with disabilities.

Close contact and communication must be established and maintained between the school district staff, each base school, and the various specialists (or consultants) providing ancillary services. These persons often serve special needs students in auxiliary (i.e., providing help) and supplementary (i.e., in addition to) ways. Thus, the principles and methods of special education must be shared with regular educators, and tenets and practices of regular education must be conveyed to special educators. Job roles and unique responsibilities and duties of support specialists like Speech/Language Therapists, Physical and Occupational Therapists, Social Workers, School Psychologists and Nurses, and others need to be known by all teachers.

Furthermore, the services which can be provided by community resources, and the support that can be given by parents and professional organizations, must be known to all in order for maximum education for exceptional students to occur. Professional services are offered on a local, state, and national level for most areas of disability. Teachers are able to stay abreast of most current practices and changes by reading professional journals, attending professional conferences, and maintaining membership in professional organizations.

Skill 15.04 Identifying principles and analyzing factors related to the coordination of efforts (e.g., information-sharing systems, scheduling) among professionals working with students with disabilities

When professionals work together to provide services for students with disabilities, it is important that they work as a cohesive teaching unit, using information sharing systems and proper scheduling procedures.

A system should be put into place for sharing program materials, tracking students' mastery of goals and objectives, and supporting the various requirements of administrative and teaching staff. Because of the variety of learning objectives and the need to make the special education curriculum appropriate for each student, information sharing is critical. It is not uncommon for a teacher in one part of the school to be completely unaware of what another teacher is doing. Two teachers may have similar students with similar intensive needs, and by sharing information, lesson plans, and behavior modification strategies, the workload is shared and students benefit from a more cohesive program.

Professionals also need to work together to ensure that students with disabilities are receiving the services outlined in the IEP. The Speech Teacher, the Occupational Therapist, the General Education teacher, and the Special Education Teacher may all be providing services to one student. In order to ensure that the proper time is allotted for each service, the professionals involved will have to work together to develop a schedule for the student to ensure that nothing is left out and that all areas outlined in the IEP are addressed. This will also help when ensuring that students with disabilities that can be taught in groups are grouped with other students who may have the same requirements. This can only be effectively done when professionals share schedules, student information, and student requirements. If they work together, they can accomplish a great deal more than when working independently.

Skill 15.05   Demonstrating an understanding of how to work effectively within school administrative structures to ensure that students with disabilities receive services as specified in their IEPs

The student's IEP must state the special education and related services and supplementary aids and services to be provided to the student, or on behalf of the student. A statement of the program modifications or supports for school personnel that will allow the student to become involved in and progress in the general curriculum should also be included in the IEP. In the past, students with disabilities were sometimes placed in the regular education classroom without any help or support for the sake of inclusion. IDEA '97 required that supplementary aids and services, accommodations, modifications, and supports play a more important role in a student's education.

The IEP should specify supports for school personnel. The decisions as to which supplementary aids and services, accommodations, modifications, or supports are appropriate for a particular student are to be made on an individualized basis by the IEP team.

The approach should be to create, from the beginning, a curriculum with built-in supports for diverse learners, rather than to fit supplementary aids and services, accommodations, modifications, or supports in after the fact.

The IEP should include ways for the parent and the teacher to objectively measure the student's progress or lack of progress (regression) in the special education program. If the student is not receiving the services specified in his/her IEP, then he/she may not be able to meet the goals outlined in the IEP, so this careful monitoring and reporting of goals and objectives every quarter should help ensure that students receive the services that they are entitled too.

If the student is entitled to additional services from a speech therapist, Occupational Therapist, or other specialist, the teachers should ensure that the specified services that are outlined in the IEP are being provided to the students. This can be done by working with the principal or other administrators and discussing how much time has been allotted for the additional services and ensuring that each student receives the time allotted and spelled out in his/her IEP.

Skill 15.06   Identify the roles of community personnel (e.g., Social Workers, case workers, psychiatrists/Psychologists) in providing services to students with special needs, including transition services.

Please refer to Skill 5.03

Skill 15.07   Demonstrate an understanding of how to communicate and work effectively with community members (e.g., interagency collaboration, establishing relationships with advocacy groups).

Parent and Professional Advocacy Activity and Parent Organizations

There have always been, and will always be, exceptional children with special needs, but special education services have not always been in existence to provide for these needs. Private school and state institutions were primary sources of education for individuals with retardation in earlier years. The 9th and 10th amendments to the U.S. Constitution leave education as an unstated power and therefore vested in the states. As was the practice in Europe, government funds in America were first appropriated to experimental schools to determine whether students with disabilities actually could be educated. During the mid-twentieth century, legislators and governors in control of funds, faced with evidence of the need and efficacy of special education programs, refused to expend funds adequately, thus creating the ultimate need for federal guidelines in PL 94-142 to mandate flow-through money. Concurrently, due process rights and procedures were outlined based on litigation and legislation enacted by parents of children with disabilities, parent organizations, and professional advocacy groups. "Public support in the form of legislation and appropriation of funds has been achieved and sustained only by the most arduous and persevering efforts of individuals who advocate for exceptional children." (Hallahan & Kauffman, 1986, p. 26).

Parents, professionals, and other members of advocacy groups and organizations finally succeeded in bringing to the attention of legislators astounding data about the population of youth with disabilities in our country. Among the findings revealed, Congress noted that: (1) there were more than eight million children with disabilities in the United States, and more than half were not receiving an appropriate education; (2) more than one million children with disabilities were excluded from the educational system, and many other children with disabilities were enrolled in regular education classes where they were not benefiting from the educational services provided because of their undetected conditions; and (3) due to inadequate educational services within the public school systems, families were forced to seek services outside the public realm. Years of advocacy effort resulted in the current laws and court decisions mandating special education at a federal level.

Teachers of exceptional students are expected to manage many roles and responsibilities, not only as concern their students, but also with respect to students' caregivers and other involved educational, medical, therapeutic and administrative professionals. Because the needs of exceptional students are by definition multidisciplinary, a teacher of exceptional children often serves as the hub of a many-pronged wheel, communicating, consulting and collaborating with the various stakeholders in a child's educational life. Managing these relationships effectively can be a challenge but is central to successful work in exceptional education.

Related Service Providers and Administrators

Related service providers and administrators offer specialized skills and abilities that are critical to an exceptional education teacher's ability to advocate for his or her student and meet a school's legal obligations to the student and his or her family. Related service providers—like speech, occupational and language therapists, Psychologists, and physicians—offer expertise and resources unparalleled in meeting a child's developmental needs. Administrators are often experts in the resources available at the school and local education agency levels and the culture and politics of a school system and can be powerful partners in meeting the needs of exceptional education teachers and students. A teacher's most effective approach to collaborating with these professional includes:

- Confirming mutual understanding of the accepted goals and objectives of the student with exceptional learning needs as documented in his or her IEP;
- Soliciting input about ways to support related service goals in classroom settings;
- Understanding the needs and motivations of each and acting in support whenever possible;
- Facilitating respectful and beneficial relationships between families and professionals; and
- Regularly and accurately communicating observations and data about the child's progress or challenges.

See also Skill 14.05.

COMPETENCY 0016   UNDERSTAND THE HISTORICAL, SOCIAL, LEGAL, AND ETHICAL FOUNDATIONS OF EDUCATION FOR STUDENTS WITH DISABILITIES.

Skill 16.01   Demonstrating an understanding of models, theories, and philosophies that provide the basis for special education practice and the beliefs, traditions, and values underlying them

Legal Mandates and Historical Aspects

Special education is precisely what the term denotes: education of a special nature for students who have special needs. The academic and behavioral techniques that are used today in special education are a culmination of "best practices" and have evolved from a number of disciplines (e.g., medicine, psychology, sociology, language, ophthalmology, otology) to include education. Each of these disciplines contributed uniquely to their field so that the needs of special students might be better met in the educational arena.

Unfortunately, during the earlier part of the 1900s and mid-1950s, too many educators placed in positions of responsibility refused to recognize their professional obligation for assuring all children a free, appropriate, public education. Today, doors can no longer be shut, eyes cannot be closed, and heads cannot be turned since due process rights have been established for special needs students and their caregivers. Specific mandates are now stated in national laws, state regulations, and local policies. These mandates are the result of many years of successful litigation and political advocacy, and they govern the delivery of special education.

What special educators do is one thing; how services are delivered is yet another. The concept if **inclusion** stresses the need for educators to rethink the continuum of services, which was designed by Evelyn Deno and has been in existence since the early 1970s. Many school districts developed educational placement sites, which contain options listed on this continuum. These traditional options extend from the least restrictive to the most restrictive special education settings. The least restrictive environment is the regular education classroom. The present trend is to team special education and regular classroom teachers in regular classrooms. This avoids pulling out students for resource room services and provides services by specialists for students who may be showing difficulties similar to those of special education students.

The competencies in this section include the mandates (i.e., laws, regulations, policies) that apply to or have a bearing upon the respective states and local districts, as well as the major provisions of federal laws implemented twenty or more years ago, such as Public Laws 94-142 (1975), 93-112 (1973) and 101-476 (1990). These laws culminated into the comprehensive statute, IDEA (Individuals with Disabilities Education Act), which requires the states to offer comprehensive special education service programs to students with disabilities and to plan for their transition into the work world. Most local districts have elaborately-articulated delivery systems, which are an extension of national or state Department of Education of Department of Public Instruction. Any inquires should be directed to the unit that administers programs for exceptional children.

Major Developments in the History of Special Education

Although the origin of special education services for youngsters with disabilities is relatively recent, the history of public attitude toward people with disabling conditions was recorded as early as 1552. The Spartans practiced infanticide, the killing or abandonment of malformed or sickly babies. The ancient Greeks and Romans thought people with disabilities were cursed and forced them to beg for food and shelter. Those who could not fend for themselves were allowed to perish. Some with mental disabilities were employed as fools for the entertainment of the Roman royalty.

In the time of Christ, people with disabilities were thought to be suffering the punishment of God. Those with emotional disturbances were considered to be possessed by the devil, and although early Christianity advocated humane treatment of those who were not normal physically or mentally, many remained outcasts of society, sometimes pitied and sometimes scorned.

During the Middle Ages, persons with disabilities were viewed within the aura of the unknown and were treated with a mixture of fear and reverence. Some were wandering beggars, while others were used as jesters in the courts. The Reformation brought about a change of attitude, however. Individuals with disabilities were accused of being possessed by the devil, and exorcism flourished. Many innocent people were put in chains and cast into dungeons.

The early seventeenth century was marked by a softening of public attitude towards persons with disabilities. Hospitals began to provide treatment for those with emotional disturbances and mental retardation. A manual alphabet for those with deafness was developed, and John Locke became the first person to differentiate between persons who were mentally retarded and those who were emotionally disturbed.

In America, however, the colonists treated people with severe mental disorders as criminals, while those who were harmless were left to beg or were treated as paupers. At one time, it was common practice to sell them to the person who would provide for them at the least cost to the public. When this practice was stopped, persons with mental retardation were put into poorhouses, where conditions were often extremely squalid.

The Nineteenth Century: The Beginning of Training

In 1799, Jean Marc Itard, a French physician, found a 12-year old boy who had been abandoned in the woods of Averyron, France. His attempts to civilize and educate the boy, Victor, established many of the educational principles presently in use in the field of special education, including developmental and multi-sensory approaches, sequencing of tasks, individualized instruction, and a curriculum geared towards functional life skills.

Itard's work had an enormous impact upon public attitude towards individuals with disabilities. They began to be seen as educable. During the late 1700s, rudimentary procedures were devised by which those with sensory impairments (i.e., deaf, blind) could be taught, closely followed in the early 1800s by attempts to teach students with mild intellectual disabilities and emotional disorders (i.e., at that time to as the "idiotic" and "insane"). Throughout Europe, schools for students with visual and hearing impairments were erected, paralleled by the founding of similar institutions in the United States. In 1817, Thomas Hopkins Galluder founded the first American school for students who were deaf, known today as Galluder College in Washington, D.C. and as one of the world's best institutions of higher learning for those with deafness. Galluder's work was followed closely by that of Samuel Gridley, however, who was instrumental in the founding of the Perkins Institute for students who were blind in 1829. The mid-1800s saw the further development of Itard's philosophy of education of students with mental disabilities. Around that time, his student, Edward Seguin, immigrated to the United States, where he established his philosophy of education for persons with mental retardation in a publication entitled *Idiocy and Its Treatment by the Physiological Method* in 1866. Seguin was instrumental in the establishment of the first residential school for individuals with retardation in the United States.

State legislatures began to assume the responsibility for housing people with physical and mental disabilities, but the institutional care was largely custodial. Institutions were often referred to as warehouses due to the deplorable conditions of many. Humanitarians like Dorthea Dix helped to relieve the anguish and suffering of persons with mental illnesses in institutions.

1900 - 1919: Specific Programs

The early twentieth century saw the publication of the first standardized test of intelligence by Alfred Binet of France. The test was designed to identify educationally sub-standard children, but by 1916, the test was revised by an American, Louis Terman, and the concept of the intelligence quotient (IQ) was introduced. Since then, the IQ test has come to be used as a predictor of both retarded (delayed) and advanced intellectual development.

At approximately the same time, the Italian physician Maria Montessori was concerned with the development of effective techniques for early childhood education. Although she is known primarily for her contributions to this field, her work included methods of education for children with mental retardation as well, and the approach she developed is used in preschool programs today.

Ironically, it was the advancement of science and the scientific method that led special education to its worst setback in modern times. In 1912, Psychologist Henry Goddard published a study based on the Killikak family, in which he traced five generations of the descendants of a man who had one legitimate child and one illegitimate child. Among the descendants of the legitimate child were numerous mental defectives and social deviates. This led Goddard to conclude that mental retardation and social deviation were inherited traits, and therefore that mental and social deviates were a threat to society, an observation that he called the Eugenics Theory. Reinforcing the concept of retardation as hereditary deviance was a popular philosophy called positivism, under which these unscientific conclusions were believed to be fixed, mechanical laws that were carrying mankind to inevitable improvement. Falling by the wayside was seen as the natural, scientific outcome for the defective person in society. Consequently, during this time mass institutionalization and sterilization of persons with mental retardation and criminals were practiced.

Nevertheless, public school programs for persons with retardation gradually increased during this same period. Furthermore, the first college programs for the preparation of Special Education Teachers were established between 1900 and 1920.

1919 - 1949: Professional and Expansion of Services

An awareness of the need for medical and mental health treatment in the community was evidenced during the 1920s. Halfway houses became a means for monitoring the transition from institution to community living, and outpatient clinics were established to provide increased medical care. Social Workers and other support personnel were dispensed into the community to coordinate services for the needy. However, the thrust toward humane treatment within the community came to an abrupt halt during the 1930s and 1940s, primarily due to economic depression and widespread dissatisfaction toward the recently enacted social programs.

Two factors related to the Word Wars I and II helped to improve public opinion towards persons with disabilities. First was the intensive screening of the population of young men with physical and mental disabilities that were in the United States. Second, patriotism caused people to regard the enormous number of young men who returned from the wars with physical and emotional disabilities in a different light than they would have been regarded before that time. People became more sensitive to the problems of the veterans with disabilities, and this acceptance generalized to other groups in the special needs population.

With increased public concern for people with disabilities, came new research. John B. Watson introduced behaviorism, which shifted the treatment emphasis from psychoanalysis to learned behavior. He demonstrated in 1920 that maladaptive (or abnormal) behavior was learned by Albert, an 11-month old boy, through conditioning. B.F. Skinner followed with a book entitled the *Behavior of Organisms*, which outlined principles of operant behavior (i.e., voluntary) behavior.

In 1922, the Council for Exceptional Children (first called the International Council for Exceptional Children) was founded. During the 1920s, many comprehensive statewide programs were initiated. The number of special education programs in public schools increased at a rapid rate until the 1930s, when the push for humane and effective treatment of people with disabilities began to diminish once again. The period of the Depression was marked by large-scale institutionalization and lack of treatment. Part of the cause was inadequately-planned programs and poorly-trained teachers. WW II did much to swing the pendulum back in the other direction, however, and inaugurated the most active period in the history of the development of special education.

1950 - 1969: The Parents, Legislators, and Courts Become Involved

The first two decades of the second half of this century were characterized by increased federal involvement in general education, gradually extending to special education. In 1950, came the establishment of the National Association of Retarded Children, later renamed the National Association of Retarded Citizens (NARC). It was the result of the efforts of concerned parents who felt the need for an appropriated public education. Increased media coverage exposed the miserable conditions in some of the institutions devoted to caring for people with disabilities, especially those with intellectual and emotional disabilities, and treatment consequently became more humane.

It was at about this time that parents of children with disabilities discovered the federal courts as a powerful agent on behalf of their children. The 1954 decision in the Brown v. the Topeka Board of Education case guaranteed equal opportunity rights to a free public education for all citizens, and the parents of children and youth with disabilities insisted that their children be included in that decision. From this point on, the court cases and public laws enacted[1] as a result of court decisions are too numerous to include in their entirety. Only those few which had the greatest impact on the development of special education, as we know it today, are listed. Collectively, they are part of a movement in U.S. Supreme Court history known as the Doctrine of Selective Incorporation, under which the states are compelled to honor various substantive rights under procedural authority of the 14th Amendment.

1954: **The Cooperative Research Act** was passed, the first designation of general funds for the use of students with disabilities.

1958: **Public Law 85-926** provided grants to intuitions of higher learning and to state education agencies for training professional personnel who would, in turn, train teachers of students with mental retardation.

1963: **Public Law 88-164** (Amendment to Public Law 85-926) extended support to the training of personnel for teaching those with other disabling conditions (i.e., hard of hearing, speech impaired, visually impaired, seriously emotionally disturbed, crippled, and other health impaired.

1965: **Elementary and Secondary Education Act** provided funds for the education of children who were disadvantaged and disabled (Public Law 89-10).

---

[1] The first cluster of two digits of each public law represents the congressional session during which the law, numbered by the last three digits, was passed.. Congressional sessions begin every two years on the odd numbered year. The first biennial session sat in 1787-88. Bills may be passed and signed into law during either of the two years during which the congressional session is being held. For example, Public Law 94-142 was the 142nd law passed by the Ninety-fourth Congress, which was in session in 1975-76 and was passed and signed in 1975.

1965: **Educational Consolidation and Improvement Act (**Public Law 89-313), State Operated Programs provided funds for children with disabilities who are or have been in state-operated or state-supported schools.

1966: **Public Law 89-750** authorized the establishment of the Bureau of Education for the Handicapped (BEH) and a National Advisory Committee on the Handicapped.

1967: **Hanson v. Hobson** ruled that ability grouping (tracking) based on student performance on standardized tests is unconstitutional.

1968: **Handicapped Children's Early Education Assistance Act** (Public Law 80-538) funded model demonstration programs for preschool students with disabilities.

1968: **Public law 90-247** included provisions for deaf-blind centers and resource centers and expansion of media services for students with disabilities.

1968: **Public Law 90-576** specified that 10 percent of vocational education funds be earmarked for youth with disabilities.

1969: **Education of the Handicapped** (Public Law 91-230: Amendments to Public Law 89-10). Previous enactments relating to children with disabilities were consolidated into one act.

1970-Present: Federal Involvement in the Education of Children and Youth with Disabilities

During early involvement of the government in the education of individuals with disabilities, states were encouraged to establish programs, and they were rewarded with monetary assistance for compliance. Unfortunately, this assistance was often abused by those in control of services and funds. Therefore, a more dogmatic attitude arose, and the states were mandated to provide education for those with disabilities or else experience the cutoff of education funds from the federal government. Federal legal authority for this action was the 14th Amendment due process denial, paralleling enforcement of the 1954 Brown v. Topeka desegregation decision. High proportions of minority students in programs for mental retardation resulted in a mandatory reexamination of placement procedures, which in turn brought about a rigid legal framework for the provision of educational services for students with disabilities.

1970: **Diana v. the State Board of Education** resulted in the decision that all children must be tested in their native languages.

1971: **Wyatt v. Stickney** established the right to adequate treatment (education) for institutionalized persons with mental retardation.

1971: **Pennsylvania Association for Retarded Children (PARC) v. the Commonwealth of Pennsylvania** prohibited the exclusion of students with mental retardation from educational treatment at state schools.

1972: **Mills v. the Board of Education of the District of Columbia** asserted the right of children and youth with disabilities to a constructive education, which includes appropriate specialized instruction.

1973: **Rehabilitation Amendments of 1973** (Public Law 93-112) was the first comprehensive federal statute to address specifically the rights of disabled youth. It prohibited illegal discrimination in education, employment, or housing on the basis of a disability.

1974: Public Law 93-380 (**Education Amendments of 1974**. Public Law 94-142 is the funding portion of this act). It requires the states to provide full educational opportunities for children with disabilities. It addressed identification, fair evaluation, alternative placements, due process procedures, and free, appropriate public education.

1975: **Education for all Handicapped Children Act** (Public Law 94-142) provided for a free, appropriate public education for all children with disabilities, defined special education and related services, and imposed rigid guidelines on the provisions of those services. It paralleled the provision for a free and appropriate public education in Section 504 of Public Law 94-142 and extended these services to preschool children with disabilities (ages 3-5) through provisions to preschool incentive grants. This was the creation of FAPE.

1975: **Goss v. Lopez** ruled that the state could not deny a student education without following due process. While this decision was not based on a special education issue, the process of school suspension and expulsion was obviously critical in assuring an appropriate public education to children with disabilities.

1978: **Gifted and Talented Children's Act** (Public Law 95-56) defined the gifted and talented population and focused upon this exceptionally category, which was not included in Public Law 94-142.

1979: **Larry P. v. Riles** ordered the reevaluation of black students enrolled in classes for educable mental retardation (EMR) and enjoined the California State Department of Education from the use of intelligence tests in subsequent EMR placement decisions.

1980: **Parents in Action on Special Education (PASE) v. Hannon** ruled that IQ tests are necessarily biased against ethnic and racial subcultures.

1982: The appeal for services of an interpreter during the school day for a deaf girl was denied by the Supreme Court in **Hendrick Hudson Board of Education v. Rowley**. Established that an "appropriate" education does not mean the "best" education has to be provided. What is required is that individuals benefit and those due process procedures are followed in developing the educational program.

1983: **Education of the Handicapped Act [EHA] Amendments** (Public Law 98-199& Public Law 94-142) was amended to provide added emphasis on parental education and preschool, secondary, and post-secondary programs for children and youth with disabilities.

1984: **Irving Independent School District v. Tarro** (468 U.S. 883) established that catheterization and similar health-type services are "related services" when they are relatively simple to provide and when medical assistance is not needed in providing them.

1985: **Public Law 99-457** mandated service systems for infants and young children.

1986: **Handicapped Children's Protection Act of 1985** (Public Law 99-372). This law allowed parents who are unsuccessful in due process hearings or reviews to seek recovery of attorney's fees.

1986: **Education of the Handicapped Act Amendments of 1986** (Public Law 99-457). It re-authorized existing EHA, amended Public Law 94-142 to include financial incentives for states to educate children 3 to 5 years old by the 1990-1991 school years, and established incentive grants to promote programs serving infants with disabilities (birth to 2 years of age).

1986: **Rehabilitation Act Amendments of 1986** (Public Law 99-506). It authorized formula grant funds for the development of supported employment demonstration projects.

1987: **School Board of Nassau County v. Arline** Established that contagious diseases are a disability under Section 504 of the Rehabilitation Act and that people with them are protected from discrimination, if otherwise qualified (actual risk to health and safety to others make persons unqualified).

1988: **Honig v. Doe** established that expulsion from school programs for more than ten days constitutes a change in placement for which all due process provisions must be met; temporary removals are permitted in emergencies.

1990: **American with Disabilities Act ADA** (Public Law 101-336) gives civil rights protection to individuals with disabilities in private sector employment, all public services, public accommodations, transportation, and telecommunications. This law is patterned after Section 504 of the Rehabilitation Act of 1973.

1990: The U.S. House of Representatives opened for citizen comment the issue of a separate exceptionality category for students with attention deficit disorders. The issue was tabled without legislative action.

1990: **Public Law 101-476 (Individuals with Disabilities Education Act IDEA)** reauthorized and renamed existing EHA. This amendment to EHA changed the term "handicapped" to "disability," expanded related services, and required individual education programs (IEPs) to contain transitional goals and objectives for adolescents (ages 16 and above, special situations).

1993 **Florence County School Dist Four v. Shannon Carter** established that when a school district does not provide FAPE for a student with a disability, the parents may seek reimbursement for private schooling. This decision has encouraged districts to be more inclusive of students with Autism who receive ABA/Lovaas therapy.

1994 **Goals 2000: Educate America Act** (Public Law 103-227), established national education goals to help guide state and local education systems

1997 **Reauthorization of IDEA**—required involvement of a regular education teacher as part of the IEP team. Provided additional strength to school administrators for the discipline of students with special needs.

2002 **No Child Left Behind Act (NCLB)** Requires all Special Education Teachers on a Secondary Level to be no less qualified than other teachers of the subject areas.

2004 **M.L. v. Federal Way School District (WA)** in the Ninth Circuit Court of Appeals ruled that absence of a regular education teacher on an IEP team was a serious procedural error.

2004 **Reauthorization of IDEA**—Enforces NCLB requirement that all Special Education Teachers on a Secondary Level to be no less qualified than other teachers of the subject areas.

Important Legislation Special Education Teachers Must Know:

SECTION 504

Section 504 is part of Public Law 93-112 was passed and signed into law in 1973. Currently Section 504 expands the older law by extending its protection to other areas that receive federal assistance, such as education.
To be entitled to protection under Section 504, the individual must meet the definition of a person with a disability, which is, any person who:

i. Has a physical or mental impairment, which substantially limits one or more of such person's major life activities,

ii Has a record of such impairment, or

iii Is regarded as having such impairment.

Major life activities are:
  caring for one's self, performing manual tasks, walking, seeing, hearing, speaking, breathing, learning and working.

The individual must also be "otherwise qualified." This has been interpreted to mean that the person must be able to meet the requirements of a particular program in spite of his or her disability. The person must be afforded "reasonable accommodations," by recipients of Federal financial assistance. The usual remedy when a violation of Section 504 is proven is the termination of federal funding assistance.

Section 504 assists with the several categories of children that are not comprehensively covered for special education under IDEA. Children in these categories may meet the definition for disabled, but are not eligible. For example, a child with an emotional disorder may not meet the criteria for "intensity and degree." Others have medical conditions but these conditions are not listed as disabilities. An exampled is the child with AIDS whose condition is not listed specifically Other Health Impaired. (Refer to Skill 1.11 for definitions)

Youth with social impairments do not qualify for special education under IDEA unless they have an emotional/behavior disorder as well. There is controversy over whether to identify or even attempt to separate youth with social maladjustments from other youth who meet the definition of emotional/behavioral disturbance. Unlike slow learners, some of whom may qualify for compensatory services; these youngsters have no safety net of services.

Attention Deficit Disorder (ADD) is another category of children who require significant assistance in schools, but for whom there is no category in special education. Youth who are addicted to drugs and alcohol are protected under IDEA only if they qualify for special education and related services under one of the disability categories such as emotional disturbance. These students, like other categories described are at-risk and while they do not qualify for special education under IDEA, they are entitled to protection under Section 504 of the Rehabilitation Act or the Americans with Disabilities Act (ADA). See competency skill 2.5 for more information about ADA.

Section 504 requires schools not to discriminate and to provide reasonable accommodations in all of its programming aspects.

AMERICANS WITH DISABILITIES ACT (ADA)

Americans with Disabilities Act (ADA) 1990 bars discrimination in employment, transportation, public accommodations, and telecommunications in all aspects of life, not just those receiving federal funding. This act gives protections to all people without regard to race, gender, national origin, religion, or disability.

Title II and Title III are applicable to special education because they cover the private sector (such as private schools) and require access to public accommodations. New and remodeled public buildings, transportation vehicles, and telephone systems now must be accessible to the handicapped. ADA also protects individuals with contagious diseases, such as AIDS, from discrimination.

> **Keep up to date on the Law and Special Education subscribe to the free Email service at:** http://wrightslaw.com

In 1990, Congress passed Public Law 101-336, the Americans with Disabilities Act, referred to as ADA. The ADA is similar to the Rehabilitation in terms of who is considered to be protected under the Act, but it does not require entities to be recipients of federal financial assistance.

IDEA '97 (PUBLIC LAW 105-17)

In 1997, IDEA was revised and reauthorized as Public Law 105-17 as progressive legislation for the benefit of school age children with special needs, their parents and those who work with these children. The 1997 reauthorization of IDEA made major changes in the areas of the evaluation procedures, parent rights, transition and, discipline.

The evaluation process was amended to require members of the evaluation team to look at previously collected data, tests and information and to use it when it is deemed appropriate. Previous to IDEA 97 a entire re-evaluation had to be conducted every three years in relation to determine if the child continued to be a "child with a disability." This was changed to allow existing information/evaluations to be considered which would prevent unnecessary assessment of students and reduce the cost of evaluations.

Parent participation was not a requirement under the previous IDEA for an evaluation team to make decisions regarding a student's eligibility for special education and related services. Under IDEA 97, parents were specifically included as members of the group making the eligibility decision.

IEP Amendments

The IEP was modified under IDEA 97 to emphasize the involvement of students with special needs in a general education classroom setting, with the services and modifications deemed necessary by the evaluation team.

The "Present Levels of Educational Performance"(PLEP) was changed to require a statement of how the child's disability affects his or her involvement and progress in the general curriculum. IDEA 97 established that there must be a connection between the special education and general education curriculum. For this reason the PLEP was required include an explanation of the extent to which the student will *not* be participating with nondisabled children in the general education class and in extracurricular and non-academic activities.

The IEP now had an established connection to the general education setting and had to provide the needed test accommodations that would be provided on all state and district wide assessments of the student with special needs. IDEA 97's emphasis on raising the standards of those in special education placed an additional requirement of a definitive reason why a standard general education assessment would not be deemed appropriate for a child, and how the child should then be assessed.

IDEA 97 looked at how parents were receiving annual evaluations on their child's IEP goals and determined that this was not sufficient feedback for parents and required Schools to make reports to parents on the progress of their child at least as frequently as progress of their nondisabled peers.

The IEP was also modified to include a review of the student's transitional needs and services specifically:

- Beginning when a student is 14, and annually thereafter, the student's IEP must contain a statement of his or her transition service needs under the various components of that IEP that focus upon the student's courses of study (e.g., vocational education or advanced placement); and

- Beginning at least one year before the student reaches the age of majority under State law, the IEP must contain a statement that the student has been informed of the rights under the law that will transfer to him or her upon reaching the age of majority.

Discipline
IDEA 97 broadened the schools' right to take a disciplinary action with children who have been classified as needing special education services with those students that knowingly possess or use illegal drugs or sell or solicit the sale of a controlled substance while at school or school functions.

Manifest Determination Review

Under IDEA 97, suspensions/disciplinary consequences could result in an alternative educational placement. This possibility was to be weighed by a Manifest Determination Review, which is held by an IEP Team. Manifest Determination Reviews must occur no more than 10 days after the disciplinary action. This review team has the sole responsibility of determining:

1) Does the child's disability impaired his/her understand the impact and consequences of the behavior under disciplinary action?
2) Did the child's disability impair the ability of the child to control the behavior subject to discipline.

Determination of a relationship of the student's disability and an inappropriate behavior could allow current placement to occur.

When no relationship between the "inappropriate" behavior is established, IDEA 97 utilized FAPE to allow the relevant disciplinary procedures applicable to children without disabilities may be applied to the child in the same manner in which they would be applied to children without disabilities,

Functional Behavioral Assessments (FBAs) and Behavior Intervention Plans (BIPs) now became a requirement in many situations for schools to both modify and provide disciplinary consequences.

No Child Left Behind Act, PL 107-110 (2002)

No Child Left Behind, Public Law 107-110, was signed on January 8, 2002. It addresses accountability of school personnel for student achievement with the expectation that every child will demonstrate proficiency in reading, math, and science. The first full wave of accountability will be in 12 years when children who attended school under NCLB graduate, but the process to meet that accountability begins now. In fact, as students progress through the school system, testing will show if an individual teacher has effectively met the needs of her students. Through testing, each student's adequate yearly progress or lack thereof will be tracked.

NCLB affects regular and special education students, gifted students and slow learners, and children of every ethnicity, culture and environment. NCLB is a document that encompasses every American educator and student. Educators are affected as follows. Elementary teachers (K-3) are responsible for teaching reading and using different, scientific-based approaches as needed. Elementary teachers of upper grades will teach reading, math and science. Middle and high school teacher will teach to new, higher standards. Sometimes, they will have the task of playing catch up with students who did not have adequate education in earlier grades.

Special educators are responsible for teaching students to a level of comparable proficiency as their non-disabled peers. This will raise the bar of academic expectations throughout the grades. For some students with disabilities, the criteria for getting a diploma will be more difficult. Although a small percentage of students with disabilities will need alternate assessment, they will still need to meet grade appropriate goals.

In order for Special Education Teachers to meet the professional criteria of this act, they must be *Highly Qualified*, that is certified or licensed in their area of special education and show proof of a specific level of professional development in the core subjects that they teach. As special education teachers received specific education in the core subject they teach, they will be better prepared to teach to the same level of learning standards as the general education teacher.

IDEIAA (IDEA 2004)

The second revision of IDEA occurred in 2004, IDEA was re-authorized as the Individuals with Disabilities Education Improvement Act of 2004 (IDEIA 2004) is commonly referred to as IDEA 2004. IDEA 2004 (effective July 1, 2005).

NYS Special Education law: http://www.vesid.nysed.gov/special ed/publications/law s andregs/ part200.htm

It was the intention to improve IDEA by adding the philosophy/understanding that special education students need preparation for further study beyond the high school setting by teaching compensatory methods. Accordingly, IDEA 2004 provided a close tie to PL 89-10, the Elementary and Special Education Act of 1965, and stated that students with special needs should have maximum access to the general curriculum. This was defined as the amount for an individual student to reach his fullest potential. Full inclusion was stated not to be the only option by which to achieve this, and specified that skills should be taught to compensate students later in life in cases where inclusion was not the best setting.

IDEA 2004 added a new requirement for Special Education Teachers on the secondary level enforcing NCLBs "Highly Qualified" requirements in the subject area of their curriculum. The rewording in this part of IDEA states that they shall be "no less qualified" than teachers in the core areas.

Free and Appropriate Public Education (FAPE), was revised by mandating that students have maximum access to appropriate general education. Additionally, LRE placement for those students with disabilities must have the same school placement rights as those students who are not disabled. IDEA 2004 recognizes that due to the nature of some disabilities, appropriate education may vary in the amount of participation / placement in the general education setting. For some students, FAPE will mean a choice as to the type of educational institution they attend (private school for example), any of which must provide the special education services deemed necessary for the student through the IEP.

The definition of *Assistive technology devices* was amended to exclude devices that are surgically implanted (i.e. cochlear implants), and clarified that students with assistive technology devices shall not be prevented from having special education services. Assistive technology devices may need to monitored by school personnel, but schools are not responsible for the implantation or replacement of such devices surgically. An example of this would be a cochlear implant.

The definition of *Child with a disability* is the term used for children ages 3-9 with a developmental delay now has been was changed to allow for the inclusion of Tourettes Syndrome.

IDEA 2004 recognized that all states must follow the National Instructional Materials Accessibility Standards which states that students who need materials in a certain form will get those at the same time their non-disabled peers receive their materials. Teacher recognition of this standard is important.

Changes in Requirements for Evaluations

The clock/time allowance between the request for an initial evaluation and the determination if a disability is present may be requested has been changed to state the finding/determination must occur within 60 calendar days of the request. This is a significant change as previously it was interpreted to mean 60 school days. Parental consent is also required for evaluations and prior to the start of special education services.

No single assessment or measurement tool may now be used to determine special education qualification. Assessments and measurements used should be in *language and form* that will give the most accurate picture of the child's abilities.

IDEA 2004's recognized that there exists a disproportionate representation of minorities and bilingual students and that pre-service interventions that are *scientifically based on early reading programs, positive behavioral interventions and support, and early intervening services)* may prevent some of those children from needing special education services. This understanding has led to a child not being considered to have a disability if he/she has not had appropriate education in math or reading, nor shall a child be considered to have a disability if the reason for his/her delays is that English is a second language.

When determining a specific learning disability, the criteria may or may not use a discrepancy between *achievement and intellectual ability* but whether or not the child responds to scientific research-based intervention. In general, children who may not have been found eligible for special education (via testing) but are known to need services (via functioning, excluding lack of instruction) are still eligible for special education services. This change now allows input for evaluation to include state and local testing, classroom observation, academic achievement, and *related developmental needs,*

Changes in Requirements for IEPs
Individualized Education Plans (IEPS) continue to have multiple sections. One section, *present levels,* now addresses *academic achievement and functional performance.* Annual IEP goals must now address the same areas.

IEP goals should be aligned to state standards, thus short term objectives are not required on every IEP. Students with IEPs must not only participate in regular education programs to the full extent possible, they must show progress in those programs. This means that goals should be written to reflect academic progress. For students who must participate in alternate assessment, there must be alignment to *alternate achievement standards.*

Significant change has been made in the definition of the IEP team as it now includes *not less than 1* teacher from each of the areas of special education and regular education be present.

IDEA 2004 recognized that the amount of required paperwork placed upon teachers of students with disabilities should be reduced if possible, for this reason a pilot program has been developed in which some states will participate using using multi-year IEPs. Individual student inclusion in this program will require consent by both the school and the parent.

Skill 16.02   Demonstrating knowledge of the rights and responsibilities of students, parents/guardians, teachers, other professionals, and schools as they relate to individual learning needs

The rights and responsibilities of individuals as they relate to ensuring that the individual learning needs of students with disabilities are met are multi-faceted.

Teacher of students with disabilities have a wide range of responsibilities. They are responsible for understanding and implementing appropriate instruction and strategies incorporating relevant curriculum frameworks; providing developmentally-appropriate learning experiences; and preparing and implementing individual education plans (IEPs).

Parents and students have rights under the No Child Left Behind (NCLB) Act of 2001. The purpose of the NCLB is to ensure that all children have a fair, equal and significant opportunity to obtain a high-quality education. The act has several parental involvement provisions which reflect shared accountability between schools and parents for high student achievement, including expanded public school choice and supplemental educational services for eligible children in low performing schools, local development of parental involvement plans with sufficient flexibility to address local needs, and building parents' capacities for using effective practices to improve their own children's academic achievement.

> **Great Resource:**
> **Printable Parents**
> **Rights Guides for the**
> **parents of your**
> **students**
> http://www.specialed
> news.com/behavior/b
> ehavnews/CECbehav
> assess021900.html

Parental involvement is important, as research has shown that families have a major influence on their children's achievement in school and through life. When schools, families, and community groups work together to support learning, children do better in school, stay in school longer, and enjoy school more.

> **The NYS Parents**
> **Rights Guide:**
> http://www.vesid
> .nysed.gov/speci
> aled/
> publications/poli

Initially, parents need to fully understand their children's disabilities and consider how their disabilities will impact their self-help skills, communication, discipline, play, and independence. Parents should be encouraged to take advantage of their daily routines to foster the development of certain concepts and skills that appear to be weak.
Whatever parents decide to do, however, should be done in the context of a social relationship that is pleasant and non-threatening. Emphasis should be placed on the child's strengths, not just the weaknesses.

IDEA requires schools to establish performance goals and indicators for children with disabilities—consistent to the maximum extent appropriate with other goals and standards for all children established by the state—and to report on progress toward meeting those goals.

The IEP team determines how the student will participate in state and district-wide assessments of student achievement. They also determine if any individual modifications in administration are needed in order for the student to participate in the assessment. Alternate assessments need to be aligned with the general curriculum standards set for all students and should not be assumed appropriate only for those students with significant cognitive impairments.

Skill 16.03 Recognizing and analyzing due process rights related to assessment, eligibility, and placement

(Please refer to the "due process" section of skill 14.07.)

Skill 16.04 Demonstrating knowledge of health and safety issues related to the definition and provision of special education services

Irving Independent School District v. Tatro 1984: IDEA lists health services as one of the "related services" that schools are mandated to provide to exceptional students. Amber Tatro, who had spina bifida, required the insertion of a catheter on a regular schedule in order to empty her bladder. The issue was specifically over the classification of clean, intermittent catheterization (CIC) as a medical service (not covered under IDEA) or a "related health service," which would be covered. In this instance, the catheterization was not declared a medical service, but a "related service" necessary for the student to have in order to benefit from special education. The school district was obliged to provide the service. The Tatro case has implications for students with other medical impairments who may need services to allow them to attend classes at the school.

School Board of Nassau County v. Arline, 1987: This case established that contagious diseases are a disability under Section 504 of the Rehabilitation Act and that people with them are protected from discrimination, if otherwise qualified (actual risk to health and safety to others may persons unqualified).

Included in Abraham Maslow's hierarchy of basic human needs is the requirement for safety and security. Children have the need to feel safe from dangers while at school and during transit to and from school. Educators must respond to this basic need by providing adequate supervision and by developing appropriate safety procedures.

Employing instructional approaches that include tasks that students are able to master and complete successfully can heighten psychological safety. Learning environments in which children feel threatened and put on the defensive in reduce psychological safety.

Life in America without reading skills is difficult, even dangerous. Reading skills can be placed upon a needs hierarchy much like the total human needs array developed by such theorists as Abraham Maslow.

At the most primitive level, reading skills provide safety and security. This realm is as important for the child or adult with a disability as for the person who has no identified disability. It is incorrect to assume that there will always be a caretaker available to the person with a disability to read for him, especially in times of danger and personal necessity.

Examples of reading requirements at this first level of the hierarchy are STOP, DO NOT TOUCH, HOT, and OFF/ON signs; directions for use with most appliances, conveyances, and facilities; and warnings in many social settings. The individual with a disability will need some reading skills in order to deal successfully with the pedestrian crossing lane at a busy intersection, the tramway at the airport, the taxicab, and the stairs in a public building, a revolving door, an escalator, and a fire exit.

In working with a special population composed of students with a variety of needs and disabling conditions, the assurance of a safe learning environment is paramount. The special education classroom, as well as regular classroom and support areas that are utilized by all students, should be set up and maintained so that students can move about freely without incurring physical harm.

The avoidance of physical barriers and the formulation of appropriate procedures for emergencies are necessary conditions for students with disabilities. Children with sensory impairments who are not able to hear audible alarms or see danger signals or those with limited intellectual capabilities who may not respond well in atypical situations, need to be protected with preestablished, well thought out procedural regulations. Further, school personnel need to be trained in handling and positioning students with physical impairments so that risk of further physical disability is minimized.

Vocational training programs involve the use of specialized machines and equipment, thus presenting modification and teaching techniques can be of benefit, such as (1) ensuring a stable and predictable training environment; (2) outlining concrete, step-by-step procedures; (3) posting a list of classroom and laboratory safety rules; and (4) reacting calmly to inappropriate behavior, while firmly enforcing set procedures and regulations.

Skill 16.05 Demonstrating knowledge of ethical practices in instruction and other professional activities (e.g., interactions with students, use of copyrighted educational materials, use of information technology) related to the education of students with disabilities

The special educator is expected to demonstrate ethical practice in all areas of his teaching responsibilities.

With regards to interaction with students, teaching and discipline practices should reflect practices that are respectful of the student as a person. Researched-based methods should be employed that will provide measurable outcomes.

The ethics of special education goes beyond methods to materials. With students of a variety of age and/or ability levels, and often limited funding, appropriate materials can become difficult to obtain. If possible, students should be included in the head count for ordering general education materials. When alternative materials are needed, it is important to secure those through special education funding sources in the school. Teaching materials that are copyrighted may not be photocopied unless they are specifically intended for such use as printed on the book. The same is true for musical materials that have a copyright. If materials are intended for reproduction, it will be stated.

Information technology brings a world of information to the special educator and student's classroom. Careful consideration should be given, however, to the validity of the information before it is incorporated into practice or curricular material. Reputable sources for education practices will have connections to recognized organizations for special educators, such as the Council for Exceptional Children, or to teacher training programs.

Likewise, students should be guided in the finding and use of valid sites for research and learning. It is important to teach the philosophy that not everything on the internet is true.

Ethical practice in communication is an additional expectation of all educators and especially of those teaching students with disabilities. Confidentiality is crucial. Specific information regarding a student's disability and IEP (Individualized Education Program) should be discussed only with the team of professionals working with the student and his family. When an exchange of information is needed with another school district, physician, therapist, or other professional outside of the school district, it is necessary to get written permission from the student's parent. Often, forms for such are available from the school district.

COMPETENCY 0017 UNDERSTAND THE PROFESSIONAL FOUNDATIONS OF EDUCATION FOR STUDENTS WITH DISABILITIES.

Skill 17.01 Demonstrating knowledge of how to advocate effectively for students with disabilities and for the special education program

Because of the unique needs of each student with disabilities, Special Education Teachers are frequently advocates for their students and for the special education program in general.

In order to be an effective advocate, the teacher must be knowledgeable in a number of areas. First, the special educator must understand the general education program that is the counterpart of her program. Factors such as student expectations (learning standards), materials used, and teacher training and inservice provide a starting point. If the special educator is familiar with the goals and overall program for all students at her grade level, she will have a clear picture of the direction she should be working with her students with disabilities.

> **Learn more about Advocating for the special education child in an inclusive setting:**
> http://www.ldonline.org/article/5690

The special educator should also have a clear understanding of each student's strengths and needs. She must consider how each student can participate in the general education curriculum to the extent that it is beneficial for that student (IDEA 2004). When should services and instruction take place outside of the general education classroom?

In addition, special educators should have an understanding of alternate materials that would be useful or necessary for her students and what resources for materials are available to her.

Knowledge of the Individual's with Disabilities Education Act (IDEA 2004) and NCLB (No Child Left Behind) provides an outline of legislative mandates for special education.

A clear understanding of the above points will allow the special educator to most effectively advocate for the most appropriate placement, programming, and materials for each student. She will be able to advocate for research-based methods with measurable outcomes.

Often, advocacy happens between regular and Special Education Teachers. A special educator may see modification or accommodation possibilities that could take place in the general education classroom. It is her responsibility to advocate those practices. The Special Education Teacher may also offer to make supplementary materials or to work with a group of students in the general education setting to achieve that goal. When students with disabilities are in an inclusion classroom, give and take on the part of both teachers as a team is crucial.The Special Education Teacher may need to be an advocate for her program (or the needs of an individual student) with the administration. Although success for all students is important to administration, often the teacher must explain the need for comparable materials written at a different reading level, the need for assistance in the classroom, or the offering of specific classes or therapies.

Occasionally, the local school district cannot provide an appropriate educational setting. The special educator must advocate with the school district for appropriate placement of the child in another, more suitable environment.

Skill 17.02 Demonstrating knowledge of the standards and policies of the profession (e.g., the codes of ethics of the Council for Exceptional Children [CEC] and other organizations)

The special educator is epected to use accepted teaching practices with measurable outcomes. She is expected to use professionalism and confidentiality in her role as a teacher. Professional organizations provide a structure for understanding those expectations.

The Council for Exceptional Children (CEC) is a national professional organization (with state chapters) that encompasses teaching in of all areas of disability. The CEC has established a *Code of Ethics for Educators of Persons with Exceptionalities.* In brief, the code charges educators with continuing to learn best practices in the education of students with disabilities, providing a quality educational program that will best meet the needs of their students and their families, and abiding by legal and ethical guidelines of the profession.

New York State Code of Ethics for Educators

Statement of Purpose

The Code of Ethics is a public statement by educators that sets clear expectations and principles to guide practice and inspire professional excellence. Educators believe a commonly held set of principles can assist in the individual exercise of professional judgment. This Code speaks to the core values of the profession. "Educator" as used throughout means all educators serving New York schools in positions requiring a certificate, including classroom teachers, school leaders and pupil personnel service providers.

Principle 1: Educators nurture the intellectual, physical, emotional, social, and civic potential of each student.

Educators promote growth in all students through the integration of intellectual, physical, emotional, social and civic learning. They respect the inherent dignity and worth of each individual. Educators help students to value their own identity, learn more about their cultural heritage, and practice social and civic responsibilities. They help students to reflect on their own learning and connect it to their life experience. They engage students in activities that encourage diverse approaches and solutions to issues, while providing a range of ways for students to demonstrate their abilities and learning. They foster the development of students who can analyze, synthesize, evaluate and communicate information effectively.

Principle 2: Educators create, support, and maintain challenging learning environments for all.

Educators apply their professional knowledge to promote student learning. They know the curriculum and utilize a range of strategies and assessments to address differences. Educators develop and implement programs based upon a strong understanding of human development and learning theory. They support a challenging learning environment. They advocate for necessary resources to teach to higher levels of learning. They establish and maintain clear standards of behavior and civility. Educators are role models, displaying the habits of mind and work necessary to develop and apply knowledge while simultaneously displaying a curiosity and enthusiasm for learning. They invite students to become active, inquisitive, and discerning individuals who reflect upon and monitor their own learning.

Principle 3: Educators commit to their own learning in order to develop their practice.

Educators recognize that professional knowledge and development are the foundations of their practice. They know their subject matter, and they understand how students learn. Educators respect the reciprocal nature of learning between educators and students. They engage in a variety of individual and collaborative learning experiences essential to develop professionally and to promote student learning. They draw on and contribute to various forms of educational research to improve their own practice.

Principle 4: Educators collaborate with colleagues and other professionals in the interest of student learning.

Educators encourage and support their colleagues to build and maintain high standards. They participate in decisions regarding curriculum, instruction and assessment designs, and they share responsibility for the governance of schools. They cooperate with community agencies in using resources and building comprehensive services in support of students. Educators respect fellow professionals and believe that all have the right to teach and learn in a professional and supportive environment. They participate in the preparation and induction of new educators and in professional development for all staff.

Principle 5: Educators collaborate with parents and community, building trust and respecting confidentiality.

Educators partner with parents and other members of the community to enhance school programs and to promote student learning. They also recognize how cultural and linguistic heritage, gender, family and community shape experience and learning. Educators respect the private nature of the special knowledge they have about students and their families and use that knowledge only in the students' best interests. They advocate for fair opportunity for all children.

Principle 6: Educators advance the intellectual and ethical foundation of the learning community.

Educators recognize the obligations of the trust placed in them. They share the responsibility for understanding what is known, pursuing further knowledge, contributing to the generation of knowledge, and translating knowledge into comprehensible forms. They help students understand that knowledge is often complex and sometimes paradoxical. Educators are confidantes, mentors and advocates for their students' growth and development. As models for youth and the public, they embody intellectual honesty, diplomacy, tact and fairness.

CEC Code of Ethics

for

Educators of Persons with Exceptionalities

We declare the following principles to be the Code of Ethics for educators of persons with exceptionalities. Members of the special education profession are responsible for upholding and advancing these principles. Members of The Council for Exceptional Children agree to judge and be judged by them in accordance with the spirit and provisions of this Code.

1. Special education professionals are committed to developing the highest educational and quality of life potential of individuals with exceptionalities.

2. Special education professionals promote and maintain a high level of competence and integrity in practicing their profession.

3. Special education professionals engage in professional activities which benefit individuals with exceptionalities, their families, other colleagues, students, or research subjects.

4. Special education professionals exercise objective professional judgment in the practice of their profession.

5. Special education professionals strive to advance their knowledge and skills regarding the education of individuals with exceptionalities.

6. Special education professionals work within the standards and policies of their profession.

7. Special education professionals seek to uphold and improve where necessary the laws, regulations, and policies governing the delivery of special education and related services and the practice of their profession.

8. Special education professionals do not condone or participate in unethical or illegal acts, nor violate professional standards adopted by the Delegate Assembly of CEC.

The Council for Exceptional Children. (1993). CEC Policy Manual, Section Three, part 2 (p. 4). Reston, VA: Author.

Originally adopted by the Delegate Assembly of The Council for Exceptional Children in April 1983.

Skill 17.03 Demonstrating the ability to exercise objective professional judgment

The Special Education Teacher comes to the job with past experiences as well as personal opinions and beliefs. It is vital that she not let those personal persuasions guide her professionally. Objective professional judgment is important in all areas of the teacher's role.

Objective professional judgment should be exercised when considering the cultural, religious, and sexual orientations of the special educator's students and their families. An unbiased approach to communication maintains positive interaction and increased cooperation between home and school. The result is a better educational program that will meet the individual student's needs.

Objectivity should also be exercised when considering assessment of a possible disability. Educator preference for a particular assessment should be secondary to matching the needs of the child with a specific instrument. Assessment tools should be researched-based and determined to be appropriate for the needs of the specific student.

When establishing the special education program, the specific student's IEP (Individualized Education Program) must be followed. If the special educator determines that the goals and objectives of the IEP no longer fit the child's needs, an IEP meeting should be called to review and possibly revise the document. Again, the revision of the IEP should be based on the needs of the child as determined objectively and not through the personal preference of the teacher for a particular type of program or schedule. This objectivity should include: materials, scheduling, activities, and evaluation.

The student's IEP should also be focused on the learning standards established by the state. In particular, learning activities should be employed that provide measurable outcomes. Such data provides objective evaluation of student progress and mastery of the targeted standards.

Professional objectivity is crucial in communication with administration for representation of students' needs for placement, programming, materials, scheduling, and staffing needs. When documented, data-driven information is presented, optimum decisions are made for students with disabilities and for the school community in general.

Skill 17.04 Identifying ways to address one's own cultural biases and differences to ensure positive regard for the culture, religion, gender, and sexual orientation of individual students

The role of the Special Education Teacher is to advocate for the most appropriate education for her students and to guide them in discovering new knowledge and developing new skills to the best of their potential. According to IDEA 2004 (Individual's with Disabilities Education Act), she is to prepare them for future, purposeful work in society with the possibility of post-secondary education or training.

Although each special educator is also a person with a set of experiences, opinions, and beliefs, it is important the she remain unbiased and positive in her professional role with students, parents, administration, and the community. Differences in culture, religion, gender, or sexual orientation should not influence the teacher's approach to instruction, student goals or expectations, or advocacy.

In order to remain unbiased, the special educator should avail herself of opportunities to learn about various cultures, religions, genders, and sexual orientations. This can be accomplished through reading, classroom awareness activities, as appropriate, and teacher inservice.

Learn more about Cultural Competence for Teachers: http://www.opb.org/ education/minisites/ culturalcompetence /teachers.html

Reading to increase awareness and acceptance of cultural differences may be done through professional, adult literature, as well as through books to be read with the class.

Cultural activities in the classroom are especially well received, including foods, dress, and games, and are easily added to curriculum and often address learning standards.

The special educator is charged with academic, social, communicative, and independent skills instruction. Education or influence in other areas is not appropriate.

When the special educator remains unbiased, she is better able to meet the needs of her students and to not react to additional factors. The students and their families are also more open to school-related suggestions.

The teacher's reaction to differences with her students and their families models the commonly taught character education trait of respect. When she demonstrates respect for all individuals in her program, it is likely that respect will also be practiced by students, parents, and administration.

Skill 17.05   Identifying professional activities, including self-reflection and self-assessment, to improve one's own effectiveness in providing services to individuals with disabilities and their families

In providing services to students with disabilities and their families, teachers need to be involved in a wide range of professional activities that will help improve their instruction and their effectiveness in the classroom. This should include self-reflection and self-assessment. Self-reflection involves reflecting on one's practice to improve instruction and to guide professional growth. In the area of special education, this would entail evaluating how successful one is in ensuring that students are meeting their short- and long-term goals in the classroom. When teachers reflect on their own performance, they can evaluate what they are doing right and where improvements should be made.

The teacher should participate in professional activities and organizations that benefit individuals with exceptional needs, their families, and their colleagues. This will ensure that they are on the cutting edge of any new legislation that applies to Special Education Teachers, as well as ensuring that they are aware of the best practices that are being implemented in teaching students with disabilities. They should also ensure that they incorporate the research into their daily teaching practice.

Other activities that improve teacher effectiveness include using available and innovative resources and technologies to enhance personal productivity and efficiency; using methods to remain current regarding evidence-based practices; and maintaining student, familial, and collegial confidentiality.

The Special Education Teacher needs to be aware of how personal cultural biases and differences impact one's teaching and learning. They should also be aware of professional organizations relevant to practice.

The self-assessment and reflection process should form the basis for decisions about programs and instructional strategies. After the teacher has reflected and assessed his performance in the classroom, he should work to improve his teaching practice, as professional growth is the practitioner's responsibility.

Skill 17.06   Recognizing strategies for establishing and maintaining ongoing communication and collaboration with other professionals in the field

(Please refer to **Skill 15.07**. Please also refer to skills about interviews, questionnaires, and conferences.)

SUBAREA IV. **PROMOTING STUDENT LEARNING AND DEVELOPMENT IN A COLLABORATIVE LEARNING COMMUNITY: CONSTRUCTED-RESPONSE ASSIGNMENT**

The content to be addressed by the constructed-response assignment is described in Subarea II, Competencies 06–13.

Post-test

1. Parents are more likely to have a child with a learning disability if: *(Skill 1.01) (Average Rigor)*

   A. They smoke tobacco.
   B. The child is less than 5 pounds at birth.
   C. If the mother drank alcohol on a regular basis until she planned for a baby.
   D. The father was known to consume large quantities of alcohol during the pregnancy.

2. Tom's Special Education Teacher became concerned about her ability to deliver the adaptations and services he needs when she heard him begin to talk to someone who was not there. He also responds to questions in a nonsensical manner. Tom's teacher is concerned because she thinks he may be exhibiting symptoms of: *(Skill 1.01) (Easy)*

   A. Sensory perceptual disorder.
   B. Mental illnesses.
   C. Depression
   D. Tactile sensory deprivation.

3. Janice is a new student in your self-contained class. She is extremely quiet and makes little if any eye contact. Yesterday she started to "parrot" what another student said. Today you became concerned when she did not follow directions and seemed not to even recognize your presence. Her cumulative file arrived today, when you review the health section, it most likely will state that she is diagnosed with: *(Skill 1.01) (Average)*

   A. Autism
   B. Central Processing Disorder
   C. Traumatic Brain Injury
   D. Mental Retardation

4. Across America there is one toxic substance that is contributing to the creation of disabilities in our children. What is it? *(Skill 1.01) (Average Rigor)*

   A. Children's Aspirin
   B. Fluoride water
   C. Chlorine Gas
   D. Lead

5. **Of the following which does not describe the term delinquency?**
    (Skill 1.01) (Average Rigor)

    A. Behavior that would be considered criminal if exhibited by an adult.
    B. Socialized aggression.
    C. Academic truancy.
    D. Inciting fights with verbal abuse.

6. **Which of these explanations would not likely account for the lack of a clear definition of behavior disorders?**
    (Skill 1.01) (Rigorous)

    A. Problems with measurement
    B. Cultural and/or social influences and views of what is acceptable
    C. The numerous types of manifestations of behavior disorders
    D. Differing theories that use their own terminology and definitions

7. **All children cry, hit, fight, and play alone at different times. Children with behavior disorders will perform these behaviors at a higher than normal:** *(Skill 1.01) (Average Rigor)*

    A. Rate
    B. Topography
    C. Duration
    D. Magnitude

8. **Which of these is not true for most children with behavior disorders?**
    (Skill 1.01) (Average Rigor)

    A. Many score in the "slow learner" or "mildly retarded" range on IQ tests
    B. They are frequently behind their classmates in academic achievement
    C. They are bright but bored with their surroundings
    D. A large amount of time is spent in nonproductive, nonacademic behaviors

9. **Jonathan has Attention Deficit Hyperactivity Disorder (ADHD). He is in a regular classroom and appears to be doing OK. But, his teacher does not want John in her class because he will not obey her when she asks him to stop doing a repetitive action such as tapping his foot. The teacher sees this as distractive during tests. John needs:** *(Skill 1.02) (Easy)*

    A. An IEP.
    B. A 504 Plan.
    C. A VESID evaluation.
    D. A more restrictive environment.

10. Otumba is a 16 year old in your class who recently came from Nigeria. The girls in your class have come to you to complain about the way he treats them in a sexist manner. When they complain you reflect that this is also the way he treats adult females. You have talked to Otumba before about appropriate behavior. You should first? *(Skill 1.03) (Rigorous)*

A. Complain to the Principal.
B. Ask for a Parent-Teacher Conference
C. Check to see if this is a cultural norm in his country.
D. Create a behavior contract for him to follow.

11. Mark is a 6th grader. You have noticed that he doesn't respond to simple requests like the other students in your class. If you ask him to erase the board he may look at you shake his head and say, but then he will clean the board. When the children gather together for recess he joins them. Yet, you observe that it takes him much longer to understand the rules to a game. Mark retains what he reads. Mark most likely has: *(Skill 1.04) (Rigorous)*

A. Autism
B. Tourette's Syndrome
C. Mental Retardation
D. A pragmatic language disability.

12. Skilled readers use all but which one of these knowledge sources to construct meanings beyond the literal text: (1.04) (Rigorous)

A. Text knowledge
B. Syntactic knowledge
C. Morphological knowledge
D. Semantic knowledge

13. **Chaz is observing Melody's interaction with others. It is apparent that the student does not know social cues, or that she is misinterpreting them. Chaz next observes Melody punch someone, after having tagged a friend during a game of tag. Chaz believes that melody may have a disability related to a:** *(Skill 1.04) (Rigorous)*

    A. Conduct Disorder
    B. Social Pragmatic Disorder
    C. Psychoses
    D. Depression

14. **Scott is in middle school but still makes statements like, "I gotted new high-tops yesterday," and "I saw three mans in the front office." Language interventions for Scott would target:** *(Skill 1.04) (Rigorous)*

    A. Morphology
    B. Syntax
    C. Pragmatics
    D. Cultural linguistics

15. **Mr. Mendez is assessing his students' written expression. Which of these is not a component of written expression?** *(Skill 1.04) (Rigorous)*

    A. Vocabulary
    B. Morphology
    C. Content
    D. Sentence structure

16. **Ray is being suspended because he will not go in Miss Smith's the classroom until after the bell rings. Ray never skips Mr. Paul's class, however, Mr. Paul does not care if the students are one to two minutes late. What is the best reason that Ray will not arrive on time to Miss Smith's class?** *(1.05) (Average Rigor)*

    A. Ray is afraid of being known as "Special Ed."
    B. Mr. Paul doesn't follow the rule.
    C. Miss Smith's class is boring.
    D. All of the above.

17. It is considered normal for a teenager to do all of the following except: *(Skill 2.01)* *(Average Rigor)*

   A. Use logical operations before applying them socially.
   B. Fail a class.
   C. Think about long term goals.
   D. Accept authority

18. Temper tantrums, disrupting the educational process or disobedience, and explosiveness are associated with those who are: *(Skill 2.01)* *(Average Rigor)*

   A. Emotionally Disturbed
   B. Diagnosed with personality disorders
   C. Immature
   D. Labeled "At Risk."

19. A person who has a learning disability has: *(Skill 2.02)* *(Easy)*

   A. An IQ two standard deviations below the norm.
   B. Congenital abnormalities.
   C. Is limited by the educational environment.
   D. Has a disorder in one of the basic psychological processes.

20. Justin, is diagnosed with Autism and is in an inclusive setting. You were called down to "Stop him from turning the lights off and remove him." When you arrive you learn that today a movie was supposed to be finished and the VCR broke, so the teacher planed another activity. What is the best way to explain to the teacher why Justin was turning off the lights? *(Skill 2.02)* *(Easy)*

   A. He is perseverating and will stop shortly.
   B. He is telling you the lights bother him.
   C. He needs forewarning before a transition. Next time you have an unexpected change in classroom schedule please let him know.
   D. Please understand, this is part of who Justin is. He will leave the lights alone after I talk to him.

21. Which of these characteristics is NOT included in the IDEA and Part 200 definition of emotional disturbance? *(Skill 2.02) (Average Rigor)*

   A. General pervasive mood of unhappiness or depression
   B. Social maladjustment manifested in a number of settings
   C. Tendency to develop physical symptoms, pains, or fear associated with school or personal problems
   D. Inability to learn that is not attributed to intellectual, sensory, or health factors

22. Students that exhibit engage in gang activity, are often in fights, and are often truant could be said to be: *(Skill 2.02) (Average Rigor)*

   A. Socially Maladjusted
   B. Emotionally Disturbed
   C. Learning Disabled
   D. Depressed

23. According to IDEA a child whose disability is related to being deaf and blind may not be classified as: *(Skill 2.02) (Rigorous)*

   A. Multiple Disabilities
   B. Other Health Impaired
   C. Mentally Retardation
   D. Visually Impaired

24. Children with behavior disorders often do not exhibit stimulus control. This means they do not display: *(Skill 2.02) (Average Rigor)*

   A. Culturally correct behaviors
   B. Where and when certain behaviors are appropriate
   C. Acceptance of others
   D. Listening skills

25. A child may be classified under the Special Education "umbrella" as having Traumatic Brain Injury (TBI) if he/she does not have the following cause? *(Skill 2.02) (Rigorous)*

   A. Stroke
   B. Anoxia
   C. Encephalitis
   D. Birth Trauma

26. Children with Visual-Spatial difficulties may not accomplish some developmental tasks, such as: (Skill 2.03) (Rigorous)

   A. Answering when called upon.
   B. Demonstrating characteristics of a certain letter in print.
   C. A delay in achieving the "th" sound.
   D. Recognition of the permanence of print.

27. A developmental delay may be indicated by a: *(Skill 2.03) (Rigorous)*

   A. Second grader having difficulty buttoning clothing.
   B. Stuttered response.
   C. Kindergartner not having complete bladder control.
   D. Withdrawn behavior.

28. A student on medication may have his/her dosage adjusted as his/her body grows. A parent may call and ask questions about their child's adjustment to the medication during the school day. During this time you should: *(Skill 2.04) (Average Rigor)*

   A. Observe the student for changes in behavior.
   B. Watch for a progression of changed behavior.
   C. Communicate with the parent concerns about sleepiness.
   D. All of the above.

29. Gerald, generally exhibits good behavior, and has been complaining that his new medicine keeps him from sleep at night and he can't help falling asleep in class. On top of that all of a sudden he seems excitable and antsy. What do you think he is on medication for? *(Skill 2.04) (Average Rigor)*

   A. Autism
   B. ADHD
   C. Conduct disorder
   D. Pervasive developmental

30. The purpose of error analysis of a test is to determine: *(Skill 3.01) (Easy)*

   A. What events were labeled in error.
   B. If the test length was the cause of error
   C. Evaluate the types of errors made by categorizing incorrect answers.
   D. Establish a baseline.

31. Formal assessment includes standardized criteria, norm-referenced instruments and____? *(Skill 3.01) (Rigorous)*

   A. Developmental rating scales.
   B. Interviews
   C. Error
   D. Performance analysis by gender, social economic status and/or ethnic groups.

32. A good assessment of whether a child may have ADHD in your classroom would include a_____.

A. Baseline
B. Monetary time sampling.
C. Age based norm criteria.
D. Construct Validity

33. Criteria for choosing behaviors to measure by frequency include all but those that: *(Skill 3.01)* *(Average Rigor)*

A. Have an observable beginning
B. Last a long time
C. Last a short time
D. Occur often

34. Criteria for choosing behaviors to measure by duration include all but those that: *(Skill 3.01)* *(Easy)*

A. Last a short time
B. Last a long time
C. Have no readily observable beginning or end
D. Do not happen often

35. You are working with a functional program and have placed a student in a vocational position at a Coffee House. You need to perform a Task Analysis of making coffee. Which task should be first in the analysis? *(Skill 3.01)* *(Average Rigor)*

A. Filling the pot with water
B. Taking the order.
C. Measuring the coffee
D. Picking the correct coffee

36. The basic tools necessary to observe and record behavior may include all BUT: *(Skill 3.01)* *(Average Rigor)*

A. Cameras
B. Timers
C. Counters
D. Graphs or charts

37. The extent that a test measures what it claims to measure is called: *(Skill 3.01)* *(Rigorous)*

A. Reliability
B. Validity
C. Factor analysis
D. Chi Square

38. A best practice for evaluating student performance and progress on IEPs is: *(Skill 3.01) (Rigorous)*

    A. Formal assessment
    B. Curriculum-based assessment
    C. Criterion-based assessment
    D. Norm-referenced evaluation

39. Statements like, "Darren is lazy," are not helpful in describing his behavior for all but which of these reasons? *(Skill 3.01) (Average Rigor)*

    A. There is no way to determine if any change occurs from the information given.
    B. The student and not the behavior becomes labeled.
    C. Darren's behavior will manifest itself clearly enough without any written description
    D. Constructs are open to various interpretations among the people who are asked to define them

40. Often, Marcie is not in her seat when the bell rings. She may be found at the pencil sharpener, throwing paper away, or fumbling through her notebook. Which of these descriptions of her behavior can be described as a pinpoint? *(Skill 3.01) (Easy)*

    A. Is tardy
    B. Is out of seat
    C. Is not in seat when late bell rings
    D. Is disorganized

41. Criteria for choosing behaviors that are in the most need of change involve all but the following: *(Skill 3.01) (Average Rigor)*

    A. Observations across settings to rule out certain interventions
    B. Pinpointing the behavior that is the poorest fit in the child's environment
    C. The teacher's concern about what is the most important behavior to target
    D. Analysis of the environmental reinforcers

42. Ms. Wright is planning an analysis of Jeffrey's out-of-seat behavior. Her initial data would be called: *(Skill 3.01) (Easy)*

    A. Pre-referral phase
    B. Intervention phase
    C. Baseline phase
    D. Observation phase

43. To reinforce Audrey each time she is on task and in her seat, Ms. Wright delivers specific praise and stickers, which Audrey may collect and redeem for a reward. The data collected during the time Ms. Wright is using this intervention is called: *(Skill 3.01) (Average Rigor)*

A. Referral phase
B. Intervention phase
C. Baseline phase
D. Observation phase

44. Which of these would be the least effective measure of behavioral disorders? *(Skill 3.01) (Average Rigor)*

A. Alternative Assessment
B. Naturalistic assessment
C. Standardized test
D. Psychodynamic analysis

45. Which would not be an advantage of using a criterion-referenced test? *(Skill 3.02) (Rigorous)*

A. Information about an individual's ability level is too specific for the purposes of the assessment.
B. It can pinpoint exact areas of weaknesses and strengths.
C. You can design them yourself.
D. You do not get comparative information.

46. Measurement of adaptive behavior should include all but: *(Skill 3.03) (Rigorous)*

A. Student's behavior in a variety of settings.
B. Student's skills displayed in a variety of settings.
C. Comparative analysis is to other students in his/her class.
D. Analysis of student's social skills.

47. Grading should be based on all of the following EXCEPT: *(Skill 3.04) (Average Rigor)*

A. Clearly-defined mastery of course objectives
B. A variety of evaluation methods
C. Performance of the student in relation to other students
D. Assigning points for activities and basing grades on a point total

48. Anecdotal Records should record? *(Skill 3.04) (Average Rigor)*

A. Observable behavior
B. End with conjecture.
C. Motivational factors
D. Note previously stated interests.

49. **Alternative Assessments include all of the following EXCEPT:** *(Skill 3.05)* *(Average Rigor)*

    A. Portfolios
    B. Interviews
    C. Teacher made tests
    D. Performance Based Tests

50. **According to NYS an initial evaluation/assessment for qualification of disability always must include all of the following EXCEPT:** *(Skill 4.01)* *(Rigorous)*

    A. Physical Evaluation
    B. Social History
    C. Psychological Evaluation
    D. Vocational Assessment

51. **If a child does not qualify for classification under Special Education the committee shall:** *(Skill 4.01)* *(Average Rigor)*

    A. Refer the parental interventions to the 504 Plan.
    B. Provide temporary remedial services for the student.
    C. Recommend to the parent possible resources outside of the committee the child may qualify for.
    D. Give the parents the information about possible reviews by an exterior source.

52. **Mark is receiving special education services within a 12:1:1. His teacher asks that he be placed in a more restrictive setting such as a residential placement. She presents good reasoning. What will the committee most likely recommend?** *(Skill 4.03)* *(Average Rigor)*

    A. 8:1:1
    B. BOCES School placement
    C. 1:1 Aide
    D. Return to placement

53. **Which of the following is NOT a feature of effective classroom rules?** *(Skill 4.05)* *(Easy)*

    A. They are about 4 to 6 in number
    B. They are negatively stated
    C. Consequences are consistent and immediate
    D. They can be tailored to individual teaching goals and teaching styles

54. **An effective classroom behavior management plan includes all but which of the following?** *(Skill 4.06)* *(Average Rigor)*

    A. Transition procedures for changing activities
    B. Clear consequences for rule infractions
    C. Concise teacher expectations for student behavior
    D. Strict enforcement

55. IDEA 2004 changed the IEP by? *(Skill 5.02) (Rigorous)*

   A. Not requiring short term objectives.
   B. Requiring an inclusive activity.
   C. Requiring parents to participate in the CSE.
   D. Establishing new criteria to be classified as learning disabled.

56. A letter must be sent to a parent informing them of a scheduled CSE. How many days prior notice must they receive? *(Skill 5.04) (Rigorous)*

   A. 7
   B. 30
   C. 10
   D. 5

57. How many contacts should be made with a parent prior to a CSE? *(Skill 5.04) (Rigorous)*

   A. 1
   B. 2
   C. Several
   D. 3

58. You have documented proof that Janice performs higher with the use of a computer on both class work and tests. Which kind of CSE/IEP Conference should be held? *(Skill 5.05) (Easy)*

   A. Manifestation Determination
   B. Post-School Transition to insure provision of lap top by outside services
   C. Amendment—Change of program/placement
   D. Annual

59. Teaching children skills that will be useful in their home life and neighborhoods is the basis of: *(Skill 5.06) (Average Rigor)*

   A. Curriculum-based instruction
   B. Community-based instruction
   C. Transition planning
   D. Academic curriculum

60. When would proximity control not be a good behavioral intervention: *(Skill 6.01) (Easy)*

   A. Two students are arguing.
   B. A student is distracting others.
   C. One student threatens another.
   D. Involve fading and shaping

61. Teacher feedback, task completion, and a sense of pride over mastery or accomplishment of a skill are examples of: (Skill 6.01) (Average Rigor)

A. Extrinsic reinforcers
B. Behavior modifiers
C. Intrinsic reinforcers
D. Positive feedback

62. Social approval, token reinforcers, and rewards, such as pencils or stickers, are examples of: (Skill 6.01) (Easy)

A. Extrinsic reinforcers
B. Behavior modifiers
C. Intrinsic reinforcers
D. Positive feedback reinforcers

63. Which of the following should be avoided when writing goals for social behavior? (Skill 6.01) (Average Rigor)

A. Non-specific adverbs
B. Behaviors stated as verbs
C. Criteria for acceptable performance
D. Conditions where the behavior is expected to be performed

64. The Integrated approach to learning utilizes all resources available to address student needs. What are the resources? (Skill 6.03) (Average Rigor)

A. The student, his/her parents, and the teacher.
B. The teacher, the parents, and the special education team.
C. The teacher the student, and an administrator to perform needed interventions.
D. The student, his/her parents, the teacher and community resources.

65. Mr. Johnson asks his students to score each of their classmates in areas such as who they would prefer to play with and work with. A Likert-type scale with non-behavioral criteria is used. This is an example of: (Skill 6.04) (Rigorous)

A. Peer nomination
B. Peer rating
C. Peer assessment
D. Sociogram

66. What is the highest goal a teacher should aim for while preparing a student for success? (Skill 6.05) (Average Rigor)

A. Reading.
B. Budgeting.
C. Cooking
D. Self-Advocacy

67. Which of the follow is does NOT have an important effect on the spatial arrangement (physical setting) of your classroom? *(Skill 6.05)* *(Average Rigor)*

   A. Adequate Physical Space
   B. Ventilation
   C. Window placement
   D. Lighting Adequacy

68. You are having continual difficulty with your classroom assistant. A good strategy to address this problem would be: *(Skill 6.08)* *(Rigorous)*

   A. To address the issue immediately.
   B. To take away responsibilities.
   C. To write a clearly establish role plan to discuss.
   D. To speak to your supervisor

69. Which of the following is a responsibility that can NOT be designated to a classroom aide? *(Skill 6.08)* *(Average Rigor)*

   A. Small group instruction
   B. Small group planning
   C. Coordination of an activity
   D. Assist in BIP implementation

70. The key to success for the exceptional student placed in a regular classroom is: *(Skill 7.01)* *(Average Rigor)*

   A. Access to the special aids and materials.
   B. Support from the ESE teacher.
   C. Modification in the curriculum.
   D. The mainstream teacher's belief that the student will profit from the placement.

71. Ability to supply specific instructional materials, programs, and methods and to influence environmental learning variables are advantages of which service model for exceptional students? *(Skill 7.01)* *(Rigorous)*

   A. Regular classroom
   B. Consultant teacher
   C. Itinerant teacher
   D. Resource room

72. A Consultant Teacher should be meeting the needs of his/her students by: *(Skill 7.01)* *(Easy)*

   A. Pushing in to do small group instruction with regular education students.
   B. Asking the student to show his/her reasoning for failing.
   C. Meeting with the teacher before class to discuss adaptations and expectations.
   D. Accompanying the student to class.

73. **Teaching techniques that stimulate active participation and understanding in the mathematics class include all but which of the following?** *(Skill 7.02)* *(Easy)*

   A. Having students copy computation facts for a set number of times.
   B. Asking students to find the error in an algorithm.
   C. Giving immediate feedback to students.
   D. Having students chart their progress.

74. **According to IDEA 2004, students with disabilities are to do what:** *(Skill 7.02)* *(Average Rigor)*

   A. Participate in the general education program to the fullest extent that it is beneficial for them.
   B. Participate in a vocational training within the general education setting.
   C. Participate in a general education setting for physical education.
   D. Participate in a modified program that meets his/her needs.

75. **Marisol has been mainstreamed into a ninth grade language arts class. Although her behavior is satisfactory, and she likes the class, Marisol's reading level is about two years below grade level. The class has been assigned to read *Great Expectations* and write a report. What intervention would be LEAST successful in helping Marisol complete this assignment?** *(Skill 7.01)(Average Rigor)*

   A. Having Marisol listen to a taped recording while following the story in the regular text.
   B. Giving her a modified version of the story.
   C. Telling her to choose a different book that she can read.
   D. Showing a film to the entire class and comparing and contrasting it with the book.

76. Mrs. Taylor takes her students to a special gymnastics presentation that the P.E. coach has arranged in the gym. The students get a chance to perform some of the simple stunts. They all easily go through the movements except for Sam, who is known as the class klutz. Carl, another student of Mrs. Taylor, helps Sam, who does not give up and finally completes the stunts. His classmates cheer him on with comments like, "Way to go". What kind of teaching technique was implemented? *(Skill 7.02) (Average Rigor)*

   A. Group share
   B. Modeling
   C. Peer Tutoring
   D. All of the above

77. Teachers in grades K-3 are mandated to teach what to all students using scientifically based methods with measurable outcomes *(Skill 7.03) (Average Rigor)*

   A. Math
   B. Reading
   C. Citizenship
   D. Writing

78. Many special education students may have trouble with the skills necessary to be successful in algebra and geometry for all but one of these reasons: *(Skill 7.03) (Average Rigor)*

   A. Prior instruction focused on computation rather than understanding
   B. Unwillingness to problem solve
   C. Lack of instruction in prerequisite skills
   D. Large amount of new vocabulary

79. Cooperative learning does NOT utilize? *(Skill 7.02) (Average Rigor)*

   A. Shared ideas
   B. Small groups
   C. Independent practice
   D. Student expertise

80. The revision of Individuals with Disabilities Education Act in 1997 required: *(Skill 7.04)(Rigorous)*

    A. Collaboration of educational professionals in order to provide equitable opportunities for students with disabilities.
    B. Removed the requirement for short term objectives with objectives with goals.
    C. School Administrator approval for an IEP to be put into place.
    D. FBAs and BIPs for all students that were suspended for 6 days.

81. Students with disabilities develop greater self-images and recognize their own academic and social strengths when they are: *(Skill 7.05)(Easy)*

    A. Included in the mainstream classroom.
    B. Provided community based internships.
    C. Socializing in the hallway.
    D. Provided 1:1 instructional opportunity.

82. An emphasis on instructional remediation and individualized instruction in problem areas, and a focus on mainstreaming, are characteristics of which model of service delivery? *(Skill 7.06) (Average Rigor)*

    A. Regular classroom
    B. Consultant teacher
    C. Itinerant teacher
    D. Resource room

83. Organizing ideas by use of a web or outline is an example of which writing activity? *(Skill 8.06) (Easy)*

    A. Revision
    B. Drafting
    C. Prewriting
    D. Final draft

84. Ryan is working on a report about dogs. He uses scissors and tape to cut and rearrange sections and paragraphs and then photocopies the paper so he can continue writing. In which stage of the writing process is Ryan? *(Skill 8.06)(Easy)*

    A. Final draft
    B. Prewriting
    C. Revision
    D. Drafting

85. You are advocating for a student who is blind and is proficient in Braille. You should: *(Skill 8.06) (Rigorous)*

A. Ask the team for a PC.
B. Tell the team you need a Mac.
C. Tell the team that it needs a special keyboard.
D. Tell the team that it doesn't need to come with a monitor.

86. When a student begins to use assistive technology it is important for the teacher to have a clear outline as to when and how the equipment should be used. Why? *(Skill 8.07) (Rigorous)*

A. To establish a level of accountability with the student.
B. To establish that the teacher has responsibility of the equipment that is in use in his/her room.
C. To establish that the teacher is responsible for the usage of the assistive technology.
D. To establish a guideline for evaluation.

87. Which is not indicative of a handwriting problem? *(Skill 9.01) (Rigorous)*

A. Errors persisting over time
B. Little improvement on simple handwriting tasks
C. Fatigue after writing for a short time
D. Occasional letter reversals, word omissions, and poor spacing

88. The Phonics approach to teaching children how to read utilizes what method? *(Skill 9.02) (Average Rigor)*

A. Reading for meaning
B. Reading for letter combinations
C. Identifying word by their position and context
D. Word configurations

89. Which of these techniques is least effective in helping children correct spelling problems? *(Skill 9.02)(Rigorous)*

A. The teacher models the correct spelling in a context
B. Student sees the incorrect and the correct spelling together in order to visualize the correct spelling
C. Positive reinforcement as the child tests the rules and tries to approximate the correct spelling
D. Copying the correct word five times

90. Ms. Tolbert is teaching spelling to her students. The approach stresses phoneme-grapheme relationships within parts of words. Spelling rules, generalizations, and patterns are taught. A typical spelling list for her third graders might include light, bright, night, fright, and slight. Which approach is Ms. Tolbert using? *(Skill 9.02)(Rigorous)*

 A. Rule-based Instruction
 B. Phonics
 C. Whole Word
 D. Both a and b

91. A teacher should consider all of the following when evaluating a student's reading comprehension EXCEPT: *(Skill 9.03) (Average Rigor)*

 A. Past experience
 B. Teacher prepared preset questions on text
 C. Level of content
 D. Oral language comprehension.

92. In a positive classroom environment, errors are viewed as: *(Skill 9.03) (Average Rigor)*

 A. Symptoms of deficiencies.
 B. Lack of attention or ability.
 C. A natural part of the learning process.
 D. The result of going too fast.

93. Which of the following sentences will NOT test recall? (Skill 9.05) *(Average Rigor)*

 A. What words in the story describe Goldilocks?
 B. Why did Goldilocks go into the three bears' house?
 C. Name in order the things that belonged to the three bears that Goldilocks tried.
 D. What did the three bears learn about leaving their house unlocked?

94. Modeling of a behavior by an adult who verbalizes the thinking process, overt self-instruction, and covert self-instruction are components of: *(Skill 10.02) (Rigorous)*

 A. Rational-emotive therapy
 B. Reality therapy
 C. Cognitive behavior modification
 D. Reciprocal teaching

95. What is considered the most effective when teaching children with special needs new concepts in math? *(Skill 10.02) (Rigorous)*

 A. Problem solving
 B. Direct instruction
 C. Repetition
 D. Ongoing Assessment

96. Mr. Ward notes that Jennifer, a 9th grade student, understands the concept for three step equations but seems unable to do problems successfully. When he reviews Jennifer's work he notes that her addition and subtraction is not correct. What strategy would be most appropriate? *(Skill 10.05) (Average Rigor)*

   A. Basic multiplication and addition charts.
   B. Checks for understanding.
   C. Private instruction on adding and subtracting.
   D. Calculator Usage

97. The most direct method of obtaining assessment data, and perhaps the most objective, is: *(Skill 10.05) (Rigorous)*

   A. Testing
   B. Self-recording
   C. Observation
   D. Experimenting

98. Laura is beginning to raise her hand first instead of talking out. An effective schedule of reinforcement should be: *(Skill 11.02) (Average Rigor)*

   A. Continuous
   B. Variable
   C. Intermittent
   D. Fixed

99. To facilitate learning instructional objectives: *(Skill 11.02) (Average Rigor)*

   A. Grade level spelling list
   B. They should be written and shared.
   C. They should be arranged in order of similarity.
   D. Should be taken from a scope and sequence.

100. Transfer of learning occurs when? *(Skill 11.02) (Rigorous)*

   A. Experience with one task influences performance on another task.
   B. Content can be explained orally.
   C. Student experiences the "I got it!" syndrome.
   D. Curricular objective is exceeded.

101. Teacher modeling, student-teacher dialogues, and peer interactions are part of which teaching technique designed to provide support during the initial stages of instruction? *(Skill 11.05) (Rigorous)*

   A. Reciprocal teaching
   B. Scaffolding
   C. Peer tutoring
   D. Cooperative learning

102. Functional curriculum focuses on all of the following EXCEPT: *(Skill 11.03) (Rigorous)*

    A. Skills needed for social living
    B. Occupational readiness
    C. Functioning in society.
    D. Remedial academic skills

103. Diversity can be identified in students by: *(Skill 12.04) (Average Rigor)*

    A. Biological factors
    B. Socioeconomic Status (SES)
    C. Ethnicity
    D. All of the above

104. Which of the following is NOT the best way to encourage and strengthen a social skill? *(Skill 12.01) (Average Rigor)*

    A. Role playing
    B. Field Trips
    C. Student story telling
    D. Reading a book on the topic

105. Distractive behavior, verbal outbursts, and passive aggressiveness should be addressed using: *(Skill 12.03) (Rigorous)*

    A. Time-out.
    B. Response cost.
    C. Planned ignoring.
    D. Rule reminders.

106. A student with a poor self-concept may manifest in all of the ways listed below EXCEPT: *(Skill 12.03) (Average Rigor)*

    A. Withdrawn actions.
    B. Aggression
    C. Consistently announcing his/her achievements.
    D. Shyness.

107. A good naturalistic assessment requires: *(Skill 12.04)(Rigorous)*

    A. Communication notebooks
    B. Portfolios
    C. Long-range planning
    D. Diverse responses

108. Mr. Smith is on a field trip with a group of high school EH students. On the way, they stop at a fast-food restaurant for lunch, and Warren and Raul get into an argument. After some heated words, Warren stalks out of the restaurant and refuses to return to the group. He leaves the parking lot, continues walking away from the group, and ignores Mr. Smith's directions to come back. What would be the best course of action for Mr. Smith? (Skill 13.05) (Rigorous)

   A. Leave the group with the class aide and follow Warren to try to talk him into coming back.
   B. Wait a little while and see if Warren cools off and returns.
   C. Telephone the school and let the crisis teacher notify the police in accordance with school policy.
   D. Call the police himself.

109. When a teacher is choosing behaviors to modify, two issues must be considered. What are they? (Skill 13.01) (Average Rigor)

   A. The need for the behavior to be performed in public and the culture of acceptance.
   B. The culture of the child and society standards to regarding the behavior.
   C. Evidence that the behavior can be changed, and society norms.
   D. Standards of the student's community and school rules.

110. Sam is working to earn half an hour of basketball time with his favorite P.E. teacher. At the end of each half hour, Sam marks his point sheet with an X if he reached his goal of no call-outs. When he has received 25 marks, he will receive his basketball free time. This behavior management strategy is an example of: (Skill 13.01) (Average)

   A. Self-recording
   B. Self-evaluation
   C. Self-reinforcement
   D. Self-regulation

111. Mark has been working on his target goal of completing his mathematics class work. Each day he records, on a scale of 0 to 3, how well he has done his work, and his teacher provides feedback. This self-management technique is an example of: *(Skill 13.01) (Average Rigor)*

    A. Self-recording.
    B. Self reinforcement.
    C. Self-regulation.
    D. Self-evaluation.

112. Token systems are popular for all of these advantages EXCEPT: (Skill 13.01) *(Average Rigor)*

    A. The number needed for rewards may be adjusted as needed.
    B. Rewards are easy to maintain.
    C. They are effective for students who generally do not respond to social reinforcers.
    D. Tokens reinforce the relationship between desirable behavior and reinforcement.

113. Alternative Assessments include all of the following EXCEPT: *(Skill 3.05) (Average Rigor)*

    A. Portfolios.
    B. Interviews.
    C. Teacher made tests.
    D. Performance Based Tests.

114. A BIP (Behavior Intervention Plan is written to teach positive behavior. Which element listed below is NOT a standard feature of the plan? *(Skill 13.03) (Rigorous)*

    A. Identification of "behavior to be modified
    B. Strategies to implement the replacement behavior
    C. Statement of distribution
    D. Team creation of BIP

115. You have a class of 8th Grade students in an English class. Sheryl sits in the back of the room by choice and rarely answers questions. You believe that she has a learning disability and begin to modify her worksheets. You are: *(Skill 13.04) (Average Rigor)*

    A. Planning for success of the student.
    B. Creating a self-fulfilled prophecy.
    C. Developing a student centered curriculum.
    D. Testing her ability.

116. All of these are effective in teaching written expression EXCEPT: *(Skill 13.04)* *(Easy)*

   A. Exposure to various styles and direct instruction in those styles.
   B. Immediate feedback from the teacher with all mistakes clearly marked.
   C. Goal setting and peer evaluation of written products according to set criteria.
   D. Incorporating writing with other academic subjects.

117. A student who has issues with truancy, gang membership, low school performance, and drug use is displaying: *(Skill 13.05)* *(Average Rigor)*

   A. Emotionally disturbed behaviors.
   B. Symptoms of self-medication.
   C. Average Rigor adolescent behavior.
   D. Warning signs of crisis.

118. Kareem's father sounds upset and is in the office demanding to see his son's cumulative record. You should: *(Skill 13.06)* *(Average Rigor)*

   A. Tell him that he will have to make an appointment.
   B. Bring the record to a private room for him to review with either an administrator or yourself.
   C. Take the record to the principals office for review.
   D. Give the record to the parent.

119. Kara's mother has requested a computer for her child to do class work and home work and the CSE does not agree. Kara complains to you. You should: *(Skill 13.06)* *(Easy)*

   A. Tell her you agree with her.
   B. Recommend an outside source that may provide a free laptop computer.
   C. Tell Kara's mother she can still fight the CSE's decision by requesting a Due Process Hearing.
   D. Tell the parent to call a lawyer.

120. Taiquan's parents are divorced and have joint custody. They both have requested to be present at the CSE. You call to make sure that they received the letter informing them of the coming CSE. Taiquan's father did not receive the notification and is upset. You should: *(Skill 13.06)* *(Rigorous)*

A. Tell him that you could review the meeting with him later.
B. Ask him if he can adjust his schedule.
C. Tell him you can reschedule the meeting.
D. Ask him to coordinate a time for the CSE to meet with his ex-wife.

121. Shyquan is in your inclusive class and she exhibits a slower comprehension of assigned tasks and concepts. Her first two grades were Bs but she is now receiving failing marks. She has seen the Resource Teacher. You should: *(Skill 13.06)* *(Rigorous)*

A. Ask for a review of current placement.
B. Tell Shyquan to seek extra help.
C. Ask Shyquan if she is frustrated.
D. Ask the regular education teacher to slow instruction.

122. According to IDEA 2004 an FBA must be: *(Skill 13.07)* *(Average Rigor)*

A. Written by the Special Education Administrator.
B. Written by the teacher who has the issue with the student.
C. Written by the primary teacher.
D. Written by a team.

123. Parent contact should first begin when: *(Skill 14.02)* *(Average Rigor)*

A. You are informed the child will be your student.
B. The student fails a test.
C. The student exceeds others on a task.
D. A CSE is coming and you have had no previous replies to letters.

124. **Parents of children with disabilities may seek your advice on several aspects regarding their child. A mother calls you and complains she can't keep her son on task so much she has to keep sending her son back to the bathroom until he finishes getting prepared for the day. What advice should you give her?** *(Skill 14.03) (Average Rigor)*

   A. Request an educational evaluation.
   B. Recommend close supervision until he does all tasks together consistently.
   C. Create a list of tasks to be completed in the bathroom.
   D. Ask for outside coordination of services advocacy that can assist with this type of issue.

125. **By November, Annette's 7th grade teacher is concerned with her sporadic attendance. What action should take place next?** *(Skill 14.04) (Average Rigor)*

   A. Notify CPS
   B. Notify the police of non-compliance with compulsory attendance.
   C. Question parents about the absences.
   D. Notify the Administrator.

126. **Which is not a goal of collaboration for a Consult Teacher?** *(Skill 14.05) (Average Rigor)*

   A. To have the regular education teacher understand the student's disability.
   B. Review content for accuracy
   C. Review Lessons for possible necessary modifications.
   D. Understanding of reasons for current grade Average Rigor.

127. **Kenny is a 9th grader enrolled in Wood Shop; he is having difficulty grasping fractions. You know that Kenny has difficulty with abstract concepts. What would be a good method to teach this concept?** *(Skill 14.06)(Rigorous)*

   A. Pie blocks that proportionately measure whole, half, 1/4, 1/8, etc.
   B. Strips of paper that proportionately measure whole, half, 1/4, 1/8, etc.
   C. One on one review of the worksheet.
   D. You work with in the wood shop privately showing him how to measure.

128. **Task related attending skills include:** *(Skill 14.06) (Hard)*

    A. Compliance to requests
    B. Writing the correct Answer: on the chalk board.
    C. Listening to the assignment
    D. Repeating instructions

129. **What legislation started FAPE?** *(Skill 16.01) (Rigorous)*

    A. Section 504
    B. EHCA
    C. IDEA
    D. Education Amendment 1974

130. **NCLB changed:** *(Skill 16.01) (Rigorous)*

    A. Special Education Teacher placement
    B. Classroom guidelines
    C. Stricter behavioral regulations.
    D. Academic content

131. **IDEA 97 changed IDEA by requiring** *(Skill 16.01) (Rigorous)*

    A. IEPs to be in Electronic format.
    B. Requiring all staff working with the student to have access to the IEP.
    C. Allowing past assessments to be used in Triennials.
    D. BIPs for many students with FBAs.

132. **Which of these groups is not comprehensively covered by IDEA?** *(Skill 16.01) (Easy)*

    A. Gifted and talented
    B. Mentally retarded
    C. Specific learning disabilities
    D. Speech and language impaired

133. **Educators who advocate educating all children in their neighborhood classrooms and schools propose the end of labeling and segregation of special needs students in special classes, and who call for the delivery of special supports and services directly in the classroom, may be said to support the:** *(Skill 16.01) (Easy)*

    A. Full service model
    B. Regular education initiative
    C. Full inclusion model
    D. Mainstream model

134. **NCLB (No Child Left Behind Act), was signed on January 8, 2002. It addresses what:** *(Skill 16.01) (Rigorous)*

   A. Accessibility of curriculum to the student
   B. Administrative incentives for school improvements
   C. The funding to provide services required.
   D. Accountability of school personnel for student achievement.

135. **Section 504 differs from the scope of IDEA because its main focus is on:** *(Skill 16.01) (Average Rigor)*

   A. Prohibition of discrimination on the basis of disability.
   B. A basis for additional support services and accommodations in a special education setting.
   C. Procedural rights and safeguards for the individual.
   D. Federal funding for educational services.

136. **Public Law 99-457 amended the EHA to make provisions for:** *(Skill 16.01) (Average Rigor)*

   A. Education services for "uneducable" children
   B. Education services for children in jail settings
   C. Special education benefits for children birth to five years
   D. Education services for medically-fragile children

137. **Under the provisions of IDEA, the student is entitled to all of these EXCEPT:** *(Skill 16.01) (Average Rigor)*

   A. Placement in the best environment
   B. Placement in the least restrictive environment
   C. Provision of educational needs at no cost
   D. Provision of individualized, appropriate educational program

138. **As a New Special Education Teacher you have responsibility to?** *(Skill 16.01) (Average Rigor)*

    A. Share new law related to special education.
    B. Discuss and plan intervention strategies for other teachers.
    C. Stay current on national and local news.
    D. Observe incoming students for possible referrals to CSE.

139. **Which law specifically states that "Full Inclusion is not the only way for a student to reach his/her highest potential?"** *(Skill 16.01) (Rigorous)*

    A. IDEA
    B. IDEA 97
    C. IDEA 2004
    D. Part 200

140. **The following words describe an IEP objective EXCEPT:** *(Skill 16.01) (Rigorous)*

    A. Specific
    B. Observable
    C. Measurable
    D. Flexible

141. **NCLB and IDEA 2004 changed Special Education Teacher requirements by:** *(Skill 16.01) (Easy)*

    A. Requiring a Highly Qualified status for job placement.
    B. Adding changes to the requirement for certifications
    C. Adding legislation requiring teachers to maintain knowledge of law.
    D. Requiring inclusive environmental experience prior to certification.

142. **IDEA 2004 stated that there is a disproportionate amount of minority students classified. The reason IDEA 2004 suggests is:** *(Skill 16.01) (Average Rigor)*

    A. Socioeconomic status where disproportionate numbers exist.
    B. Improper evaluations – Not making allowances for students who have English as a second language.
    C. Growing population of minorities.
    D. Percentage of drug abuse per ethnicity.

143. Which of the following statements was not offered as a rationale for Inclusion? *(Skill 16.01) (Average Rigor)*

   A. Special education students are not usually identified until their learning problems have become severe
   B. Lack of funding will mean that support for the special needs children will not be available in the regular classroom.
   C. Putting children in segregated special education placements is stigmatizing
   D. There are students with learning or behavior problems who do not meet special education requirements but who still need special services

144. Guidelines for an Individualized Family Service Plan (IFSP) would be described in which legislation? *(Skill 16.01) (Rigorous)*

   A. Education of the Handicapped Act Amendments
   B. IDEA (1990)
   C. IDEA 2004
   D. ADA

145. Cheryl is a 15-year old student receiving educational services in a full-time EH classroom. The date for her IEP review is planned for two months before her 16th birthday. According to the requirements of IDEA, what must ADDITIONALLY be included in this review? *(Skill 16.01) (Average Rigor)*

   A. Graduation plan
   B. Individualized transition plan
   C. Vocational assessment
   D. Transportation planning

146. Previous to IDEA97 what was not accepted? (Skill 16.01) (Hard)

   A. Using previous assessments to evaluate placement.
   B. Parent refusal of CSE determination (No Due Process)
   C. Student input on placement and needs.
   D. All of the Above

147. Hector is a 10th grader in a program for the severely emotionally handicapped. After a classmate taunted him about his mother, Hector threw a desk at the other boy and attacked him. A crisis intervention team tried to break up the fight, and one teacher hurt his knee. The other boy received a concussion. Hector now faces disciplinary measures. How long can he be suspended without the suspension reviewing a possible "change of placement"? *(Skill 16.01) (Rigorous)*

A. 5 days
B. 10 days
C. 10 + 30 days
D. 60 days

148. The concept that a handicapped student cannot be expelled for misconduct that is a manifestation of the handicap itself is not limited to students which are labeled "seriously emotionally disturbed". Which reason does not explain this concept? *(Skill 16.01) (Easy)*

A. Emphasis on individualized evaluation
B. Consideration of the problems and needs of handicapped students
C. Right to a free and appropriate public education
D. Students in special education get special privileges.

149. What is required of a Special Education Teacher when approaching an administrator regarding a request to change placement of a student: *(Skill 17.03) (Rigorous)*

A. Observation.
B. Objectivity.
C. Assessments.
D. Parent permission.

150. Teachers have a professional obligation to do all of the following except: *(Skill 17.05)* *(Average Rigor)*

   A. Join a professional organization such as CEC, or LDA.
   B. Attend inservices or seminars related to your position.
   C. Stay after school to help students.
   D. Run school clubs.

Post-test Answer Key

1.	B	39.	C	77.	B	115.	B
2.	B	40.	C	78.	A	116.	B
3.	A	41.	C	79.	C	117.	D
4.	D	42.	C	80.	A	118.	B
5.	D	43.	B	81.	A	119.	C
6.	C	44.	C	82.	D	120.	C
7.	A	45.	D	83.	C	121.	A
8.	C	46.	C	84.	C	122.	D
9.	B	47.	C	85.	A	123.	A
10.	C	48.	A	86.	A	124.	C
11.	D	49.	C	87.	D	125.	C
12.	C	50.	A	88.	C	126.	B
13.	B	51.	C	89.	D	127.	B
14.	A	52.	A	90.	A	128.	C
15.	B	53.	B	91.	B	129.	A
16.	A	54.	D	92.	C	130.	A
17.	D	55.	A	93.	D	131.	D
18.	A	56.	C	94.	C	132.	C
19.	D	57.	D	95.	A	133.	C
20.	C	58.	C	96.	D	134.	D
21.	B	59.	B	97.	C	135.	A
22.	A	60.	C	98.	A	136.	C
23.	A	61.	C	99.	C	137.	A
24.	B	62.	A	100.	A	138.	A
25.	D	63.	A	101.	B	139.	C
26.	B	64.	D	102.	D	140.	D
27.	A	65.	A	103.	D	141.	A
28.	D	66.	B D	104.	D	142.	B
29.	B	67.	C	105.	C	143.	B
30.	C	68.	C	106.	C	144.	B
31.	D	69.	C	107.	C	145.	B
32.	B	70.	D	108.	C	146.	B
33.	B	71.	B	109.	B	147.	B
34.	A	72.	A	110.	A	148.	D
35.	C D	73.	A	111.	D	149.	B
36.	A	74.	A	112.	B	150.	D
37.	B	75.	C	113.	C		
38.	B	76.	D	114.	C		

Post-test Rigor Table

Number	Level of Question	Skill Reference	Number	Level of Question	Skill Reference
1	Average Rigor	1.01	36	Average Rigor	3.01
2	Easy Rigor	1.01	37	Hard	3.01
3	Average Rigor	1.01	38	Hard	3.01
4	Average Rigor	1.01	39	Average Rigor	3.01
5	Hard	1.01	40	Easy Rigor	3.01
6	Hard	1.01	41	Average Rigor	3.01
7	Average Rigor	1.01	42	Easy Rigor	3.01
8	Average Rigor	1.01	43	Average Rigor	3.01
9	Easy Rigor	1.02	44	Average Rigor	3.01
10	Hard	1.03	45	Hard	3.02
11	Hard	1.04	46	Hard	3.03
12	Hard	1.04	47	Average Rigor	3.04
13	Hard	1.04	48	Average Rigor	3.04
14	Hard	1.04	49	Average Rigor	3.05
15	Hard	1.04	50	Hard	4.01
16	Average Rigor	1.05	51	Average Rigor	4.01
17	Average Rigor	2.01	52	Average Rigor	4.03
18	Easy Rigor	2.01	53	Easy Rigor	4.05
19	Average Rigor	2.02	54	Average Rigor	4.06
20	Easy Rigor	2.02	55	Hard	5.02
21	Average Rigor	2.02	56	Hard	5.04
22	Average Rigor	2.02	57	Hard	5.04
23	Hard	2.02	58	Easy Rigor	5.05
24	Average Rigor	2.02	59	Average Rigor	5.06
25	Hard	2.02	60	Easy Rigor	6.01
26	Hard	2.03	61	Average Rigor	6.01
27	Hard	2.03	62	Easy Rigor	6.01
28	Average Rigor	2.04	63	Average Rigor	6.01
29	Average Rigor	2.04	64	Average Rigor	6.03
30	Easy Rigor	3.01	65	Hard	6.04
31	Hard	3.01	66	Average Rigor	6.05
32	Easy Rigor	3.01	67	Average Rigor	6.05
33	Average Rigor	3.01	68	Hard	6.08
34	Easy Rigor	3.01	69	Average Rigor	6.08
35	Average Rigor	3.01	70	Average Rigor	7.01
			71	Hard	7.01
			72	Easy Rigor	7.01

73	Easy Rigor	7.02	112	Average Rigor	13.01
74	Average Rigor	7.02	113	Hard	13.02
75	Average Rigor	7.02	114	Hard	13.03
76	Average Rigor	7.02	115	Average Rigor	13.04
77	Average Rigor	7.03	116	Easy Rigor	13.04
78	Average Rigor	7.03	117	Average Rigor	13.05
79	Average Rigor	7.03	118	Average Rigor	13.06
80	Hard	7.04	119	Easy Rigor	13.06
81	Easy Rigor	7.04	120	Hard	13.06
82	Average Rigor	7.06	121	Hard	13.06
83	Easy Rigor	8.06	122	Average Rigor	13.07
84	Easy Rigor	8.06	123	Average Rigor	14.02
85	Hard	8.06	124	Average Rigor	14.03
86	Hard	8.07	125	Average Rigor	14.04
87	Hard	9.01	126	Average Rigor	14.05
88	Average Rigor	9.02	127	Hard	14.06
89	Hard	9.02	128	Hard	14.06
90	Hard	9.02	129	Hard	16.01
91	Average Rigor	9.03	130	Hard	16.01
92	Average Rigor	9.03	131	Hard	16.01
93	Average Rigor	9.05	132	Easy Rigor	16.01
94	Hard	10.02	133	Easy Rigor	16.01
95	Hard	10.02	134	Hard	16.01
96	Average Rigor	10.05	135	Average Rigor	16.01
97	Hard	10.05	136	Average Rigor	16.01
98	Average Rigor	11.02	137	Average Rigor	16.01
99	Average Rigor	11.02	138	Average Rigor	16.01
100	Hard	11.02	139	Hard	16.01
101	Hard	11.05	140	Hard	16.01
102	Hard	11.06	141	Easy Rigor	16.01
103	Average Rigor	12.01	142	Average Rigor	16.01
104	Average Rigor	12.01	143	Average Rigor	16.01
105	Hard	12.03	144	Hard	16.01
106	Average Rigor	12.03	145	Average Rigor	16.01
107	Hard	12.04	146	Hard	16.01
108	Hard	13.01	147	Easy Rigor	16.01
109	Average Rigor	13.01	148	Easy Rigor	17.01
110	Average Rigor	13.01	149	Hard	17.03
111	Average Rigor	13.01	150	Average Rigor	17.05

Post-test Rationales with Sample Questions

1.   Parents are more likely to have a child with a learning disability if: (Skill 1.01) (Average Rigor)

    A. They smoke tobacco.
    B. The child is less than 5 pounds at birth.
    C. If the mother drank alcohol on a regular basis until she planned for a baby.
    D. The father was known to consume large quantities of alcohol during the pregnancy.

Answer: B. The child is less than 5 pounds at birth.

Babies that are born weighing less than 5 pounds at birth are more likely to have a form of learning disability. The reasoning is that the babies may not have fully developed before birth.

2.   Tom's Special Education Teacher became concerned about her ability to deliver the adaptations and services he needs when she heard him begin to talk to someone who was not there. He also responds to questions in a nonsensical manner. Tom's teacher is concerned because she thinks he may be exhibiting symptoms of: (Skill 1.01) (Easy)

    A. Sensory perceptual disorder.
    B. Mental illnesses.
    C. Depression
    D. Tactile sensory deprivation.

Answer: B.   Mental illnesses.

Tom is demonstrating delusional or hallucinogenic symptoms. These symptoms may indicate a need for psychiatric treatment within a more restrictive environment.

3.   Janice is a new student in your self-contained class. She is
       extremely quiet and makes little if any eye contact. Yesterday she
       started to "parrot" what another student said. Today you became
       concerned when she did not follow directions and seemed not to
       even recognize your presence. Her cumulative file arrived today,
       when you review the health section, it most likely will state that she
       is diagnosed with: (Skill 1.01) (Average)

       A. Autism
       B. Central Processing Disorder
       C. Traumatic Brain Injury
       D. Mental Retardation

Answer: A. Autism

Janice is exhibiting 3 symptoms of Autism. While a child may demonstrate some
of these behaviors, if they are diagnosed with Traumatic Brain Injury or Mental
Retardation, the combination of these symptoms are more likely to indicate
Autism.

4.   Across America there is one toxic substance that is contributing to
       the creation of disabilities in our children. What is it? (Skill 1.01)
       (Average Rigor)

       A. Children's Aspirin
       B. Fluoride water
       C. Chlorine Gas
       D. Lead

Answer: D Lead

Lead poisoning is still a major factor influencing /causing disabilities. Today
many homes in Urban, suburban and rural neighborhoods are still working to
remove the lead paint in houses.

5.   **Of the following which does not describe the term delinquency? (Skill 1.01) (Average Rigor)**

   A. Behavior that would be considered criminal if exhibited by an adult.
   B. Socialized aggression. ⁻
   C. Academic truancy.
   D. Inciting fights with verbal abuse.

Answer: D. Inciting fights with verbal abuse.

Socialized aggression, and criminal behavior are characteristics of gang membership and delinquency. Truancy is also characteristic of this behavior. Verbal abuse however is not descriptive of this as it is not seen as criminal behavior.

6.   **Which of these explanations would not likely account for the lack of a clear definition of behavior disorders? (Skill 1.01) (Rigorous)**

   A. Problems with measurement
   B. Cultural and/or social influences and views of what is acceptable
   C. The numerous types of manifestations of behavior disorders
   D. Differing theories that use their own terminology and definitions

Answer: C. Cultural and/or social influences and views of what is acceptable

A, B, and D are factors that account for the lack of a clear definition of some behavioral disorders. C is not a factor.

7.   **All children cry, hit, fight, and play alone at different times. Children with behavior disorders will perform these behaviors at a higher than normal: (Skill 1.01) (Average Rigor)**

   A. Rate
   B. Topography
   C. Duration
   D. Magnitude

Answer: A. Rate

Children with behavior disorders display them at a much higher rate than normal children.

8. **Which of these is not true for most children with behavior disorders? (Skill 1.01) (Average Rigor)**

   A. Many score in the "slow learner" or "mildly retarded" range on IQ tests
   B. They are frequently behind their classmates in academic achievement
   C. They are bright but bored with their surroundings
   D. A large amount of time is spent in nonproductive, nonacademic behaviors

Answer: C. They are bright but bored with their surroundings

Most children with conduct disorders display the traits found in A, B, and D.

9. **Jonathan has Attention Deficit Hyperactivity Disorder (ADHD). He is in a regular classroom and appears to be doing OK. But, his teacher does not want John in her class because he will not obey her when she asks him to stop doing a repetitive action such as tapping his foot. The teacher sees this as distractive during tests. John needs: (Skill 1.02) (Easy)**

   A. An IEP.
   B. A 504 Plan.
   C. A VESID evaluation.
   D. A more restrictive environment.

Answer: B. A 504 Plan.

John is exhibiting normal grade level behavior with the exception of the ADHD behaviors, which may need some acceptance for his academic success. John has not shown any academic deficiencies. John needs a 504 Plan to provide small adaptations to meet his needs.

10. Otumba is a 16 year old in your class who recently came from Nigeria. The girls in your class have come to you to complain about the way he treats them in a sexist manner. When they complain you reflect that this is also the way he treats adult females. You have talked to Otumba before about appropriate behavior. You should first? (Skill 1.03) (Rigorous)

   A. Complain to the Principal.
   B. Ask for a Parent-Teacher Conference
   C. Check to see if this is a cultural norm in his country.
   D. Create a behavior contract for him to follow.

Answer: C. Check to see if this is a cultural norm in his country.
While a, b, and d are good actions it is important to remember that Otumba comes from a culture where woman are treated differently than they are here in America. Learning this information will enable the school as a whole to address this behavior.

11. Mark is a 6th grader. You have noticed that he doesn't respond to simple requests like the other students in your class. If you ask him to erase the board he may look at you shake his head and say, but then he will clean the board. When the children gather together for recess he joins them. Yet, you observe that it takes him much longer to understand the rules to a game. Mark retains what he reads. Mark most likely has: (Skill 1.04) (Rigorous)

   A. Autism
   B. Tourette's Syndrome
   C. Mental Retardation
   D. A pragmatic language disability.

Answer: D. A pragmatic language disability.

Pragmatics is the basic understanding of a communicator's intent. The issue here is Mark's ability to respond correctly to another person.

12. Skilled readers use all but which one of these knowledge sources to construct meanings beyond the literal text: (1.04) (Rigorous)

A. Text knowledge
B. Syntactic knowledge
C. Morphological knowledge
D. Semantic knowledge

Answer: C. Morphological knowledge

The student is already skilled, so morphological knowledge is already in place.

13. Chaz is observing Melody's interaction with others. It is apparent that the student does not know social cues, or that she is misinterpreting them. Chaz next observes Melody punch someone, after having tagged a friend during a game of tag. Chaz believes that melody may have a disability related to a: (Skill 1.04) (Rigorous)

A. Conduct Disorder
B. Social Pragmatic Disorder
C. Psychoses
D. Depression

Answer: B. Social Pragmatic Disorder

Pragmatics involves the way that language is used to communicate and interact with others. When this is misinterpreted as in the example above, a tag is interpreted as a hit, a response occurs for the person's interpretation of the social pragmatic interpretation, however inappropriate.

14. Scott is in middle school but still makes statements like, "I gotted new high-tops yesterday," and "I saw three mans in the front office." Language interventions for Scott would target: (Skill 1.04) (Rigorous)

A. Morphology
B. Syntax
C. Pragmatics
D. Cultural linguistics

Answer: A. Morphology

Morphology is the process of combining phonemes into meaningful words.

15. Mr. Mendez is assessing his students' written expression. Which of these is not a component of written expression? (Skill 1.04) (Rigorous)

    A. Vocabulary
    B. Morphology
    C. Content
    D. Sentence structure

Answer: B. Morphology

Morphology is correct. Vocabulary consists of words, content is made up of ideas, which are expressed in words, and sentences are constructed from words. Morphemes, however, are not always words. They may be prefixes or suffixes.

16. Ray is being suspended because he will not go in Miss Smith's the classroom until after the bell rings. Ray never skips Mr. Paul's class, however, Mr. Paul does not care if the students are one to two minutes late. What is the best reason that Ray will not arrive on time to Miss Smith's class? (1.05) (Average Rigor)

    A. Ray is afraid of being known as "Special Ed."
    B. Mr. Paul doesn't follow the rule.
    C. Miss Smith's class is boring.
    D. All of the above.

Answer: A. Ray is afraid of being known as "Special Ed."

Ray is probably more concerned about being seen going to a special class. Children who are labeled as having special needs are generally ostracized especially if they do not look "special," and have the ability to "fit in." Mr. Paul seems to understand this and makes an allowance for the students to sneak in to his room.

17. It is considered normal for a teenager to do all of the following except: (Skill 2.01) (Average Rigor)

   A. Use logical operations before applying them socially.
   B. Fail a class.
   C. Think about long term goals.
   D. Accept authority

Answer: is D   Accept authority

The teen years are the time teens begin to question authority, rules and the reasons they are given.

18. Temper tantrums, disrupting the educational process or disobedience, and explosiveness are associated with those who are:___ (Skill 2.01) (Average Rigor)

   A. Emotionally Disturbed
   B. Diagnosed with personality disorders
   C. Immature
   D. Labeled "At Risk."

Answer: A. Emotionally Disturbed

While all of the answers may be considered related to the stated behaviors the only one which encompasses all is the label is Emotionally Disturbed.

19. A person who has a learning disability has: (Skill 2.02) (Easy)

   A. An IQ two standard deviations below the norm.
   B. Congenital abnormalities.
   C. Is limited by the educational environment.
   D. Has a disorder in one of the basic psychological processes.

Answer: D. Has a disorder in one of the basic psychological processes.

The definition of "learning disability" begins: a disorder in one or more of the basic psychological processes involved in understanding or in using language, spoken or written.

20.   Justin, is diagnosed with Autism and is in an inclusive setting. You were called down to "Stop him from turning the lights off and remove him." When you arrive you learn that today a movie was supposed to be finished and the VCR broke, so the teacher planed another activity. What is the best way to explain to the teacher why Justin was turning off the lights? (Skill 2.02) (Easy)

   A. He is perseverating and will stop shortly.
   B. He is telling you the lights bother him.
   C. He needs forewarning before a transition. Next time you have an unexpected change in classroom schedule please let him know.
   D. Please understand, this is part of who Justin is. He will leave the lights alone after I talk to him.

Answer: C. He needs forewarning before a transition. Next time you have a unexpected change in classroom schedule please let him know.

The teacher already knows that Justin will stop after you talk to him. That is why she called you. She needs to know what to do if this happens again. Explaining the problem with transition may enable the teacher to see a problem before it occurs, or to prevent a possible problem.

21.   Which of these characteristics is NOT included in the IDEA and Part 200 definition of emotional disturbance? (Skill 2.02) (Average Rigor)

   A. General pervasive mood of unhappiness or depression
   B. Social maladjustment manifested in a number of settings
   C. Tendency to develop physical symptoms, pains, or fear associated with school or personal problems
   D. Inability to learn that is not attributed to intellectual, sensory, or health factors

Answer: B. Social maladjustment manifested in a number of settings

Social maladjustment is not considered a disability.

22.   **Students that exhibit engage in gang activity, are often in fights, and are often truant could be said to be: (Skill 2.02) (Average Rigor)**

      A. Socially Maladjusted
      B. Emotionally Disturbed
      C. Learning Disabled
      D. Depressed

Answer: A. Socially Maladjusted

These behaviors do not demonstrate a disability, and may be placed under the description of social maladjustment.

23.   **According to IDEA a child whose disability is related to being deaf and blind may not be classified as: (Skill 2.02) (Rigorous)**

      A. Multiple Disabilities
      B. Other Health Impaired
      C. Mentally Retardation
      D. Visually Impaired

Answer: A. Multiple Disabilities

The only stated area where deaf-blindness is not accepted is in Multiple Disabilities.

24.   **Children with behavior disorders often do not exhibit stimulus control. This means they do not display: (Skill 2.02) (Average Rigor)**

A. Culturally correct behaviors
B. Where and when certain behaviors are appropriate
C. Acceptance of others
D. Listening skills

Answer: B. Where and when certain behaviors are appropriate

Children with behavioral disorders often do not have the ability to understand what behavior is appropriate where. Inappropriate cultural behavior however, is often a learned response as an expression of prejudice.

25.   **A child may be classified under the Special Education "umbrella" as having Traumatic Brain Injury (TBI) if he/she does not have the following cause? (Skill 2.02) (Rigorous)**

A. Stroke
B. Anoxia
C. Encephalitis
D. Birth Trauma

Answer: D. Birth Trauma

According to IDEA and Part 200, a child may not be labeled as having Traumatic Brain injury if the injury is related to birth

26.   **Children with Visual-Spatial difficulties may not accomplish some developmental tasks, such as: (Skill 2.03) (Rigorous)**

A. Answering when called upon.
B. Demonstrating characteristics of a certain letter in print.
C. A delay in achieving the "th" sound.
D. Recognition of the permanence of print.

Answer: B Demonstrating characteristics of a certain letter in print.

Visual spatial difficulties misinterpret direct compositions of objects and symbols. The characteristics of a letter are samples of items/symbols that could be wrongly misinterpreted.

27. **A developmental delay may be indicated by a: (Skill2.03) (Rigorous)**

    A. Second grader having difficulty buttoning clothing.
    B. Stuttered response.
    C. Kindergartner not having complete bladder control.
    D. Withdrawn behavior

Answer: A. Second grader having difficulty buttoning clothing.

Buttoning of clothing is generally mastered by the age of 4. While many children have full bladder control by age 4, it is not unusual for "embarrassing accidents" to occur.

28. **A student on medication may have his/her dosage adjusted as his/her body grows. A parent may call and ask questions about their child's adjustment to the medication during the school day. During this time you should: (Skill2.04) (Average Rigor)**

    A. Observe the student for changes in behavior.
    B. Watch for a progression of changed behavior.
    C. Communicate with the parent concerns about sleepiness.
    D. All of the above.

Answer: D. All of the above.

If you have a student on medication, it is important to communicate with the parent changes in behavior, because their bodies are constantly growing. Being informed about the medication(s) your student is on allows you to assist the student and the parent as an objective observer.

29.   Gerald, generally exhibits good behavior, and has been complaining that his new medicine keeps him from sleep at night and he can't help falling asleep in class. On top of that all of a sudden he seems excitable and antsy. What do you think he is on medication for? (Skill 2.04) (Average Rigor)

    A. Autism
    B. ADHD
    C. Conduct disorder
    D. Pervasive developmental Answer: disorder

Answer: B.

Students with ADHD are often placed on stimulants. This medication can create insomnia. Quite often it easy to tell the moment the medicine wears off because the symptoms of ADHD become apparent at that moment.

30.   The purpose of error analysis of a test is to determine: (Skill 3.01) (Easy)

    A. What events were labeled in error.
    B. If the test length was the cause of error
    C. Evaluate the types of errors made by categorizing incorrect answers.
    D. Establish a baseline.

Answer: C. Evaluate the types of errors made by categorizing incorrect answers.

Error Analysis examines how and why a person makes a mistake. In an Informal Reading Inventory like Burns and Roe, questions are given to specifically address possible errors. Other tests that utilize error analysis provide specific possible answers to denote which error was made. The purpose of both is to see where problems lie and to provide clues to assist the learning process.

31. **Formal assessment includes standardized criteria, norm-referenced instruments and_____. (Skill 3.01) (Rigorous)**

   A. Developmental rating scales.
   B. Answer: Interviews
   C. Error
   D. Performance analysis by gender, social economic status and/or ethnic groups.

Answer: D. Performance analysis by gender, social economic status and/or ethnic groups.

While some assessments include both formal and informal assessment tools, a standard feature of the Formal Assessment is performance Analysis by gender, social economic status, and/or ethnic groups.

32. **A good assessment of whether a child may have ADHD in your classroom would include a_____.**

   A. Baseline
   B. Monetary time sampling.
   C. Age based norm criteria.
   D. Construct Validity

Answer: B. Monetary time sampling.
Assessing ADHD should include measurements of time on task. A simple box chart of 5 to 10 minute intervals that record on task versus off task is a good example of this.

33. **Criteria for choosing behaviors to measure by frequency include all but those that: (Skill 3.01) (Average Rigor)**

   A. Have an observable beginning
   B. Last a long time
   C. Last a short time
   D. Occur often

Answer: B. Last a long time

We use frequency to measure behaviors that do not last a long time.

34.   Criteria for choosing behaviors to measure by duration include all but those that: (Skill 3.01) (Easy)

   A. Last a short time
   B. Last a long time
   C. Have no readily observable beginning or end
   D. Do not happen often

Answer: A. Last a short time

We use duration to measure behaviors that do not last a short time.

35.   You are working with a functional program and have placed a student in a vocational position at a Coffee House. You need to perform a Task Analysis of making coffee. Which task should be first in the analysis? (Skill 3.01) (Average Rigor)

   A. Filling the pot with water
   B. Taking the order.
   C. Measuring the coffee
   D. Picking the correct coffee

Answer: ~~C. Measuring the coffee~~   D. Picking

While the student is in a coffee house the task was to make coffee not to wait on customers. There are different kinds of coffee, decaffeinated, regular, etc. and they all have there appropriate canisters. The student must be able to choose the correct coffee before measuring the coffee.

36.   The basic tools necessary to observe and record behavior may include all BUT: (Skill 3.01) (Average Rigor)

   A. Cameras
   B. Timers
   C. Counters
   D. Graphs or charts

Answer: A. Cameras

The camera gives a snapshot. It does not record behavior.

37.   **The extent that a test measures what it claims to measure is called: (Skill 3.01) (Rigorous)**

        A. Reliability
        B. Validity
        C. Factor analysis
        D. Chi Square

Answer: B. Validity

The degree to which a test measures is what it claims to measure.

38.   **A best practice for evaluating student performance and progress on IEPs is: (Skill 3.01) (Rigorous)**

        A. Formal assessment
        B. Curriculum-based assessment
        C. Criterion-based assessment
        D. Norm-referenced evaluation

Answer: B. Curriculum-based assessment

This is a teacher-prepared test that measures the student's progress, but at the same time shows the teacher whether or not the accommodations are effective.

39.   **Statements like, "Darren is lazy," are not helpful in describing his behavior for all but which of these reasons? (Skill 3.01) (Average Rigor)**

        A. There is no way to determine if any change occurs from the information given
        B. The student and not the behavior becomes labeled
        C. Darren's behavior will manifest itself clearly enough without any written description
        D. Constructs are open to various interpretations among the people who are asked to define them

Answer: C. Darren's behavior will manifest itself clearly enough without any written description

'Darren is lazy' is a label. It can be interpreted in a variety of ways, and there is no way to measure this description for change. A description should be measurable.

40. Often, Marcie is not in her seat when the bell rings. She may be found at the pencil sharpener, throwing paper away, or fumbling through her notebook. Which of these descriptions of her behavior can be described as a pinpoint? (Skill 3.01) (Easy)

    A. Is tardy
    B. Is out of seat
    C. Is not in seat when late bell rings
    D. Is disorganized

Answer: C. Is not in seat when late bell rings

Even though A, B, and D describe the behavior, C is most precise.

41. Criteria for choosing behaviors that are in the most need of change involve all but the following: (Skill 3.01) (Average Rigor)

    A. Observations across settings to rule out certain interventions
    B. Pinpointing the behavior that is the poorest fit in the child's environment
    C. The teacher's concern about what is the most important behavior to target
    D. Analysis of the environmental reinforcers

Answer: C. The teacher's concern about what is the most important behavior to target.

The teacher must take care of the criteria in A, B, and D. Her concerns are of the least importance.

42. Ms. Wright is planning an analysis of Jeffrey's out-of-seat behavior. Her initial data would be called: (Skill 3.01) (Easy)

    A. Pre-referral phase
    B. Intervention phase
    C. Baseline phase
    D. Observation phase

Answer: C. Baseline phase

Ms Wright is a teacher. She should begin at the baseline phase.

43. To reinforce Audrey each time she is on task and in her seat, Ms. Wright delivers specific praise and stickers, which Audrey may collect and redeem for a reward. The data collected during the time Ms. Wright is using this intervention is called: (Skill 3.01) (Average Rigor)

    A. Referral phase
    B. Intervention phase
    C. Baseline phase
    D. Observation phase

Answer: B. Intervention phase

Ms Wright is involved in behavior modification. This is the intervention phase.

44. Which of these would be the least effective measure of behavioral disorders? (Skill 3.01) (Average Rigor)

    A. Alternative Assessment
    B. Naturalistic Assessment
    C. Standardized test
    D. Psychodynamic analysis

Answer: C. is Standardized test.

These tests make comparisons, rather than measure skills.

45. Which would not be an advantage of using a criterion-referenced test? (Skill 3.02) (Rigorous)

    A. Information about an individual's ability level is too specific for the purposes of the assessment.
    B. It can pinpoint exact areas of weaknesses and strengths.
    C. You can design them yourself.
    D. You do not get comparative information.

Answer: D. You do not get comparative information.

Criterion-referenced tests measure mastery of content rather than performance compared to others. Test items are usually prepared from specific educational objectives and may be teacher made or commercially prepared. Scores are measured by the percentage of correct items for a skill (e.g., adding and subtracting fractions with like denominators).

46. **Measurement of adaptive behavior should include all but: (Skill 3.03) (Rigorous)**

    A. Student's behavior in a variety of settings.
    B. Student's skills displayed in a variety of settings.
    C. Comparative analysis is to other students in his/her class.
    D. Analysis of student's social skills.

Answer: C. Comparative analysis to other students in his/her class.

Evaluating a student's adaptability requires analysis only of that person, and does not allow for comparative analysis. Comparing to people and how they interact with others or comparing skill levels is not a good measure of adaptability.

47. **Grading should be based on all of the following EXCEPT: (Skill 3.04)(Average Rigor)**

    A. Clearly-defined mastery of course objectives
    B. A variety of evaluation methods
    C. Performance of the student in relation to other students
    D. Assigning points for activities and basing grades on a point total

Answer: C. Performance of the student in relation to other students

Grading should never be based on the comparison of performance of other students. It should always be based on the student's mastery of course objectives, the methods of evaluation, and the grading rubric (how points are assigned).

48. **Anecdotal Records should record? (Skill 3.04) (Average Rigor)**

    A. Observable behavior
    B. End with conjecture.
    C. Motivational factors
    D. Note previously stated interests.

Answer: A. Observable behavior

Anecdotal records should only record observable behavior, describing the actions and not possible interest or motivational factors that may lead to possible prejudicial reviews.

49. **Alternative Assessments include all of the following EXCEPT: (Skill 3.05) (Average Rigor)**

   A. Portfolios
   B. Interviews
   C. Teacher made tests
   D. Performance Based Tests

Answer: C. Teacher made tests

Teacher made tests are normally created on worksheets, not on observations. It is a standard form of evaluation.

50. **According to NYS an initial evaluation/assessment for qualification of disability always must include all of the following EXCEPT: (Skill 4.01) (Rigorous)**

   A. Physical Evaluation
   B. Social History
   C. Psychological Evaluation
   D. Vocational Assessment

Answer: A. Physical Evaluation

The Vocational Assessment evaluation requirement starts at age 12.

51. **If a child does not qualify for classification under Special Education the committee shall: (Skill 4.01) (Average Rigor)**

   A. Refer the parental interventions to the 504 Plan.
   B. Provide temporary remedial services for the student.
   C. Recommend to the parent possible resources outside of the committee the child may qualify for.
   D. Give the parents the information about possible reviews by an exterior source.

Answer: C. Recommend to the parent possible resources outside of the committee the child may qualify for.

A student may qualify for a 504 Plan or not. The student may however be in need of additional resources such as outside counseling with an agency, or a mentor situation similar to what Big Brother provides.

52.   Mark is receiving special education services within a 12:1:1. His teacher recommends that he be placed in a more restrictive setting such as a residential placement. She presents good reasoning. What will the committee most likely recommend? (Skill 4.03) (Average Rigor)

   A. 8:1:1
   B. BOCES School placement
   C. 1:1 Aide
   D. Return to placement

Answer: A. 8:1:1

The teacher presents well, but the committee most likely will attempt the next level down of services before placing a child in a special school setting. This is believed to be the best way of following the LRE requirement.

53.   Which of the following is NOT a feature of effective classroom rules? (Skill 4.05) (Easy)

   A. They are about 4 to 6 in number
   B. They are negatively stated
   C. Consequences are consistent and immediate
   D. They can be tailored to individual teaching goals and teaching styles

Answer: B. They are negatively stated

Rules should be positively stated, and they should follow the other three features listed.

54.   An effective classroom behavior management plan includes all but which of the following? (Skill 4.06)(Average Rigor)

   A. Transition procedures for changing activities
   B. Clear consequences for rule infractions
   C. Concise teacher expectations for student behavior
   D. Strict enforcement

Answer: D. Strict enforcement

There are always situations where rules must be flexible. Not all of the rules need to be flexible, But allowing a student to stop a behavior with a reminder of the rule is not being too flexible.

55.   IDEA 2004 changed the IEP by? (Skill 5.02) (Rigorous)

A. Not requiring short term objectives.
B. Requiring an inclusive activity.
C. Requiring parents to participate in the CSE.
D. Establishing new criteria to be classified as learning disabled.

Answer: A. Not requiring short term objectives.

Until IDEA 2004 short term goals/objectives needed to be in place to see progress towards a goal.

56.   **A letter must be sent to a parent informing them of a scheduled CSE. How many days prior notice must they receive? (Skill 5.04) (Rigorous)**

A. 7
B. 30
C. 10
D. 5

Answer: C. 10

Parents must receive a letter 10 days before the meeting.

57.   **How many contacts should be made with a parent prior to a CSE? (Skill 5.04) (Rigorous)**

A. 1
B. 2
C. Several
D. 3

Answer: D. 3

A minimum of three contacts with the parent are expected before a CSE.

58. **You have documented proof that Janice performs higher with the use of a computer on both class work and tests. Which kind of CSE/IEP Conference should be held? (Skill 5.05) (Easy)**

   A. Manifestation Determination
   B. Post-School Transition to insure provision of lap top by outside services
   C. Amendment—Change of program/placement
   D. Annual

Answer: C. Amendment—Change of program/placement

The Amendment CSE's should be held to add or remove services. Adding a test modification or service is a change in program.

59. **Teaching children skills that will be useful in their home life and neighborhoods is the basis of: (Skill 5.06) (Average Rigor)**

   A. Curriculum-based instruction
   B. Community-based instruction
   C. Transition planning
   D. Academic curriculum

Answer: B. Community-based instruction

Transitional training is a standard for all students labeled as having special needs after age 12. Student's can learn how to balance a check book, shop, and understand how to use mass transit, etc..

60. **When would proximity control not be a good behavioral intervention: (Skill 6.01) (Easy)**

   A. Two students are arguing.
   B. A student is distracting others.
   C. One student threatens another.
   D. Involve fading and shaping

Answer: C. One student threatens another.

Threats can break into fights. Standing in the middle of a fight can be threatening to your ability to supervise the class as a whole or to get the help needed to stop the fight.

61.   Teacher feedback, task completion, and a sense of pride over
        mastery or accomplishment of a skill are examples of: (Skill 6.01)
        (Average Rigor)

        A. Extrinsic reinforcers
        B. Behavior modifiers
        C. Intrinsic reinforcers
        D. Positive feedback

Answer: C. Intrinsic reinforcers

These are intangibles.

Motivation may be achieved through intrinsic reinforcers or extrinsic reinforcers.
Intrinsic reinforcers are usually intangible, and extrinsic reinforcers are usually
tangible rewards and from an external source.

62.   Social approval, token reinforcers, and rewards, such as pencils or
        stickers, are examples of: (Skill 6.01) (Easy)

        A. Extrinsic reinforcers
        B. Behavior modifiers
        C. Intrinsic reinforcers
        D. Positive feedback reinforcers

Answer: A. Extrinsic reinforcers

These are rewards from external sources.

63.   Which of the following should be avoided when writing goals for
        social behavior? (Skill 6.01) (Average Rigor)

        A. Non-specific adverbs
        B. Behaviors stated as verbs
        C. Criteria for acceptable performance
        D. Conditions where the behavior is expected to be performed

Answer: A. Non-specific adverbs

Behaviors should be specific. The more clearly the behavior is described, the
less the chance for error.

64. The Integrated approach to learning utilizes all resources available to address student needs. What are the resources? (Skill 6.03) (Average Rigor)

   A. The student, his/her parents, and the teacher.
   B. The teacher, the parents, and the special education team.
   C. The teacher the student, and an administrator to perform needed interventions.
   D. The student, his/her parents, the teacher and community resources.

Answer: D. The student, his/her parents, the teacher and community resources.

The integrated response encompasses all possible resources including the resources in the community.

65. Mr. Johnson asks his students to score each of their classmates in areas such as who they would prefer to play with and work with. A Likert-type scale with non-behavioral criteria is used. This is an example of: (Skill 6.04)(Rigorous)

   A. Peer nomination
   B. Peer rating
   C. Peer assessment
   D. Sociogram

Answer: A. Peer nomination

Students are asked for their preferences on non-behavioral criteria.

66. What is the highest goal a teacher should aim for while preparing a student for success? (Skill 6.05) (Average Rigor)

   A. Reading.
   B. Budgeting
   C. Cooking
   D. Self-Advocacy

Answer: B. Budgeting

When a student is able to self-advocate well he/she is on the road to independence, with an understanding of his/her limits and needs to find success in their endeavors.

67. Which of the follow is does NOT have an important effect on the spatial arrangement (physical setting) of your classroom? (Skill 6.05) (Average Rigor)

   A. Adequate Physical Space
   B. Ventilation
   C. Window placement
   D. Lighting Adequacy

Answer: C. Window placement

Many classrooms today do not have windows, as they may be placed in the middle of a building. It is also the only factor listed which can not be controlled/adjusted by you or the administration.

68. You are having continual difficulty with your classroom assistant. A good strategy to address this problem would be: (Skill 6.08) (Rigorous)

   A. To address the issue immediately.
   B. To take away responsibilities.
   C. To write a clearly establish role plan to discuss.
   D. To speak to your supervisor

Answer: C. To write a clearly establish role plan to discuss.

If you are having difficulty with your classroom assistant, it is most likely is over an issue or issues that have happened repeatedly, and you have attempted to address them. Establishing clear roles between the two of you will provide a good step in the right direction. It may also provide you with the ability to state you have made an attempt to address the issue/issues to an administrator should the need arise.

69. Which of the following is a responsibility that can NOT be designated to a classroom aide? (Skill 6.08) (Average Rigor)

   A. Small group instruction
   B. Small group planning
   C. Coordination of an activity
   D. Assist in BIP implementation

Answer: C. Coordination of an activity

Teachers are responsible for all lesson planning.

70.   The key to success for the exceptional student placed in a regular classroom is: (Skill 7.01) (Average Rigor)

A. Access to the special aids and materials.
B. Support from the ESE teacher.
C. Modification in the curriculum.
D. The mainstream teacher's belief that the student will profit from the placement.

Answer: D. The mainstream teacher's belief that the student will profit from the placement.

Without the regular teacher's belief that the student can benefit, no special accommodations will be provided.

71.   Ability to supply specific instructional materials, programs, and methods and to influence environmental learning variables are advantages of which service model for exceptional students? (Skill 7.01) (Rigorous)

A. Regular classroom
B. Consultant teacher
C. Itinerant teacher
D. Resource room

Answer: B. Consultant teacher

Consultation is usually done by specialists.

72.   A Consultant Teacher should be meeting the needs of his/her students by: (Skill 7.01) (Easy)

A. Pushing in to do small group instruction with regular education students.
B. Asking the student to show his/her reasoning for failing.
C. Meeting with the teacher before class to discuss adaptations and expectations.
D. Accompanying the student to class.

Answer: A. Pushing in to do small group instruction with regular ed. students.

Students that receive consult services are receiving minimum instructional services. They require little modification to their educational program.

73. **Teaching techniques that stimulate active participation and understanding in the mathematics class include all but which of the following? (Skill 7.02) (Easy)**

    A. Having students copy computation facts for a set number of times.
    B. Asking students to find the error in an algorithm.
    C. Giving immediate feedback to students.
    D. Having students chart their progress.

Answer: A. Having students copy computation facts for a set number of times.

Copying does not stimulate participation or understanding.

74. **According to IDEA 2004, students with disabilities are to do what; (Skill 7.02) (Average Rigor)**

    A. Participate in the general education program to the fullest extent that it is beneficial for them.
    B. Participate in a vocational training within the general education setting.
    C. Participate in a general education setting for physical education.
    D. Participate in a modified program that meets his/her needs.

Answer: A. Participate in the general education program to the fullest extent that it is beneficial for them.

B,C, and D are all possible settings related to participating in the general education setting to the fullest extent possible. This still can mean that a student's LRE may restrict him/her to a 12:1:1 for the entire school day.

75.   Marisol has been mainstreamed into a ninth grade language arts class. Although her behavior is satisfactory, and she likes the class, Marisol's reading level is about two years below grade level. The class has been assigned to read Great Expectations and write a report. What intervention would be LEAST successful in helping Marisol complete this assignment? (Skill 7.01)(Average Rigor)

    A. Having Marisol listen to a taped recording while following the story in the regular text.
    B. Giving her a modified version of the story.
    C. Telling her to choose a different book that she can read.
    D. Showing a film to the entire class and comparing and contrasting it with the book.

Answer: C. Telling her to choose a different book that she can read.

A, B, and D are positive interventions. C is not an intervention.

76.   Mrs. Taylor takes her students to a special gymnastics presentation that the P.E. coach has arranged in the gym. The students get a chance to perform some of the simple stunts. They all easily go through the movements except for Sam, who is known as the class klutz. Carl, another student of Mrs. Taylor, helps Sam, who does not give up and finally completes the stunts. His classmates cheer him on with comments like, "Way to go". What kind of teaching technique was implemented?   (Skill 7.02) (Average Rigor)

    A. Group share
    B. Modeling
    C. Peer Tutoring
    D. All of the above

Answer: D. All of the above

Sam observed the gymnastics; he was encouraged by his group of peers, and received assistance to accomplish the task from a peer.

77. Teachers in grades K-3 are mandated to teach what to all students using scientifically based methods with measurable outcomes (Skill 7.03) (Average Rigor)

A. Math
B. Reading
C. Citizenship
D. Writing

Answer: B. Reading

Reading is the mandated subject as it is looked at as the fountain from which all learning can be secured.

78. Many special education students may have trouble with the skills necessary to be successful in algebra and geometry for all but one of these reasons: (Skill 7.03) (Average Rigor)

A. Prior instruction focused on computation rather than understanding
B. Unwillingness to problem solve
C. Lack of instruction in prerequisite skills
D. Large amount of new vocabulary

Answer: A. Prior instruction focused on computation rather than understanding

In order to build skills in math, students must be able to understand math concepts.

79. Cooperative learning does NOT utilize? (Skill 7.02) (Average Rigor)

A. Shared ideas
B. Small groups
C. Independent practice
D. Student expertise

Answer: C. Independent practice

Cooperative learning focuses on group cooperation allowing for sharing of student expertise and provides some flexibility for creative presentation of the students as they share with others.

80. The revision of Individuals with Disabilities Education Act in 1997 required: (Skill 7.04)(Rigorous)

   A. Collaboration of educational professionals in order to provide equitable opportunities for students with disabilities.
   B. Removed the requirement for short term objectives with objectives with goals.
   C. School Administrator approval for an IEP to be put into place.
   D. FBAs and BIPs for all students that were suspended for 6 days.

Answer: A. Collaboration of educational professionals in order to provide equitable opportunities for students with disabilities.

Teachers must collaborate professionally to render the best possible education to the student.

81. Students with disabilities develop greater self-images and recognize their own academic and social strengths when they are: (Skill 7.05)(Easy)

   A. Included in the mainstream classroom.
   B. Provided community based internships.
   C. Socializing in the hallway.
   D. Provided 1:1 instructional opportunity.

Answer: A. Included in the mainstream classroom.

When a child with a disability is included in the regular classroom it raises the expectations of the child's academic performance and their need to conform to "acceptable peer behavior."

82. An emphasis on instructional remediation and individualized instruction in problem areas, and a focus on mainstreaming, are characteristics of which model of service delivery? (Skill 7.06) (Average Rigor)

   A. Regular classroom
   B. Consultant teacher
   C. Itinerant teacher
   D. Resource room

Answer: D. Resource room

The resource room is a bridge towards mainstreaming.

83.   Organizing ideas by use of a web or outline is an example of which writing activity? (Skill 8.06) (Easy)

   A. Revision
   B. Drafting
   C. Prewriting
   D. Final draft

Answer: C. Prewriting.

Organizing ideas come before Drafting, Final Draft, and Revision.

84.   Ryan is working on a report about dogs. He uses scissors and tape to cut and rearrange sections and paragraphs and then photocopies the paper so he can continue writing. In which stage of the writing process is Ryan? (Skill 8.06)(Easy)

   A. Final draft
   B. Prewriting
   C. Revision
   D. Drafting

Answer: C. Revision

Ryan is revising and reordering before final editing.

85.   You are advocating for a student who is blind and is proficient in Braille. You should: (Skill 8.06) (Rigorous)

   A.   Ask the team for a PC.
   B.   Tell the team you need a Mac.
   C.   Tell the team that it needs a special keyboard.
   D.   Tell the team that it doesn't need to come with a monitor.

Answer: A. is correct.

The monitor can be useful for situations where the student has created a project and has not yet printed the material. It also can be helpful when students are doing a group edit. The student must have a PC because it has the ability to perform a function when more than two keys are pressed.

86.　When a student begins to use assistive technology it is important for the teacher to have a clear outline as to when and how the equipment should be used. Why? (Skill 8.07) (Rigorous)

A.　To establish a level of accountability with the student.
B.　To establish that the teacher has responsibility of the equipment that is in use in his/her room.
C.　To establish that the teacher is responsible for the usage of the assistive technology.
D.　To establish a guideline for evaluation.

Answer: A. To establish a level of accountability with the student.

Clear parameters as to the usage of assistive technology in a classroom creates a level of accountability in the student as he/she now knows the teacher knows the intended purpose and appropriate manner of use of the device.

87.　Which is not indicative of a handwriting problem? (Skill 9.01) (Rigorous)

A.　Errors persisting over time
B.　Little improvement on simple handwriting tasks
C.　Fatigue after writing for a short time
D.　Occasional letter reversals, word omissions, and poor spacing

Answer: D. Occasional letter reversals, word omissions, and poor spacing

A, B, and C are physical handwriting problems. D, however, is a problem with language development.

88.　The Phonics approach to teaching children how to read utilizes what method? (Skill 9.02) (Average Rigor)

A.　Reading for meaning
B.　Reading for letter combinations
C.　Identifying word by their position and context
D.　Word configurations

Answer: C. Identifying word by their position and context

The Phonics program utilizes a "Bottom-up/Code Emphasis" approach to reading.

89. **Which of these techniques is least effective in helping children correct spelling problems? (Skill 9.02)(Rigorous)**

    A. The teacher models the correct spelling in a context
    B. Student sees the incorrect and the correct spelling together in order to visualize the correct spelling
    C. Positive reinforcement as the child tests the rules and tries to approximate the correct spelling
    D. Copying the correct word five times

Answer: D. Copying the correct word five times

Copying the word is not as effective because it utilizes the least amount of positive reinforcement and correction.

90. **Ms. Tolbert is teaching spelling to her students. The approach stresses phoneme-grapheme relationships within parts of words. Spelling rules, generalizations, and patterns are taught. A typical spelling list for her third graders might include light, bright, night, fright, and slight. Which approach is Ms. Tolbert using? (Skill 9.02)(Rigorous)**

    A. Rule-based Instruction
    B. Phonics
    C. Whole Word
    D. Both a and b

Answer: A. Rule-based Instruction

Rule-based Instruction employs a system of rules and generalizations. It may be taught using the linguistic or phonics approach.

91. **A teacher should consider all of the following when evaluating a student's reading comprehension EXCEPT: (Skill 9.03) (Average Rigor)**

    A. Past experience
    B. Teacher prepared preset questions on text
    C. Level of content
    D. Oral language comprehension.

Answer: B. Teacher prepared preset questions on text

Preset question will influence the evaluation of a student's reading comprehension so a true score will not be given.

92. **In a positive classroom environment, errors are viewed as: (Skill 9.03) (Average Rigor)**

    A. Symptoms of deficiencies.
    B. Lack of attention or ability.
    C. A natural part of the learning process.
    D. The result of going too fast.

Answer: C. A natural part of the learning process.

We often learn a great deal from our mistakes and shortcomings. It is normal. Where it is not normal, fear develops. This fear of failure inhibits children from working and achieving. Copying and other types of cheating result from this fear of failure.

93. **Which of the following sentences will NOT test recall? (Skill 9.05) (Average Rigor)**

    A. What words in the story describe Goldilocks?
    B. Why did Goldilocks go into the three bears' house?
    C. Name in order the things that belonged to the three bears that Goldilocks tried.
    D. What did the three bears learn about leaving their house unlocked?

Answer: D. What did the three bears learn about leaving their house unlocked?

Recall requires the student to produce from memory ideas and information explicitly stated in the story. Answer: d requires an inference.

94. **Modeling of a behavior by an adult who verbalizes the thinking process, overt self-instruction, and covert self-instruction are components of: (Skill 10.02) (Rigorous)**

    A. Rational-emotive therapy
    B. Reality therapy
    C. Cognitive behavior modification
    D. Reciprocal teaching

Answer: C. Cognitive behavior modification

Neither A, B, nor D involves modification or change of behavior.

95. **What is considered the most effective when teaching children with special needs new concepts in math? (Skill 10.02) (Rigorous)**

    A. Problem solving
    B. Direct instruction
    C. Repetition
    D. Ongoing Assessment

Answer: A. Problem solving.

Teaching problem solving techniques relevant to the task create the possibility that student an address the problem independently. Allowing students to problem solve in groups where peer instruction and group review can be addressed allows for higher developed understanding of the concept.

96. **Mr. Ward notes that Jennifer, a 9th grade student, understands the concept for three step equations but seems unable to do problems successfully. When he reviews Jennifer's work he notes that her addition and subtraction is not correct. What strategy would be most appropriate? (Skill 10.05) (Average Rigor)**

    A. Basic multiplication and addition charts.
    B. Checks for understanding.
    C. Private instruction on adding and subtracting.
    D. Calculator Usage

Answer D. Calculator Usage.

If Jennifer is in 9th grade and still has difficulty adding and subtracting correctly, it is likely that this is part of her disability. The correct compensatory intervention would be a calculator and brief tutoring on how to correctly use it.

97.   The most direct method of obtaining assessment data, and perhaps the most objective, is: (Skill 10.05) (Rigorous)

A. Testing
B. Self-recording
C. Observation
D. Experimenting

Answer: C. Observation

Observation is often better than testing, due to language, culture, or other factors.

98.   Laura is beginning to raise her hand first instead of talking out. An effective schedule of reinforcement should be: (Skill 11.02) (Average Rigor)

A. Continuous
B. Variable
C. Intermittent
D. Fixed

Answer: A. Continuous

Note that the behavior is new. The pattern of reinforcement should not be variable, intermittent, or fixed. It should be continuous.

99.   To facilitate learning instructional objectives: (Skill 11.02) (Average Rigor)

A. Grade level spelling list
B. They should be written and shared.
C. They should be arranged in order of similarity.
D. Should be taken from a scope and sequence.

Answer C. They should be arranged in order of similarity.

Spelling instruction should include words misspelled in daily writing, generalizing spelling knowledge, and mastering objectives in progressive stages of development.

100. Transfer of learning occurs when? (Skill 11.02) (Rigorous)

   A. Experience with one task influences performance on another task.
   B. Content can be explained orally.
   C. Student experiences the "I got it!" syndrome.
   D. Curricular objective is exceeded.

Answer: A. Experience with one task influences performance on another task.

Consultation programs cannot be successful without people skills.

101. Teacher modeling, student-teacher dialogues, and peer interactions are part of which teaching technique designed to provide support during the initial stages of instruction? (Skill 11.05) (Rigorous)

   A. Reciprocal teaching
   B. Scaffolding
   C. Peer tutoring
   D. Cooperative learning

Answer: B. Scaffolding.

Scaffolding provides support through building new knowledge on previous knowledge much like one layer is placed on another.

102. Functional curriculum focuses on all of the following EXCEPT: (Skill 11.03) (Rigorous)

   A. Skills needed for social living
   B. Occupational readiness
   C. Functioning in society.
   D. Remedial academic skills

Answer: D. Remedial academic skills

Remedial academics may be applied but are not a focus. The primary goal is to achieve skills for functioning in society if possible, on an independent basis.

103. **Diversity can be identified in students by: (Skill 12.04) (Average Rigor)**

   A. Biological factors
   B. Socioeconomic Status (SES)
   C. Ethnicity
   D. All of the above

Answer: D. All of the above

Biological factors can place students apart from other. Students who are genetically predisposed to being muscular or being overweight are examples of this diversity.

104. **Which of the following is NOT the best way to encourage and strengthen a social skill? (Skill 12.01) (Average Rigor)**

   A. Role playing
   B. Field Trips
   C. Student story telling
   D. Reading a book on the topic

Answer: D. Reading a book on the topic

Rationale: All of the other answers are interactive, and involve student input on possible ethical dilemmas.

105. **Distractive behavior, verbal outbursts, and passive aggressiveness should be addressed using: (Skill 12.03) (Rigorous)**

   A. Time-out.
   B. Response cost.
   C. Planned ignoring.
   D. Rule reminders.

Answer: C. Planned ignoring.

Planned ignoring takes away from the attention the student may be seeking to receive. It is also a good way to model appropriate response to the behavior for the other students in the room.

106. **A student with a poor self-concept may manifest in all of the ways listed below EXCEPT: (Skill 12.03) (Average Rigor)**

    A. Withdrawn actions.
    B. Aggression
    C. Consistently announcing his/her achievements.
    D. Shyness.

Answer C. Consistently announcing his/her achievements.

A poor self-concept is not seen in someone who boasts of his/her achievements.

107. **A good naturalistic assessment requires: (Skill 12.04)(Rigorous)**

    A. Communication notebooks
    B. Portfolios
    C. Long-range planning
    D. Diverse responses

Answer: C. Long-range planning

Naturalistic assessment must take place in a variety of settings which also requires instruction in a variety of settings.

108. **Mr. Smith is on a field trip with a group of high school EH students. On the way, they stop at a fast-food restaurant for lunch, and Warren and Raul get into an argument. After some heated words, Warren stalks out of the restaurant and refuses to return to the group. He leaves the parking lot, continues walking away from the group, and ignores Mr. Smith's directions to come back. What would be the best course of action for Mr. Smith?**
(Skill 13.05) (Rigorous)

    A. Leave the group with the class aide and follow Warren to try to talk him into coming back.
    B. Wait a little while and see if Warren cools off and returns.
    C. Telephone the school and let the crisis teacher notify the police in accordance with school policy.
    D. Call the police himself.

Answer: C. Telephone the school and let the crisis teacher notify the police in accordance with school policy.

Mr. Smith is still responsible for his class. This is his only option.

109. When a teacher is choosing behaviors to modify, two issues must be considered. What are they? (Skill 13.01) (Average Rigor)

    A. The need for the behavior to be performed in public and the culture of acceptance.
    B. The culture of the child and society standards to regarding the behavior.
    C. Evidence that the behavior can be changed, and society norms.
    D. Standards of the student's community and school rules.

Answer: B. The culture of the child and society standards to regarding the behavior.

American society standards may/may not be the same standards of other cultures. It may be important to check the standards of the specific behavior in the student's cultural background before attempting to modify it.

110. Sam is working to earn half an hour of basketball time with his favorite P.E. teacher. At the end of each half hour, Sam marks his point sheet with an X if he reached his goal of no call-outs. When he has received 25 marks, he will receive his basketball free time. This behavior management strategy is an example of: (Skill 13.01) (Average)

    A. Self-recording
    B. Self-evaluation
    C. Self-reinforcement
    D. Self-regulation

Answer: A. Self-recording.

Sam is recording his behavior.

Self-Management: This is an important part of social skills training, especially for older students preparing for employment. Components for self-management include:

1. Self-monitoring: choosing behaviors and alternatives and monitoring those actions.
2. Self-evaluation: deciding the effectiveness of the behavior in solving the problem.
3. Self-reinforcement: telling oneself that one is capable of achieving success.

111.	Mark has been working on his target goal of completing his mathematics class work. Each day he records, on a scale of 0 to 3, how well he has done his work, and his teacher provides feedback. This self-management technique is an example of: (Skill 13.01) (Average Rigor)

A.	Self-recording.
B.	Self reinforcement.
C.	Self-regulation.
D.	Self-evaluation.

Answer: D. Self-evaluation.

Sam is evaluating his behavior, not merely recording it.

112.	Token systems are popular for all of these advantages EXCEPT: (Skill 13.01) (Average Rigor)

A.	The number needed for rewards may be adjusted as needed.
B.	Rewards are easy to maintain.
C.	They are effective for students who generally do not respond to social reinforcers.
D.	Tokens reinforce the relationship between desirable behavior and reinforcement.

Answer: B. Rewards are easy to maintain.

The ease of maintenance is not a valid reason for developing a token system.

113.	Alternative Assessments include all of the following EXCEPT: (Skill 3.05) (Average Rigor)

A.	Portfolios.
B.	Interviews.
C.	Teacher made tests.
D.	Performance Based Tests.

Answer: C. Teacher made tests.

Teacher made tests are normally created on worksheets, not on observations. It is a standard form of evaluation.

114. **A BIP (Behavior Intervention Plan is written to teach positive behavior. Which element listed below is NOT a standard feature of the plan? (Skill 13.03) (Rigorous)**

    A. Identification of "behavior to be modified
    B. Strategies to implement the replacement behavior
    C. Statement of distribution
    D. Team creation of BIP

Answer: C. Statement of distribution

There is no statement on how or who shall receive the BIP on the student.

115. **You have a class of 8th Grade students in an English class. Sheryl sits in the back of the room by choice and rarely answers questions. You believe that she has a learning disability and begin to modify her worksheets. You are: (Skill 13.04) (Average Rigor)**

    A. Planning for success of the student.
    B. Creating a self-fulfilled prophecy.
    C. Developing a student centered curriculum.
    D. Testing her ability.

Answer: B. Creating a self-fulfilled prophecy.

If a person does not Answer: questions orally, he/she may not be as expressive as those around her, but it does not mean that they have a learning disability. Handing this type of worksheet out could create frustration and a lack of will to work to her ability.

116. **All of these are effective in teaching written expression EXCEPT: (Skill 13.04) (Easy)**

    A. Exposure to various styles and direct instruction in those styles.
    B. Immediate feedback from the teacher with all mistakes clearly marked.
    C. Goal setting and peer evaluation of written products according to set criteria.
    D. Incorporating writing with other academic subjects.

Answer: B. Immediate feedback from the teacher with all mistakes clearly marked.

Teacher feedback is not always necessary. The student can have feedback from his peers, or emotional response, or apply skills learned to other subjects.

117. **A student who has issues with truancy, gang membership, low school performance, and drug use is displaying: (Skill 13.05) (Average Rigor)**

    A. Emotionally disturbed behaviors.
    B. Symptoms of self-medication.
    C. Average Rigor adolescent behavior.
    D. Warning signs of crisis.

Answer: D. Warning signs of crisis.

The student is acting out by using aggression. This gives him a sense of belonging.

118. **Kareem's father sounds upset and is in the office demanding to see his son's cumulative record. You should: (Skill 13.06) (Average Rigor)**

    A. Tell him that he will have to make an appointment.
    B. Bring the record to a private room for him to review with either an administrator or yourself.
    C. Take the record to the principals office for review.
    D. Give the record to the parent.

Answer: B. Bring the record to a private room for him to review with either an administrator or yourself.

Parents have the rights to see their children's cumulative record. You do not have the right to remove something from the cum so that the parent may not see it.. However, it is important to remember that the documents should remain in the folde, and that the parent may need information explained or interpreted so someone should be present.

119. Kara's mother has requested a computer for her child to do class work and home work and the CSE does not agree. Kara complains to you. You should: (Skill 13.06) (Easy)

    A. Tell her you agree with her.
    B. Recommend an outside source that may provide a free laptop computer.
    C. Tell Kara's mother she can still fight the CSE's decision by requesting a Due Process Hearing.
    D. Tell the parent to call a lawyer.

Answer: C. Tell Kara's mother she can still fight the CSE's decision by requesting a Due Process Hearing.

It is your legal obligation to let Kara's mother know that she does not have to accept the CSE decision if she does not like it and that she can request a Due Process Hearing.

120. Taiquan's parents are divorced and have joint custody. They both have requested to be present at the CSE. You call to make sure that they received the letter informing them of the coming CSE. Taiquan's father did not receive the notification and is upset. You should: (Skill 13.06) (Rigorous)

    A. Tell him that you could review the meeting with him later.
    B. Ask him if he can adjust his schedule.
    C. Tell him you can reschedule the meeting.
    D. Ask him to coordinate a time for the CSE to meet with his ex-wife.

Answer: C. Tell him you can reschedule the meeting.

A parent should be informed if he/she is divorced and both have joint custody and have expressed a desire to be present at the CSE. In this case, if the one of the parents want to be at the meeting, and is unable to attend the meeting should be rescheduled.

121. **Shyquan is in your inclusive class and she exhibits a slower comprehension of assigned tasks and concepts. Her first two grades were Bs but she is now receiving failing marks. She has seen the Resource Teacher. You should: (Skill 13.06) (Rigorous)**

   A. Ask for a review of current placement.
   B. Tell Shyquan to seek extra help.
   C. Ask Shyquan if she is frustrated.
   D. Ask the regular education teacher to slow instruction.

Answer: A. Ask for a review of current placement.

All of the responses listed above can be deemed correct, but you are responsible for reviewing her ability to function in the inclusive environment. Shyquan may or may not know she is not grasping the work, and she has sought out extra help with the Resource Teacher. Also, if the regular education class students are successful, the class should not be slowed to adjust to Shyquan's learning rate. It is more likely that she may require a more modified curriculum to stay on task and to succeed academically. This would require a more restrictive environment.

122. **According to IDEA 2004 an FBA must be: (Skill 13.07) (Average Rigor)**

   A. Written by the Special Education Administrator.
   B. Written by the teacher who has the issue with the student.
   C. Written by the primary teacher.
   D. Written by a team.

Answer: D. Written by a team.

FBAs (Functional Behavioral Assessments) should be written and reviewed as a team. This approach is the most effective for improving student behavior.

123.   Parent contact should first begin when: (Skill 14.02) (Average Rigor)

      A. You are informed the child will be your student.
      B. The student fails a test.
      C. The student exceeds others on a task.
      D. A CSE is coming and you have had no previous replies to letters.

Answer: A. You are informed the child will be your student.

Student contact should begin as a getting to know you piece, which allows you to begin on a non-judgmental platform. It also allows the parent to receive a view that you are a professional that is willing to work with them.

124.   Parents of children with disabilities may seek your advice on several aspects regarding their child. A mother calls you and complains she can't keep her son on task so much she has to keep sending her son back to the bathroom until he finishes getting prepared for the day. What advice should you give her? (Skill 14.03) (Average Rigor)

      A. Request an educational evaluation.
      B. Recommend close supervision until he does all tasks together consistently.
      C. Create a list of tasks to be completed in the bathroom.
      D. Ask for outside coordination of services advocacy that can assist with this type of issue.

Answer: C. Create a list of tasks to be completed in the bathroom.
The child is independent on each task. Calling outside resources is a good idea, but it does not address the issue. The student may simply have a short-term memory loss, and may need a reminder to keep on task.

125.   By November, Annette's 7th grade teacher is concerned with her sporadic attendance. What action should take place next? (Skill 14.04) (Average Rigor)

      A. Notify CPS
      B. Notify the police of non-compliance with compulsory attendance.
      C. Question parents about the absences.
      D. Notify the Administrator.

Answer: C. Question parents about the absences.

The parents should be contacted initially they may be willing to file a report with the police (PINS) or have a rational reason for the absences.

126. **Which is not a goal of collaboration for a Consult Teacher? (Skill 14.05) (Average Rigor)**

    A. To have the regular education teacher understand the student's disability.
    B. Review content for accuracy
    C. Review Lessons for possible necessary modifications.
    D. Understanding of reasons for current grade Average Rigor.

Answer: B. Review content for accuracy.

The regular education teacher is responsible for the content. You are responsible for seeing that the child's necessary modifications are adapted.

127. **Kenny is a 9th grader enrolled in Wood Shop; he is having difficulty grasping fractions. You know that Kenny has difficulty with abstract concepts. What would be a good method to teach this concept? (Skill 14.06)(Rigorous)**

    A. Pie blocks that proportionately measure whole, half, 1/4, 1/8, etc.
    B. Strips of paper that proportionately measure whole, half, 1/4, 1/8, etc.
    C. One on one review of the worksheet.
    D. You work with in the wood shop privately showing him how to measure.

Answer: B. Strips of paper that proportionately measure whole, half, 1/4, 1/8, etc.

Strips of paper can be used to teach the concept by tearing a whole sheet into proportionate pieces. They can also be used like a tape measure to measure a length of wood. This instruction would enable him to transfer knowledge easily when the topic is grasped.

128. **Task related attending skills include: (Skill 14.06) (Hard)**

    A. Compliance to requests
    B. Writing the correct Answer: on the chalk board.
    C. Listening to the assignment
    D. Repeating instructions

Answer: C. Listening to the assignment

Attending skills are used to receive a message. Compliance may have nothing to do with what was said at the moment. Repetition of instructions may ne a compensatory strategy.

129. **What legislation started FAPE? (Skill 16.01) (Rigorous)**

    A. Section 504
    B. EHCA
    C. IDEA
    D. Education Amendment 1974

Answer: A. Section 504

FAPE stands for Free Appropriate Public Education. Section 504 of the Rehabilitation Act in 1973 is the legislation, which enacted/created FAPE stands for Free Appropriate Public Education.

130. **NCLB changed: (Skill 16.01) (Rigorous)**

    A. Special Education Teacher placement
    B. Classroom guidelines
    C. Stricter behavioral regulations.
    D. Academic content

Answer: A. Special Education Teacher placement

Special education teachers are now required to meet the same criteria as those of the content teachers in their area to be Highly Qualified.

131. **IDEA 97 changed IDEA by requiring (Skill 16.01) (Rigorous)**

    A. IEPs to be in Electronic format.
    B. Requiring all staff working with the student to have access to the IEP.
    C. Allowing past assessments to be used in Triennials.
    D. BIPs for many students with FBAs.

Answer D. BIPs for many students with FBAs

IDEA 97 created a mandate to provide interventions to change inappropriate behaviors to increase the possibility that the student could avoid the consequences of repeating the behavior.

132. **Which of these groups is not comprehensively covered by IDEA? (Skill 16.01) (Easy)**

    A. Gifted and talented
    B. Mentally retarded
    C. Specific learning disabilities
    D. Speech and language impaired

Answer: C. Specific learning disabilities

IDEA did not cover all exceptional children. The Gifted and Talented Children's Act, was passed in 1978.

133. **Educators who advocate educating all children in their neighborhood classrooms and schools propose the end of labeling and segregation of special needs students in special classes, and who call for the delivery of special supports and services directly in the classroom, may be said to support the: (Skill 16.01) (Easy)**

    A. Full service model
    B. Regular education initiative
    C. Full inclusion model
    D. Mainstream model

Answer: C. Full inclusion model.

All students must be included in the regular classroom.

134. **NCLB (No Child Left Behind Act), was signed on January 8, 2002. It addresses what: (Skill 16.01) (Rigorous)**

    A. Accessibility of curriculum to the student
    B. Administrative incentives for school improvements
    C. The funding to provide services required.
    D. Accountability of school personnel for student achievement.

Answer: D. Accountability of school personnel for student achievement.

All behavior is learned. This behavior is different from the norm. It is different because of something the child has experienced or learned.

135. **Section 504 differs from the scope of IDEA because its main focus is on: (Skill 16.01) (Average Rigor)**

    A. Prohibition of discrimination on the basis of disability.
    B. A basis for additional support services and accommodations in a special education setting.
    C. Procedural rights and safeguards for the individual.
    D. Federal funding for educational services.

Answer: A. Prohibition of discrimination on the basis of disability.

Section 504 prohibits discrimination on the basis of disability.

136. **Public Law 99-457 amended the EHA to make provisions for: (Skill 16.01) (Average Rigor)**

    A. Education services for "uneducable" children
    B. Education services for children in jail settings
    C. Special education benefits for children birth to five years
    D. Education services for medically-fragile children

Answer: C. Special education benefits for children birth to five years.

P.L. 99-457 amended EHA to provide Special Education programs for children 3-5 years, with most states offering outreach programs to identify children with special needs from birth to age 3.

137. **Under the provisions of IDEA, the student is entitled to all of these EXCEPT: (Skill 16.01) (Average Rigor)**

   A. Placement in the best environment
   B. Placement in the least restrictive environment
   C. Provision of educational needs at no cost
   D. Provision of individualized, appropriate educational program

Answer: A. Placement in the best environment

IDEA mandates a **least restrictive environment, an IEP, (individual education plan) and a free public education.**

138. **As a New Special Education Teacher you have responsibility to? (Skill 16.01) (Average Rigor)**

   A. Share new law related to special education.
   B. Discuss and plan intervention strategies for other teachers.
   C. Stay current on national and local news.
   D. Observe incoming students for possible referrals to CSE.

Answer: A. Share new law related to special education.

Quite often school administrators are not knowledgeable of the changes in special education laws until a court case becomes public, or an angry parent approaches and tells them they are in violation of the law. You as the Special Education Teacher must keep current on the law. Sharing that knowledge is a collegial responsibility, if you believe people who need to be informed of the changes are not aware of them.

139. **Which law specifically states that "Full Inclusion is not the only way for a student to reach his/her highest potential?" (Skill 16.01) (Rigorous)**

   A. IDEA
   B. IDEA 97
   C. IDEA 2004
   D. Part 200

Answer: C. IDEA 2004.

IDEIAA (IDEA 2004) full inclusion stated that this was not always best for the individual student. This allows for students who need more restrictive services to be served appropriately when people who push full inclusion are confronted.

140. The following words describe an IEP objective EXCEPT: (Skill 16.01) (Rigorous)

A. Specific
B. Observable
C. Measurable
D. Flexible

Answer: D. Flexible.

IEPs are not flexible for interpretation. They are enforceable legal documents that must be followed, or modified by the CSE team.

141. NCLB and IDEA 2004 changed Special Education Teacher requirements by: (Skill 16.01) (Easy)

A. Requiring a Highly Qualified status for job placement.
B. Adding changes to the requirement for certifications
C. Adding legislation requiring teachers to maintain knowledge of law.
D. Requiring inclusive environmental experience prior to certification.

Answer: A. Requiring a Highly Qualified status for job placement.

NCLB and IDEA 2004 place a requirement that all teacher shall be equally qualified to tech in their content area.

142. IDEA 2004 stated that there is a disproportionate amount of minority students classified. The reason IDEA 2004 suggests is: (Skill 16.01) (Average Rigor)

A. Socioeconomic status where disproportionate numbers exist.
B. Improper evaluations – Not making allowances for students who have English as a second language.
C. Growing population of minorities.
D. Percentage of drug abuse per ethnicity.

Answer: B. Improper evaluations – Not making allowances for students who have English as a second language.

IDEA 2004 questioned the acceptance or inclusion of students who have English as a second language as being over represented.

143. **Which of the following statements was not offered as a rationale for Inclusion? (Skill 16.01) (Average Rigor)**

    A. Special education students are not usually identified until their learning problems have become severe
    B. Lack of funding will mean that support for the special needs children will not be available in the regular classroom.
    C. Putting children in segregated special education placements is stigmatizing
    D. There are students with learning or behavior problems who do not meet special education requirements but who still need special services

Answer: B. Lack of funding will mean that support for the special needs children will not be available in the regular classroom.

All except lack of funding were offered in support of Inclusion.

144. **Guidelines for an Individualized Family Service Plan (IFSP) would be described in which legislation? (Skill 16.01) (Rigorous)**

    A. Education of the Handicapped Act Amendments
    B. IDEA (1990)
    C. IDEA 2004
    D. ADA

Answer: B. IDEA (1990).

Education for All Handicapped Children Act, was passed in the Civil Rights era, and its amendment in 1986 provided financial incentive to educate children with disabilities who are 3 to 5 years of age. ADA is the Americans with Disabilities Act.

145.   Cheryl is a 15-year old student receiving educational services in a full-time EH classroom. The date for her IEP review is planned for two months before her 16th birthday. According to the requirements of IDEA, what must ADDITIONALLY be included in this review? (Skill 16.01) (Average Rigor)

A. Graduation plan
B. Individualized transition plan
C. Vocational assessment
D. Transportation planning

Answer: B. Individualized transition plan

This is necessary, as the student should be transitioning from school to work.

146.   Previous to IDEA97 what was not accepted? (Skill 16.01) (Hard)

A. Using previous assessments to evaluate placement.
B. Parent refusal of CSE determination (No Due Process)
C. Student input on placement and needs.
D. All of the Above

Answer: B. Using previous assessments to evaluate placement.

Previous to IDEA97 evaluation of placement always required assessments. No acceptance of previous testing was accepted. This was recognized as creating needless testing for students as IQs generally do not change, while the student's knowledge base grows.

147. Hector is a 10th grader in a program for the severely emotionally handicapped. After a classmate taunted him about his mother, Hector threw a desk at the other boy and attacked him. A crisis intervention team tried to break up the fight, and one teacher hurt his knee. The other boy received a concussion. Hector now faces disciplinary measures. How long can he be suspended without the suspension reviewing a possible "change of placement"? (Skill 16.01) (Rigorous)

   A. 5 days
   B. 10 days
   C. 10 + 30 days
   D. 60 days

Answer: B. 10 days

According to **Honig versus Doe,** 1988, Where the student has presented an immediate threat to others, that student may be temporarily suspended for up to 10 school days to give the school and the parents time to review the IEP and discuss possible alternatives to the current placement.

148. The concept that a handicapped student cannot be expelled for misconduct that is a manifestation of the handicap itself is not limited to students which are labeled "seriously emotionally disturbed". Which reason does not explain this concept? (Skill 16.01) (Easy)

   A. Emphasis on individualized evaluation
   B. Consideration of the problems and needs of handicapped students
   C. Right to a free and appropriate public education
   D. Students in special education get special privileges.

Answer: D. Students in special education get special privileges.

A, B, and C are tenets of IDEA and should take place in the least restrictive environment. D does not explain this concept.

149. What is required of a Special Education Teacher when approaching an administrator regarding a request to change placement of a student:
(Skill 17.03) (Rigorous)

   A. Observation.
   B. Objectivity.
   C. Assessments.
   D. Parent permission.

Answer: B. Objectivity.

Presenting a case for change of placement to your supervisor does not require parental permission. It requires your ability to objectively analyze the needs of the student versus current placement.

150. Teachers have a professional obligation to do all of the following except: (Skill 17.05) (Average Rigor)

   A. Join a professional organization such as CEC, or LDA.
   B. Attend inservices or seminars related to your position.
   C. Stay after school to help students.
   D. Run school clubs.

Answer: D. Run school clubs.

Teachers are not obligated to run a school club. It is often considered volunteering of your time.

References

Ager, C.L. & Cole, C.L. (1991). A review of cognitive-behavioral interventions for children and adolescents with behavioral disorders. *Behavioral Disorders,* 16(4), 260-275.

Aiken, L.R. (1985). *Psychological testing and assessment* (5th ed.). Boston: Allyn and Bacon.

Alberto, P.A. & Trouthman, A.C. (1990). *Applied behavior analysis for teachers: Influencing student performance.* Columbus, Ohio: Charles E. Merrill.

Algozzine, B. (1990). *Behavior problem management: Educator's resource service.* Gaithersburg, MD: Aspen Publishers.

Algozzine, B., Ruhl, K., & Ramsey, R. (1991). *Behaviorally disordered: Assessment for identification and instruction CED mini-library.* Renson, VA: The Council for Exceptional Children.

Ambron, S.R. (1981). *Child development* (3rd ed.). New York: Holt, Rinehart and Winston.

Anerson, V., & Black, L. (Eds.). (1987, Winter). National news: U.S. Department of Education releases special report (Editorial). *GLRS Journal* [Georgia Learning Resources System].

Anguili, R. (1987, Winter). The 1986 amendment to the Education of the Handicapped Act. *Confederation* [A quarterly publication of the Georgia Federation Council for Exceptional Children].

Ashlock, R.B. (1976). *Error patterns in computation: A semi-programmed approach* (2nd ed.). Columbus, Ohio: Charles E. Merrill.

Association of Retarded Citizens of Georgia (1987). *1986-87 Government report.* College Park, GA: Author.

Ausubel, D.P. & Sullivan, E.V. (1970). *Theory and problems of child development.* New York: Grune & Stratton.

Banks, J.A., & McGee Banks, C.A. (1993). *Multicultural education* (2nd ed.). Boston: Allyn and Bacon.

Barrett, T.C. (Ed.). (1967). *The evaluation of children's reading achievement. in perspectives in reading, No. 8.* Newark, Delaware: International Reading Association.

Bartoli, J.S. (1989). An ecological response to Cole's interactivity alternative. *Journal of Learning Disabilities*, 22 (5), 292-297.

Basile-Jackson, J. *The exceptional child in the regular classroom.* Augusta, GA: East Georgia Center, Georgia Learning Resources System.

Bauer, A.M., & Shea, T.M. (1989). *Teaching exceptional students in your classroom.* Boston: Allyn and Bacon.

Bentley, E.L. Jr. (1980). *Questioning skills* (Videocassette & manual series). Northbrook, IL: Hubbard Scientific Company. (Project STRETCH [Strategies to Train Regular Educators to Teach Children with Handicaps], Module 1, ISBN 0-8331-1906-0).

Berdine, W.H., & Blackhurst, A.E. (1985). *An introduction to special education.* (2nd ed.) Boston: Little, Brown and Company.

Blake, K. (1976). *The mentally retarded: An educational psychology.* Englewood Cliff, NJ: Prentice-Hall.

Bohline, D.S. (1985). *Intellectual and affective characteristics of attention deficit disordered children.* Journal of Learning Disabilities, 18 (10),604-608.

Boone, R. (1983). Legislation and litigation. In R.E. Schmid, & L. Negata (Eds.). *Contemporary Issues in Special Education.* New York: McGraw Hill.

Brantlinger, E.A., & Guskin, S.L. (1988). Implications of social and cultural differences for special education. In Meten, E.L. Vergason, G.A., & Whelan, R.J. *Effective Instructional Strategies for Exceptional Children.* Denver, CO: Love Publishing.

Brewton, B. (1990). Preliminary identification of the socially maladjusted. In Georgia Psycho-educational Network, Monograph #1. *An Educational Perspective On: Emotional Disturbance and Social Maladjustment.* Atlanta, GA Psychoeducational Network.

Brolin, D.E., & Kokaska, C.J. (1979). *Career education for handicapped children approach.* Renton, VA: The Council for Exceptional Children.

Brolin, D.E. (Ed). (1989). *Life centered career education: A competency based approach.* Reston, VA: The Council for Exceptional Children.

Brown, J.W., Lewis, R.B., & Harcleroad, F.F. (1983). *AV instruction: Technology, media, and methods* (6TH ed.). New York: McGraw-Hill.

Bryan, T.H., & Bryan, J.H. (1986). *Understanding learning disabilities* (3rd ed.). Palo Alto, CA: Mayfield.

Bryen, D.N. (1982). *Inquiries into child language*. Boston: Allyn & Bacon.

Bucher, B.D. (1987). *Winning them over*. New York: Times Books.

Bush, W.L., & Waugh, K.W. (1982). *Diagnosing learning problems* (3rd ed.). Columbus, OH: Charles E. Merrill.

Campbell, P. (1986). *Special needs report* [Newsletter]. 1(1), 1-3.

Carbo, M., & Dunn, K. (1986). *Teaching students to read through their individual learning styles*. Englewood Cliffs, NJ: Prentice Hall.

CArtwright, G.P., & Cartwright, C.A., & Ward, M.E. (1984). *Educating special learners* (2nd ed.). Belmont, CA: Wadsworth.

Cejka, J.M. (Consultant), & Needham, F. (Senior Editor). (1976). *Approaches to mainstreaming*. (Filmstrip and cassette kit, units 1 & 2). Boston: Teaching Resources Corporation. (Catalog Nos. 09-210 & 09-220).

Chalfant, J. C. (1985). *Identifying learning disabled students: A summary of the national task force report*. Learning Disabilities Focus, 1, 9-20.

Charles, C.M. (1976). *Individualizing instructions*. St Louis: The C.V. Mosby Company.

Chrispeels, J.H. (1991). *District leadership in parent involvement: Policies and actions in San Diego*. Phi Delta Kappa, 71, 367-371.

Clarizio, H.F. (1987). Differentiating characteristics. In Georgia Psychoeducational Network, Monograph #1, *An educational perspective on: Emotional disturbance and social maladjustment*. Atlanta, GA: Psychoeducational Network.

Clarizio, H.F. & McCoy, G.F. (1983). *Behavior disorders in children* (3rd ed.). New York: Harper & Row.

Coles, G.S. (1989). *Excerpts from the learning mystique: A critical look at disabilities*. Journal of Learning Disabilities, 22 (5), 267-278.

Collins, E. (1980). *Grouping and special students*. (Videocassette & manual series). Northbrook, IL: Hubbard Scientific Company. (Project STRETCH [Strategies to Train Regular Educators to Teach Children with Handicaps], Module 17, ISBN 0-8331-1922-2).

Craig, E., & Craig, L. (1990). *Reading In the Content Areas*. (Videocassette & manual series). Northbrook, IL: Hubbard Scientific Company. (Project STRETCH [Strategies to Train Regular Educators to Teach Children with Handicaps], Module 13, ISBN 0-8331-1918-4).

Compton, C., (1984). A Guide to 75 Tests for Special Education. Belmont, CA., Pitman Learning.

Council for Exceptional Children. (1976). Introducing P.L. 94-142. [Filmstrip-cassette kit manual]. Reston, VA: Author.

Council for Exceptional Children. (1987). The Council for Exceptional Children's Fall 1987. Catalog of Products and Services. Renton, VA: Author.

Council for Exceptional Children Delegate Assembly. (1983). Council for Exceptional Children Code of Ethics (Adopted April 1983). Reston, VA: Author.

Czajka, J.L. (1984). Digest of Data on Person With Disabilities (Mathematics Policy Research, Inc.). Washington, D.C.: U.S. Government Printing Office.

Dell, H.D. (1972). Individualizing Instruction: Materials and Classroom Procedures. Chicago: Science Research Associates.

Demonbreun, C., & Morris, J. Classroom Management [Videocassette & Manual series]. Northbrook, IL: Hubbard Scientific Company. Project STRETCH (Strategies to Train Regular Educators to Teach Children with Handicaps]. Module 5, ISBN 0-8331-1910-9).

Department of Education. Education for the Handicapped Law Reports. Supplement 45 (1981), p. 102: 52. Washington, D.C.: U.S. Government Printing Office.

Department of Health, Education, and Welfare, Office of Education. (1977, August 23). Education of Handicapped Children. Federal Register, 42, (163).

Diana vs. State Board of Education, Civil No. 70-37 R.F.P. (N.D.Cal. January, 1970).

Digangi, S.A., Perryman, P., & Rutherford, R.B., Jr. (1990). Juvenile Offenders in the 90's A Descriptive Analysis. Perceptions, 25(4), 5-8.

Division of Educational Services, Special Education Programs (1986). <u>Fifteenth Annual Report to Congress on Implementation of the Education of the Handicapped Act.</u> Washington, D.C.: U.S. Government Printing Office.

Doyle, B.A. (1978). <u>Math Readiness Skills.</u> Paper presented at National Association of School Psychologists, New York. K.J. (1978). <u>Teaching Students Through Their Individual Learning Styles</u>.

Dunn, R.S., & Dunn, K.J. (1978). <u>Teaching Students Through Their Individual Learning Styles: A Practical Approach.</u> Reston, VA: Reston.

Epstein, M.H., Patton, J.R., Polloway, E.A., & Foley, R. (1989). Mild retardation: Student characteristics and services. <u>Education and Training of the Mentally Retarded,</u> 24, 7-16.

Ekwall, E.E., & Shanker, J.L. 1983). <u>Diagnosis and Remediation of the Disabled Reader</u> (2nd ed.) Boston: Allyn and Bacon.

Firth, E.E. & Reynolds, I. (1983). Slide tape shows: A creative activity for the gifted students. <u>Teaching Exceptional Children.</u> 15(3), 151-153.

Frymier, J., & Gansneder, B. (1989). <u>The Phi Delta Kappa Study of Students at Risk.</u> Phi Delta Kappa. 71(2) 142-146.

Fuchs, D., & Deno, S.L. 1992). Effects of curriculum within curriculum-based measurement. <u>Exceptional Children 58</u> (232-242).

Fuchs, D., & Fuchs, L.S. (1989). Effects of examiner familiarity on Black, Caucasian, and Hispanic Children. A Meta-Analysis. <u>Exceptional Children.</u> 55, 303-308.

Fuchs, L.S., & Shinn, M.R. (1989). Writing CBM IEP objectives. In M.R. Shinn, <u>Curriculum-based Measurement: Assessing Special Students.</u> New York: Guilford Press.

Gage, N.L. (1990). <u>Dealing With the Dropout Problems?</u> Phi Delta Kappa. 72(4), 280-285.

Gallagher, P.A. (1988). <u>Teaching Students with Behavior Disorders: Techniques and Activities for Classroom Instruction</u> (2nd ed.). Denver, CO: Love Publishing.

Gearheart, B.R. (1980). <u>Special Education for the 80s.</u> St. Louis, MO: The C.V. Cosby Company.

Gearhart, B.R. & Weishahn, M.W. (1986). The Handicapped Student in the Regular Classroom (2nd ed.). St Louis, MO: The C.V. Mosby Company.

Gearhart, B.R. (1985). Learning Disabilities: Educational Strategies (4th ed.). St. Louis: Times Mirror/ Mosby College of Publishing.

Georgia Department of Education, Program for Exceptional Children. (1986). Mild Mentally Handicapped (Vol. II), Atlanta, GA: Office of Instructional Services, Division of Special Programs, and Program for Exceptional Children. Resource Manuals for Program for Exceptional Children.

Georgia Department of Human Resources, Division of Rehabilitation Services. (1987, February). Request for Proposal [Memorandum]. Atlanta, GA: Author.

Georgia Psychoeducational Network (1990). An Educational Perspective on: Emotional Disturbance and Social Maladjustment. Monograph #1. Atlanta, GA Psychoeducational Network.

Geren, K. (1979). Complete Special Education Handbook. West Nyack, NY: Parker.

Gillet, P.K. (1988). Career Development. Robinson, G.A., Patton, J.R., Polloway, E.A., & Sargent, L.R. (eds.). Best Practices in Mild Mental Disabilities. Reston, VA: The Division on Mental Retardation of the Council for Exceptional Children.

Gleason, J.B. (1993). The Development of Language (3rd ed.). New York: Macmillan Publishing.

Good, T.L., & BROPHY, J.E. (1978). Looking into Classrooms (2nd Ed.). New York: Harper & Row.

Hall, M.A. (1979). Language-Centered Reading: Premises and Recommendations. Language Arts, 56 664-670.

Halllahan, D.P. & Kauffman, J.M. (1988). Exceptional Children: Introduction to Special Education. (4th Ed.). Englewood Cliffs, NJ; Prentice-Hall.

Hallahan, D.P. & Kauffman, J.M. (1994). Exceptional Children: Introduction to Special Education 6th ed.). Boston: Allyn and Bacon.

Hammill, D.D., & Bartel, N.R. (1982). Teaching Children With Learning and Behavior Problems (3rd ed.). Boston: Allyn and Bacon.

Hammill, D.D., & Bartel, N.R. (1986). Teaching Students with Learning and Behavior Problems (4th ed.). Boston and Bacon.

Hamill, D.D., & Brown, L. & Bryant, B. (1989) A Consumer's Guide to Tests in Print. Austin, TX: Pro-Ed.

Haney, J.B. & Ullmer, E.J. ((1970). Educational Media and the Teacher. Dubuque, IA: Wm. C. Brown Company.

Hardman, M.L., Drew, C.J., Egan, M.W., & Wolf, B. (1984). Human Exceptionality: Society, School, and Family. Boston: Allyn and Bacon.

Hardman, M.L., Drew, C.J., Egan, M.W., & Worlf, B. (1990). Human Exceptionality (3rd ed.). Boston: Allyn and Bacon.

Hargrove, L.J., & Poteet, J.A. (1984). Assessment in Special Education. Englewood Cliffs, NJ: Prentice-Hall.

Haring, N.G., & Bateman, B. (1977). Teaching the Learning Disabled Child. Englewood Cliffs, NJ: Prentice-Hall.

Harris, K.R., & Pressley, M. (1991). The Nature of Cognitive Strategy Instruction: Interactive strategy instruction. Exceptional Children, 57, 392-401.

Hart, T., & Cadora, M.J. (1980). The Exceptional Child: Label the Behavior [Videocassette & manual series], Northbrook, IL: Hubbard Scientific Company. (Project STRETCH [Strategies to Train Regular Educators to Teach Children with Handicaps], Module 12, ISBN 0-8331-1917-6). HART, V. (1981) Mainstreaming Children with Special Needs. New York: Longman.

Henley, M., Ramsey,R.S., & Algozzine, B. (1993). Characteristics of and Strategies for Teaching Students with Mild Disabilities. Boston: Allyn and Bacon.

Hewett, F.M., & Forness, S.R. (1984). Education of Exceptional Learners. (3rd ed.). Boston: Allyn and Bacon.

Howe, C.E. (1981) Administration of Special Education. Denver: Love.

Human Services Research Institute (1985). Summary of Data on Handicapped Children and Youth. (Digest). Washington, D.C.: U.S. Government Printing Office.

Johnson, D.W. (1972) Reaching Out: Interpersonal Effectiveness and Self-Actualization. Englewood Cliffs, NJ: Prentice-Hall.

Johnson, D.W. (1978) Human Relations and Your Career: A Guide to Interpersonal Skills. Englewood Cliffs, NJ: Prentice-Hall.

Johnson, D.W., & Johnson, R.T. (1990). Social Skills for Successful Group Work. Educational Leadership. 47 (4) 29-33.

Johnson, S.W., & Morasky, R.L. Learning Disabilities (2nd ed.) Boston: Allyn and Bacon.

Jones, F.H. (1987). Positive Classroom Discipline. New York: McGraw-Hill Book Company.

Jones, V.F., & Jones, L. S. (1986). Comprehensive Classroom Management: Creating Positive Learning Environments. (2nd ed.). Boston: Allyn and Bacon.

Jones, V.F. & Jones, L.S. (1981). Responsible Classroom Discipline: Creating Positive Learning Environments and Solving Problems. Boston: Allyn and Bacon.

Kauffman, J.M. (1981) Characteristics of Children's Behavior Disorders. (2nd ed.). Columbus, OH: Charles E. Merrill.

Kauffman, J.M. (1989). Characteristics of Behavior Disorders of Children and Youth. (4th ed.). Columbus, OH: Merrill Publishing.

Kem, M., & Nelson, M. (1983). Strategies for Managing Behavior Problems in the Classroom. Columbus, OH: Charles E. Merrill.

Kerr, M.M., & Nelson, M. (1983) Strategies for Managing Behavior Problems in the Classroom. Columbus, OH: Charles E. Merrill.

Kirk, S.A., & Gallagher, J.J. (1986). Educating Exceptional Children (5th ed.). Boston: Houghton Mifflin.

Kohfeldt, J. (1976). Blueprints for construction. Focus on Exceptional Children. 8 (5), 1-14.

Kokaska, C.J., & Brolin, D.E. (1985). Career Education for Handicapped Individuals (2nd ed.). Columbus, OH: Charles E. Merrill.

Lambie, R.A. (1980). A systematic approach for changing materials, instruction, and assignments to meet individual needs. Focus on Exceptional Children, 13(1), 1-12.

Larson, S.C., & Poplin, M.S. (1980). Methods for Educating the Handicapped: An Individualized Education Program Approach. Boston: Allyn and Bacon.

Lerner, J. (1976) Children with Learning Disabilities. (2nd ed.). Boston: Houghton Mifflin.

Lerner, J. (1989). Learning Disabilities,: Theories, Diagnosis and Teaching Strategies (3rd ed.). Boston: Houghton Mifflin.

Levenkron, S. (1991). Obsessive-Compulsive Disorders. New York: Warner Books.

Lewis, R.B., & Doorlag, D.H. (1991). Teaching Special Students in the Mainstream. (3rd ed.). New York: Merrill.

Lindsley, O. R. (1990). Precision Teaching: By Teachers for Children. Teaching Exceptional Children, 22. (3), 10-15.

Linddberg, L., & Swedlow, R. (1985). Young Children Exploring and Learning. Boston: Allyn and Bacon.

Long, N.J., Morse, W.C., & Newman, R.G. (1980). Conflict in the Classroom: The Education of Emotionally Disturbed Children. Belmont, CA: Wadsworth.

Losen, S.M., & Losen, J.G. (1985). The Special Education Team. Boston: Allyn and Bacon.

Lovitt, T.C. (1989). Introduction to Learning Disabilities. Boston: Allyn and Bacon.

Lund, N.J., & Duchan, J.F. (1988)/ Assessing Children's Language in Naturalist Contexts. Englewood Cliffs, NJ: Prentice Hall

Male, M. (1994) Technology for Inclusion: Meeting the Special Needs of all Children. (2nd ed.). Boston: Allyn and Bacon.

Mandelbaum, L.H. (1989). Reading. In G.A. Robinson, J.R., Patton, E.A., Polloway, & L.R. Sargent (eds.). Best Practices in Mild Mental Retardation. Reston, VA: The Division of Mental Retardation, Council for Exceptional Children.

Mannix. D. (1993). Social Skills for Special Children. West Nyack, NY: The Center for Applied Research in Education.

Marshall, et al. vs. Georgia U.S. District Court for the Southern District of Georgia. C.V. 482-233. June 28, 1984.

Marshall, E.K., Kurtz, P.D., & Associates. Interpersonal Helping Skills. San Francisco, CA: Jossey-Bass Publications.

Marston, D.B. (1989) A curriculum-based measurement approach to assessing academic performance: What it is and why do it. In M. Shinn (Ed.). Curriculum-Based Measurement: Assessing Special Children. New York: Guilford Press.

McDowell, R.L., Adamson, G.W., & Wood, F.H. (1982). Teaching Emotionally Disturbed Children. Boston: Little, Brown and Company.
MCGINNIS, E., GOLDSTEIN, A.P. (1990). Skill Streaming in Early

Childhood: Teaching prosocial skills to the preschool and kindergarten child. Champaign, IL: Research Press.

Mcloughlin, J.A., & Lewis, R.B. (1986). Assessing Special Students (3rd ed.). Columbus, OH: Charles E. Merrill.

MERCER, C.D. (1987). Students with Learning Disabilities. (3rd. ed.). Merrill Publishing.

MERCER, C.D., & MERCER, A.R. (1985). Teaching Children with Learning Problems (2nd ed.). Columbus, OH: Charles E. Merrill.

MEYEN, E.L., VERGASON, G.A., & WHELAN, R.J. (Eds.). (1988). Effective Instructional Strategies for Exceptional Children. Denver, CO: Love Publishing.

MILLER, L.K. (1980). Principles of Everyday Behavior Analysis (2nd ed.). Monterey, CA: Brooks/Cole Publishing Company.
MILLS VS. THE BOARD OF EDUCATON OF THE DISTRICT OF COLUMBIA, 348F. Supp. 866 (D.C. 1972).

MOPSICK, S.L. & AGARD, J.A. (Eds.) (1980). Cambridge, MA: Abbott Associates.

MORRIS, C.G. (1985). Psychology: An Introduction (5th ed.). Englewood Cliffs, NJ: Prentice-Hall.

MORRIS, J. (1980). Behavior Modification. [Videocassette and manual series]. Northbrook, IL: Hubbard Scientific Company. (Project STRETCH [Strategies to Train Regular Educators to Teach Children with Handicaps,] Module 16, Metropolitan Cooperative Educational Service Agency.).
MORRIS, J. & DEMONBREUN, C. (1980). Learning Styles [Videocassettes & Manual series]. Northbrook, IL: Hubbard Scientific Company. (Project STRETCH [Strategies to Train Regular Educators to Teach Children with Handicaps], Module 15, ISBN 0-8331-1920-6).

MORRIS, R.J. (1985). Behavior Modification with Exceptional Children: Principles and Practices. Glenview, IL: Scott, Foresman and Company.

MORSINK, C.V. (1984). Teaching Special Needs Students in Regular Classrooms. Boston: Little, Brown and Company.

MORSINK, C.V., THOMAS, C.C., & CORREA, V.L. (1991). Interactive Teaming, Consultation and Collaboration in Special Programs. New York: MacMillan Publishing.

MULLSEWHITE, C.R. (1986). Adaptive Play for Special Needs Children: Strategies to Enhance Communication and Learning. San Diego: College Hill Press.

NORTH CENTRAL GEORGIA LEARNING RESOURCES SYSTEM/CHILD SERVE. (1985). Strategies Handbook for Classroom Teachers. Ellijay, GA.

PATTON, J.R., CRONIN, M.E., POLLOWAY, E.A., HUTCHINSON, D., & ROBINSON, G.A. (1988). Curricular considerations: A life skills orientation. In Robinson, G.A., Patton, J.R., Polloway, E.A., & Sargent, L.R. (Eds.). Best Practices in Mental Disabilities. Des Moines, IA: Iowa Department of Education, Bureau of Special Education.

PATTON, J.R., KAUGGMAN, J.M., BLACKBOURN, J.M., & BROWN, B.G. (1991). Exceptional Children in Focus (5th ed.). New York: MacMillan.

PAUL, J.L. (Ed.). (1981). Understanding and Working with parents of Children with Special Needs. New York: Holt, Rinehart and Winston.

PAUL, J.L. & EPANCHIN, B.C. (1991). Educating Emotionally Disturbed Children and Youth: Theories and Practices for Teachers. (2nd ed.). New York: MacMillan. PENNSYLVANIA ASSOCIATION FOR RETARDED CHILDREN VS. COMMONWEALTH OF PENNSYLVANIA, 334 F. Supp. 1257 (E.D., PA., 1971), 343 F. Supp. 279 (L.D. PA., 19972).

PHILLIPS, V., & MCCULLOUGH, L. (1990). Consultation based programming: Instituting the Collaborative Work Ethic. Exceptional Children. 56 (4), 291-304.

PODEMSKI, R.S., PRICE, B.K., SMITH, T.E.C., & MARSH, G.E., IL (1984). Comprehensive Administration of Special Education. Rockville, MD: Aspen Systems Corporation.

POLLOWAY, E.A., & PATTON, J.R. (1989). Strategies for Teaching Learners with Special Needs. (5th ed.). New York: Merrill.

POLLOWAY, E.A., PATTON, J.R., PAYNE, J.S., & PAYNE, R.A. 1989). Strategies for Teaching Learners with Special Needs, 4th ed.). Columbus, OH: Merrill Publishing.

PUGACH, M.C., & JOHNSON, L.J. (1989a). The challenge of implementing collaboration between general and special education. Exceptional Children, 56 (3), 232-235.

PUGACH, M.C., & JOHNSON, L.J. (1989b). Pre-referral interventions: Progress, Problems, and Challenges. Exceptional Children, 56 (3), 217-226.

RADABAUGH, M.T., & YUKISH, J.F. (1982). Curriculum and Methods for the Mildly Handicapped. Boston: Allyn and Bacon.

RAMSEY, R.S. (1981). Perceptions of disturbed and disturbing behavioral characteristics by school personnel. (Doctoral Dissertation, University of Florida) Dissertation Abstracts International, 42(49), DA8203709.

RAMSEY, R.S. (1986). Taking the practicum beyond the public school door. Journal of Adolescence. 21(83), 547-552.

RAMSEY, R.S., (1988). Preparatory Guide for Special Education Teacher competency Tests. Boston: Allyn and Bacon, Inc.

RAMSEY, R.S., DIXON, M.J., & SMITH, G.G.B. (1986) Eyes on the Special Education: Professional Knowledge Teacher Competency Test. Albany, GA: Southwest Georgia Learning Resources System Center.

RAMSEY R.W., & RAMSEY, R.S. (1978). Educating the emotionally handicapped child in the public school setting. Journal of Adolescence. 13(52), 537-541.

REINHEART, H.R. (1980). Children I Conflict: Educational Strategies for the Emotionally Disturbed and Behaviorally Disordered. (2nd ed.). St Louis, MO: The C.V. Mosby Company.

ROBINSON, G.A., PATTON, J.R., POLLOWAY, E.A., & SARGENT, L.R. (Eds.). (1989a). Best Practices in Mental Disabilities. Des Moines, IA Iowa Department of Education, Bureau of Special Education.

ROBINSON, G.A., PATTON, J.R., POLLOWAY, E.A., & SARGENT, L.R. (Eds.). (1989b). Best Practices in Mental Disabilities. Renton, VA: The Division on Mental Retardation of the Council for Exceptional Children.

ROTHSTEIN, L.F. (1995). Special education Law (2nd ed.). New York: Longman Publishers.

SABATINO, D.A., SABATION, A.C., & MANN, L. (1983). Management: A Handbook of Tactics, Strategies, and Programs. Aspen Systems Corporation.

SALVIA, J., & YSSELDYKE, J.E. (1985). Assessment in Special Education (3rd. ed.). Boston: Houghton Mifflin.

SALVIA J., & YSSELDYKE, J.E. (1991). Assessment (5th ed.). Boston: Houghton Mifflin.

SALVIA, J. & YSSELDYKE, J.E. (1995) Assessment (6th ed.). Boston: Houghton Mifflin.

SATTLER, J.M. (1982). Assessment of Children's Intelligence and Special Abilities (2nd ed.). Boston: Allyn and Bacon.

SCHLOSS, P.J., HARRIMAN, N., & PFIEFER, K. (in press). Application of a sequential prompt reduction technique to the independent composition performance of behaviorally disordered youth. Behavioral Disorders.

SCHLOSS, P.J.., & SEDLAK, R.A.(1986). Instructional Methods for Students with Learning and Behavior Problems. Boston: Allyn and Bacon.

SCHMUCK, R.A., & SCHMUCK, P.A. (1971). Group Processes in the Classroom. Dubuque, IA: William C. Brown Company.

SCHUBERT, D.G. (1978). Your teaching - the tape recorder. Reading Improvement, 15(1), 78-80.

SCHULZ, J.B., CARPENTER, C.D., & TURNBULL, A.P. (1991). Mainstreaming Exceptional Students: A Guide for Classroom Teachers. Boston: Allyn and Bacon.

SEMMEL, M.I., ABERNATHY, T.V., BUTERA G., & LESAR, S. (1991). Teacher perception of the regular education initiative. Exceptional Children, 58 (1), 3-23.

SHEA, T.M., & BAUER, A.M. (1985). Parents and Teachers of Exceptional Students: A Handbook for Involvement. Boston: Allyn and Bacon.

SIMEONSSON, R.J. (1986). Psychological and Development Assessment of Special Children. Boston: Allyn and Bacon.

SMITH, C.R. (1991). Learning Disabilities: The Interaction of Learner, Task, and Setting. Boston: Little, Brown, and Company.

SMITH, D.D., & LUCKASSON, R. (1992). Introduction to Special Education: Teaching in an Age of Challenge. Boston: Allyn and Bacon.

SMITH, J.E., & PATTON, J.M. (1989). A Resource Module on Adverse Causes of Mild Mental Retardation. (Prepared for the President's Committee on Mental Retardation).

SMITH, T.E.C., FINN, D.M., & DOWDY, C.A. (1993). Teaching Students With Mild Disabilities. Fort Worth, TX: Harcourt Brace Jovanovich College Publishers.

SMITH-DAVIS, J. (1989a April). A National Perspective on Special Education. Keynote presentation at the GLRS/College/University Forum, Macon, GA.

STEPHENS, T.M. (1976). Directive Teaching of Children with Learning and Behavioral Disorders. Columbus, OH Charles E. Merrill.

STERNBURG, R.J. (1990). Thinking Styles: Key to Understanding Performance. Phi Delta Kappa, 71(5), 366-371.
SULZER, B., & MAYER, G.R. (1972). Behavior Modification Procedures for School Personnel. Hinsdale, IL: Dryden.

TATEYAMA-SNIEZEK, K.M. (1990.) Cooperative Learning: Does it improve the academic achievement of students with handicaps? Exceptional Children, 57(2), 426-427.

THIAGARAJAN, S. (1976). Designing instructional games for handicapped learners. Focus on Exceptional Children. 7(9), 1-11.

THOMAS, O. (1980). Individualized Instruction [Videocassette & manual series]. Northbrook, IL: Hubbard Scientific Company. (Project STRETCH [Strategies to Train Regular Educators to Teach Children with Handicaps]. Module 14, ISBN 0- 8331-1919-2).

THOMAS, O. (1980). Spelling [Videocassette & manual series]. (Project STRETCH [Strategies to Train Regular Educators to Teach Children with Handicaps]. Module 10, ISBN 0-83311915-X).

THORNTON, C.A., TUCKER, B.F., DOSSEY, J.A., & BAZIK, E.F. (1983). Teaching Mathematics to Children with Special Needs. Menlo Park, CA: Addison-Wesley.

TURKEL, S.R., & PODEL, D.M. (1984). Computer-assisted learning for mildly handicapped students. Teaching Exceptional Children. 16(4), 258-262.

TURNBULL, A.P., STRICKLAND, B.B., & BRANTLEY, J.C. (1978). Developing Individualized Education Programs. Columbus, OH: Charles E. Merrill.

U.S. DEPARTMENT OF EDUCATION. (1993). To Assure the Free Appropriate Public Education of all Children with Disabilities. (Fifteenth annual report to Congress on the Implementation of The Individuals with Disabilities Education Act.). Washington, D.C.

WALKER, J.E., & SHEA, T.M. (1991). Behavior Management: A Practical Approach for Educators. New York: MacMillan.

WALLACE, G., & KAUFFMAN, J.M. (1978). Teaching Children with Learning Problems. Columbus, OH: Charles E. Merrill.

WEHMAN, P., & MCLAUGHLIN, P.J. (1981). Program Development in Special Education. New York: McGraw-Hill.

WEINTRAUB, F.J. (1987, March). [Interview].

WESSON, C.L. (1991). Curriculum-based measurement and two models of follow-up consultation. Exceptional Children. 57(3), 246-256.

WEST, R.P., YOUNG, K.R., & SPOONER, F. (1990). Precision Teaching: An Introduction. Teaching Exceptional Children. 22(3), 4-9.

WHEELER, J. (1987). Transitioning Persons with Moderate and Severe Disabilities from School to Adulthood: What Makes it Work? Materials Development Center, School of Education, and Human Services. University of Wisconsin-Stout.

WHITING, J., & AULTMAN, L. (1990). Workshop for Parents. (Workshop materials). Albany, GA: Southwest Georgia Learning Resources System Center.

WIEDERHOLT, J.L., HAMMILL, D.D., & BROWN, V.L. (1983). The Resource Room Teacher: A Guide to Effective Practices (2nd ed.). Boston: Allyn and Bacon.

WIIG, E.H., & SEMEL, E.M. (1984). Language Assessment and Intervention for the Learning Disabled. (2nd ed.). Columbus, OH: Charles E. Merrill.

WOLFGANG, C.H., & GLICKMAN, C.D.(1986). Solving Discipline Problems: Strategies for Classroom Teachers (2nd ed.). Boston: Allyn and Bacon.

YSSELKYKE, J.E., ALGOZZINE, B., (1990). Introduction to Special Education (2nd ed.). Boston: Houghton Mifflin.

YSSELDYKE, J.E., ALGOZZINE, B., & THURLOW, M.L. (1992). Critical Issues in Special Education (2nd ed.). Boston: Houghton Mifflin Company.

YSSEDLYKE, J.E., THURLOW, M.L., WOTRUBA, J.W., NANIA, PA.A (1990). Instructional arrangements: Perceptions From General Education. Teaching Exceptional Children, 22(4), 4-8.

ZARGONA, N., VAUGHN, S., 7 MCINTOSH, R. (1991). Social Skills Interventions and children with behavior problems: A review. Behavior Disorders, 16(4), 260-275.

ZIGMOND, N., & BAKER, J. (1990). Mainstream experiences for learning disabled students (Project Meld): Preliminary report. Exceptional Children, 57(2), 176-185.

ZIRPOLI, T.J., & MELLOY, K.J. (1993). Behavior Management. New York: Merrill.

Resources

Autism Society of America
7910 Woodmont Avenue, Suite 300
Bethesda, Maryland 20814

www.autism-society.org

1-800-328-8476

Open to all who support the mission of ASA

To increase public awareness about autism and the day-to-day issues faced by individuals with autism, their families and the professionals with whom they interact. The Society and its chapters share a common mission of providing information and education, and supporting research and advocating for programs and services for the autism community.

Brain Injury Association of America
8201 Greensboro Drive
Suite 611
McLean, VA 22102

http://www.biausa.org/

Phone: (703) 761-0750

Open to all

Provides information, education and support to assist the 5.3 million Americans currently living with traumatic brain injury and their families.

Child and Adolescent Bipolar Association (CABF)
1187 Wilmette Ave.
P.M.B. #331
Wilmette, IL 60091

http://www.bpkids.org

Physicians, scientific researchers, and allied professionals (therapists, Social Workers, educators, attorneys, and others) who provide services to children and adolescents with bipolar disorder or do research on the topic

educates families, professionals, and the public about pediatric bipolar disorder; **connects** families with resources and support; **advocates** for and **empowers** affected families; and **supports research** on pediatric bipolar disorder and its cure.

Children and Adults with Attention Deficit/Hyperactive Disorder (CHADD) 8181 Professional Place - Suite 150 Landover, MD 20785 www.chadd.org Tel: 301-306-7070 / Fax: 301-306-7090 Email: national@chadd.org	Open to all	providing resources and encouragement to parents, educators and professionals on a grassroots level through CHADD chapters
Council for Exceptional Children 1110 N. Glebe Road Suite 300 Arlington, VA 22201 www.cec.sped.org 1-888-232-7733 TTY: 1-866-915-5000 FAX 703-264-9494	Teachers, administrators, teacher educators, and related service personnel	Advocate for services for [disabled] and gifted individuals. A professional organization that addresses service, training, and research relative to exceptional persons.
Epilepsy Foundation of America 8301 Professional Place Landover, MD 20785 www.epilepsyfoundation.org/ (800) 332-1000	A non-membership organization	works to ensure that people with seizures are able to participate in all life experiences; and to prevent, control and cure epilepsy through research, education, advocacy and services
Family Center on Technology and Disability (FCTD) 1825 Connecticut Avenue, NW 7th Floor Washington, DC 20009 http://www.fctd.info/ phone: (202) 884-8068 fax: (202) 884-8441 email: fctd@aed.org	Non member association	a resource designed to support organizations and programs that work with families of children and youth with disabilities.

Hands and Voices P.O. Box 371926 Denver CO 80237 www.handsandvoices.org Toll Free: (866) 422-0422 parentadvocate@handsandvoices.org	families, professionals, other organizations, pre-service students, and deaf and hard of hearing adults who are all working towards ensuring successful outcomes for children who are deaf and hard of hearing.	supporting families and their children who are deaf or hard of hearing, as well as the professionals who serve them.
The International Dyslexia Association Chester Building, Suite 382 8600 LaSalle Road Baltimore, Maryland 21286 http://www.interdys.org/ 410-296-0232 Fax: 410-321-5069	Anyone interested in IDA and its mission can become a member	Provides information and referral services, research, advocacy and direct services to professionals in the field of learning disabilities.
Learning Disabilities Association of America 4156 Library Road Pittsburgh, PA 15234 http://www.ldanatl.org/ Phone (412) 341-1515 Fax (412) 344-0224	Anyone interested in LDA and its mission can become a member	• provides cutting edge information on learning disabilities, practical solutions, and a comprehensive network of resources. • provides support to people with learning disabilities, their families, teachers and other professionals.

National Association of the Deaf (NAD) 8630 Fenton Street, Suite 820, Silver Spring, MD 20910-3819 301-587-1789 TTY, 301-587-1788 Voice, 301-587-1791 FAX Email: NADinfo@nad.org http://nad.org	Anyone interested in NAD and its mission can become a member	to promote, protect, and preserve the rights and quality of life of deaf and hard of hearing individuals in the United States of America.
National Mental Health Information Center P.O. Box 42557 Washington, DC 20015 http://www.mentalhealth.samhsa.gov/ 1-800-789-2647	Government Agency	developed for users of mental health services and their families, the general public, policy makers, providers, and the media.
National Dissemination Center for Children with Disabilities (NIHCY) P.O. Box 1492 Washington, DC 20013 (800) 695-0285 · v/tty (202) 884-8441 · fax nichcy@aed.org	Non membership association	a central source of information on: • disabilities in infants, toddlers, children, and youth, • IDEA, which is the law authorizing special education, • No Child Left Behind (as it relates to children with disabilities), and • research-based information on effective educational practices.
Office of Special Education and Rehabilitative Services US Department of Education http://www.ed.gov/about/offices/list/osers/index.html	Government Resource	Committed to improving results and outcomes for people with disabilities of all ages.

Wrights Law Wrightslaw.com webmaster@wrightslaw.com	Non membership organization	Parents, educators, advocates, and attorneys come to Wrightslaw for accurate, reliable information about special education law, education law, and advocacy for children with disabilities. Provides parent Advocacy training and updates on the law through out the country.
TASH (Formerly **The Association for Persons with Severe Handicaps**) 29 W. Susquehanna Ave., Suite 210 Baltimore, MD 21204 www.tash.org Phone: 410-828-8274 Fax: 410-828-6706	Anyone interested in TASH and its mission can become a member	**To create change and build capacity so that all people, no matter their perceived level of disability, are included in all aspects of society.**
American Psychological Association 750 First Street, NE, Washington, DC 20002-4242 **Telephone: 800-374-2721; 202-336-5500. TDD/TTY: 202-336-6123** www.apa.org	Psychologists and professors of Psychology	Scientific and professional society working to improve mental health services and to advocate for legislation and programs that will promote mental health; facilitate research and professional development.
Association for Children and Adults with Learning Disabilities 4156 Library Road Pittsburgh, PA 15234 http://www.acldonline.org/	Parents of children with learning disabilities and interested professionals	Advanced the education and general well-being of children with adequate intelligence who have learning disabilities arising from perceptual, conceptual, or subtle coordinative problems, sometimes accompanied by behavior difficulties.

The Arc of the United States (Formerly the National Association of Retarded Citizens) 1010 Wayne Avenue Suite 650 Silver Springs, MD 20910

www.the arc.org (301) 565-3842 FAX: (301) 565-3843 | Parents, professionals, and others interested in individuals with mental retardation | Work on local, state, and national levels to promote treatment, research, public understanding, and legislation for persons with mental retardation; provide counseling for parents of students with mental retardation. |
| National Association for Gifted Children 1707 L Street, NW Suite 550 Washington, DC 20036

http://nagc.org

Phone: (202) 785-4368 FAX: (202) 785-4248 Email: nagc@nagc.org | Parents, educators, community leaders and, other professionals who work with Gifted children. | To address the unique needs of children and youth with demonstrated gifts and talents. |
| Council for Children with Behavioral Disorders CEC Two Ballston Plaza 1110 N. Glebe Road Arlington, VA 22201

ccbd.net

800-224-6830 (business) 888-232-7733 (membership line) 703-264-9494 fax. | Members of the Council for Exceptional Children who teach children with behavior disorders or who train teachers to work with those children | Promote education and general welfare of children and youth with behavior disorders or serious emotional disturbances. Promote professional growth and research on students with behavior disorders and severe emotional disturbances. |

Council for Educational Diagnostic Services, CEC Two Ballston Plaza 1110 N. Glebe Road Arlington, VA 22201	Members of the Council for Exceptional Children who are school Psychologists, educational diagnosticians, [and] Social Workers who are involved in diagnosing educational difficulties	Promote the most appropriate education of children and youth through appraisal, diagnosis, educational intervention, implementation, and evaluation of a prescribed educational program. Work to facilitate the professional development of those who assess students. Work to further development of better diagnostic techniques and procedures.
Council for Exceptional Children Two Ballston Plaza 1110 N. Glebe Road Arlington, VA 22201	Teachers, administrators, teacher educators, and related service personnel	Advocate for services for [disabled] and gifted individuals. A professional organization that addresses service, training, and research relative to exceptional persons.
Council of Administrators of Special Education Two Ballston Plaza 1110 N. Glebe Road Arlington, VA 22201	Members of the Council for Exceptional Children who are administrators, directors, coordinators, or supervisors of programs, schools, or classes for exceptional children; college faculty who train administrators	Promote professional leadership; provide opportunities for the study of problems common to its members; communicate through discussion and publications information that will facilitate improved services for children with exceptional needs.

Division for Children with Communication Disorders Two Ballston Plaza 1110 N. Glebe Road Arlington, VA 22201	Members of the Council for Exceptional Children who are speech-language pathologists, audiologists, teachers of children with communication disorders, or educators of professionals who plan to work with children who have communication disorders	Promote the education of children with communication disorders. Promote professional growth and research.
Division for Early Childhood Two Ballston Plaza 1110 N. Glebe Road Arlington, VA 22201	Members of the Council for Exceptional Children who teach preschool children and infants or educate teachers to work with young children	Promote effective education for young children and infants. Promote professional development of those who work with young children and infants. Promote legislation and research.
Division for the Physically Handicapped Two Ballston Plaza 1110 N. Glebe Road Arlington, VA 22201	Members of the Council for Exceptional Children who work with individuals who have physical disabilities or educate professionals to work with those individuals	Promote closer relationships among educators of students who have physical impairments or are homebound. Facilitate research and encourage development of new ideas, practices, and techniques through professional meetings, workshops, and publications.

Division for the Visually Handicapped Two Ballston Plaza 1110 N. Glebe Road Arlington, VA 22201	Members of the Council for Exceptional Children who work with individuals who have visual disabilities or educate professionals to work with those individuals	Work to advance the education and training of individuals with visual impairments. Work to bring about better understanding of educational, emotional, or other problems associated with visual impairment. Facilitate research and development of new techniques or ideas in education and training of individuals with visual problems.
Division on Career Development Two Ballston Plaza 1110 N. Glebe Road Arlington, VA 22201	Members of the Council for Exceptional Children who teach or in other ways work toward career development and vocational education of exceptional children	Promote and encourage professional growth of all those concerned with career development and vocational education. Promote research, legislation, information dissemination, and technical assistance relevant to career development and vocational education.

Division on Mental Retardation Two Ballston Plaza 1110 N. Glebe Road Arlington, VA 22201	Members of the Council for Exceptional Children who work with students with mental retardation or educate professionals to work with those students	Work to advance the education of individuals with mental retardation, research mental retardation, and the training o professionals to work with individuals with mental retardation. Promote public understanding of mental retardation and professional development of those who work with persons with mental retardation.
Gifted Child Society P.O. Box 120 Oakland, NJ 07436	Parents and educators of children who are gifted	Train educators to meet the needs of students with gifted abilities, offer assistance to parents facing special problems in raising children who are gifted, and seek public recognition of the needs of these children.
National Association for the Education of Young Children 1313 L St. N.W. Suite 500, Washington DC 20005 (202) 232-8777 || (800) 424-2460 || webmaster@naeyc.org		Promote service and action on behalf of the needs and rights of young children, with emphasis on provision of educational services and resources.
http://www.naeyc.org/ National Association for Retarded Citizens 5101 Washington Ave., N.W. Washington, D.C www.thearc.org		Work to promote the general welfare of persons with mental retardation; facilitate research and information dissemination relative to causes, treatment, and prevention of mental retardation.

National Easter Seal Society 230 West Monroe Street, Suite 1800 Chicago, IL 60606 800-221-6827 (toll-free) 312-726-4258 (tty) 312-726-1494 (fax) http://www.easterseals.com/	State units (49) and local societies (951); no individual members	Establish and run programs for individuals with physical impairments, usually including diagnostic services, speech therapy, preschool services, physical therapy, and occupational therapy.
The National Association of Special Education Teachers 1201 Pennsylvania Avenue, N.W., Suite 300Washington D.C. 20004 **Call us at:** 800-754-4421 **Fax us at:** 800-424-0371 **Or email us at:** contactus@naset.org	Special Education Teachers	to render all possible support and assistance to professionals who teach children with special needs. to promote standards of excellence and innovation in special education research, practice, and policy in order to foster exceptional teaching for exceptional children.

XAMonline, INC. 21 Orient Ave. Melrose, MA 02176

Toll Free number 800-509-4128

TO ORDER Fax 781-662-9268 OR www.XAMonline.com

NEW YORK STATE TEACHER CERTIFICATION
EXAMINATION - NYSTCE - 2007

PO#   Store/School:

Address 1:

Address 2 (Ship to other):

City, State Zip

Credit card number_____-_____-_____-_____   expiration_____

EMAIL _____

PHONE   **FAX**

13# ISBN 2007	TITLE	Qty	Retail	Total
978-1-58197-866-7	NYSTCE ATS-W ASSESSMENT OF TEACHING SKILLS- WRITTEN 91			
978-1-58197-867-4	NYSTCE ATAS ASSESSMENT OF TEACHING ASSISTANT SKILLS 095			
978-1-58197-854-4	CST BIOLOGY 006			
978-1-58197-855-1	CST CHEMISTRY 007			
978-1-58197-865-0	CQST COMMUNICATION AND QUANTITATIVE SKILLS TEST 080			
978-1-58197-856-8	CST EARTH SCIENCE 008			
978-1-58197-851-3	CST ENGLISH 003			
978-1-58197-862-9	CST FAMILY AND CONSUMER SCIENCES 072			
978-1-58197-858-2	CST FRENCH SAMPLE TEST 012			
978-1-58197-868-1	LAST LIBERAL ARTS AND SCIENCE TEST 001			
978-1-58197-863-6	CST LIBRARY MEDIA SPECIALIST 074			
978-1-58197-861-2	CST LITERACY 065			
978-1-58197-852-0	CST MATH 004			
978-1-58197-872-8	CST MULTIPLE SUBJECTS 002 SAMPLE QUESTIONS			
978-1-58197-850-6	CST MUTIPLE SUBJECTS 002			
978-1-58197-864-3	CST PHYSICAL EDUCATION 076			
978-1-58197-857-5	CST PHYSICS SAMPLE TEST 009			
978-1-58197-853-7	CST SOCIAL STUDIES 005			
978-1-58197-859-9	CST SPANISH 020			
978-1-58197-860-5	CST STUDENTS WITH DISABILITIES 060			

	SUBTOTAL	
FOR PRODUCT PRICES VISIT WWW.XAMONLINE.COM	**Ship**	$8.25
	TOTAL	

WITHDRAWN

Printed in the United States
106467LV00005B/9/A

9 781581 978605